Habitus in Habitat I

Emotion and Motion

natur, wissenschaft und die künste
nature, science et les arts
nature, science and the arts

Band 3

PETER LANG
Bern · Berlin · Bruxelles · Frankfurt am Main · New York · Oxford · Wien

Sabine Flach, Daniel Margulies &
Jan Söffner (eds)

Habitus in Habitat I

Emotion and Motion

PETER LANG
Bern · Berlin · Bruxelles · Frankfurt am Main · New York · Oxford · Wien

Bibliographic information published by Die Deutsche Nationalbibliothek
Die Deutsche Nationalbibliothek lists this publication in the Deutsche Nationalbibliografie; detailed bibliographic data is available on the Internet at ‹http://dnb.d-nb.de›.

British Library and Library of Congress Cataloguing-in-Publication Data:
A catalogue record for this book is available from *The British Library*, Great Britain

Library of Congress Cataloging-in-Publication Data

Habitus in Habitat I : Emotion and Motion / Sabine Flach, Daniel Margulies & Jan Söffner (eds). – 1st ed.
p. cm.
ISBN 978-3-0343-0530-3
1. Conditioned response. 2. Habituation (Neuropsychology) 3. Emotions. I. Flach, Sabine. II. Margulies, Daniel (Daniel Shendelman). III. Söffner, Jan.
IV. Title: Habitus in habitat 1. V. Title: Habitus in habitat one. VI. Title: Emotion and motion.
BF319.H28 2010
152–dc22

2010046967

The proceedings are result of a conference which was supported by the German Federal Ministry of Education and Research (promotional reference: 01UG07129).
The authors of this publication are responsible for its content.

Cover illustration: Suzanne Anker: *The Glass Veil*, 2009, digital print mounted on sintra, 96"x120" / 243.8cm x 304.8cm.

Cover design: Thomas Jaberg, Peter Lang AG

ISBN 978-3-0343-0530-3

Hochfeldstrasse 32, CH-3012 Bern
info@peterlang.com, www.peterlang.com, www.peterlang.net

Printed in Switzerland

Contents

Introduction

SABINE FLACH, DANIEL MARGULIES, AND JAN SÖFFNER

Theories of habituation reflect their diversity through the myriad disciplines from which they emerge. They entail several issues of trans-disciplinary interest – such as embodiment, aesthetics and phenomenology, which on the other hand have profoundly influenced the discussion. Embodiment has become a prominent issue in disciplines such as the cognitive sciences, neurosciences and psychology – but it has equally had an impact on the social sciences, art history, and cultural, literary, and media studies, as well as philosophy of mind and phenomenology. Since the 1980s, from the interaction of these various perspectives, interdisciplinary fields of research have emerged. Phenomenological and neurophenomenological issues play a key role in the discussions, and this is one of the most promising fields of cultural, social and psychological interest. At the same time the issue of aesthetic experiencing, and especially of the relation between the senses and the emotions, has provided vivid and fruitful debates – and they are essential for artistic fields of knowledge as well. One major issue here is not just the senses, but also phenomena of 'sense' (meaning) and 'sense' (sensuality) in their intricate interaction.

This interaction includes the 'sense' emerging in environmental relations, but also its subjective manifestations through perception; and it is based upon the correspondence of the sensual organs and the modalities of the senses.[1] The interdependence of sense and the senses, of cultural meaning and sensuality, can only be conceived as being a complex relation of stability and flexibility, of habituations and readjustments, considering both a shared reality and private experience. The meaning emerging from the balance and the adjustments of these interrelations cannot accordingly be analyzed by referring to concepts of the intelligible world alone – as would be the case when reducing it to concepts of inscribed meanings. Embodiment entails a phenomenology that cannot just be reduced to concepts or metaphors of scripture. Rather the approach to these phenomena must be profoundly based on concepts of performance and performativi-

1 Cf. Krämer: "Sinnlichkeit, Denken, Medien", p. 24. Krämer argues that the distinction between the Sense (sensing) and sense (meaning) has not always been a cultural given: "Sense derives from traveling or following a track; originally it implies a movement in space and most of all the pursuit of a certain direction in the act of doing something", p. 29. Cf. also Flach: *Sensing Senses*.

ty, regarding the interrelation of sense and sensing[2] as a relation as inextricably linked to the interrelation of habitus and habitat.

Despite the fact that similar discussions have always been inherently interdisciplinary, the disparate nature of disciplinary approaches continues to thwart the necessary exchange of ideas. To grant a common base for the whole project, we have developed the unifying theme: *habitus in habitat*, because it constitutes a fundamental issue concerning all these fields of interest, and it allows for contributions from a variety of disciplines.

The term habitus, in a general sense, refers to habituated embodied and mental schemata, implied in social communication, in personal attitudes, in social identity, in cultural experience and in the production of cultural meaning. On the other hand subjectivity is not only constituted by habitus – a habitus is also deeply rooted in subjectivity and depends on subjective experiencing as well.

The concept of habitus is also profoundly 'emotional' from its very origin and its antique predecessors. The Greek word for habitus is *hexis* – i.e., the 'having' also rendered in the Latin word habitus – and as such it is already used in Aristotle, most prominently in the *Nicomachean Ethics*. Aristotle thinks of hexis as a tendency or disposition, induced by our habits, to have feelings and to act (1105b 25–6). Hexis is a stance on oneself and on the environment. Moral virtue, in his eyes, is therefore the right hexis, i.e. the disposition to have appropriate feelings and act appropriately. It is thereby a form of cognition and judgment as well – even though it does not necessarily imply conscious reasoning.

Indeed, emotions have always been central to human experience and behavior. They condition our actions and are inherent in all forms of communication.[3] It has also become widely accepted that there is no cognition without emotion, suggesting that every formation of cognitive skills and epistemological faculties, every cultural practice and any form of human communication is accompanied by specific emotional habituations and the formation of an *emotional* habitus – a set of habits involved in emotional communication.

Since these habituations always imply a stance on the surrounding environment, they are closely linked to a habitat as well. In the current discussions on the emotions, this is true, e.g. for Jesse J. Prinz, who conceives of emotions as "not merely perceptions of the body but also perceptions of our relations to the world"[4]; it is true for Peter Goldie, who develops a concept of conscious "feeling towards"[5] and focuses on emotions "by subtly identifying the thoughts which are involved" in order to open up "a space to consider the ethical and sometimes the political dimensions of an emotion"[6]; it is true for Joseph LeDoux, who con-

2 Emrich: "Illusionen, die Wirklichkeit und das Kino", p. 41/46, and Krämer: "Sinnlichkeit, Denken, Medien", p. 33.

3 Damasio: *Descartes' Error*.

4 Jesse J. Prinz: *Gut Reactions*, p. 20.

5 Peter Goldie: *The Emotions: A Philosophical Exploration*, pp. 58–62.

6 Ibid., p. 27.

ceives of conscious feelings as being grounded in a subjective "capacity to be consciously aware of one's self and the relation of oneself to the rest of the world"[7]; and it is true for Matthew Ratcliffe, who developed a theory of existential feelings, i.e. of feelings as "finding oneself in the world"[8]. This is just to name four recent theories considering the emotional relation with an environment in very different ways. According to each of them, habitus is nevertheless closely tied to issues of both subjectivity and environmental interaction.

Habitus, though, is not just individually acquired, but it also forms a foundation for habituation to collectively shared patterns of embodied communication. For Marcel Mauss habitus is closely related to the *Techniques du corps* – techniques of the body, which consist of a "work of individual and collective practical reason"[9]. This remains stable in Pierre Bourdieu's vast theory of habitus as a fact of the production of social meaning and social distinctions – which are embodied in human interaction. His concept of habitus – at least in his later writings[10] – can be understood as an enactive way of the social production of meaning, referring to the whole body and including cognition, judgement and aesthetics. Moreover, Bourdieu elaborates on the *habitat* as well. For him *habitus* stems from the habituation with an *environment*. It is a fact of being habituated with what one *inhabits*. And at the same time it is a fact of being inhabited by one's own habitat. Habitus is formed *by* and constitutes a ground *for* embodied interaction. Bourdieu's notion of habitus has recently been extended by his former student Loïc Wacquant, who focuses even more on embodiment than did his mentor. In opting for a "carnal sociology" of habitus, taking more seriously the knowledge gained by "bodily and sensual apprenticeship"[11], he opens up the term for phenomenological considerations drawing upon Edmund Husserl,[12] Maurice Merleau-Ponty[13] and Martin Heidegger,[14] for the discussion of "dispositional representations" in the brain (such as conceived of by Joseph LeDoux)[15], for considerations about cultural meaning – and for the knowledge sometimes implied in artistic practises.

All this makes the concepts of habitus and habitat apt for describing the cultural aspects of embodied cognition, perception, appreciation, judgment and taste – of being more or less attuned with situations or people, of practical knowledge, and of subjective experiencing. Habitus, hence, can be understood as a set of behavioural attitudes and habits that make up both a subjective and a cultural

7 LeDoux: *The Emotional Brain*, p. 125
8 Ratcliffe: *Feelings of Being*, p. 2.
9 Mauss: "Body Techniques", p. 101.
10 Cf. Bourdieu: *Pascalian Meditations*.
11 Loïc Wacquant: "Habitus as Topic and Tool", p. 146.
12 Husserl: *Cartesianische Meditationen*.
13 Merleau-Ponty: *Phénoménologie de la perception*, Paris: Gallimard 1945.
14 Heidegger: *Sein und Zeit*, Tübingen: Niemeyer 1986.
15 Joseph LeDoux: *The Synaptic Self*.

identity. Habituation refers to experiencing within a culturally shaped environment, it refers to what one gets habituated to. Habitus, on the other hand, as a form of stance relating to an environment and to oneself, draws to the foreground both subjective and culturally shaped issues about the 'sense of senses' and the 'sense' of motor actions.

Indeed, in considering the interrelation between habitus and emotion, scholars tend to focus progressively more on the connection between emotions and motor actions (usually understood as 'expressions'). In other words: The habitualization of emotions is constituted by more than simply psychological aspects (in the narrow sense of the word), it must rather be described by considering the moving body – and how this body, by means of its (often subliminal) motions, relates to its environment. In reflecting on the etymology of the word 'emotion' (i.e. *ex motus* – out of the motion) in an embodied sense, and not just related to a mental, and hence metaphorical 'movement of the soul' (a *motus animi*), the relation of motion and emotion becomes an issue of the embodied mind, implicating literal movements of the body as well. The term "emotion", hence, should no more just refer to something disembodied and inner, but it should also refer to an environmentally related behavioral pattern involving cognitive, motivational and sensorimotor aspects of experience. And moreover, emotions involve embodied interaction with an environment – as much including the interrelation of subjective expressions and impressions as involving trans-subjective emotionality (observable in affect-driven mass phenomena or moods and atmospheres).

Discussing the embodiment of emotions also leads to discussing questions about how emotions present themselves to others. This question is an important issue for aesthetic and artistic theory and art history. Here habitus in habitat does not allow for privileging facial expression (as is often the case in research on emotional expressiveness). Rather the focus must be on the whole body in motion. Moreover, it must include considerations about the media implied in every human habitat.[16] These questions figure paramount in the arts. Just to pick two famous examples from the vast discussion of expressive movements in the visual arts: Konrad Fiedler, in his *Schriften zur Kunst* (Writings on Art)[17], develops a concept of artistic autonomy based upon a critical and psychophysiologically grounded re-interpretation of Kant. He thereby liberates art from being a mere ornament accompanying scientific insights – he rather describes its autonomous and legitimate production of knowledge. Fiedler's point of departure is the 'production of reality' as a fact of sensual mediation.[18] With reference to the works of Wilhelm Wundt, he establishes the category of 'expressive movement' in order to describe all modes of articulation: "The problem of artistic means of expres-

16 See for instance: Flach: "Realfiktionen. Versuchsanordnungen von Olafur Eliasson"; Flach: "It's not easy being green!", Flach: "Withdrawal as an Artform".

17 Fiedler: *Schriften zur Kunst*

18 Cf. Boehm: "Anschauung als Sprache", p. IX.

sion will not gain a scientific setting until one gets habituated to seeing them as expressive movements (...): Only by means of such an inquiry can the fact slowly come to the light which aspects of human consciousness are assisted by the diverse modes of expression."[19] In aiming to establish a new form of verifiable knowledge, Fiedler establishes a concept of insight leading the sensual "matter of reality" to the "expression of itself"[20]. While challenging concepts of art as the imitation or representation of reality, Fiedler establishes the concept of an expressive movement joining visual perception and gestalt perception – thereby producing a mental figure without reference to anything pre-existing. Aby Warburg's concept of the "pathos formula", to give the second example, allows for describing the manifold emotional articulations of bodies – pointing to the fact that iconic figurations are essential for the knowledge of and about emotions. Warburg's pathos formula is a methodological instrument which is suitable for bringing to light the epistemological relevance of the detail – or the "moved accessories" ("bewegtes Beiwerk"), as Warburg calls it. As Warburg explains: These moved accessories, the increased motion of the garment and the hair (as Warburg exemplifies with regards to Botticelli's *Birth of Venus*) constitute the way in which the work of art relates to its antique tradition. Not the motif or the composition of the image, but the "bewegtes Beiwerk", the moved detail, carries on the historical correspondences and articulates their inherent energetic momentum. The pathos formula thereby does not only display or represent affects and passions, but it rather is understood as affective itself. Warburg does not just describe this element, but regards it as a methodological instrument[21] – thereby making the specific moved detail an epistemological instrumentarium as well. Moreover, the concept allows for analysing the intricate *historical* dimension of iconic figurations.

Indeed, habitus and habitat cannot be discussed without shedding light on their temporal dimension, which makes them crucial for historical research and considerations as well. They are not just focused on a given moment – they also include questions about perpetuation, and therefore the relation of shorter and longer spans of time. A habitus is always something provided with a past one carries on. One's own past, and the past of the collective, is something which one has been dealing with for the duration of one's lifetime.

This is essential for personal impressions and for and formative events – as prominently discussed in psychoanalysis. Indeed, relating to a past and – so to speak – embodying one's own past in one's habits is not only about remembering past events. But the habitus-based organization of the past is apparent on the level of the episodic memory too. Neurobiological research has provided evi-

19 Boehm (ed.): *Konrad Fiedler. Schriften zur Kunst II*, p. 74.

20 Fiedler: "Der Ursprung der künstlerischen Tätigkeit", p. 266.

21 With regard to Warburg's theory it is also possible to draw parallels with Charles Darwin's *The Expression of the Emotion in Man and Animals* (1872) and Robert Vischer's *Über das optische Formgefühl* (1873).

dence that it is not the original experience that is remembered, but the latest actualization of it. Memory is hence a fact of changing habits of remembering, transforming and reconsolidating the remembered issues.[22] Neuro-psychoanalytic research on this fact closely relates to Freud, who some 100 years earlier already claimed that the present transforms the remembered past – which lead him to the assumption that memories acquire new forms and functions over the course of time: the concept of 'Nachträglichkeit' (James Strachey translated this as 'deferred action', which falls short of ideal. The literal translation is 'belatedness' or 'posteriority', and the term is difficult to render in English).[23] The process of inventing one's own past, indeed, cannot be separated from emotional experience; and it was, again, Aristotle who pointed out this fact by noting the neat relation between emotion and memory – and conceiving of memory as a simulacrum (*eidolon*). But to return to Freud:[24] Unconscious processes of both a self-organizing formative and a self-organizing episodic memory must be considered when considering habitus. And this is equally true for conceiving of the interrelation of habitus and habitat. The interrelation of past and present holds a memory that is both personal and collective.

These are the most important reasons why we consider habitus and habitat to be useful concepts for engaging the question of how *emotion* can be thought of. And we think that this relation is especially crucial when it comes to questions of the cultural production of meaning and the cultural shaping of experience in exchange with a material cultural heritage partially *embodied* in its members. But this is not all there is to say about it: The habitus of one individual is also a part of the habitat for others. Not only is habitus shaped by the environment – it is also the environment which is shaped by habitus. Furthermore, this issue cannot be discussed without considering issues of subjective experiencing – i.e. without raising the question of how an emotional relation of habitus in habitat is brought forth as an experience. The formation of an *emotional habitus*, i.e. the development of a set of habits involving the moving body is, hence, as fundamental to understanding emotions as understanding emotions is fundamental for conceiving of habitus in habitat.[25]

The project of *habitus in habitat* is to reciprocally open the sciences and the humanities, and face both the opportunities and challenges. The interdisciplinary issue of this volume is hence to describe concrete interdependences of subjectivity, habituation and embodied environmental relations – and to address the ques-

22 Cf. e.g. Kaplan-Solms / Solms: *Clinical Studies in Neuro-Psychoanalysis.*

23 The notion of *Nachträglichkeit* first appears in a letter which Freud wrote to Wilhelm Fließ 1896, and is consistently used in his writings.

24 These considerations impressively figure in the recent work of Hustvedt: *Die zitternde Frau.* For Freud and Aristoteles see pp. 120, 121 and 125.

25 Cf. for a more elaborate discussion: Flach / Söffner: *Emotionaler Habitus.*

tion of how these interdependencies relate the social and subjective production of meaning and the field of the artistic knowledge.

The issue of subjectively relating to the world and the development of personal emotional habits is crucial for this discussion. Moreover the focus must be on how emotions present themselves, how they are mediated and what role cultural and artistic habits or styles play in this formation. One further point of departure for considering *habitus in habitat* is that neither a culture, nor a community, nor cognition, nor the formation of individual and cultural systems of meaning is possible without the habituation of bodies. Habituation and habitualization, as the relationship and interface of the body to the environment, therefore must not only be considered as a matter of cultural 'inscriptions', but be taken as an embodied interaction in the full material meaning of the term.[26] From this material perspective, the scientific debates about the embodied mind[27] and the plasticity of the human brain[28,29] always take part in a culturally meaningful habitat, which is in turn partly constituted by their participation[30] – with deep impact on the humanities, social sciences and the issue of knowledge for the arts. Purely material approaches to embodiment, from any disciplinary perspective, fundamentally require the consideration of interrelations with cultural, social, and aesthetic productions of meaning in order to achieve philosophical purchase on issues previously only discussed within the humanities.

The approach of a habitus in habitat accordingly cannot be limited to issues of embodiment only. Indeed, the term *embodiment* itself only achieves full meaning when discussed with respect to practices of transmission, which can be context-independent, and hence, in a way, disembodied as well. This fact is essential for conceiving of the interrelations of subjective, cultural and social habituations. More concretely: What can be embodied might also have an option for transmission or contagion via the relation of a body with its environment, thus raising the issue of relating embodied subjectivity to the environment. While this question constitutes a major issue in the cognitive sciences, it also has deep impact on the neurosciences (relating to mirror phenomena and neuronal plasticity), for affective psychology (intercorporeal phenomena of emotional communication are at

26 Gallagher / Zahavi: *The Phenomenological Mind.*

27 Varela / Thompson / Rosch: *The Embodied Mind*; Gallagher: *How the Body Shapes the Mind;* Johnson: *The Meaning of the Body.*

28 Cf. Doidge: *The Brain That Changes Itself*, and Schwartz and Begley: *The Mind and the Brain.*

29 The birth of new neurons during human adult life was dogmatically disregarded by neuroscientists until well into the past three decades. Even in the face of prior evidence to the contrary, the persistence of such beliefs, and their eventual overturning was dependent on factors beyond the scientific evidence alone.

30 One example, provided by Catherine Malabou, is the concordance of the rise of the neoliberal market economy, which demands the flexibility of the individual, and the turn in neuroscience towards research on the malleability of the human brain. Malabou: *What Should We Do with Our Brain?*

stake), psychology of perception (focusing on the 'ecological' conditions of sensing), as well as phenomenological philosophy (which must relate to sensorimotoric habitualization when discussing issues of embodied reasoning). These discussions have also contributed to constructivist and cybernetic theories. Moreover, current evolutionary biology focuses on the meaning of expressions and accessories of the whole body in motion, while art history investigates the relation of images to the body[31] (considering concepts of pictorial anthropology and the relation of vision, motion and emotion), and together with performance studies, and literary and music theory, focuses on the relation of embodiment to practices of showing and hiding, simulating and dissimulating. Images, in this sense, can be understood neither as mere carriers of meanings nor as representations or expressions of reality – they must rather be conceived of as a relation between cognition and experience, inner images and externalized images, imagination and representation. In the line with Richard Wollheim's theory of "Sehen-In" (seeing-in),[32] Max Imdahl's concept of an iconicity of "sehendes Sehen" (seeing seeing),[33] and the notion of echo-objects as introduced by Barbara Stafford,[34] the image here is understood as a performative act (a picture act or image action) addressing the complete sensorium. And it is here that image theory relates to theories of embodiment as put forth by Shaun Gallagher[35] and Alva Noë, who conceived of the *Action in Perception*[36] – or, alternatively the "Theory of Response" as developed by the art historian David Freedberg in collaboration with the neurologist Vittorio Gallese.[37] Together with performance studies, and literary and music theory, art history focuses on the relation of embodiment to practices of showing and hiding, simulating and dissimulating. In all of these issues, the interrelation of cultural questions with neuroscientific and neurological perspectives is becoming more and more potent.

Discussing both subjectivity and environmental embodiment on the basis of asking about *habitus in habitat*, first of all, means building a bridge between the sciences and both social and cultural theories. Indeed, in these disciplines, such aspects of embodiment had been discussed long before the term had been coined – and sometimes they are discussed when focusing on related issues such as *aisthesis* and aesthetics, theatrical and cultural performativity, [38] production of pres-

31 Cf. Flach / Schneider / Treml (eds.): *Warburgs Denkraum.*
32 Wollheim: *Objekte der Kunst.*
33 Boehm*: Die Arbeit des Blickes. Hinweise zu Max Imdahls theoretischen Schriften.*
34 Stafford: *Echo-Objects.*
35 Gallagher: *How the Body Shapes the Mind.*
36 Noë: *Action in Perception.*
37 Freedberg: *The Power of Images*, and Gallese / Freedberg: "Motion, Emotion and Empathy in Aesthetic Experience".
38 Fischer-Lichte: *Ästhetik des Performativen.*

ence[39] in religious cults and sociocultural events or social rituals,[40] swarm and mass phenomena and the relation of meaning to the senses.

These issues can be social – but they are not limited to sociological questions (as the term habitus might suggest to readers well acquainted with Bourdieu than with different traditions of it). This fact becomes more striking when considering that emotions extend beyond solely anthropological issues. In current research they are understood as being a fundamental aspect of animal behavior as well – and hence human emotions can be investigated through experiments with animals or by referring to comparative ethology. Taking research on animal emotions and animal behavior into the study of evolutionary heritage of human emotions provides for a vivid discussion about the interrelations of phylogenetic and ontogenetic aspects of emotions[41] – in other words: the evolutionary development of specific 'animal' emotions through interaction with a 'natural' habitat – and the habitualization of human emotions in and with a culturally produced habitat. This discussion regarding evolution, development and culture has even become intertwined in the current discussion about neuronal plasticity and mirror neurons, paving the ground for a more productive discourse on the interrelation of 'nature' and 'nurture' in emotions: It allows for conceiving of the formation of an emotional habitus, which exists beyond the dichotomous alternatives of solely classical conditioning or cultural production of meaning, allowing rather for the articulation of a *habitus in habitat* relation as well. The advantage here is that the *interrelation* of culture and evolution are emphasized rather than opposed.

Focusing on the interrelation of motion and emotion thus expands the scope of *habitus in habitat*, providing a foundation for broader discussion. Emotional habitus and emotional habitat constitute the foundation of personal and shared experiencing, of subjective attitudes and sociocultural communities, of the psychology of emotions and cultural practices.[42] And they have much to contribute to the study of emotions, both for cognition and aesthetics. Habitualizing embodied emotionality is hence crucial for communicative and social sciences, psychology, philosophy, and all cultural fields of research.

The papers assembled in this volume address a variety of issues related to these premises. These include questions of appearance and representation, which are central to regarding emotions as emerging from motion, such as: How do emotions present themselves? How are they represented in motion? What is their relation to the specific media contexts of the arts? How can an embodied relation

39 Gumbrecht: *Production of Presence.*

40 Victor Turner: *The Ritual Process: Structure and Anti-Structure*; Dissanayake: *Art and Intimacy.*

41 For the discussion about more or less basic and more or less secondary emotions, which is – of course – highly relevant for this discussion, see: Panksepp: *Affective Neuroscience*; Solms / Turnbull: *The Grain and the Inner World.*

42 Cf. Söffner: "Non-Representational Mimesis".

with, for instance, a printed text or a two-dimensional image, be conceived of and habitualized? How are embodied emotions brought into visibility, audibility or readability? How can media processes relate to neuronal processes, and vice versa?

Focusing on the embodied interrelation of *habitus* and *habitat*, moreover, means going beyond concepts of emotionality as 'something inner' expressed by 'something outer'. Encoding and decoding are part of the emotional process themselves. This suggests the question of emotional 'meaning', 'sense' or 'meaningfulness' of emotional articulations, the relation between cognition and sensorimotoric aspects of habitualized emotions and their relation to the imaginary as well as proprioception. These issues can also be focused on by considering the specific habitualizations of the senses – and hence include concepts of the iconic or the pictorial.

As stated above, current research on the articulation of emotions is primarily focused on facial expressions. The papers assembled here rather attempt to conceptualize a broader view on the articulation of emotions by addressing the whole body – as well as its environmental interrelations. They focus on *mises-en-scène* of the body as a whole, on body practices, and on the immanent cognitive and emotional processes involved. Moreover they investigate the way in which articulations can be culturally 'coined' and have their own 'lives' by travelling not only from body to body, but also through time and space, and hence from one culture to another. This is especially true when relating emotionality to the process of embodied communication and of time-related media practices (e.g., in film, literature, music and performance).

The first section of this volume, *Socially Shared Emotions*, concerns issues of how the transmission of or the contagion by emotions works and how emotions can be socially shared. The opening paper of Erika Fischer-Lichte focuses on how emotions figure in theatrical performance. A central issue of the paper is the notion of emotional contagion leading to the transformation of the spectators. Defining this contagion as a liminal experience (a term borrowed from the theory of rituals) is especially important when conceiving of shifts in the habitus produced in a special segment of the social life (especially the theatre – but not only) and needing repetition to become stabilized. The paper traces historic notions of emotional contagions leading to a variety of insights concerning its transformations. The chapter is followed by Thomas Fuchs' insightful paper on embodied interaction, opening up the discussion for neuroscientific and psychological issues by conceiving of the brain as a social organ. Social habituation and embodied socialization here figure as facts of the ontogenetic development, based upon the plasticity of the brain. The important issue is intercorporal interaction leading to issues of shared meanings, which link individuals in a common system through mutual perceptions and reactions. A similar approach of social interaction has been developed in the phenomenological works of Shaun Gallagher. In this volume he focuses on issues of participatory sense-making, drawing upon his interactive approach to social phenomenology – as opposed to 'Simulation Theory' and 'Theory Theory', as they are discussed in the philosophical discussions about the 'Theory of Mind'. The notion of habitus here figures prominently as a set of attitudes, which are embodied rather than mentalized. It is discussed by focusing on phenomena of joint attention. Marta Braun instead turns to issues of habitus as a means of social distinction. In focusing on Eadweard Muybridge's famous photographic practises of moved bodies, she discusses a mediatic habitat allowing body morphologies to be traced. Her criticism especially concerns racial differences that are addressed by this practise. Jan Söffner focuses on nostalgia and homesickness as deeply rooted in shared intercorporality. Experiencing that one's own habitus does not fit into the cultural habitat of a foreign place is examined as a liminal experience of embodied interaction.

The second section of the volume turns to discussing *Expressivity and Interaction* grounded in an emotional habitus in habitat. Erik Porath here traces ways of dealing with the unconscious and its interpretation as linked to and rooted in expressive interactivity. Focusing on works of Sigmund Freud and Conrad Fiedler, he develops a notion of self-referential expressiveness without the distinction of a subjective inside and an objective outside. Especially Fiedler's thoughts upon a 'field' shaping the visual world figures as a habitat for expressive interaction. Christine Kirchhoff's article, instead, deals with psychoanalytical conceptions of emotional affectedness. In discussing the "inner outside", she traces notions of how the unconscious of a self and an other interrelate. Crucial for her approach is the constructedness and mediatedness of the unconscious. A further dimension of emotional communication is approached by Burkhard Meyer-Sickendiek, who focuses on theories of grace as both beauty in movement and an expression of a moral sentiment present in Kant, Schiller, Kleist, Hegel and Wieland. Meyer-Sickendiek discusses this issue through the background of its opposite, shame, as an important emotion relating to social coersion. The important issue is how an expression of the 'beautiful soul' *in actu* was conceived of, and how it related to notions of consciousness. The section closes with the important insights of Arno Villringer, who offers a neuroscientific approach to the body and its representation in the brain. This paper not only regards the most updated theories about the topic, but also provides for a broad basis concerning theories of embodiment by focusing on the human homunculus and what is to be considered conscious and unconscious – thereby rounding up the second major topic of the section, which is subliminal or unconscious enaction.

The Arts Embodied is the topic of the final section of the volume. It starts with Sabine Flach's interview with Suzanne Anker, concerning nearly all major issues of this volume by focusing on Anker's work *The Glass Veil*, which was exhibited at the conference. The knowledge of the arts is rendered in an especially vivid way throughout the interview, and hence, it also provides an introduction into the issues of the section. In the second paper John Michael Krois focuses on the emotional brain as it is linked to image theory. Starting with what he calls the scandal of emotion without motion (due to 'frozen' images), he elaborates on embodiment in spatial interaction with pictures, their gestalt-effects and their work with image-schemas (the term is borrowed from Mark Jonson – but linked with theories of the body schema). In conceiving of first person experiences that are private, Krois puts forth a theory of the structure of emotions as an essential aspect of picture acts. The paper is followed by Sabine Flach's profound insights into figurations of lament in contemporary art (she focuses on the video installations *Silent Mountain* by Bill Viola and *Pent Up* by Sam Taylor-Wood). Flach outlines a theory of the image act grounded on the notion of a "habitus of an image" inextricably linked to the embodied act of showing. Gestures – especially the smallest movements of the body, known as 'accessories' – are understood as both visually present and presented; and their iconic dimension provides them with their own intrinsic emotionality. From this, Flach concludes that the images presented in the video installations "do not show emotions; far rather *they are* [...] the emotion." In furthering Aby Warburg's concept of pathos formulae, Robert Vischer's thoughts on the optical sense and Rudolf Arnheim's notion of "isomorphic symbolism", she develops a highly innovative account on what it means to depict life in motion. Heike Schlie focuses on emotional habituations with Renaissance images. Compassion, the emotion she prevalently discusses, is conceived of as mediated through and staged by the genre of 'eccentric crucifiction'. Simulating the emotional habitus by providing for an emotional space as its congenial habitat is conceived of with references to the neurosciences. Especially, the notion of mirror neurons as present in current art history is critically discussed. The relation of artistic abstraction and embodiment is vividly discussed in Barbara Larson's chapter dealing with Twentieth Century Avant-Garde cycles. The issue of shared emotions and collective realities is exposed as crucial for habituations through an artistic habitat. Larson especially elaborates on Kupka's embodied situatedness as related to abstraction. She draws the conclusion that Kandinsky even goes as far as to develop a theory of neuroplasticity *avant la lettre*. The section closes with Jin Hyun Kim's chapter, displaying how embodiment-based research on musical expressiveness can be conceived of. Kim argues against a mind/culture vs. nature dichotomy in musical theory, and rather puts forth the notion of a cognitive system embodied and embedded in a biological and socio-cultural environment. Musical expressiveness is understood as emerging from recurrent sensorimotor patterns present as action-perception loops – which can be simulated in human-robot interaction design. She concludes that embodiment of emotions takes place in an act of going along with music rather than listening to an expression of private emotions – thereby rounding up the discussion about emotional artistic knowledge.

The conference *Habitus in Habitat I – Emotion and Motion* was the first major event organized by the research project *Habitus in Habitat*, primarily based in the research department "WissensKünste – Kunst und Wissenschaft" at the Zentrum für Literatur- und Kulturforschung (ZfL) in Berlin. We wish to thank all of our colleagues at the ZfL for the fruitful discussions about the topic and for participating at the conference as speakers or chairs. And we are also very grateful for the great help of Jana Wolf and Andrea Schulz for this publication. Our special thanks go to the director of the ZfL, Prof. Dr. Dr. h.c. Sigrid Weigel, for her confidence in our research work and for engagement in the project. We are equally grateful about the collaboration of our colleagues from the Berlin School of Mind and Brain – and we are especially thanking the directors Prof. Dr. Arno Villringer and Prof. Dr. Michael Pauen, for being long-term cooperation partners on the project and for discussing the insights of the cognitive sciences, philosophy and the neuro-sciences with us, which are all of equal importance for our project.

We also thank the "Medizinhistorisches Museum der Charité", and here especially Prof. Dr. Thomas Schnalke and Inga Franke, who provided an unforgettable conference site, namely the *Hörsaalruine*, which is located in the Museum – and who, moreover made it possible to realize the art exhibition, "The Glass Veil" by Suzanne Anker, within the rooms of the museum.

We are very grateful that Suzanne Anker, in collaborating with Sabine Flach, has been engaged in the project for years now, travelling to and fro between Berlin and the United States in order to realize this art project and to successfully conclude the exhibition *The Glass Veil*. We are very proud that several pictures of this exhibition will be published for the first time in this volume (a catalogue of the exhibition is forthcoming in 2011). We also thank Henry Sanchez for his great help.

Very special thanks are due to our colleagues from the research group "Habitus in Habitat", which – independently from the research project at the ZfL – has been working together in regular meetings for several years now, consisting of members of the ZfL, the Berlin School of Mind and Brain and the research group "Picture Act and Embodiment" at the Humboldt Universität zu Berlin. We are grateful for the vivid, critical and enthusiastic discussions of this research group; without the existence of the forum, the topics realized in this volume would not have been possible.

Berlin, October 2010
Sabine Flach, Daniel Margulies and Jan Söffner

References

Boehm, Gottfried: "Anschauung als Sprache", in: Gottfried Boehm (ed.): *Konrad Fiedler. Schriften zur Kunst I*, Munich (Fink), 2nd edition 1991, pp. VII–XXIII.

Boehm, Gottfried (ed.): *Konrad Fiedler. Schriften zur Kunst II*, Munich (Fink), 2nd edition 1991.

Boehm, Gottfried: "Die Arbeit des Blickes. Hinweise zu Max Imdahls theoretischen Schriften", in: Boehm, Gottfried (ed.): *Max Imdahl, Gesammelte Schriften, Bd. 3: Reflexion – Theorie – Methode*, Frankfurt a.M. (Suhrkamp) 1996, pp. 7–41.

Bourdieu, Pierre: *Pascalian Meditations*, Stanford (Stanford University Press) 1997/2000.

Damasio, Antonio: *Descartes' Error: Emotion, Reason and the Human Brain*, New York (G.P. Putnam's Sons) 1994.

Darwin, Charles: *The Expression of the Emotions in Man and Animals* (1872), Chicago and London (University of Chicago Press) 1965.

Dissanayake, Ellen: *Art and Intimacy: How the Arts Began*, Washington (University of Washington Press) 2000.

Doidge, Norman: *The Brain That Changes Itself: Stories of Personal Triumph from the Frontiers of Brain Science*, New York (Viking Press) 2007.

Emrich, Hinderk M.: "Illusionen, die Wirklichkeit und das Kino", in: Gertrud Koch / Christiane Voss (eds.): *...kraft der Illusion*, Munich (Fink) 2006, pp. 39–53.

Fiedler, Konrad: *Schriften zur Kunst* (1913/14), ed. by Gottfried Boehm, Munich (Fink), 2nd edition 1991.

Fiedler, Konrad: "Der Ursprung der künstlerischen Tätigkeit", in: Gottfried Boehm (ed.): *Konrad Fiedler. Schriften zur Kunst I*, Munich (Fink), 2nd edition 1991.

Flach, Sabine: "Withdrawal as an Artform. Between Withdrawal and Presentation – The Body in the Media Arts", in: Schieren, Mona (ed.): *Present Continuous Past(s). Media Art. Strategies of Presentation, Mediation and Dissemination*, Vienna (Springer) 2005, pp. 48–62.

Flach, Sabine: "'It's not easy being green!' Schnittpunkte von Kunst, Medientechnik und Naturwissenschaften am Beispiel der Transgenic Art", in: Hessler, Martina (ed.): *Konstruierte Sichtbarkeiten. Wissenschafts- und Technikbilder seit der frühen Neuzeit*, Munich (Fink) 2006, pp. 281–303.

Flach, Sabine: "Realfiktionen. Versuchsanordnungen von Olafur Eliasson", in Matthias Bruhn / Kai Uwe Hemken (eds.): *Modernisierung des Sehens. Sehweisen zwischen Künsten und Medien*, Bielefeld (transcript) 2008, pp. 287–298.

Flach, Sabine / Pablo Schneider / Martin Treml (eds.): *Warburgs Denkraum. Formen. Motive. Materialien*, Munich (Fink) 2010.

Flach, Sabine: *Sensing Senses. Die Kunst der Avantgarden. Künstlerische Theorie und Praxis zwischen Wahrnehmungswissenschaft, Kunst und Medientechniken. 1910–1930* (post-doctoral dissertation, in final preparation).

Flach, Sabine / Jan Söffner: *Emotionaler Habitus. Verkörperte Sinnlichkeit zwischen Subjektivität und Umweltrelation*, Munich (Fink) 2011 (in preparation).

Freedberg, David: *The Power of Images*, Chicago (University of Chicago Press) 1989.

Fischer-Lichte, Erika: *Ästhetik des Performativen*, Frankfurt am Main (Suhrkamp) 2004.

Gallagher, Shaun / Dan Zahavi: *The Phenomenological Mind: An Introduction to Philosophy of Mind and Cognitive Science*, London (Routledge) 2008.

Gallagher, Shaun: *How the Body Shapes the Mind*, New York (Oxford University Press) 2004.

Gallese, Vittorio / David Freedberg: "Motion, Emotion and Empathy in Aesthetic Experience", in: *Trends in Cognitive Sciences* 11 (2007), pp. 197–203.

Goldie, Peter: *The Emotions: A Philosophical Exploration*, Oxford (Oxford University Press) 2002, pp. 58–62.

Heidegger, Martin: *Sein und Zeit* (1927), reprint Tübingen (Niemeyer) 1986.

Husserl, Edmund: *Cartesianische Meditationen* (1950), Hamburg (Meiner) 1995.

Hustvedt, Siri: *Die zitternde Frau. Eine Geschichte meiner Nerven*, Reinbek bei Hamburg (Rowohlt), 2010.

Gumbrecht, Hans Ulrich: *Production of Presence: What Meaning Cannot Convey*, Stanford (Stanford University Press) 2004.

Johnson, Mark: *The Meaning of the Body. Aesthetics of Human Understanding*, Chicago (University of Chicago Press) 2007.

Kaplan-Solms, Karen / Mark Solms: *Clinical Studies in Neuro-Psychoanalysis*, London (Other Press) 2000.

Krämer, Sybille: "Sinnlichkeit, Denken, Medien: Von der 'Sinnlichkeit als Erkenntnisform' zur 'Sinnlichkeit als Performanz'", in: Kunst- und Ausstellungshalle der Bundesrepublik Deutschland GmbH (ed.): *Der Sinn der Sinne*, Bonn/Göttingen, 1998, pp. 24–40.

LeDoux, Joseph: *The Emotional Brain*, London (Phoenix) 1999.

LeDoux, Joseph: *The Synaptic Self: How Our Brains Become Who We Are*, New York (Penguin) 2002.

Malabou, Catherine: *What Should We Do with Our Brain?* Translated by Sebastian Rand, New York (Fordham University Press) 2008.

Mauss, Marcel: "Body Techniques", in: *Sociology and Psychology: Essays*, London (Routledge and Kegan Paul) 1939/1979, pp. 95–123.

Merleau-Ponty, Maurice: *Phénoménologie de la perception*, Paris (Gallimard) 1945.

Noë, A.: *Action in Perception*, Cambridge, MA (MIT Press) 2004.

Panksepp, Jaak: *Affective Neuroscience: The Foundations of Human and Animal Emotions*, New York (Oxford University Press) 1998.

Prinz, Jesse J.: *Gut Reactions: A Perceptual Theory of Emotion*, Oxford (Oxford University Press) 2004.

Ratcliffe, Matthew: *Feelings of Being: Phenomenology, Psychiatry and the Sense of Reality*, New York (Oxford University Press) 2008.

Schwartz, Jeffrey M. / Sharon Begley: *The Mind and the Brain: Neuroplasticity and the Power of Mental Force*, New York (Regan Books) 2002.

Solms, Mark / Oliver Turnbull: *The Brain and the Inner World – An Introduction to the Neuroscience of Subjective Experience*, London (Other Press) 2002.

Söffner, Jan: "Non-Representational Mimesis (Grönemeyer with Plato)", in: *Etnofoor* 22 (2010), pp. 91–102.

Stafford, Barbara Maria: *Echo-Objects. The Cognitive Work of Images*, Chicago/London (University of Chicago Press) 2007.

Turner, Victor: *The Ritual Process: Structure and Anti-Structure*, London (Routledge and Kegan Paul) 1969.

Varela, Francisco J. / Evan Thompson / Eleanor Rosch: *The Embodied Mind. Cognitive Science and Human Experience*, Cambridge MA (MIT Press) 1991.

Vischer, Robert: *Über das optische Formgefühl. Ein Beitrag zur Ästhetik*, Leipzig 1873.

Wacquant, Loïc: "Habitus as Topic and Tool", in: Shaffir, William / Antony Puddephatt / Steven Kleinknecht (eds.): *Ethnographies Revisited*, New York (Routledge) 2009, pp. 137–151.

Wollheim, Richard: *Objekte der Kunst*, translated by Max Looser, Frankfurt a.M. (Suhrkamp) 1982.

Socially Shared Emotions

Performing Emotions
How to Conceptualize Emotional Contagion in Performance

ERIKA FISCHER-LICHTE

The two oldest treatises on theatre, Aristotle's *Poetics* in Europe and the *Natya-sastra* in India, establish that the main purpose of performance is to excite strong emotions in the spectator. Aristotle described the effect of tragic theatre as the excitement of ἔλεος and φόβος (pity and terror), i.e. exceptional affective states leading to cleansing. *Catharsis*, the term he introduced for this process of cleansing, is rooted in healing rituals. While the excitement of emotions transfers the spectator into a liminal state, catharsis brings about the actual transformation.

The *Natyasastra*, written between the second century before and the first century after Christ, is ascribed to the legendary sage Bharata. Its central focus lies on exploring the particular experience made possible by performance for actors/dancers and spectators alike. This experience is called *rasa* and entails specific emotional states. *Rasa* is differentiated into eight expressions, such as the erotic or the heroic *rasa*, which correspond to different modes of being or emotional dispositions assumed to be shared by all human beings. Triggered in the actor/dancer and the spectator through gesture, costume, music, etc., *rasa* transforms this disposition into an actual emotional state. Rasa thus also implies a liminal and transformative experience.

In the same way as the concept of *rasa* is relevant to different aesthetic theories in India today, the concept of *catharsis* significantly influenced the discussion of aesthetic experience in performance in Europe until the late 18th century. In the 20th century, it experienced a revival: discussions of *Wirkungsästhetik* (aesthetics of effect) were inextricably linked to the notion of *catharsis*. In these periods, it was considered an unquestionable fact that theatre's main purpose was to excite strong emotions.

In order to fulfill this purpose, each period developed specific devices. In the 17th century, for example, the three main devices were the art of acting, music and the use of various machines. The task of machines – used for lighting, flying and many other special effects – was to arouse awe, wonder and amazement in the spectator. As Claude-François Ménestrier remarked: "Tout ce qui se fait par Machines a toujours paru admirable, extraordinaire et surprenant."[1]

In the performance of Gian Lorenzo Bernini's *Fontana di Trevi*, for instance, machines were used to particularly powerful effect. It showed the flood-

1 Ménestrier: *Traité des tournois*, p. 141.

ing of the Tiber and was presented in Rome during the 1638 carnival season, one year after the Tiber actually flooded its banks. On stage, houses collapsed with loud bangs, burying their occupants. The "victims" looked so dreadfully disfigured that their sight triggered in the spectators a feeling of "pleasant horror". The flooding was staged in front of a backdrop featuring St. Peter's Basilica, clearly establishing the location as Rome. Gradually, real water rose on stage in a dam-like construction at its front. Suddenly, the dam broke and the water threatened to spill onto the spectators and flood the auditorium. Spectators, particularly those seated in the first rows, jumped up and ran out to save themselves from the tidal wave, struck by horror and fear. At that moment, another dam rose from the stage floor and "the water dispersed without having harmed anyone."[2] Spectators have probably rarely felt as frightened by a performance as they did that night.

Music, in turn, was supposed to represent the passions perfectly – not so much to express affects (*affectus exprimere*), but to excite them (*affectus excitare*). As Monteverdi wrote: "It is the contradictions (of affections) which greatly move our minds and hearts, the goal of good music must be to move us."[3] In 1650, Athanasius Kircher reported on the effect of the opera performances he had witnessed in Rome: "The miraculous effects of music in the theatre today in Rome are indescribable; the emotion is often so strong that the auditores begin to scream, sigh, and cry out loud, particularly in casibus tragicis."[4] He described how spectators responded to certain actors and how listeners were often unable to control themselves ("contineri nescii"), how they began to lament ("gemitus"), sigh ("suspiria") and burst into tears ("lacrimas"). Their bodies were compelled to move ("exoticos corporum motus erumpentes") as inner emotions ("interiorum affectuum") expressed themselves in external, bodily signs ("signis extrinsecis").[5]

The Jesuit priest Franciscus Lang wrote about the third – and in some respects most important – device, the art of acting: "The more forcefully, energetically, and grippingly the art of acting affects the person speaking on stage, the more forceful will be the emotions that befall the spectator. For our senses are the gates through which the appearance of things enters the chamber of affects."[6] By way of calculated and varied emotions, spectators were to be transformed into *viri perculsi* – deeply moved subjects.[7] Thus, the representation of a particular emotion was thought to arouse that emotion in the spectator. Lang provided a whole list of the most effective physical signs for different emotions, to be displayed by the actor in order to excite this emotion in the spectator.

2 Bernini: *Fontana di Trevi*, annex to documents, p. 96.

3 Preface to Monteverdi's eighth madrigal book (1638), quoted from Ehrmann: "Claudio Monteverdi", p. 143.

4 Kircher: *Musurgia universalis*, p. 546.

5 Ibid., pp. 546–547.

6 Lang: *Dissertatio de actione scenica*, p. 163.

7 Ibid., p. 164.

1. *Admiration:* Both hands outstretched above the chest and palms towards the audience.
2. *Shame:* The face turned away over the left shoulder and the hands calmly joined behind the back. This same result can be achieved by just the right hand when it is clenched and unclenched repetitively.
3. *Entreating:* Both hands upraised with the palms turned to the listener again and again. Also with the arms hanging down. Also with the hands clenched together.
4. *Weeping and Melancholy:* Both hands joined in the middle of the chest, either high on the chest or lower about the belt. Also accomplished by extending the right hand gently and motioning towards the chest ...
5. *Reproach:* Three fingers folded and the forefinger extended ...
6. *Imploring:* Both hands extended towards the one being spoken to as if about to embrace him ...
7. *Repentance:* Pressing the hands to the breast.
8. *Fear:* The right hand reaching towards the breast with the four digits visible while the rest of the body is bent, relaxed and bowed.[8]

These examples suggest the idea of theatre as a special habitat particularly suited to bringing forth and shaping emotions. However, they also raise two fundamental questions:

1) How is it possible for emotions to be excited in the spectator during a performance, more particularly when they are triggered not by the miraculous or shocking working of machines, but by representations of emotions, especially as carried out by actors (rather than music)? And in case emotions are excited in spectators, does this happen as a consequence of the representation of any given emotion or only of specific emotions?
2) Assuming that the arousal of emotions during a single performance is unlikely to have a lasting effect on the emotional habitus of a spectator, is it however conceivable that the repeated participation in performances in which actors display the same types of emotion may contribute to a shift in emotional habitus?

In order to address these questions, I shall focus my considerations on such emotions as are excited by an actor's representation of the respective emotions (rather than by the use of machines or music).

1. Emotional contagion

In recent years, in the debate on theatre's ability to stir emotions in the spectator, a term was introduced which, like that of *catharsis*, originates in medical discourse – the term *contagion.* Both concepts imply a process of somatic transfor-

8 Ibid., pp. 186 f., here quoted from Engle: "Franz Lang and the Jesuit Stage", p. 107.

mation – in one case the physical cleansing of passions with a healing effect, and in the other the transfer of a disease from one body to another. Both point to passages that transfer the body from one state to another: from illness to health and vice versa. Such processes are triggered by imperceptible forces, which emanate from the body of one person, affect the body of another and transfer it to a state of in-between – between health and illness. In this sense, the terms *catharsis* and *contagion* signify a passage, a state of liminality.[9]

As noted earlier, the term *catharsis* was introduced into the theory of theatre by Aristotle. Since its reception in the late 16th century, the concept has assumed pivotal importance in debates on theatre and art, undergoing definition and redefinition both within and without the realm of aesthetics. The concept of *contagion*, however, evolved in a very different manner. It only recently became the focus of aesthetic and cultural debates.[10] Even though it was not theorized as early as the concept of *catharsis*, it should not be ignored that, beyond medical discourse, it has enjoyed a long history in debates on the notion of emotion in theatre from the 17th century onwards. However, *contagion* as it was discussed in these writings does not operate in accordance with medical knowledge of the time: it occurs neither through direct or indirect contact, nor due to a *miasma*, nor to an exhalation spreading through the air. Rather, it finds its way via spectators' perception, more precisely via their gaze, through which they perceive the actor's body, facial expression and gestures. The spectator's own gaze was thought of as unfolding a transformative power and thus causing physical change. Contagion happened in the act of spectating, it happened *as* spectating.

In theoretical writings on theatre from the 17th and 18th centuries, the term *contagion* was used in a way that related it to a kind of magical process, by which invisible, mysterious forces worked on the body of the spectator and transformed it. This process was denounced as harmful by theatre opponents and hailed as salutary by theatre enthusiasts. No matter whether theatre was condemned or praised, all parties to the debate identified the bodily co-presence of actors and spectators, as well as the presentness of actions and events represented on stage, as necessary conditions for the possibility of contagion. The Church Fathers and, following in their wake much later, participants in the *Querelle de la moralité du théâtre* (fought fiercely in the 17th century)[11] all acknowledged theatre's ability to exercise an immediate sensual effect on the spectator and trigger strong, even overwhelming emotions based on its presentness. The atmosphere inside a theatre was interpreted and described as highly infectious. Actors perform passionate actions on stage, whereas spectators perceive and are infected by them: they, too, begin to feel passionate. Through the act of perception, the emo-

9 Regarding the concept of liminality cf. Turner: *The Ritual Process*; Turner: "Variations on a Theme of Liminality", pp. 36–52.

10 Cf. among others Haas / Nägele / Rheinberger (eds.): *Kontaminationen*; Schaub, Suthor, and Fischer-Lichte (eds.): *Ansteckung*; Sperber: *La contagion des idées*.

11 Cf. Nicole: *Traité de la comédie*.

tion is transferred from the actor's present body to the spectator's present body. The representation of emotions by the actors using their bodies unleashes forces that, the very moment the spectator's gaze turns on them and via this very gaze, invade the spectator's body and transform it – they transfer it into a state of passionate excitement. Both theatre enthusiasts and theatre opponents agreed on this point. They only differed in their assessment of the phenomenon. They either saw it as a healing catharsis or as a profoundly harmful, destructive and estranging (from oneself and from God) disturbance, as Rousseau still argued in the second half of the 18th century. Both emphasized that the contagion leads to a transformation of the spectator: it "heals" the sickness of passion, or results in the loss of self-control or a change of one's identity. In both cases, even long-lasting effects were thought possible – be it life-long immunization against the passions or chronic disease.

Such transformative potential was conceptualized as arising from the bodily co-presence of actors and spectators, understood as the foundation and the cause of such contagion. It is the spectator's gaze, directed towards the body of an actor displaying all the signs of an emotion, which infects him with this very emotion.

1.1 Eighteenth-century theories

While those parties to the *Querelle* opposed to theatre quite often replaced the term *contagion* with the term *poisoning* or *contamination* (*empoisonnement*) in order to underline its harmfulness,[12] 18th-century theoreticians quite generally used it with positive connotations. Contagion was thought of as furthering the coming into being of an aesthetic illusion, which was the aim of the new psychological-realistic art of acting advocated by Denis Diderot, Gotthold Ephraim Lessing, Johann Jakob Engel, Louis-Sébastien Mercier and others. Perceiving the modifications in the actor's body, displayed as representation of an emotion, causes a physical transformation of the perceiving subject by infecting him with the emotion represented. According to Engel, this can in turn only happen if the aesthetic illusion is successful. In his *Mimik* (1785/6), he therefore chided actors for drawing the spectator's attention away from the dramatic figure represented and towards the actor's own phenomenal body. In the theatre, spectators were to exclusively perceive and empathize with the dramatic figure. If their attention was diverted to the actor's phenomenal body, it would "invariably destroy the illusion"[13]. Spectators would be forced to leave the fictive world of the play and enter the world of real physicality. In this case, contagion would be impossible. The "contagiousness of another's gesture"[14] can work only in case the spectator is immersed in the illusion created by the acting.

12 Cf. Nicole: *Traité de la comédie*, pp. 82 ff., 219, 235, 487.

13 Engel: *Mimik,* in J.J. Engel: *Schriften*, vol. 7/8, p. 58.

14 Ibid., p. 100.

Johann Wilhelm Gleim referred to just such a situation in his letter dated July 25, 1755, reporting on the first night of Lessing's *Miss Sara Sampson* performed by Ackermann's troupe in Frankfurt/Oder on July 10, 1755: "The spectators listened for three and a half hours, sitting motionless like statues, and cried"[15]. This is one of the first in a long series of reports of tearful theatre audiences in the second half of the 18th century. Considering that 18th-century audiences were usually loud and noisy – eating and drinking, talking across several seats, coming and going – this letter by contrast suggests that in this case, spectators were completely immersed in the aesthetic illusion, empathizing with the weeping Sir William and his virtuous daughter.

Another key condition for contagion to occur is highlighted by Johann Georg Sulzer. Under the entry *Schauspiel* (theatre, performance) in his *Allgemeine Theorie der schönen Künste* (General Theory of the Fine Arts, 1792), he wrote:

> It is certain that people express their impressions and emotions most vividly in public performances ... Nothing in the world is more contagious and powerful than the perception of emotions that affect a crowd of people at the same time.[16]

While Engel reflects on the relationship between actor and dramatic figure on the one hand, and between dramatic figure and spectator on the other hand as the condition for contagion to occur, Sulzer focuses on what goes on *between* spectators who are infected by the emotion displayed by an actor. Performance, here, is understood as a particular social situation, in which spectators, after being infected, infect each other or reinforce the contagion.

For Sulzer, it is not only the aesthetic illusion that serves as a prerequisite for contagion to happen. It is also the gathering of a number of people who are displaying signs of the same emotion. In his memoirs from 1798, the actor and later director of the Berlin Royal Theatre, August Wilhelm Iffland, described a situation that strongly supports Sulzer's assumption. The performance of *The Barber of Seville* (music by Paisiello) that took place on the occasion of the Princess' name day on November 20, 1785 at the Mannheim Court and National Theatre began with a prologue written and recited by Iffland himself. Iffland wrote:

> The audience seriously considered the action unfolding on stage. When the first relationships were introduced, there was a momentary commotion that, however, ceased again immediately. Gradually, one heard a violently repressed "Ach!" – silence – then again the suppressed mumbling of happy emotion. In one scene, the old countryman said that he had planted the trees in front of his hut on the occasion of the birth of the prince and that he wanted to add a young tree whenever a good prince was born, that he wanted to turn the entire area into a forest, dense, strong, and mighty, which would withstand any storm in the

15 Schüddekopf (ed.): *Briefwechsel zwischen Gleim und Ramler*, vol. 2, p. 206.
16 Sulzer: *Allgemeine Theorie der schönen Künste*, p. 255.

> whole world. Loud voices erupted from the audience: "My God! Oh my God!" The spectators rose from their seats, their calls finally turned into general, wild shouting – arms were raised – hats were waved in cheer! "Live on, live on! God bless you!" Their love, loyalty, and delight called out to the family. The young princesses kissed the hand of their great-aunt, who had broken into tears – the princely brothers embraced with loud wails – the cheers erupted once again – the performance had to be paused for people's emotions to be released.[17]

Here, emotions are brought forth and shaped by a social situation defined by the performance. They are articulated physically and presented in order to be perceived – they are performed both by the actors and by the spectators. The emotions are located neither within nor without the individuals, but in the field between them. They circulate and reinforce each other in the shared space. With regard to 18th-century theatre, emotional contagion in performance can be conceptualized as a particular state of "being in between", as a liminal state made possible by the theatrical frame. This frame entailed three conditions for emotional contagion to occur: 1) the perception of an actor as a dramatic figure; 2) the perception of the actor displaying signs of a particular emotion felt by the figure; and 3) a lit auditorium in which, in response to such perception, a crowd of people themselves display the signs of the same emotion and perceive other spectators displaying them as well. Spectating as emotional contagion was thus defined as a somatic process.

This might explain why, over the course of the 19th century (i.e. as a consequence of the demise of *Wirkungsästhetik*, aesthetics of effect), the term *contagion* gradually disappeared from theoretical discourse on theatre. Spectating in the theatre was no longer regarded as a physical process, but as an "inner", "mental-psychic" process, which would have been contaminated by somatic interventions. The positive meaning of the term *contagion* as it had become accepted over the course of the 18th century was undone. *Contagion* now meant damage, weakening, and contamination of the body, and thus referred to an exclusively negative process. This would appear to be in line with the obsession with notions of purity that developed during the 19th century.[18]

In this context, the term *contagion* could hold only negative connotations, for it pointed to the contamination of the body and, applied to theatre, inadmissibly blended cognitive and hermeneutic with somatic processes. It was replaced by the term *empathy*, defined by Friedrich Theodor Vischer as "the act of lending one's soul".[19] The two leading theoreticians of empathy, Vischer and his son Robert, were quite unambiguous in describing the phenomenon as an inner "psychic-mental" process. The soul of the spectator, so to speak, leaves his body and enters the dramatic figure. To feel empathy meant to understand intentions, motivation and impulses. It meant a bodiless, purely mental act, which does not

17 Iffland: *Meine theatralische Laufbahn*, p. 69.
18 Cf. Haas, Nägele, and Rheinberger: "Kontaminationen" pp. 7–10.
19 Vischer: "Das Symbol", p. 435.

cause any physical symptoms and therefore cannot be perceived by others. The idea of performance as a social situation, enabling or even demanding the display of emotions among spectators, was thus rendered obsolete. The invention of electric lighting, which made it possible to completely darken the auditorium (as happened in Germany for the first time at the Bayreuther Festspiele in 1876), assisted the spectator in learning this new kind of spectatorship. Indeed, a dark auditorium guarded against the danger of emotional contagion as caused by the perception of one's fellow spectators' facial expressions and gestures (spectators, notwithstanding the new theories, still displaying the emotions excited in them by the acting).

In the 1990s, the discovery by neuroscientists working with macaque monkeys of what they called mirror neurons in the animals' brain[20] seemed like a rehabilitation of 18th-century theories of emotional contagion in theatre. Indeed, it made clear that perception is the basis of any kind of empathy, putting an end to the notion of empathy as a purely "mental-psychic" act or process. 18th-century theories could explain why emotional contagion occurs in the theatre – whereas it does not necessarily occur in everyday social life – by defining aesthetic illusion as a precondition. By contrast, mirror neuron theory has so far not been able to define the conditions under which mirror neurons are activated, allowing empathy in its new definition to take place.

1.2 Emotional contagion in contemporary theatre

The conditions defined by 18th-century theoreticians can no longer be taken for granted in contemporary theatre. In many performances, no aesthetic illusion is created or, when it is, it is regularly disrupted. Spectators' perception is not focused on the dramatic figure but oscillates and shifts between the actor's/performer's phenomenal body and a dramatic figure – if such a thing is conjured up at all. Since the 1960s, experimental theatre and performance art have developed a number of devices to focus the spectator's attention on the specific corporeality of the actor/performer. Actors address spectators directly, try to draw them into the play or abuse them, as was for example often the case in Frank Castorf's productions in the 1990s. In some of Christoph Schlingensief's productions, spectators were expressly asked to perform particular actions in front of their fellow audience, but left unclear about the status of these actions, i.e. whether they were to be regarded as part of an art event or of their own everyday life. The Viennese Actionists in the 1960s and many performance artists such as Marina Abramovic, Vito Acconci, Chris Burden, Denis Oppenheim or Gina Pane in the 1970s violated

20 Cf. Gallese and Goldman: "Mirror Neurons and the Simulation Theory of Mind-Reading", pp. 493–501; Gallese et al.: "The Mirror Matching System", pp. 35–36.

their own body before the eyes of an audience without even pretending they were doing so while embodying a dramatic figure.

In all these cases, the theatre frame quite obviously was/is quite different from the one which 18th-century theoreticians had in mind. If emotional contagion still does occur, what are its preconditions?

There is no doubt that all these examples point towards a new *Wirkungsästhetik* (aesthetics of effect). In this context, it must be noted that a revival of *Wirkungsästhetik* had already taken place in the first decades of the 20th century. The historical avant-garde movements, each striving for the advent of their own, specifically defined "new man", proclaimed that performances should contribute to this aim by deeply affecting spectators. In order to explain how theatre had to change in order to be able to bring about this "new man", Antonin Artaud reintroduced the term *contagion* into theoretical discourse on theatre. In his critique of contemporary European culture, he identified logocentrism, rationalism and individualism as the diseases of the time. In order to overcome them, theatre was to bring Western man into contact with his pre-logical, pre-rational and pre-individualistic origins. Theatre would have to "induce trance", i.e. states of liminality, in the spectator. By directly affecting the spectator's subconsciousness, theatre would allow him to "attain ... awareness and a possession of certain dominant forces ... that control all others."[21] Theatre would heal Western man, who was diseased with civilization, by restoring the spectator to "life" and "humanness"[22]. Artaud was not referring to "psychological man, with his well-dissected character and feelings" nor to "social man, submissive to laws and misshapen by religions and precepts" but to "total man"[23]. Again and again, Artaud emphasized that theatre performances aim at liminal states: "The theatre, like the plague, is a crisis which is resolved by death or cure."[24] With the image of the plague, the concept of *contagion* found its way back into theatrical discourse: "First of all we must recognize that the theatre, like the plague, is a delirium and is contagious."[25] It immediately infects the spectators' bodies, altering their somatic states.

Since the 1960s, Artaud's idea of theatre as a highly contagious disease has been taken up by a number of performance artists and stage directors. The question thus arises as to how emotional contagion in performance is re-conceptualized as a consequence of this idea. This question will be explored with reference to a production that took place in the first years of the new millennium – Christoph Schlingensief's *Kunst und Gemüse. Theater ALS Krankheit* (Art and Vegetables. Theatre A(L)S Disease) at the Volksbühne am Rosa-Luxemburg-Platz in 2004. In this performance, the notion of emotional contagion in theatre was redefined.

21 Artaud: *The Theatre and Its Double*, pp. 83/80.
22 Artaud: *Die Tarahumaras*, p. 167.
23 Artaud: *The Theatre and Its Double,* p. 123.
24 Ibid., p. 31.
25 Ibid., p. 27.

A bed was placed at the centre of the auditorium, in which lay Angela Jansen – not an actress, but a person suffering from amyotrophic lateral sclerosis (ALS). The insidious disease, which had already reached an advanced stage, had left her completely paralyzed. She could communicate only via movements of her eyes, interpreted by a computer. Over the course of the performance, her sentences appeared on large screens. She talked, for instance, of her struggle with her health insurance provider, who initially had refused to fund the computer because it was not deemed worthwhile to invest such a large amount on behalf of someone unlikely to survive the next six months.

In the beginning, the presence of the sick woman and her willingness to make her illness part of the performance were felt as a deep irritation by many spectators. As the auditorium was illuminated, spectators could see Angela Jansen and each other. This gave rise to the type of social situation Sulzer had described as a key condition for emotional contagion to occur, challenging spectators to deal with their own and each other's visibly displayed emotions.

The production referred back to Schlingensief's *Parsifal* at Bayreuth earlier the same year, as well as to the Wagner family. As usual for Schlingensief's productions, disabled people appeared on stage side-by-side with professional actors to form the so-called Schlingensief family. While they usually perform *in propria persona*, here they took on certain roles. They played the twelve tones of Schoenberg's twelve-tone scale, members of the Wagner family or Johannes Heesters. Their imperfect acting, which regularly diverted the spectators' attention from the "characters" they were playing and focused it on their own person instead, was offered as matter-of-factly as the presence of Angela Jansen.

When the spectators realized that a terminally ill woman was among them, who did not hide herself and her disease away in a hospital but preferred to communicate with them in this public space, they at first displayed all the signs of irritation and dismay, but also of pity, fear, horror, and even shame. All kinds of emotional contagion were circulating amongst the spectators. However, over the course of the performance, the spectators' emotional states shifted. Neither Angela Jansen's presence, nor the messages she sent via the computer, nor the unprofessional and clearly imperfect acting of the disabled people triggered emotions of anxiety, fear or shame anymore. The situation became increasingly "natural". It gave rise to serenity, even laughter, and did not appear to violate anyone's feelings. It involved neither exhibitionism nor voyeurism. Rather, the shared theatrical space enabled an encounter and communication between "healthy" people, a sick person and a group of disabled people – a space in which everyone was granted equal rights, even if the action revolved around the terminally ill Angela Jansen.

The performance made it possible for spectators to shift not only their emotional states, but also the value systems that caused or justified them. For the initial emotions of fear, anxiety, shame or pity were grounded in the socially sanctioned discourse of "purity" and "impurity", "health" and "illness". Performing these emotions in the beginning, spectators attested to a crisis caused by their perception of the terminally ill woman. The further course of the performance freed them from such emotions and thus allowed them to overcome the crisis by re-assessing underlying value systems. The longer the performance proceeded, the more this re-assessment became a lived experience, and thus reality. This made a certain serenity possible. In the end, the performance allowed spectators to experience catharsis by shifting their value systems.

Obviously, contagion operated very differently in *Kunst und Gemüse* than in the first performance of *Miss Sara Sampson* in 1755. While in the earlier production spectators started to weep after perceiving Sir William doing so, here the audience's anxiety, shame or fear was not triggered by the perception of dramatic figures displaying these emotions. If we want to apply the term *contagion* to this case, it must be expanded to encompass a crisis brought about by perceiving a genuinely sick woman at the center of the auditorium, and not a sick dramatic figure within a fictive world. Because of the underlying value system, it was perceived as a threat to be confronted with the brutal facts of illness and death, even though there was no risk of medical contagion.

However, over the further course of the performance, spectators became infected by Angela Jansen's serenity and the cheerful atmosphere emanating from the Schlingensief family. While in *Miss Sara Sampson* emotional contagion was enabled by aesthetic illusion – the perception of the actors as dramatic figures and of their facial expressions, gestures and movements as signs for the emotions of the dramatic figures – here it was enabled by a confrontation with reality – with an actually terminally ill woman whom no one knew before. This situation transferred spectators into a state of a radical "betwixt and between". Hitherto valid rules and norms were invalidated, and new ones had to be invented and tried out. Spectators remained on the threshold between the no-longer-valid and the not-yet-valid. The performance thus plunged them into a crisis, which could not be overcome by taking refuge in generally accepted standards of behavior, as these did not apply and new ones had not yet been agreed upon. Obviously, for most spectators such a state of liminality proved a real challenge. It alienated them from their everyday life precisely by creating a situation of everyday life, and not by offering an aesthetic illusion. It was the perception of this woman that "infected" them with irritation, fear or shame and the perception of the signs of irritation, fear or shame displayed by other spectators that reinforced these emotions.

Thus, two different kinds of contagion occurred: the first one between spectators themselves and the second one between "actors" (Angela Jansen and the Schlingensief family) and spectators.

In contrast to the conditions identified by 18th-century theoreticians, emotional contagion in this case was not made possible by an aesthetic illusion. It was the perception within the theatre frame of an actually ill woman and of the imperfect acting of disabled people that allowed emotional contagion to occur.

This contagion was in turn reinforced by the visibility of spectators to each other, infecting each other via their perception. By reinstating a lit auditorium – which makes spectators' responses visible to other spectators as well as to the performers, as was the case in 18th-century theatres – and, at the same time, replacing aesthetic illusion by reality or having it imperfectly created and disrupted time and again, Schlingensief succeeded in bringing about emotional contagion. A crisis took place, to be overcome by emotional infection. The contagion by Angela Jansen's serenity and the cheerfulness of the Schlingensief family operated as a form of cure. Over the course of the performance, spectators visibly adopted a shifting emotional stance towards their encounter with actual disease. They were, so to speak, "cleansed" of their anxiety, fear and shame. Instead, they seemed to feel that the terminally ill Angela Jansen deserved the right to appear in a public space such as the theatre and to draw attention to herself and to her illness. It looked as if they had undergone a cathartic experience.

Not only are the conditions for emotional contagion to occur different in 18th-century theatre and today; the types of emotion that are highlighted also vary. As available sources suggest, in 18th-century theatre it was mostly emotions such as pity, sympathy or compassion that proved contagious. References to weeping spectators are thus frequent, whereas there are no reports of spectators experiencing fury along with a dramatic figure. It would appear that the only emotions performed in the auditorium were those considered important in supporting and realizing the new values of bourgeois family life and society.

The situation at the turn of the 21st century is markedly different. In the context of a culture driven by entertainment and events, in which it is possible to witness catastrophes on TV and which bans physical and mental handicaps as well as sickness and death from the public sphere, it seems that crises are needed to startle the senses and the mind of spectators. Irritation, the collision of frames, the destabilization of perceptions of oneself, others and the world are required. Shock, horror, anxiety, fear or shame thus seem to be the most appropriate emotions to be excited in spectators. Such emotions, which are characteristic of crises, make deeply disturbing experiences possible which may effect a transformation in those who are infected by them. Theatre as an emotional habitat thus changes according to society's varying emotional needs.

2. Theatre's contribution to the shaping of a new emotional habitus

In the debates of the 17th and 18th centuries, the assumption prevailed that emotional contagion in theatre could result in long-lasting effects such as, for instance, life-long immunization against the passions or, in the case of self-loss, chronic disease. Even if this were to be the case, it is hard to believe that such long-lasting effects could occur as a consequence of participating in one performance only. Tales about such effects seem rather legendary or mere propaganda, as in the following case: After the performance of Jakob Bidermann's *Cenodoxus* at the Jesuit school in Augsburg in 1602, which presented the life of the hypocritical doctor of Paris, who was highly respected by his fellow citizens but was condemned to eternal damnation by God after his death, several spectators supposedly joined the Jesuit order, following the example of the dramatic figures who, having witnessed the damnation, decided to found a monastic order. Even if we concede that such dramatic life changes may happen as the consequence of participating in a performance as a spectator, it is much more likely that long-lasting effects will occur as a result of repeated participation.

I have called the particular aesthetic experience spectators undergo in a performance when being infected by the emotions of others a liminal experience, the experience of being betwixt and between, of standing on a threshold. The term *liminal* is taken from ritual theory and describes the state of passage from one identity to another – e.g. from boy to warrior or from illness to health. The state of liminality is the necessary precondition for the intended transformation to happen. Whereas in ritual this transformation is irreversible and has to be accepted by the community – the boy who has become a warrior cannot return to the status of a boy once the community has accepted him as warrior – the same does not apply to the consequences of aesthetic experience as liminal experience.[26] The transformations caused by liminality in a theatre performance are predominantly temporary; they take effect only for the duration of the performance or even for limited periods of time within the performance. Such transformations include physiological, emotional, energetic and motoric changes. They can also lead to an actual change of status – from spectator to actor – or produce emotional communities. Whether the experience of the concerned subjects leads to a lasting transformation and reorientation depends on each individual case. It therefore does not seem a promising avenue to discuss the question of whether and how theatre may contribute to shaping a specific emotional habitus with reference to participation and emotional contagion in only a single performance.

Such an effect of theatre is plausible if two conditions are met. First, within the segment of society from which spectators are drawn (also in other cultural spheres than the theatre), a shift in emotional habitus is advocated and initiated. Second, over a long stretch of time, spectators repeatedly participate in performances that infect them with those very emotions that are fundamental to the new emotional habitus.

In the case of 18th-century bourgeois theatre, in performances of domestic plays actors often displayed signs of pity and compassion, tears in particular.

26 Regarding liminality in ritual theory cf. Turner: *The Ritual Process*; regarding the concept of aesthetic experience as liminal experience see Fischer-Lichte: *The Transformative Power of Performance,* especially pp. 174–180 and 190–200.

When infecting spectators with such emotions, they thus worked towards an important shift in their emotional habitus. As Lessing put it:

> *Compassionate human beings are the best human beings,* always eager to exercise all social virtues and all forms of generosity. Who ever makes us feel compassionate makes us a better, more virtuous person, and tragedies that achieve this have the same effect, or rather – this is their purpose.[27]

The 18th century, the "weeping century"[28], quite obviously favored compassionate behavior in different cultural spheres – it was one of the leading ideologies of bourgeois society, which could thus only be realized once the bourgeois subject had developed a corresponding emotional habitus. It is likely that participating frequently in performances that infected spectators with compassion contributed to the shaping of such an emotional habitus.

The liminal experience, made possible by emotional contagion, thus has to be lived through repeatedly: the accumulation of such liminal experiences appears to be an important prerequisite for the shaping of a new emotional habitus, such as evolved, for example, over the course of the 18th century.

However, it is only possible to reach such a conclusion in historical retrospect, and not with reference to our own times. Schlingensief's production was chosen as an example because it caused perceptible, strong emotions in spectators that, in my view, were closely linked to ongoing debates in our society on disease and death, as well as the ever-present possibility of infection. A few years before the production was staged, Michael Hardt and Antonio Negri stated that, at a time of globalization, in which the borders of nation states have become permeable to all kinds of streams, fear of contagion has become ubiquitous. Medieval fences against the plague and cholera live on in quarantine stations at airports.[29] The consequence is the exclusion of anyone who might infect us.

Without doubt, Schlingensief's production can be viewed as an intervention in this debate and as an attempt to shift the dominant emotional habitus. Other productions of his testify to the same ambition. After his own lung cancer was diagnosed, he staged the trilogy *Eine Kirche der Angst vor dem Fremden in mir* (Church of Fear, Ruhr Triennial 2008), *Zwischenstand der Dinge* (As Things Currently Stand, Gorki Studio Berlin 2008) and *Mea Culpa* (Burgtheater Vienna 2009), dealing with his own disease; he performed himself, together with the Schlingensief family and famous professional actors. For those who participated as spectators in all these performances, an accumulation of specific liminal experiences caused by emotional contagion, and maybe even a shift towards a new emotional habitus, seem likely effects. However, this remains a guess.

27 Lessing: "Letter to Nicolai", p. 163.

28 Arbeitsstelle 18. Jahrhundert der Universität Münster: "Das *weinende Saeculum*".

29 Hardt and Negri: *Empire.*

In conclusion: Judging from the example of the 18th century, it would seem a promising project to examine the theatre of different past periods with reference to the questions of which emotions it predominantly triggered in spectators; how these emotions were related to emotions dominant or repressed in the respective society; and finally, whether a series of performances, repeated over an extended stretch of time and triggering these emotions, allowed for an accumulation of liminal experiences that may have resulted in a long-lasting transformation, thus most likely contributing to shaping a new emotional habitus. Such a research program remains to be realized.

Bibliography

Arbeitsstelle 18. Jahrhundert der Universität Münster (ed.): *Das weinende Saeculum. Colloquium der Arbeitsstelle 18. Jahrhundert, Gesamthochschule Wuppertal, Universität Münster, Schloß Dyck, 7–9 October 1981,* Heidelberg (Winter) 1983.

Artaud, Antonin: *The Theatre and Its Double* (1938), transl. by M.C. Richards, New York (Grove Press) 1958.

Artaud, Antonin: *Die Tarahumaras. Revolutionäre Botschaften* (1937), transl. by Brigitte Weidmann, Munich (Rogner & Bernhard) 1975.

Bernini, Gian Lorenzo: "Fontana di Trevi", ed. by Cesare d'Onofrio (ed.), Rome (Staderini) 1963.

Ehrmann, Sabine: Claudio Monteverdi: *Die Grundbegriffe seines musiktheoretischen Denkens* (= Musikwissenschaftliche Studien 2), Pfaffenweiler (Centaurus) 1989.

Engel, Johann Jakob: *Mimik* (1785/6), reprint in: ibid., *Schriften,* vol. 7/8, Berlin 1804 [Reprint Frankfurt am Main {Athenäum}, vol. 7, 1971].

Engle, Ronald Gene: *Franz Lang and the Jesuit Stage*, Ph.D. dissertation, University of Illinois, Ann Arbor (University Microfilms) 1968.

Fischer-Lichte, Erika: *The Transformative Power of Performance: A New Aesthetics,* transl. by Saskya Jain, London/New York (Routledge) 2008.

Gallese, Vittorio / Alvin Goldman: "Mirror Neurons and the Simulation Theory of Mind-Reading", in: *Trends in Cognitive Sciences,* vol. 2 (1998) 12, Dec., pp. 493–501.

Gallese Vittorio et al.: "The Mirror Matching System. A Shared Manifold for Intersubjectivity", in: *Behavioral and Brain Sciences* 25 (2002), pp. 35–36.

Haas, Norbert / Rainer Nägele / Hans-Jörg Rheinberger (eds.): "Kontaminationen", in: *Liechtensteiner Exkurse IV*, Eggingen (Edition Isele) 2001.

Hardt, Michael / Antonio Negri: *Empire*, Cambridge, Mass. (Harvard University Press) 2000.

Iacoboni, Marco: *Mirroring People. The New Science of How We Connect with Others*, New York (Farrar, Straus and Giroux) 2008.

Iffland, August Wilhelm: *Meine theatralische Laufbahn* (1798), Stuttgart (Reclam) 1976.

Kircher, Athanasius: *Musurgia universalis sive ars magna consoni et dissoni*, vol. 1, Rome 1650.

Lang, P. Franciscus: *Dissertatio de actione scenica* (1727), translated into German by Alexander Rudin, Munich/Bern (Francke) 1975.

Lessing, Gotthold Ephraim: "Brief an Nicolai/ Letter to Nicolai", November 1756, in: Herbert G. Goepfer (ed.): *Werke*, vol. 4, Munich (Hanser) 1974.

Ménestrier, Claude-François: *Traité des Tournois, Joustes, Carrousels et autres Spectacles publics*, Lyon 1664.

Monteverdi, Claudio: "Preface to Monteverdi's eighth madrigal book" (1638), in: Sabine Ehrmann: *Claudio Monteverdi. Die Grundbegriffe seines musiktheoretischen Denkens, Musikwissenschaftliche Studien 2*, Pfaffenweiler (Centaurus) 1989.

Rizzolatti, Giacomo / Corrado Sinigaglia: *Mirrors in the Brain. How Our Minds Share Actions and Emotions*, Oxford (Oxford University Press) 2008.

Schaub, Mirjam / Nicola Suthor / Erika Fischer-Lichte: *Ansteckung. Zur Körperlichkeit eines ästhetischen Prinzips,* Munich (Fink) 2005.

Schüddekopf, Carl (ed.): *Briefwechsel zwischen Gleim und Ramler* (1753–59), vol. 2, Tübingen (Literarischer Verein in Stuttgart) 1907.

Sperber, Dan: *La contagion des idées. Théorie naturaliste de la culture*, Paris (Jacob) 1996.

Sulzer, Johann Georg: *Allgemeine Theorie der schönen Künste,* new enlarged second edition, vol. 4, Leipzig (Weidmannsche Buchhandlung) 1794.

Nicole, Pierre: *Traité de la comédie et autres pièces d'un procès du théâtre*, ed. by Laurent Thirouin, Paris (Champion) 1998.

Turner, Victor: *The Ritual Process – Structure and Anti-Structure,* London/New York (Routledge) 1969.

Turner, Victor: "Variations on a Theme of Liminality" in: S. F. Moore / B. C. Myerhoff (eds.): *Secular Ritual,* Assen (Van Garcun) 1977, pp. 36–52.

Vischer, Friedrich Theodor: "Das Symbol" (1887), in: Robert Vischer (ed.): *Kritische Gänge*, Munich (Meyer & Jessen) 1922, vol. 4.

Movement and Emotion in Joint Attention[1]

SHAUN GALLAGHER

When we see another person look at something, or in a certain direction, we automatically tend to follow their gaze to the object or the location. This may be the initiation of an instance of joint attention, which is a phenomenon that developmentally starts to emerge at around 9 months of age.[2] Joint attention has tremendous importance for social interaction and for our ability to generate meaning through such interaction. I'll refer to this co-constitution of meaning as *participatory sense-making*.[3] Not only does the direction of another person's gaze indicate current interest in an object, but their facial expression, which may reflect specific emotional content, will also have an effect on the way I may come to feel about that object, and it may lead to subsequent action.[4] The way this develops into an instance of joint attention, which involves me and the other person being aware that we are attending to the same object, requires a certain coordination between the two of us. In this paper I want to explore the nature of that coordination. I will suggest that rather than being a case of coordinating mental or psychological states, joint attention, and the participatory sense-making that issues from it, involves primarily a coordination of movement and emotion.

Three approaches to social cognition

Intersubjective interactions involved in joint attention play important roles in two areas: social cognition and participatory sense-making. The first concerns our

1 This chapter continues and builds on previous essays by this author (Gallagher 2010; "Interactive Coordination in Joint Attention"). The author's work on this topic has been supported by research grants from the École Normale Supérieure de Lyon and from CNRS while a visiting professor at the ENS in Lyon (2010), and visiting researcher at the Centre de Recherche en Epistémologie Appliquée, École Polytechnique, Paris (2009).

2 Reddy: *How Infants Know Minds*.

3 Cf. De Jaegher and Di Paolo: "Participatory Sense-Making"; De Jaegher, Di Paolo and Gallagher; "Can Social Interaction Constitute Social Cognition?"; Gallagher: "Two Problems of Intersubjectivity."

4 Bayliss et al.: "Gaze Cuing and Affective Judgments of Objects"; "Affective Evaluations of Objects".

understanding of others; the second concerns our understanding of the world in coordination with others.[5] These are closely related issues, and both of them involve social interaction. Explanations of how we understand others also play into accounts of how, with others, we make sense of the world. For this reason a brief review of the current theories of social cognition will help to set the stage for further discussion of joint attention and participatory sense-making. The two standard "theory of mind" (ToM) approaches which have dominated the discussions of social cognition are theory theory (TT) and simulation theory (ST).

TT claims that one takes a theoretical stance toward the other in order to infer or "mindread" their beliefs, desires, or intentions.[6] That is, the ability to understand others is based on having a certain kind of knowledge, a theory (or folk psychology) of how people behave in general. According to some theory theorists, folk psychology may be learned via experience; other theorists contend that it is based on innate capacities that emerge developmentally. There is also disagreement about whether we use the theory explicitly (consciously) or implicitly (non-consciously). All theory theorists, however, embrace three suppositions, although sometimes only implicitly.

(1) Understanding others means understanding their mental states, which are perceptually inaccessible. Thus, in the process of "mindreading" we must infer their beliefs and desires (the mentalizing supposition);
(2) In our encounters with others we are primarily third-person observers;
(3) For many theory theorists, use of folk psychological theory is our primary and pervasive way of understanding others. Based on experiments on judgments of false belief, it is thought that a full-scale ToM starts at around the age of four years.

In contrast to the knowledge-rich approach of TT, ST claims that in our attempt to understand others we do not require folk psychology; rather, we use our own mind as a model on which we simulate the other's mind by creating "as if" or pretend beliefs, desires, intentional states.[7] We put ourselves in the other person's shoes, run our mental simulations, and then attribute the results to the other person. As in TT, there is debate about whether our simulating ability is a product of experience or is an innate capacity activated by experience. Traditional ST suggests that simulation is explicit (conscious or introspective, involving imaginary enactments).[8] A more implicit version of ST suggests that

5 Gallagher: "Two Problems of Intersubjectivity".

6 See e.g. Baron-Cohen: "Precursors to a Theory of Mind"; Carruthers and Smith: *Theories of Theories of Mind*; Premack and Woodruff: "Does a Chimpanzee Have a Theory of Mind?".

7 See e.g. Goldman: *Simulating Minds*; Gordon: "'Radical' Simulationism"; Heal: "Simulation, Theory and Content".

8 Goldman, for example, describes it this way: "When a mindreader tries to predict or retrodict someone else's mental state by simulation, she uses pretense or imagination to put herself in

simulation routines are non-conscious, and are performed automatically and sub-personally. The discovery of mirror neurons has been used to support this idea.[9]

Simulation theorists also adopt versions of the three suppositions listed above.

(1) Understanding others means understanding their mental states, which are perceptually inaccessible. Mindreading involves simulating the beliefs and desires of the other person (the mentalizing supposition).
(2) In our encounters with others we are primarily third-person observers, although we depend on a first-person process of using the resources of our own minds to simulate theirs.
(3) For many simulation theorists, use of simulation is our primary and pervasive way of understanding others.

Consider the claim about taking an observational stance. Both TT and ST are based on the idea that our attempts to understand others are always made in the mode of observation. Person A observes the behavior of person B and then resorts to either theory or simulation to predict or explain B's action. In TT this observational stance involves an explicit third-person perspective. As a third-person observer I consult the theory and infer what is in the other's mind and accordingly predict or explain the other's behavior. In ST this observational stance involves a first-person perspective in the sense that the simulation process is accomplished in a model of my own first-person thoughts, beliefs, desires, etc. I simulate from a first-person perspective, and then infer or project beliefs or desires to the other in order to predict or explain their behavior.

In contrast to TT and ST, consider an alternative view, interaction theory (IT).[10] On this view our primary and pervasive way of encountering others is not characterized by observation, but by interaction, characterized in terms of sensory-motor processes (primary intersubjectivity) and context (secondary intersubjectivity).[11] That is, the others we try to understand are usually people

the target's 'shoes' and generate the target state" (Goldman "Mirror Systems"; see Goldman "Interpretation Psychologized").

9 See e.g. Gallese and Goldman: "Mirror Neurons and the Simulation Theory of Mindreading"; Goldman: *Simulating Minds*.

10 Gallagher: "The Practice of Mind", "Understanding Interpersonal Problems in Autism", *How the Body Shapes the Mind*, "Understanding Others", "Inference or Interaction".

11 Primary and secondary intersubjectivity are Trevarthen's ("Communication and Cooperation in Early Infancy"; "The Concept and Foundations of Infant Intersubjectivity"; Trevarthen and Hubley: "Secondary Intersubjectivity") terms for processes that begin in infancy, but they also certainly continue through our adult interactions. Primary intersubjectivity includes sensory-motor processes involved in the perception of and response to the movements, gestures, facial expressions, and intentional actions of others; secondary intersubjectivity includes our use of particular contexts and social roles to guide our understanding of others. For IT, these intersubjective processes replace belief-desire psychology (or folk psychology) as the level of basic intentional description; for the more subtle and sophisticated interpretations found in

with whom we are interacting. We are communicating with them, or working on some common task with them, or situated with them in some common setting. Our primary way of understanding others is worked out in real second-person interactions within pragmatic and social contexts. As an alternative to TT and ST, interaction theory (IT) appeals to evidence from phenomenology and developmental psychology. IT challenges the suppositions of TT and ST.

(1) IT rejects the mentalizing supposition, the Cartesian idea that other minds are hidden away and inaccessible. It cites evidence that in many cases knowing the other person's intentions, emotions, and dispositions is simply a matter of perceiving their embodied behavior in the situation. In most cases of everyday interaction no inference or simulation beyond that is necessary.
(2) IT rejects the spectatorial supposition that we are primarily observers of others' behaviors. Our normal everyday stance toward the other person is second-person interaction. For the most part we are interacting with them on some project, or in some communicative practice, or in some pre-defined relation.
(3) IT rejects the supposition that mindreading is our primary or pervasive way of understanding others. Rather, mindreading, as either TT or ST describes it, is at best a specialized activity that is relatively rarely employed. Our everyday understanding of others depends more on embodied and situated ways of perceiving and interacting with them, and is enhanced by narrative practices.

Coordination in joint attention

The onset of abilities for joint attention (at 9 months to 1 year of age) marks an important transition from primary to secondary intersubjectivity. "In joint attention the child coordinates her attention to the object and the adult at the same time as the adult coordinates her attention to the same object and the child."[12] What exactly does it mean to coordinate attention? One view, consistent with the mentalizing supposition, is that since attention is a psychological state, then the coordination must be a psychological coordination. The notion of psychological coordination is often framed in terms of propositional attitudes, or being in certain mental states, like belief, desire – states where we mentally recognize something to be the case. Moreover, on this view, with respect to joint

adult interactions, it points to the role of action narrative rather than theory or mental simulation (see Gallagher and Hutto: "Understanding Others Through Primary Interaction and Narrative Practice"; Hutto: "Articulating and Understanding the Phenomenological Manifesto").

12 Tomasello: "Joint Attention as Social Cognition", p. 107.

attention, the object of such propositional states is the other person's mental states – i.e., we recognize or know that the other person is attending, and the other person knows that we are attending. John Campbell summarizes this view.

> There are various ways in which propositional states could be involved in coordination. Propositional states might enter into the control of attention itself and they might enter into my recognition of how my attention, or your attention, is being controlled. First, it might be that I know what you are attending to, and that this knowledge is a factor in sustaining my attention on the thing. Secondly, I might intend to attend to whatever you are attending to. And thirdly, it might be that I know that the reason I am attending to the thing is, in part, that you are attending to it. And finally, it might be that I know that the reason you are attending to the thing is, in part, that I am attending to it.[13]

Such accounts suggest that joint attention involves mindreading (of the 'theory theory' [TT] or simulation theory [ST] variety) rather than embodied interaction. I not only have to know that you are attending, but I have to know that you are capable of having such a mental state as attending to something, and that is something I have to infer or simulate. Such mindreading, as Campbell points out, "is 'off-line' in that its upshot is not permanent and it is decoupled from action."[14] *Decoupled from action* because TT and ST, as noted, have traditionally been cast in terms of third-person observation rather than second-person interaction. Just this by itself should tell us that TT and ST are going to have a difficult time explaining the interactional nature of joint attention.

The fact that joint attention capability develops between 9 months and 1 year of age is already problematic for TT and explicit versions of ST – that is, for any account of social cognition that depends on some kind of complex cognition or some additional step of interpretation beyond what is available perceptually and contextually. Johannes Roessler makes this point clearly.

> The problem is that while there is compelling intuition to the effect that 1-year-olds have some grasp of others' attention, there is also prima facie grounds for doubting that they have the conceptual abilities for interpretation (such as the ability to give causal explanations).[15]

TT and ST, however, want to know, if it is not theory or simulation that provides access to others' minds, then what? What is the nature of the perceptual and contextual factors that seemingly give us access to the other person's mental state of attention? This, however, is just the wrong way to frame the problem, because once we admit that what is required for joint attention is the discernment of mental states that are not accessible and that must be inferred or simulated, then joint attention in young infants is problematic in the way Roessler explains, and anything so simple as perception and context seem insufficient to the job.

13 Campbell: "Joint Attention and Common Knowledge", p. 245.
14 Ibid. p. 242.
15 Roessler: "Joint Attention and the Problem of Other Minds", p. 236.

IT suggests that the task is not to access interior propositional attitudes, but to perceive intentions and dispositions in the embodied behaviors, movements, facial expressions, gestures, and actions of others (even if there is an undeniable interior dimension of experience and affect associated with these externalities). We can pursue this approach if we do not rig the problem in such a way that only theory or simulation could solve. On this view, the coordination required is a coordination in the movement of interaction rather than a psychological coordination of propositional attitudes. Joint attention decoupled from action is the rare case (perhaps the case in which my connection or coordination with the other person breaks down). Instead, the kind of coordination at stake in joint attention is primarily both motoric and emotional.

Movement

Campbell[16] suggests a couple of examples that are relevant. In the first one I find myself in a pasture looking at some cattle that start to move toward me. As the individual cow moves, Campbell suggests, it seems to be checking that its fellow cows are coming along. I'm not sure what to say about what it might mean for cows to engage in social referencing among themselves. In any case, my own response is not to try to get into their minds, or to work out some set of propositional attitudes that I attribute to them. Rather, my understanding of their joint attention on a particular object (me, in this case) and my own coordinated joint attention on the same object (i.e., me as I try to figure out what to do) translates immediately into movement on my part.

I might put this in terms of trying to figure out their intentions. If I try to discern whether they are going to change direction before they reach me, I don't try to mindread their mental states, I try to see it in their movements – or in the movement of the herd as a whole – and this in reference to the shape of the field and the possibilities for their moving this way or that. I can *see* that they have me as a target, and I can *see* that there is nothing else in this pasture that would capture their attention. My coordinated attention to what and where they are attending sets my feet in motion.

I want to claim that in most cases, attention that I share with other humans involves nothing more than something like this. If, for example, my friend and I happen to be in the pasture looking at a stampede coming towards us, if we catch each other's eye, as they say, if she grabs my arm and yells and we start to run, is there anything more to the coordination that we have to explain? Is there any reason to engage in mindreading? Do I have to consider her beliefs and desires?

16 "Joint Attention and Common Knowledge".

Do I need folk psychology or do I need to employ a theory to understand why someone grabs another person's arm? Do I need to simulate my friend's situation or what she might be thinking? No, the kind of knowledge I need is a very practical kind that is based on occurrent perception.

To get a better sense of what perception and context can do for us in this respect, and to get a good sense of what one might mean by claiming that some kind of "understanding" is involved – Roessler worries about this term[17], as does Hutto[18] – let's look at another example, also suggested by Campbell. This is the kind of joint attention coordination required when playing team sports like football.

Campbell puts it this way: "a team playing football are continuously monitoring one another's attention. But this does not require them to be engaged in conceptual thought, or to have even iterated knowledge of the direction of each other's attention."[19]

I think we can put this more positively by extending what Merleau-Ponty had already said about this.

> For the player in action the football field is not an "object," that is, the ideal term which can give rise to an indefinite multiplicity of perspectival views and remain equivalent under its apparent transformations. It is pervaded with lines of force (the "yard line"; those lines that demarcate the "penalty area") and is articulated in sectors (for example, the "openings" between the adversaries) which call for a certain mode of action and which initiate and guide the action as if the player were unaware of it. The field is not given to him, but present as the immanent term of his practical intentions; the player becomes one with it and feels the direction of the "goal", for example, just as immediately as the vertical and the horizontal planes of his own body.[20]

The player's intentions and actions are shaped by the physical environment and by the nature of the game he is playing. Controlling the ball on this field, and strategizing on how to get to the goal are not things accomplished in the player's head, but necessarily are processes that are laid out on this field from the perspective of the player as he is positioned and as he moves across the grid. As Merleau-Ponty acknowledges, this field is not empty of others. And many of these others are clearly in relations of joint attention with the one who controls the ball. Everyone is attending to the ball (among other things), and the player knows that everyone is attending; and everyone knows that he is attending, and so forth.

More than this, everyone's intentions are quite transparent and are specified by the context and rules of the game. No need for theory of mind (TT or ST) here; I don't have to infer anything about your propositional attitudes if you wear

17 "Joint Attention and the Problem of Other Minds", pp. 237ff.
18 "Articulating and Understanding the Phenomenological Manifesto".
19 Campbell: "Joint Attention and the Problem of Other Minds", p. 245.
20 Merleau-Ponty: *The Structure of Behavior*, p. 168–69.

a different colored jersey. I don't have to put myself in your place and work up some pretend beliefs in order to know your intentions. Your specific intentions are quite apparent in the way you are moving towards me or positioning yourself between me and the goal.

My football-field-understanding of particular others is pragmatic and enactive in the sense of being a knowing-how to deal with them, rather than a knowing-what. It's geared to action and interaction with them, in the context of the game. Theory-theorists might argue that all of this presupposes a theory of or a set of rules about how players will act on the field. But it's not clear that any such theory is what enters into the pragmatic understanding which helps to constitute the meaning of the others' behavior. One learns football by *practice*; and one comes to understand the precise actions of others on the field in terms of that practice, rather than in terms of some general theory.

One might object that practices on the football field are rather limited in terms of what we need to understand. One's intentions are, as we said, transparent; movements have well-defined goals even if they are sometimes fabulously complex. So on the football field there is not much of a challenge when it comes to working out patterns of coordination in joint attention. But again I think this applies to many human situations, circumscribed by time, place, and custom.

We know, for example, that things change dramatically when after the game we go out to have a few pints at the pub. Our immediate relations to others clearly change. Yet, we continue to engage them in joint attentional ways that remain pragmatic or specifically social. The game changes; the rules change; but the basic capacities of primary and secondary intersubjectivity, including joint attention, continue to give us access to the other person's meaning. This is the case even if the rare puzzling circumstance comes up and I have to employ theory or simulation – in such cases the only starting point I have is the ongoing interaction, now perhaps uncoordinated. But here it becomes clear that we have not been telling the whole story.

Emotion

Back in the cow pasture, when my friend grabs my arm and shouts and we start to move, I can tell quite readily whether she is shouting because this looks like good fun – she may think the situation of cows chasing philosophers is rather funny – or because she is afraid of being trampled. I will be able to tell this from the grip on my arm, from the intonation in her voice, from the expression on her face, and so on. It may or may not be so easy on the football field; but one can often tell whether your opponents feel defeated or victorious by their postures and movements.

More generally, in joint attention, not only the direction of gaze, but also the emotional expression on the face of the other has a measurable effect. In studies of object evaluation, for example, the gaze of the other person towards an object can draw one's attention to the object. Subjects presented with a face looking towards (or away from) an object evaluate the object as more (or less) likeable than those objects that don't receive much attention from others. When you add an emotional expression to the face, the effect is stronger.[21] In addition, the quality of the other person's movement is important. Seeing another person act with ease (or without ease) toward an object will influence one's feelings about the object.[22] Indeed, my awareness of the gaze of others towards objects or in joint attention influences my perception of objects in regard to motor action, significance, and emotional salience.[23]

Developmental studies support this view and trace these processes to the beginnings of joint attention. Infants are highly responsive to attentional and emotional cues as part of their secondary intersubjective abilities. Infants often share emotions, e.g., exchange smiles, when playing with a toy in joint attention with another, and they get visibly upset if the other person they are interacting with assumes a passive face.[24] They follow another person's gaze to the appropriate target[25] and reference the other's emotional expressions to know whether to approach novel objects.[26] Hornik, Risenhoover and Gunnar[27] showed that when an infant of 12-18 months saw a positive, negative, or neutral emotional expression by a parent toward a particular toy, they later, and in a different context, avoided playing with that toy. Repacholi and Meltzoff[28] showed that the emotional expressions of one person while watching the action of another (showing anger or a neutral facial expression) will influence an 18-month old infant's inclination to imitate the actions of the second person.[29]

These connections between perception of gaze, joint attention, and emotion have been show to correlate significantly with emotion regulation later in

21 Bayliss et al.: "Gaze Cuing and Affective Judgments of Objects: I Like What You Look At"; "Affective Evaluations of Objects are Influenced by Observed Gaze Direction and Emotional Expression".

22 Hayes et al.: "Self Produced and Observed Actions Influence Emotion".

23 Becchio et al.: "How the Gaze of Others Influences Object Processing".

24 See e.g. Messinger et al.: "Early Emotion Sharing and Later Joint Attention".

25 Butterworth and Jarrett: "What Minds Have in Common Is Space".

26 Klinnert et al.: "Social Referencing"; Moses et al.: "Evidence for Referential Understanding".

27 "The Effects of Maternal Positive, Neutral, and Negative Affective Communications".

28 "Emotional Eavesdropping"; Repacholi, Olsen and Meltzoff: "How Infants Integrate Attentional and Emotional Cues"; Repacholi, Meltzoff and Olsen: "Infants' Understanding of the Link Between Visual Perception and Emotion".

29 See also Walden and Ogan: "The Development of Social Referencing".

development.[30] Further, they have been shown to break down in autism, where lack of emotional connectedness between young autistic children and others correlates with the lack of engagement with the other's attitudes towards a shared world.[31] One also finds in autism a lack of social emotions, feelings such as coyness, embarrassment, guilt, pride, jealousy or shame, as well as empathic concern.[32]

With respect to participatory sense-making, where humans share a meaningful world, and through their interactions help to co-constitute that meaning, something that appears to be a feature of typically developing infants' social relations (Hobson, in press), not only joint attention – the coordination of attention – but also affective engagements with the *attitudes* of another are essential.

Conclusion

Affective engagements with the *attitudes* of others does not mean mentalizing engagement with their *propositional* attitudes, their mental states, but engaged interactions with their motoric and emotional attitudes. Our engaged interactions happen between two or more embodied individuals, and in some cases can take on a certain autonomy that multiplies and sometimes magnifies the emotional aspects of our experience. In other cases, the emotional content remains subtle and nuanced, yet still capable of affecting our intersubjective life. In still other cases the emotional dimension seems to be embedded in social practices and contexts and can have a contagious character, e.g., at the athletic event when the music of the national anthem plays.

In life, as in football, there are, on the one side, the external scaffolds – the physical place or architecture, the field of play, the game, the customs, the rules – and on the other side my embodied emotional and cognitive abilities – abilities that start out and continue as perceptual and action-oriented, that are enhanced in joint attention as we participate in sense-making, and are made more subtle and sophisticated via communicative and narrative practices – many of which take place in the pub after the game.

30 Morales et al.: "Individual Differences in Infant Attention Skills, Joint Attention, and Emotion Regulation Behaviour".

31 See Garcia-Perez, Lee and Hobson "On Intersubjective Engagement in Autism"; Hobson: "Autism and the Self"; Hobson, Lee, and Hobson: "Only Connect? Communication, Identification, and Autism"; Sigman et al.: "Responses to the Negative Emotions of Others".

32 Hobson et al.: "Foundations for Self-Awareness; Hobson, Harris, Garcia-Perez, and Hobson: "Anticipatory Concern".

References

Baron-Cohen, S.: "Precursors to a Theory of Mind: Understanding Attention in Others", in: A. Whiten (ed.): *Natural Theories of Mind: Evolution, Development and Simulation of Everyday Mindreading*, Cambridge, MA (Basil Blackwell) 1991, pp. 233–251.

Bayliss, A. P. / M. A. Paul / P. R. Cannon et al.: "Gaze Cuing and Affective Judgments of Objects: I Like What You Look At", in: *Psychonomic Bulletin & Review* 13 (2006) 6, pp. 1061–1066.

Bayliss, A. P. / M. A. Paul / P. R. Cannon et al.: "Affective Evaluations of Objects are Influenced by Observed Gaze Direction and Emotional Expression", in: *Cognition*, 104 (2007), pp. 644–653.

Becchio, C. / C. Bertone / U. Castiello: "How the Gaze of Others Influences Object Processing", in: *Trends in Cognitive Sciences*, 12 (2008) 7, pp. 254–58.

Becchio, C. / A. Pierno / M. Mari et al.: "Motor Contagion from Eye Gaze. The Case of Autism", in: *Brain*, 130 (2007), pp. 2401–2411.

Butterworth, G / N. Jarrett: "What Minds Have In Common Is Space: Spatial Mechanisms Serving Joint Visual Attention in Infancy", in: *British Journal of Developmental Psychology*, 9 (1991), pp. 55–72.

Campbell, J.: "Joint Attention and Common Knowledge", in: N. Eilan / C. Hoerl / T. McCormack et al. (eds.): *Joint Attention: Communication and Other Minds*, Oxford (Oxford University Press) 2005, pp. 287–97.

Carruthers, P. / P. K. Smith (eds.): *Theories of Theories of Mind,* Cambridge (Cambridge University Press) 1996.

De Jaegher, H. / E. Di Paolo: "Participatory Sense-Making: An Enactive Approach to Social Cognition", in: *Phenomenology and the Cognitive Sciences*, 6 (2007), pp. 485–507.

De Jaegher, H. / E. Di Paolo / S. Gallagher: "Does Social Interaction Constitute Social Cognition?", in: *Trends in Cognitive Sciences.* 14 (2010) 10, pp 441–447.

Gallagher, S.: "Interactive Coordination in Joint Attention", in: A. Seeman (ed.): *Joint Attention: Developments in Philosophy of Mind, Developmental and Comparative Psychology, and Cognitive Science*, Cambridge, MA (IT Press), in press.

Gallagher, S.: "Joint Attention and Participatory Sense-Making", in: *Alter: Revue de phénoménologie* 18, 2010.

Gallagher, S.: "Two Problems of Intersubjectivity", in: *Journal of Consciousness Studies*, 16 (2009) 6–8, pp. 289–308.

Gallagher, S.: "Understanding Others: Embodied Social Cognition", in: P. C. Garzón (ed.): *Elsevier Handbook of Embodied Cognitive Science*, London (Elsevier) 2008, pp. 439–52.

Gallagher, S.: "Inference or Interaction: Social Cognition Without Precursors", in: *Philosophical Explorations*, 11 (2008) 3, pp. 163–73.

Gallagher, S.: *How the Body Shapes the Mind*, Oxford (Oxford University Press) 2005.

Gallagher, S.: "Understanding Interpersonal Problems in Autism: Interaction Theory as an Alternative to Theory of Mind", in: *Philosophy, Psychiatry, and Psychology*, 11 (2004) 3, pp. 199–217.

Gallagher, S.: "The Practice of Mind: Theory, Simulation, or Interaction?", in: *Journal of Consciousness Studies*, 8 (2001) 5–7, pp. 83–107.

Gallagher, S. / D. Hutto: "Understanding Others Through Primary Interaction and Narrative Practice", in: J. Zlatev, T. Racine, C. Sinha et al. (eds): *The Shared Mind: Perspectives on Intersubjectivity*, Amsterdam (John Benjamins) 2008, pp. 17–38.

Gallese, V. / A. Goldman: "Mirror Neurons and the Simulation Theory of Mindreading", in: *Trends in Cognitive Sciences*, 2 (1998) 12, pp. 493–501.

Garcia-Perez, R. M. / A. Lee / R. P. Hobson: "On Intersubjective Engagement in Autism: A Controlled Study of Nonverbal Aspects of Conversation", in: *Journal of Autism and Developmental Disorders,* 37 (2007), pp. 1310–1322.

Goldman, A.: *Simulating Minds: The Philosophy, Psychology and Neuroscience of Mindreading,* Oxford (Oxford University Press) 2006.

Goldman, A.: "Mirror Systems, Social Understanding and Social Cognition", in: *Interdisciplines* (2005) <http://www.interdisciplines.org/mirror/papers/3>

Goldman, A.: "Interpretation Psychologized", in: *Mind and Language*, 4 (1989), pp. 161–185.

Gordon, R. M.: "'Radical' Simulationism", in: P. Carruthers / P. K. Smith (eds.): *Theories of Theories of Mind*, Cambridge (Cambridge University Press) 1996, pp. 11–21.

Hayes, A. E. / M. A. Paul / B. Beuger et al.: "Self Produced and Observed Actions Influence Emotion: The Roles of Action Fluency and Eye Gaze", in: *Psychol. Res.*, 72 (2007), pp. 461–472.

Heal, J.: "Simulation, Theory and Content", in: P. Carruthers / P. K. Smith (eds.): *Theories of Theories of Mind*, Cambridge (Cambridge University Press) 1996, pp. 75–89.

Hobson, J. A. / R. Harris / R. Garcia-Perez et al.: "Anticipatory Concern: A Study in Autism", in: *Developmental Science*, 12 (2009), pp. 249–263.

Hobson, R. P.: "Autism and the Self", in: S. Gallagher (ed.): *Oxford Handbook of the Self,* Oxford (Oxford University Press) 2001, pp. 571–591.

Hobson, R. P. / G. Chidambi / A. Lee et al.: "Foundations for Self-Awareness: An Exploration through Autism", in: *Monographs of the Society for Research in Child Development, 284, 71* (2006), pp. 1–165.

Hobson, R. P. / A. Lee / J. A. Hobson: "Only Connect? Communication, Identification, and Autism", in: *Social Neuroscience,* 2 (2007), pp. 320–335.

Hobson, R. P. / A. Lee: "Imitation and Identification in Autism", in: *Journal of Child Psychology and Psychiatry*, 40 (1999), pp. 649–59.

Hornik, R. / N. Risenhoover / M. Gunnar: "The Effects of Maternal Positive, Neutral, and Negative Affective Communications on Infant Responses to New Toys", in: *Child Development*, 58 (1987) 4, pp. 937–944.

Hutto, D.: "Articulating and Understanding the Phenomenological Manifesto", in: *Abstracta* 2, 2008, pp. 10–19.

Hutto, D.: *Folk Psychological Narratives: The Sociocultural Basis of Understanding Reasons,* Cambridge, MA (MIT Press) 2008.

Klinnert, M. D. / R. N. Emde / P. Butterfield et al.: "Social Referencing: The Infant's Use of Emotional Signals from a Friendly Adult with Mother Present", in: *Developmental Psychology*, 22 (1986) 4, pp. 427–432

Merleau-Ponty, M.: *The Structure of Behavior,* translated by A. Fischer, Pittsburgh (Duquesne University Press) 1983.

Messinger, D. / T. Cassel / J. D. Haltigan et al.: "Early Emotion Sharing and Later Joint Attention Among the Infant Siblings of Children with Autism", in: *Paper presented at the annual meeting of the XVth Biennial International Conference on Infant Studies, Westin Miyako, Kyoto, Japan*. 2006. <http://www.allacademic.com/meta/p93900_index.html>

Morales, M. / P. Mundy / M. Crowson et al.: "Individual Differences in Infant Attention Skills, Joint Attention, and Emotion Regulation Behaviour", in: *International Journal of Behavioral Development*, 29 (2005) 3, pp. 259–63.

Moses, L. J. / D. A. Baldwin / J.G. Rosicky et al.: "Evidence for Referential Understanding in the Emotions Domain at Twelve and Eighteen Months", in: *Child Development* 72 (2001), pp. 718–735.

Premack, D. and Woodruff, G.: "Does a Chimpanzee Have a Theory of Mind?", in: *Behavioral and Brain Sciences*, 4 (1979), pp. 515–26.

Reddy, V.: *How Infants Know Minds*, Cambridge, MA (Harvard University Press) 2008.

Repacholi, B. M. / A. N. Meltzoff: "Emotional Eavesdropping: Infants Selectively Respond to Indirect Emotional Signals", in: *Child Development,* 78 (2007), pp. 503–521.

Repacholi, B. M. / A. N. Meltzoff / B. Olsen: "Infants' Understanding of the Link Between Visual Perception and Emotion: 'If she can't see me doing it, she won't get angry'", in: *Developmental Psychology,* 44 (2008), pp. 561–574.

Repacholi, B. / B. R. Olsen / A. N. Meltzoff: "How Infants Integrate Attentional and Emotional Cues in Order to Regulate Their Imitative Responses", in: *Paper presented at the annual meeting of the XVth Biennial International Conference on Infant Studies, Westin Miyako, Kyoto, Japan,* 2006. http://www.allacademic.com/meta/p93887_index.html

Roessler, J.: "Joint Attention and the Problem of Other Minds", in: N. Eilan / C. Hoerl / T. McCormack et al. (eds.): *Joint Attention: Communication and Other Minds*, Oxford (Oxford University Press) 2005 pp. 230–359.

Sigman, M. D. / C. Kasari / J. H. Kwon et al.: "Responses to the Negative Emotions of Others by Autistic, Mentally Retarded, and Normal Children", in: *Child Development,* 63 (1992), pp. 796–807.
Tomasello, M.: "Joint Attention as Social Cognition", in: C. Moore / P. J. Dunham (eds.): *Joint Attention: Its Origin and Role in Development*, Hillsdale, N.J. (Lawrence Erlbaum) 1995, pp. 103–130.
Trevarthen, C.: "The Concept and Foundations of Infant Intersubjectivity", in: S. Braten (ed.): *Intersubjective Communication and Emotion in Early Ontogeny*, Cambridge (Cambridge University Press) 1998, pp. 15–46.
Trevarthen, C. B.: "Communication and Cooperation in Early Infancy: A Description of Primary Intersubjectivity", in: M. Bullowa (ed.): *Before Speech*, Cambridge (Cambridge University Press) 1979.
Trevarthen, C. / Hubley, P.: "Secondary Intersubjectivity: Confidence, Confiding and Acts of Meaning in the First Year", in: A. Lock (ed.): *Action, Gesture and Symbol: The Emergence of Language*, London (Academic Press) 1978, pp. 183–229.
Walden, T. A. / T. A. Ogan: "The Development of Social Referencing", in: *Child Development,* 59 (1988), pp. 1230–1240.

Intercorporality
How Embodied Interaction Shapes Mind and Brain

THOMAS FUCHS

Abstract

Cognitive neuroscience has been driven by the idea that by reductionist analysis of mechanisms within a solitary brain one can best understand how the human mind is constituted and what its nature is. This view separates the brain from the living body and from its interactions with others. In contrast, I will argue for an *embodied and enactive approach* which regards mind and brain as being rooted in bodily experience and interaction with other individuals. According to this view, the mind is not confined within the head, but is distributed among the brain, the living body, and the environment. The brain acts as a mediating and relational organ, not as the "producer" of the mind.

This applies in particular for the ontogenetic development of mind and brain. Due to its singular plasticity, the human brain is fundamentally adapted to develop within a social context. There is increasing evidence that mirror neurons and other systems necessary for social understanding have to be "trained" by embodied interaction in order to function in a meaningful context. Thus, maturational processes and interactive learning work together to form what has been called the "social brain". Nevertheless, neuroscience still favours a 3rd-person paradigm of social cognition as a passive observation of others' behaviour, attributing it to an inferential, simulative or projective process in the individual brain. In contrast to this, I will argue that intersubjectivity is not a solitary task of deciphering or simulating the movements of others, but means entering a process of intercorporal interaction and generating common meaning through it. This approach will be further illustrated by an analysis of primary dyadic interaction in early childhood and its role for brain development.

Introduction

Until now, cognitive neuroscience has mainly been driven by the idea that by analysis of mechanisms within a solitary brain one can best understand the origin and nature of the human mind. Consequently, subjectivity has been regarded as a by-product of the brain's activity as a symbol-manipulating machine. This view separates the brain not only from the living body, but also from its interactions with the environment. As a consequence, mind and world are treated separately from each other, with the outside world being mirrored by the mind as a representational system inside the head. As Thompson[1] (2007, 36) remarks, this has yielded "abstract and reified models of the mind as a disembodied and cultureless physical symbol system" in the brain of a solitary individual.

Similarly, current theories of intersubjectivity are also based on a representationalist view: Concepts such as Theory of Mind, mentalization or simulation all have in common that they conceive of social understanding as implying some kind of inner representations of others' presumed mental states that we then have to project on them. Moreover, research into the "social brain" has favoured a 3rd-person paradigm of social cognition as a passive observation of others' behaviour, based upon an inner modelling process in the individual brain.

Obviously, cognitive neuroscience is still based on the Cartesian divide between the 'mental' and the 'physical', or between the subjective mind and the objective body. The one is assumed to be only accessible from within, or from the 1st person perspective, the other only accessible from without, or from the 3rd person perspective. As a result, social cognitive neuroscience basically assumes a disembodied sender-receiver relation between two Cartesian minds, with their bodies only serving as signal transmission devices. One could even say that according to these concepts the person who perceives another does not actually interact with him or her, but deals with internal models or simulations of her actions.

In the following I start from a quite different assumption: *The mind is not in the brain; nor is the other.* For the brain as such is a physiological abstraction, an organ separated from the totality of organic life. The brain is only an organ of the mind insofar as it is connected to a human body and, through it, to other embodied human beings. Just as respiration cannot be restricted to the lungs but only functions in a systemic unity with the environment, the mind is not confined within the brain – rather, it extends throughout the living body and includes the world beyond the skin. Similarly, intersubjectivity is not a state in the head, but is based on the reciprocity of embodied agents who interact with each other in the *2nd person* perspective. Moreover, it is in the course of these interactions particularly in early childhood that the brain structures necessary for social cognition are

1 *Mind in Life*, p. 36

formed. The central question for an integrative research program would then be *how embodied interactions shape the human mind and brain.* I will try to point out some steps in this direction.

Enactive and interactive cognitive science

The alternative view which I present is based on the notions of embodiment and enaction, referring to the embedding of mental processes in the living organism and its sensorimotor interaction with the environment. The brain is primarily an organ of a living, sensing and moving being, and only in this way does it become an organ of the mind. For both life and mind are essentially related to what is beyond them, dependent on the continuous exchange with the world. The dynamic and interactive character of consciousness is not covered by the concept of passive 'mental states' or 'events' that could be translated into corresponding brain states. Consciousness is not a 'state' at all, but something that we *live and enact.*[2] Therefore the neurocognitive system cannot be grasped separately either; it functions only in interconnection with the world in which we move and live with others through our bodily existence.

In what follows, I will take a closer look at two modes of embodiment which form the basis of the human mind:[3]

(1) cycles of sensorimotor coupling between organism and environment
(2) cycles of intersubjective interaction between embodied agents.

1) Sensorimotor cycles

In the traditional view, a cognitive being's world is seen as a pregiven external realm, represented by the brain. From an enactive point of view, however, organisms do not passively receive information from their environment which they then translate into internal representations; rather, they actively participate in the generation of meaning. Cognition is the result of a dialogue between the sense-making activity of an agent and the responses it receives from the environment. Thus, it implies an intrinsic connection of perception and bodily action, as already developed in the concepts of Uexküll's *Funktionskreis*[4] and Weizsäcker's

2 See Noë: *Out Of Our Heads*, p. 47ff., for a similar view on the dynamics of consciousness.
3 Cf. Thompson and Varela: "Radical Embodiment".
4 Uexküll: *Theoretische Biologie.*

Gestaltkreis[5]. What the organism senses is a function of how it moves, and how it moves is a function of what it senses.

In a classical experiment, Held and Hain[6] investigated two groups of newborn kitten: one group was only carried around in their environment in a basket, while the other group was able to move freely. After six weeks the first group was incapable of any spatial perception, only stumbling around helplessly, while the others had learnt to perceive and move perfectly. This shows that perceptual space is not a pregiven external container, but rather a medium or working-space, moulded by our sensing and moving bodies from undifferentiated visual stimuli. The enactive approach to cognition generalizes this insight: A cognitive being's world is not a pregiven external realm, represented internally by the brain, but a relational domain created by that being's agency and coupling with the environment.[7] In other words: Living systems *enact their environment* as inseparable from their own structure and actions, an *Umwelt* in Uexküll's sense.

To illustrate this, let us look at perception from a representationalist point of view: There is an object "out there", say a knife, whose features are transmitted to the retina, then further processed by the brain using an internal representation of the object; once this is activated, a conscious representation of the knife is created. Instead of this linear model, the enactive approach regards the object as being constituted by the organism through sensorimotor functional cycles. On this view, perceptual experience is not an inner state of the brain but a skilful activity constituted by the perceiver's implicit, practical knowledge of the object and of the way sensory stimulation varies with movement. In vision, for example, when the eyes rotate, the sensory stimulation on the retina shifts and distorts in precise ways, similarly when the body moves forward or backward etc.[8] In touch, the sensorimotor dependencies are even more obvious. Moreover, objects are always perceived as affording possible actions, or in Heidegger's terms, as objects "ready-to-hand", as is obvious in the case of the knife. The object can indeed only be perceived by an embodied agent capable of somehow interacting with it, e.g. by having suitable limbs to walk around the knife, grasp it, etc. In other words: *To recognize a thing is to know how to deal with it.*

Thus, the world is constituted for us in the course of a living interaction, linking our ongoing perceptual and motor experiences to each other. In these interactions, the brain works as a mediating or *relational organ*, not as the sole producer of perception. Instead of inner maps or models we are equipped with neuronal networks derived from earlier sensorimotor experiences that underlie the complementary skills of perceptually interacting with objects. The brain provides neuronal *open loops* that are only closed to full functional cycles by suita-

5 Weizsäcker: *Der Gestaltkreis.*

6 "Movement-Produced Stimulation".

7 See Varela et al.: *The Embodied Mind.*

8 This sensorimotor account of visual perception has been elaborated in particular by O'Regan and Noë: "A Sensorimotor Account on Vision".

ble counterparts of the environment. This is supported by the discovery of so-called *canonical neurons* in the premotor cortex that are activated both when dealing with tools and when only looking at them.[9] The knife is perceived as "ready-to-hand" in an embodied sense, because the motor system is actually involved in its perception. Therefore neural states should be described not as mere correlates of mental states, but rather in terms of how they participate in dynamic sensorimotor patterns involving the organism as a whole.

This applies for motor action as well. My actions are embodied, that means, they are not somehow triggered by an inner mind, but they are enacted by me as an embodied subject. When I am writing a letter, for example, there is no point in the unity of action where my 'self' ends and the 'world' begins, no border that separates 'inner' and 'outer world'. Neural networks, muscular movements of my hand, pencil and paper synergically work together to put my thoughts down, and the whole body-environment system creates my experience of agency. I am not a pure consciousness outside of my own writing, but an *'ecological self'* whose borders do not stop at my skin.[10] In the skilful handling of tools, in writing with a pencil, playing piano or driving a car, I incorporate these instruments. Thus, I feel the paper scratching at the top of the pencil, and I feel the roughness of the street below the wheels of my car, just as the blind man feels the ground at the top of his stick, not in his hand.

2) Cycles of intersubjective interaction: Embodied social cognition

If cognition is the activity of an embodied subject, this applies in particular to the domain of social cognition or the perception of the other. According to the enactive approach, social cognition is based on a special form of human action, namely *social interaction*.

Currently, social cognitive neuroscience is still largely based on representational concepts. Social cognition is regarded as something the brain does by means of certain social modules. Similarly, present concepts of so-called mind-reading, mentalization or simulation take social cognition to be a matter of how we infer or model unobservable mental states from outward behaviour. We are hidden to each other in principle, therefore understanding others must be based on internally mapping or modelling their actions and thus explaining or predicting their behaviour. Moreover, current research paradigms in cognitive neuroscience focus on one-way, detached social situations and are biased towards localizing social cognition in one participant, or in his brain only. However, our primary and everyday encounters with others are not solitary observations, but interactions in the 2nd-person perspective. In these, we normally don't use any

9 Grafton et al.: "Premotor Cortex Activation During Observation"; Gallese & Umiltà: "From Self-Modeling to the Self Model".

10 Neisser: "Five Kinds of Self-Knowledge".

imaginative, introspective simulation or inference; instead, we immediately perceive the other's intentions and emotions in his expressive behaviour as related to a meaningful context.[11]

To illustrate this, let us imagine a football game in which one player sees his team-mate raise his arms rejoicing over a goal. According to representationalism, he will internally represent the other's body, but combined with a theory of mind or simulation mechanism which tells him: "he is happy". Instead of this linear concept, the enactive approach looks at the circular dynamics within the dyad of embodied agents. Both partners are linked to form a common system through mutual perceptions and reactions. Grasping, pointing, handing-over, moving-towards, smiling, crying, etc. – all these are not just external behaviours that we have to furnish with a meaning by way of inference, but they are inherently meaningful and goal-directed actions. Thus, the footballer will immediately perceive the other as cheering, and, empathically sharing his pleasure, he will also perceive him as a body "ready-to-hug", as it were. His understanding is interactive from the start, and might easily result in spontaneously embracing his team-mate. No simulation or introspection is necessary to share the pleasure – the embrace is just the manifestation of both players' interaffectivity and, to use Merleau-Ponty's term, intercorporality.[12]

Accordingly, phenomenological analyses of intersubjectivity are grounded on the idea that we recognize each other first and foremost as interacting embodied subjects, not as inner spectators of another's impenetrable body surface. I immediately see the triumph in his face and in his raised arms; I see the shame in another's blushing, the grief in his tears, the anger in his glowering gaze or in his bodily tension. This is based on a circular sensorimotor process in which each partner constantly influences the other by his actions.[13] The other's angry face will elicit an expressive response in my face and body which in turn finds resonance in his body. Thus, we feel the other's affect by the resonance it arouses in our own body. Understanding is jointly created in the moment-to-moment process of interaction, with both partners being engaged in what has been called "participatory sense-making."[14] This includes processes of synchronization and resonance, rhythmic co-variation of gestures, facial or vocal expression, complementary or antagonistic behaviour etc. In other words: *To understand others is to know how to deal and to interact with them.*

Now if social understanding arises from, and is constantly modified by, the moment-to-moment interaction, then the concept of inner mapping or representation is too static to be an adequate description of the process. Instead, we are dealing with a dynamical coordination of two embodied subjects coupled to

11 Scheler: *The Nature of Sympathy*; Merleau-Ponty: *Phenomenology of Perception*, pp 215ff; Gallagher: "The Practice of Mind", "Direct Perception".

12 Merleau-Ponty: *L'œil et l'esprit.*

13 Fuchs and De Jaegher: "Enactive Intersubjectivity".

14 De Jaegher and Di Paolo: "Making Sense in Participation".

each other. Interactional social understanding is not an inner modelling in a detached observer; on the contrary, the other's lived body reaches out to my own, and my own reaches out to the other, resulting in what may be termed "*mutual incorporation*"[15]. As an example, think of eye contact where the gazes of both partners enter into an often intense dialogue: I may feel the other's gaze as a pull, a suction, or also as an arrow that hits me and causes a bodily tension; I may feel his gaze right on my face (e.g. when blushing with shame); I may be fascinated by the gaze or withstand it, "cast it back" etc. This mutual incorporation is tacitly effective in every encounter, or to quote Merleau-Ponty:

> The communication or comprehension of gestures comes about through the reciprocity of my intentions and the gestures of others, of my gestures and the intentions discernible in the conduct of other people. It is as if the other person's intentions inhabited my body and mine his.[16]

A developmental perspective

This intercorporal concept is confirmed when we take a look at the development of social cognition in early childhood. Infant research has shown that even newborn babies are able to imitate the facial expressions of others.[17] By the mimetic capacity of their body, they transpose the seen gestures and mimics of others into their own proprioception and movement. Perception, proprioception and action are integrated within a common sensorimotor space. The infant does not need to carry out any process of inner simulation or inference. Its body schema is characterized by a transmodal openness that immediately allows it to incorporate and imitate others. So what primary intersubjectivity starts with is not mind-reading, but embodied interaction or intercorporality.

Since bodily mimesis evokes corresponding feelings as well, a mutual affective resonance gradually develops within the dyad. 6- to 8-week-olds already engage in proto-conversation with their mothers by smiling and vocalizing.[18] They both exhibit a finely tuned coordination of movements, rhythmic synchrony and mirroring of expressions, that has often been compared to a couple dance. Stern has emphasized the temporal flow patterns and vitality affects that are shared by both partners.[19] Infants perceive affects as the intermodal extract of

15 Fuchs and De Jaegher: "Enactive Intersubjectivity".

16 Merleau-Ponty: *Phenomenology of Perception*, p. 215.

17 Meltzoff and Moore: "Imitation of Facial and Manual Gestures", "Imitation in Newborn Infants".

18 Trevarthen: "Communication and Cooperation in Early Infancy", "The Self Born in Intersubjectivity".

19 Stern: *The Interpersonal World of the Infant.*

rhythmic, melodic, vocal, facial and gestural characteristics. These intermodal characters and contours are one of the main bridges of mutual incorporation, and with it, of primary understanding. Affect attunement and mutual incorporation create *dyadic affective states*,[20] often an intense pleasure or joy: The emerging affect during a joyful playing situation between mother and infant may not be divided, nor may its respective distribution between the two parties be identified. It arises from the "between", or from the over-arching common situation in which both are immersed. The origin of emotional life lies in interaffectivity.

Let us take a look at the brain side of this development. Research into the mirror neuron system has also supported the linkage between perception and action in social cognition, namely a close functional coupling between actions produced by the self and actions perceived in others.[21] The movement of the other is already understood as a goal-directed action because of its match to a self-performed action. This seems to apply for the emotional coupling or empathy as well: the perceived expression of pain, disgust or fear activates corresponding brain areas linked to one's own emotional experience.[22] Thus, proprioceptive, kinesthetic and emotional self-awareness is tacitly implied in perceiving the face and expression of another person. The neural systems involved in mutual understanding and empathy appear to be of a practical nature, rather than inferential, for they involve the dynamic pairing of the bodies of self and other.

However, brain mechanisms such as the mirror neuron system can hardly be taken as a sufficient basis for mutual understanding. First, 'mirrors' certainly do not exist in physical nature. A mirror on the wall does not mirror anything except *for a subject* who is able to take its reflections *as* a mirror image. Thus, the infant has to learn itself that others are 'like me' in the course of mutual exchange and interaction. There is increasing evidence that the neuronal mirror system has to be 'trained' through sensorimotor and interactive experiences in order to adequately react to social situations.[23] Hence, a merely cross-sectional view misses the embedded and biographical character of social brain systems. They only develop and function within in a common space of embodied and meaningful interactions.

20 Tronick: "Dyadically Expanded States of Consciousness".

21 Gallese: "The Roots of Empathy"; Gallese et al.: "A Unifying View of the Basis of Social Cognition".

22 Wicker et al.: "Both Of Us Are Disgusted in My Insula"; Singer et al.: "Empathy for Pain".

23 Catmur et al.: "Sensorimotor Learning Configures the Human Mirror System." – Assuming an embodied and developmental view of mirror neurons, infants are not expected to understand others' action goals by means of the mirror system before they can perform the action themselves. Accordingly, studies of anticipatory eye movement during observation of a goal-directed action showed that it is present in 12-months-olds but non in 6-months-olds (Falck-Ytter et al.: "Infants Predict Other People's Action Goals"). Moreover, there is evidence from ERP studies that the joint triadic interaction with the infant has an effect on brain structures, probably localized in the prefrontal cortex, associated with the allocation of attentional processing resources (Striano: "Neural Mechanisms of Joint Attention in Infancy").

Due to the neuroplasticity of the human brain, the history of the interactions continuously influences the infant's dispositions and skills. The patterns of interaction are sedimented in their implicit memories, resulting in what Lyons-Ruth et al.[24] have called *implicit relational knowing*. This means a prereflective knowledge or skill of how to deal with others – how to share pleasure, elicit attention, avoid rejection, re-establish contact etc. The infant acquires specific interactive schemes ("*schemes of being-with*")[25] and body micropractices that are needed for keeping up the respective interaction. Implicit relational knowing is a temporally organised, 'musical' memory for the rhythm, dynamics and affects that are present in the interaction with others. It may also be regarded as an *intercorporal memory* which shapes the actual relationship as a procedural field that encompasses both partners.

To illustrate this, let us take the example of the football players once more: The interaction cycle is based on neural networks that may be regarded as open loops which are functionally closed by the actual situation. These loops are the result of similar interactions mainly experienced in early childhood: Embracing the partner still reactualizes the first embraces between mother and child. Both partners' body memories are re-enacted in their encounter, mediating the specific 'feel' of the interaction, its timing and affective loading. However, this shared affective state does not arise in their individual brains, but from the intercorporal system constituted by both players. The understanding is achieved by the interaction itself, and no independent inner states are transmitted to the other through certain cues that he would first have to figure out and interpret in order to go on.

To repeat: A merely brain-centered and cross-sectional view misses the embedded and biographical character of the neural systems involved in social understanding. They only develop in the course of embodied and meaningful interactions. Therefore, explanations of social cognition by means of special brain modules single out *one fragment only* of the whole cycle and history of organism-environment interaction. As a result, intersubjectivity is taken as an inferential or projective process encapsulated in the brain. However, social cognition is not about representing or deciphering the movement of others, but about skilfully coping in social interactions and generating common meaning through them. The patterns of interaction in turn have a direct influence on the dispositions of the individuals involved, for due to its singular plasticity, the human brain is fundamentally adapted to develop within a social context. Thus, maturational processes and interactive learning work together to form what has been called the "social brain".

24 "Implicit Relational Knowing".

25 Stern: *The Interpersonal World of the Infant.*

Conclusion

I have outlined a concept of non-representational intersubjectivity, based on the coordinated moment-to-moment interaction of embodied agents.

According to this concept, social understanding is primarily based on intercorporality; it emerges from the interactive practice and coordination of the persons involved. We do not need to form internal models or representations of others in order to understand and communicate with them. Social cognition rather develops as a practical sense, a musicality for the rhythms and patterns of the early dialogue. In a non-mentalizing way, children are already able to see the intentions and emotions in the actions of others, in their postures, gestures and facial expressions, as related to the context of the common situation. This provides a primary understanding without recourse to a concept of mental states.

Certainly enactive cognition does not stop here. Language and narrativity in particular play a decisive role for the later stages of intersubjectivity. However, "it is only gradually and with considerable input from adults that children eventually come to conceive of something like 'bodies' on the one hand and 'minds' on the other."[26] Concepts of social cognition as based on individual simulation or mentalization are derived from special forms of intersubjectivity which rather arise from states of detached observation or disturbed interaction – states that create the need to explain another's behaviour and to infer his intentions from a 3rd person perspective. However, these situations should not be taken as the core of social cognition. Despite those later developments, enactive intersubjectivity remains the basis of our everyday social understanding.

Let us have a final look at the role of the brain for intersubjectivity. From an enactive point of view, the brain is essentially a relational organ, not the producer of social cognition.[27] It does not create, but only mediates and modulates the cycles of embodied interaction. The brain may be regarded as a system of open loops that are constantly complemented by the environment, but it cannot construct the social world or the other on its own. Thus, the mirror neuron system may in fact be an important component of enactive social perception. But as Gallagher has put it, neither neurons nor larger brain modules face the world alone.[28] Subpersonal processes do not observe, perceive or simulate. They only function as parts of an interconnected system that includes the brain and the body as a whole, the body of the other, and finally, the environmental context that encompasses both partners.

Therefore an activation of the mirror neuron system is by no means equivalent to simulation, mind reading or attribution of one's own states to another

26 Hobson: *The Cradle of Thought.*

27 Fuchs: *Das Gehirn – ein Beziehungsorgan.*

28 Gallagher: "Phenomenological Contributions to a Theory of Social Cognition".

agent. These systems should rather be interpreted as underlying an implicit bodily resonance process that informs the perception with respect to others and imbues it with a felt similarity. Thus, mirror neurons serve as only one component of the overarching action-perception cycle. Moreover, neuronal mirror systems have to be shaped and to be embedded into 'schemes of being-with' through interactive experience in order to adequately react to social situations. After all, the brain is not inserted into the world as a prefabricated apparatus, but is structured epigenetically by the continuous interaction of organism and environment. Thus, embodied and meaningful social experiences form the structure of the brain, as is evident from the development of implicit relational knowing. We may speak of an "embodied socialisation", for it is only in the course of these interactions that the neural systems necessary for social cognition can mature. Consequently, insufficient social interaction might also compromise the development of the mirror neuron system and other modules of the so-called "social brain."[29] On this background, the further elaboration of a concept of embodied and enactive social cognition is also of considerable importance for our understanding of mental disorders such as autism or schizophrenia.

References

Catmur, C. / V. Walsh / C. Heyes: "Sensorimotor Learning Configures the Human Mirror System", in: *Current Biology* 17 (2007) pp. 1527–1531.

De Jaegher, H. / E. Di Paolo: "Participatory Sense-Making: An Enactive Approach to Social Cognition", in: *Phenomenology and the Cognitive Sciences*, 6 (2007), pp. 485–507.

De Jaegher, H. / E. Di Paolo: "Making Sense In Participation. An Enactive Approach to Social Cognition", in Morganti, F. / A. Carassa / G. Riva (eds.): *Enacting Intersubjectivity: A Cognitive and Social Perspective to the Study of Interactions*, Amsterdam (IOS Press) 2008.

Falck-Ytter, T. / G. Gredebäck / C. von Hofsten: "Infants Predict Other People's Action Goals", in: *Nature Neuroscience* 9 (2006), pp. 1320–1326.

Fuchs, T.: *Das Gehirn – ein Beziehungsorgan. Eine phänomenologisch-ökologische Konzeption*, Stuttgart (Kohlhammer) 2008.

Fuchs, T. / H. De Jaegher: "Enactive Intersubjectivity: Participatory Sense-Making and Mutual Incorporation", in: *Phenomenology and the Cognitive Sciences* 8 (2009), pp. 465–486.

Gallagher, S.: "The Practice of Mind: Theory, Simulation or Primary Interaction?", in: *Journal of Consciousness Studies*, 8 (2001), pp. 83–108.

29 Iacoboni & Dapretto: "The Mirror Neuron System".

Gallagher, S.: "Phenomenological Contributions to a Theory of Social Cognition", in: *Husserl Studies* 21 (2005), pp. 95–110.

Gallagher, S.: "Direct Perception in the Intersubjective Context", in: *Consciousness and Cognition* 17 (2008), pp. 535–543.

Gallese, V.: "The Roots of Empathy: The Shared Manifold Hypothesis and the Neural Basis of Intersubjectivity", in: *Psychopathology* 36 (2002), pp. 171–180.

Gallese, V. / C. Keysers / G. Rizzolatti: "A Unifying View of the Basis of Social Cognition", in: *Trends in Cognitive Sciences* 8 (2004), pp. 396–403.

Gallese, V. / M. A. Umiltà: "From Self-Modeling to the Self Model: Agency and the Representation of the Self", in: *Neuro-Psychoanalysis* 4 (2002), pp. 35–40.

Grafton, S. T. / L. Fadiga / M. A. Arbib et al.: "Premotor Cortex Activation During Observation and Naming of Familiar Tools", in: *Neuroimage* 6 (1997), pp. 231–236.

Held, R. / A. Hein: "Movement-Produced Stimulation in the Development of Visually Guided Behavior", in: *Journal of Comparative Physiology and Psychology* 56 (1963), pp. 872–876.

Hobson, R. P.: *The Cradle of Thought*, London (Macmillan) 2002.

Iacoboni, M. / M. Dapretto: "The Mirror Neuron System and the Consequences of Its Dysfunction", in: *Nature Reviews Neuroscience* 7 (2006), pp. 942–951.

Lyons-Ruth, K. / N. Bruschweiler-Stern / A. M. Harrison et al.: "Implicit Relational Knowing: Its Role in Development and Psychoanalytic Treatment", in: *Infant Mental Health Journal* 19 (1998), pp. 282–289.

Meltzoff, A. / M. K. Moore: "Imitation of Facial and Manual Gestures by Human Neonates", in: *Science* 198 (1977), pp. 75–78.

Meltzoff, A. / M. K. Moore: "Imitation in Newborn Infants: Exploring the Range of Gestures Imitated and the Underlying Mechanisms", in: *Developmental Psychology* 25 (1989), pp. 954–962.

Merleau-Ponty, M.: *Phénoménologie de la perception.* Paris (Gallimard) 1945/1962. Engl. transl.: Smith, Colin: *Phenomenology of Perception.* London (Routledge and Kegan Paul) 1962.

Merleau-Ponty, M.: *L'œil et l'esprit*, Paris (Gallimard) 1985.

Neisser, U.: "Five Kinds of Self-knowledge", in: *Philosophical Psychology* 1 (1988), pp. 35–59.

Noë, A.: *Out Of Our Heads. Why You Are Not Your Brain, And Other Lessons From the Biology of Consciousness,* New York (Hill & Wang) 2009.

O'Regan, J. K. / A. Noë: "A Sensorimotor Account of Vision and Visual Consciousness", in: *Behavioral and Brain Sciences* 24 (2001), pp. 939–1011.

Scheler, M.: *The Nature of Sympathy*, translated by P. Heath, London (Routledge) 1954/1923.

Singer, T. / B. Seymour / J. P. O'Doherty et al.: "Empathy For Pain Involves the Affective But Not the Sensory Components of Pain", *Science* 303 (2004), pp. 1157–1162.

Stern, D. N.: *The Interpersonal World of the Infant: A View from Psychoanalysis and Developmental Psychology*, New York (Basic Books) 1985/1998.

Striano, P. / V. M. Reid / S. Hoehl: "Neural Mechanisms of Joint Attention in Infancy", in: *European Journal of Neuroscience* 23 (2006), pp. 2819–2823.

Thompson, E.: *Mind in Life. Biology, Phenomenology, and the Sciences of the Mind.* Cambridge MA (Harvard Univ Press) 2007.

Thompson, E. / F. Varela: "Radical Embodiment: Neural Dynamics and Consciousness", in: *Trends in Cognitive Sciences* 5 (2001), pp. 418–425.

Trevarthen, C.: "Communication and Cooperation in Early Infancy: A Description of Primary Intersubjectivity", in: M. Bullowa (ed.): *Before Speech,* Cambridge (Cambridge University Press) 1979, pp. 321–347.

Trevarthen, C.: "The Self Born in Intersubjectivity", in: U. Neisser (ed.): *The Perceived Self: Ecological and Interpersonal Sources of Self-knowledge*, Cambridge (Cambridge University Press) 1993, pp. 121–173.

Tronick, E. Z.: "Dyadically Expanded States of Consciousness and the Process of Therapeutic Change", in: *Infant Mental Health Journal* 19 (1998), pp. 290–299.

Uexküll, J. V.: *Theoretische Biologie*, Frankfurt am Main (Suhrkamp), 1920/1973.

Varela, F. J. / E. Thompson / E. Rosch: *The Embodied Mind: Cognitive Science and Human Experience*, 6th edition, Cambridge, MA (MIT Press) 1991.

Weizsäcker, V. v.: *Der Gestaltkreis. Theorie der Einheit von Wahrnehmen und Bewegen,* 6th edition, Stuttgart (Thieme) 1940/1986.

Wicker, B. / C. Keysers / J. Plailly et al.: "Both Of Us Are Disgusted in My Insula: The Common Neural Basis of Seeing and Feeling Disgust", in: *Neuron* 40 (2003), pp. 644–655.

Animal Locomotion

MARTA BRAUN

The 'habitus' I wish to write about belong to the bodies that appear in Eadweard Muybridge's magnum opus *Animal Locomotion.*[1] Muybridge, an Anglo-American landscape photographer who, after murdering his wife's lover and being acquitted (by a jury of 12 married men) of justifiable homicide, had succeeded, in 1878, in capturing instantaneous pictures of the movements of horses with a battery of 12 cameras. Made in Palo Alto, California for its ex-governor Leland Stanford, the pictures revealed positions of the animal – all four hooves off the ground – never before detected by the eye, and were internationally acclaimed. In 1881, Muybridge embarked on a successful lecture tour to Europe, animating drawings made from his photographs with his zoopraxiscope, but also on the look-out for a new patron. Back in America, he found a sponsor in the University of Pennsylvania when in 1883 the Provost, William Pepper, offered him the grounds of the veterinary hospital and an initial outlay of five thousand dollars to undertake a scientific study of movement to be entitled *Animal Locomotion.* The culmination of this study was published in 1887 under the auspices of the university. Its eleven volumes comprised 781 large collotype plates, each of which contained between 12 and 36 frames, for a total of almost 20 thousand single images.

Animal Locomotion is what an atlas of human and animal locomotion should look like by nineteenth-century standards. It is organized by categories, starting with gender and costume, or rather, lack of costume. The first four volumes are devoted to the male and, subsequently, the female nude. Semi-nude follows: men precede women again; then photographs of children are followed by those of men and women clothed, photographs of pathological locomotion and finally of animals. This logic, in other words, follows a hierarchy from the movements of the highest subject – the nude male – through the female, children, the crippled, and animals. It also moves from the more visually intelligible – walking and running – to the more obscure – movements with props, and miscellaneous movements: the placement of the more difficult pictures, in which the movement which is hardest to determine, is towards the end of the work, where they are less noticeable.

But that hierarchical organization, as I hope I will show, is probably the result of a decision made by the committee brought together by William Pepper,

1 Muybridge: *Animal Locomotion.*

the Provost of the University of Pennsylvania, to guarantee the scientific accuracy of Muybridge's work. It is not the order in which Muybridge originally took the photographs. But by reconstructing Muybridge's original sequences we can separate the bodies that interested Muybridge from those that interested the University committee Pepper set up, and consequently we can discern the competing claims of science and art in the work, as well as identifying those bodies inflected by race, those that exemplify late nineteenth-century notions of masculinity, and those that emphasize the performance of gender.

The earliest surviving photographs Muybridge made were taken in August 1884 of an artist's model, Mrs. Cooper, walking carrying a child, whom she pretended to be spanking, and of three unidentified male models leaping, sparring and throwing a rock. Mrs. Cooper and the athletes were photographed not with a battery of cameras, but with five or six cameras placed in a semicircle around them, the shutters triggering simultaneously to give the eye the effect of moving around the subject. Using the cameras in this way produced a single and spectacular frozen gesture seen from six different points of view, but not a sequence of the phases of motion. Instead we read the images as if walking around the model, each picture adding to the view of the figure in the three dimensions, each angle of the action suspended in time.

Produced by a technique first used by Muybridge for Stanford at Palo Alto five years earlier, these 'tracking shots' made with a semi-circle of cameras focus our attention on the spectacular nature of that single frozen moment which only the camera can capture, that instant in which the laws of gravity no longer seem to prevail. Here, for the first time, are all the motifs that would reappear obsessively throughout *Animal Locomotion*. Not just the body suspended in mid-air, but also the frozen arc of water thrown from a bucket or bowl, the fluttering of drapery, the handling of vases, jugs and baskets. These are gestures and motifs unlikely to interest his commission or to be studied by the scientists or doctors on his committee, but those which Muybridge would return to over and over again whenever he was beyond the scrutiny of their eyes.

In these early pictures taken at the University of Pennsylvania, we also first locate the bodies that the members of the committee wanted to be photographed. First the disabled, patients of committee member and professor of nervous diseases at the university Francis X. Dercum, and second, university athletes, the special interest of Provost William Pepper. For these, Muybridge reverted to his battery of 12 cameras which he used again after a winter of lecturing when he began his second summer of work on 2 June, 1885. His subject was the "mulatto pugilist" Ben Bailey, and it is with Bailey that the familiar grid found in the background of all the subsequent *Animal Locomotion* pictures first appears. The grid – the most important constituent of the Pennsylvania habitat – was made up of white threads borrowed from one first used in 1869 by the English ethnologist J. H. Lamprey, who devised it as an aid in making ethnographic photographs of Malay men and women. For Lamprey, the grid allowed comparison of general body morphology, "which no verbal description can convey and but few artists could delineate."[2] In other words, by increasing the scientific readability of the photograph, the use of the grid could authenticate the subject of the photograph as an object of anthropological scrutiny. At this time, anthropological description was aimed at collecting comparative data in order to produce pictorial evidence of racial typologies. These descriptions, in turn, were used to support an evolutionary hierarchy of races of which whiteness was the apex. The presumed superiority of the white man to the non-white was based upon assumptions that circulated with popularized Darwinism. The most fundamental of these was the particular definition of "race" itself, which joined the physical, biological nature of man to his cultural, moral and intellectual nature. This conflation of physical and cultural traits allowed nineteenth-century scientists to claim culture as biologically determined and consequently to see the advanced technological culture of the west as proof of the biological superiority of the white man. In this construction, "civilization" was an explicitly racial concept. It denoted a precise stage in human racial evolution – following the more primitive stages of "savagery" and "barbarism"[3]. The emergence of scientific anthropology at this time was supported by positivist beliefs about the validity of observation, recording and classification, and photography helped to transform these activities into a visible, permanent and measurable form.

Although artists had long used grids to ensure the accuracy of bodily proportions in their drawings, in Bailey's case the grid marks the use of sequence photography to determine racial differences. The presence of the grid in the images of Ben Bailey can be attributed to Dercum and fellow committee members Harrison Allen and Joseph Leidy, a member of the Ethnological Society of London. These men would be the founding members (in 1889) of the American Association of Anthropometry, an anthropological subdiscipline that used the measurement of physical difference such as skull size to define racial types and hierarchies. Of ninety-five models who appear in *Animal Locomotion*, Bailey is the only black man. And while Muybridge photographed the other pairs of boxers, fencers and wrestlers in combat, Bailey is photographed alone, punching the air. More: unlike the others who only fight and fence, Bailey was also instructed to walk and run for the cameras. The grid behind Bailey cues us to the fact that he is an example of "primitive" masculinity. It transforms him from a subject into an object, part of taxonomy of race constructed by *Animal Locomotion*.

In the days following Bailey's appearance, Muybridge photographed more students from the university for Provost Pepper. They are less muscle-bound than Ben Bailey, and their evenly developed bodies contrast sharply with the boxer's overdeveloped physiognomy. The athletes are the product of Pepper's new sys-

2 Lamprey: "On a Method of Measuring the Human Form", cited in Spencer: "Some Notes on the Attempt to Apply Photography to Anthropometry", p. 103.

3 See Stocking: *Victorian Anthropology*.

tem of physical education at the University, meant to develop an overall fitness and vigor, key, according to Pepper, to the "cultivation of manly and courageous qualities" that defined white masculinity.[4] Since the 1870s, elite American universities had attempted to reshape American sports on the English model, both as a way of establishing the social distinctiveness of the new American middle class, and as a way of separating it from the growing working class (who also appeared in front of Muybridge's cameras), particularly immigrants. The upper-class men that Pepper trained had to embody a notion of white "manliness" that distinguished their bodies from Bailey's. In this turn-of-the-century construction, which I can only touch upon briefly in this essay, manliness was the achievement of a perfect man, just as civilization was the achievement of a perfect race. Different from the concept of masculinity that dealt with attributes that all men had, including "savages," manliness dealt with moral achievements that only the most civilized men could attain. In the minds of pioneers like Pepper, the physical prowess of the university athlete would be a manifestation of his moral superiority, representative of the values of the American way of life, given that the athletes were amateurs, not professional sportsmen. Their physical education would also allow them to withstand neurasthenia, or "American nervousness." This "disease of civilization", seen by the medical profession as a result of the inhuman pace of modern life, was perceived as a threat to America's "brain workers", the college-educated professionals. Peter Daley and Morris Hacker, students at the University of Pennsylvania noted for their prowess in the university athletic club, were photographed because they were the beneficiaries of Pepper's system, the paradigms of the specimens he hoped to develop.

With the photographs of the athletes in June, 1885 Muybridge also expanded his apparatus. He placed two additional cameras, each with a bank of twelve lenses, shutters and plate holders, at 60 and 90 degrees to his subject. From this point, he would use his battery of twelve single cameras parallel to the model to make what he called "lateral" views, at the same time as the other two cameras made the "foreshortened" views. At least that was the intention. But as we know from the prospectus and catalogue to *Animal Locomotion*, Muybridge had difficulties.[5] The cameras would not go off in the correct sequence or at all, negatives fogged or were broken, and some exposure times and intervals were not recorded. A close look at the plates shows unexpected inconsistencies. There are gaps between the individual images, missing phases of movements, some accounted for by Muybridge, some not; there is no movement at all in some images, while in others two contrasting sets of consecutive numbers could be seen; there are horizontal and vertical images, purportedly taken simultaneously, in which the position of the figures do not match each other; supposedly chronological sequences of images marked by two different sets of consecutive numbers,

4 Cited in Brown: "Racialising the Virile Body".

5 Muybridge: *Prospectus and Catalogue of Plates.*

one in the negative and one in the print, and what were clearly separate sequences taken at different times pieced together in a single plate. Plate 504, for example, shows Blanche Epler walking up and down stairs with a bowl of water in her hands. In the third image, a water jug has taken the place of the bowl. Two sets of numbers can be seen in each image. The assemblages which constitute the published plates show how Muybridge compensated for such problems. The inconsistencies are invisible because the images are in sequences and each sequence dictates a relation among the individual images it contains. The sequence allows us to perceive movement, even when there is none.

If the assemblages of the laterals and foreshortenings in the final prints hide the problems Muybridge had with his apparatus, the cyanotypes make those problems visible. The cyanotypes – like blueprints, they are images made with iron rather than silver salts – were unearthed from storage in Washington's Smithsonian Institution in 1999. They are the contact proofs Muybridge made from his Pennsylvania negatives, and they constitute the only evidence we have of what he originally photographed. The cyanotypes are mounted roughly on board; each board is labeled with a pre-printed sheet inscribed with the *Animal Locomotion* plate number, a negative series number, the costume category and the number of lateral and foreshortened views Muybridge took.

From 2 June 1885, the day Ben Bailey and the grid first appeared in front of his cameras, Muybridge began to keep notebook entries for each sequence of images that he made. He recorded the negative series number, the model's name, a brief description of his or her movement, the number of images made, the time spent with the model, and the mechanical details of the session. Before the cyanotypes came to light, it was not possible to apply the notebook descriptions to the corresponding plate, because the published plates are numbered and ordered in a sequence that is unrelated to the negative series number, which, as explained above, is important in itself. But the cyanotypes are a kind of Rosetta stone, because their labels bear both the negative series number and its corresponding plate number, so the notebook entries can now be deciphered and their descriptions applied to the plates. This is how it is possible to reconstruct the chronology of the work and trace its progress, as well as finally ascribe names to Muybridge's models, and follow their roles in the project.

Much has been written about the social construction of gender in these images, how the women's bodies are directed to undertake activities not usually associated with science, and proscribed by modesty and social norms, how they use props that over-determine the narrative function of the images. With the identification of the models, we can make even finer distinctions. We can show, for example, how their representation indicates their social and material inequality. Muybridge identifies the artist's models only by their first names in the notebooks – Mamie, Nellie and Lily. They are represented only in the nude. The wife of J. Liberty Tadd, the director of Philadelphia's School of Industrial Art who supplied Muybridge with his artist's models, is always "Mrs. Tadd" and is only pictured fully clothed. Muybridge records the full name of Peter Daley, as he does all the students, and he tends to represent them as idealized Greek nudes, as befits their youth and status. But Redinger and Breen the blacksmiths, and Madeleine the bricklayer, are known only by their last names, and are never without the "pelvis-cloth," out of concern, according to Muybridge, for their working-class modesty. When it comes to self-consciousness, however, the artist's models' pleasure in performing for the camera parallels that of the students, while the more proper wives and mothers go about their activities with the same solemn demeanor as the laborers and professionals.

Muybridge's photographs – of the university athletes, of the labourers, carpenters, brick-layers, blacksmiths who were all "experts in their particular trades,"[6] of the boxers, fencers and other professionals who demonstrated their prowess for the cameras, and the hospital patients with locomotive disorders – all make visible his committee's concerns with health, class and race at the end of the nineteenth century. Such concerns are almost entirely absent in his photographs of women, particularly the artist's models, whom he paid by the hour. Wanting, so he said, to photograph them in everyday activities, Muybridge complained that they lacked poise. "I have experienced a great deal of difficulty in securing proper models," he wrote. In the first place, artists' models, as a rule are ignorant and not well-bred. As a consequence, their movements are not graceful and it is essential for the thorough execution of my work to have my models of a graceful bearing."[7] While the women's everyday activities often parallel those of the men – they walk, run, jump and lift objects and throw buckets of water – the men are usually involved in feats of strength: they carry big rocks and heave logs so the movement of their muscles can be seen. The women, on the other hand, carry out domestic chores; they sweep, dust, scrub floors and spend a remarkable amount of their time with cups, bowls, jugs and vases. And even though both men and women engage with occupations deemed natural to their gender by contemporary social mores, the women's movements are sometimes difficult to interpret. What physiological laws are to be found, for example in the photograph of one woman chasing another with a broom, or throwing herself down in a heap of hay? Their voluminous long dresses often hide the limbs or muscles necessary for a study of their movement, or they engage in awkward or ungainly actions and what at the time were risqué activities such as smoking. What the women do most, however (and the men not at all), is participate in narrative scenarios that Muybridge invents such as "Inspecting a Slave, White," "Crossing a Brook over a stepping stone," "Woman kneels and drinks from the water jar of another woman and both walk off," "Walking in a gale" and even "Relinquishing drapery for nature's garb" (his notebook title for almost every sequence of a woman undressing). Very few of these images depict the *habitus* of the modern American

6 Muybridge: *Prospectus and Catalogue of Plates*, p. 12.
7 Muybridge: "Animal Motion".

woman of 1885. Instead Muybridge directs his most "graceful" models, in fantasies from a distant pastoral age, as peasants and Greeks, playing with hay, fishing rods, goblets and "ancient" water jugs.

Muybridge is interested in a narrative, rather than a scientific logic. And, as the notebooks reveal, aside from the narrative arcs elicited by many single plates, even longer stories can be found by following the negatives' series numbers which show the order in which Muybridge photographed a particular model's movements. On 10 July 1885, for example, Catherine Aimer descends the stairs to pick up a pitcher, goes back up, sits, pours water into a glass from the pitcher, turns, runs (this is the print entitled 'Ashamed' in the notebooks and 'turning around in surprise and running away' in the published plate), runs again, picks up a basin and wipes it and then – perhaps tired from these activities – she lies down to read. Immediately after, she kneels with a basket, then with a bucket, and prepares to scrub.

The next day, July 11 we find her sitting down again. She crosses her legs (this gesture seems important to Muybridge, as he bothers to note it), drinks from a cup, raises a 'Goblet' from the table, and then raises a pitcher and pours water from it. Next, perhaps to do something with the props Muybridge favours, she pours the water from the pitcher into a basin, washes her face and dries it. In a kind of free association, the basin becomes the cue for a dog to enter, and she feeds it. The basin is picked up and the water tossed out.

At this point the story falters, and Miss Aimer is reduced to throwing a baseball, walking with a fan and a jar, stumbling and falling, rising and sprinkling water (again, water is never far from the set). It is unclear what Muybridge might have meant her to do next. A soldier, a certain Mr Madison, was waiting in the wings to be photographed.

Let me conclude: Poised between the discourses of art and science and operating in the ambiguous interval that separates them, *Animal Locomotion* is an atlas not only of movement but also of social mores and erotic imagery. The scientific-looking grid and the university imprimatur define the habitat of the models; the sequential structure of the images and their published order organize the habitat constructed for the viewer: these have legitimized the *habitus* of the models whom Muybridge directed. The very nature of photography as guarantor of the visible is called into question by *Animal Locomotion*: these instantaneous photographs depict what the eye could never grasp, as they allow us to immediately recognize what we have never seen before.

References

Brown, E. H.: "Racialising the Virile Body: Eadweard Muybridge's Locomotion Studies, 1883–1887", in: *Gender & History*, 17 (2005) 3, p. 47.
Stocking, George W. Jr.: *Victorian Anthropology*, New York (Free Press), 1987.
Lamprey, J. H.: "On a Method of Measuring the Human Form for the Use of Students of Ethnology", *Journal of the Ethnological Society of London* 1 (1869), pp. 84–85.
Muybridge, Eadweard: "Animal Motion", *Philadelphia Times*, August 2, 1885.
Muybridge, Eadweard: *Animal Locomotion: An Electro-Photographic Investigation of Consecutive Phases of Animal Movements, 1872–1885*, 11 vols, Philadelphia (University of Pennsylvania) 1887.
Muybridge, Eadweard: *Animal Locomotion: An Electro-Photographic Investigation of Consecutive Phases of Animal Movements – Prospectus and Catalogue of Plates*, Philadelphia (J. B. Lippincott) 1887.
Spencer, Frank: "Some Notes on the Attempt to Apply Photography to Anthropometry during the Second Half of the Nineteenth Century", in: Edwards, Elizabeth (ed.), *Anthropology and Photography 1860-1920*, New Haven and London (Yale University Press and The Royal Anthropological Institute) 1992, pp. 99–107.

List of figures

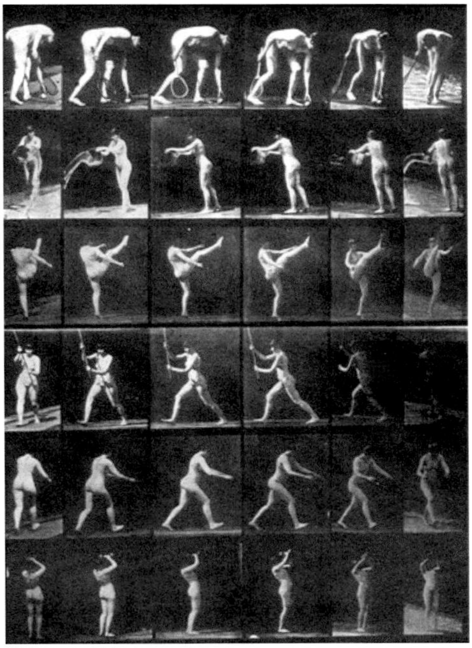

Fig. 1. Eadweard Muybridge, *Animal Locomotion*, Plate 526.

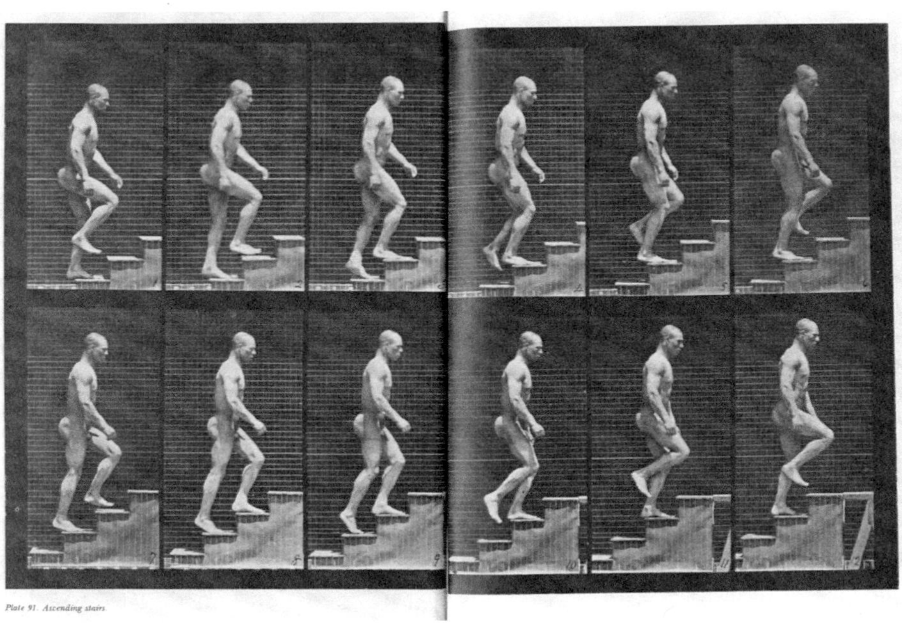

Fig. 2. Eadweard Muybridge, *Animal Locomotion*, Plate 91.

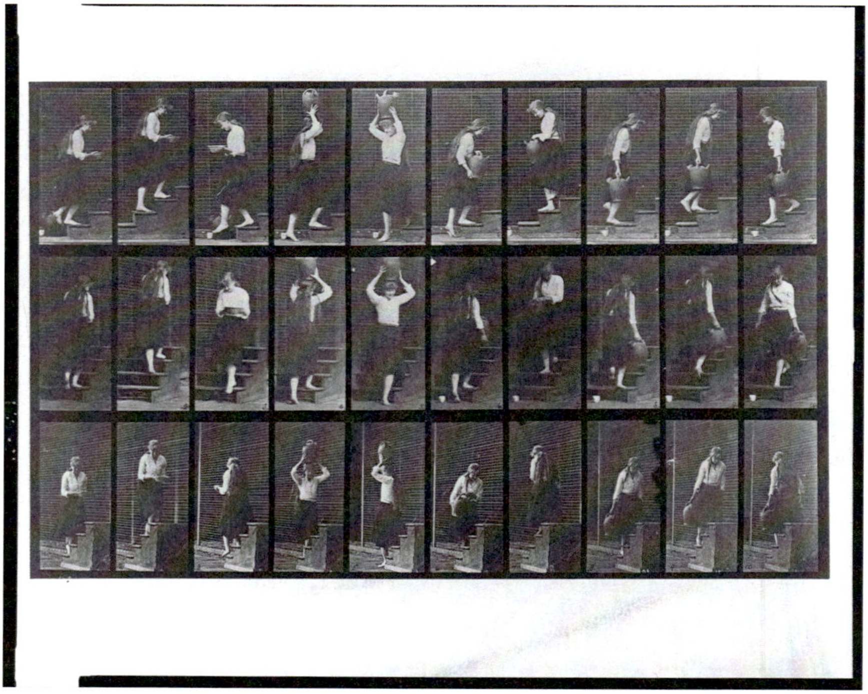

Fig. 3. Eadweard Muybridge, *Animal Locomotion*, Plate 504.

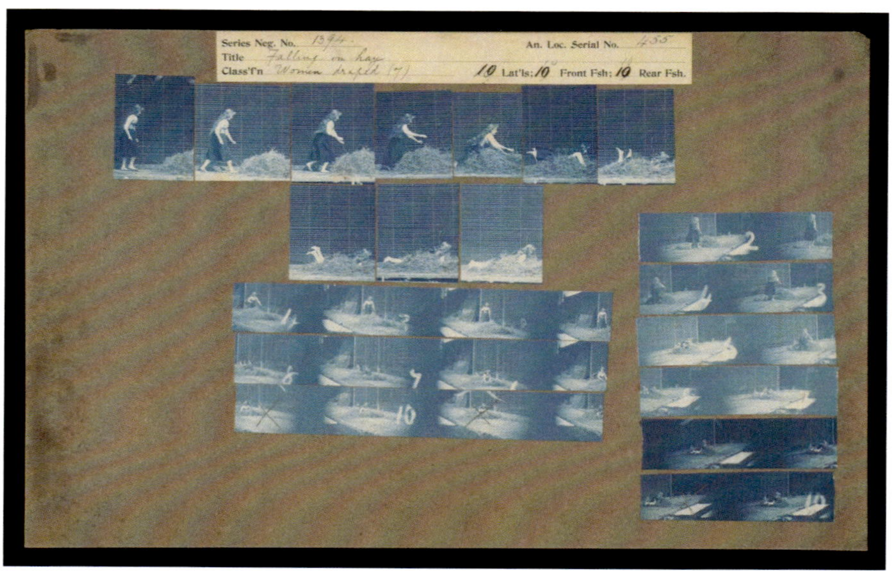

Fig. 4. Cyanotype for Eadweard Muybridge, *Animal Locomotion*, Plate 455.

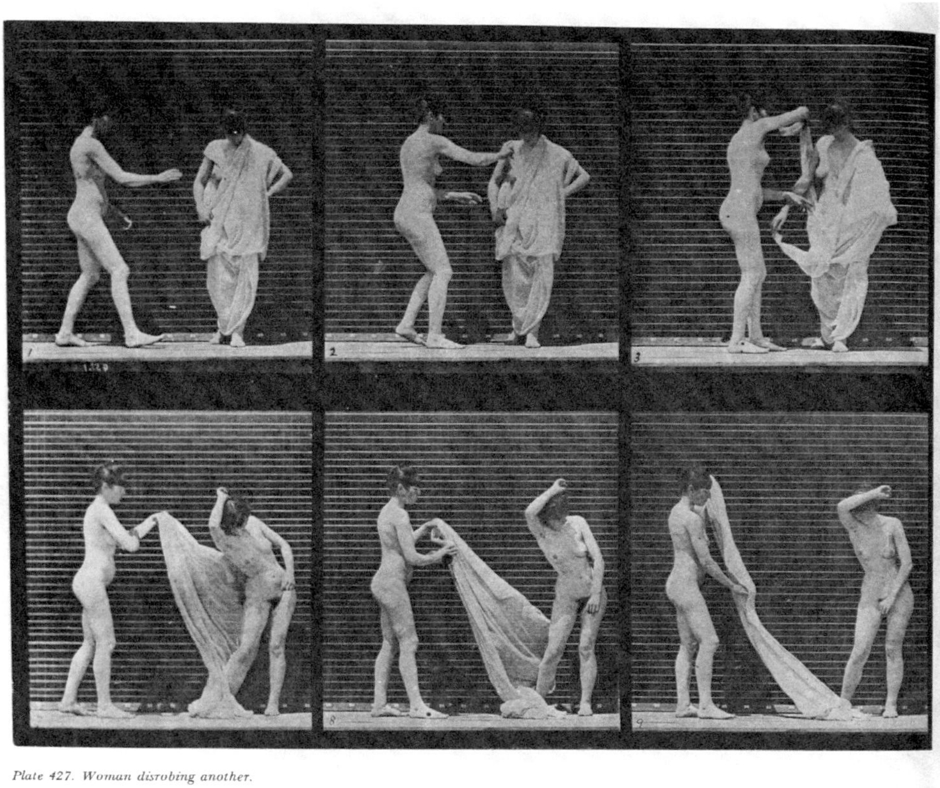

Fig. 5. Eadweard Muybridge, *Animal Locomotion*, from Plate 427.

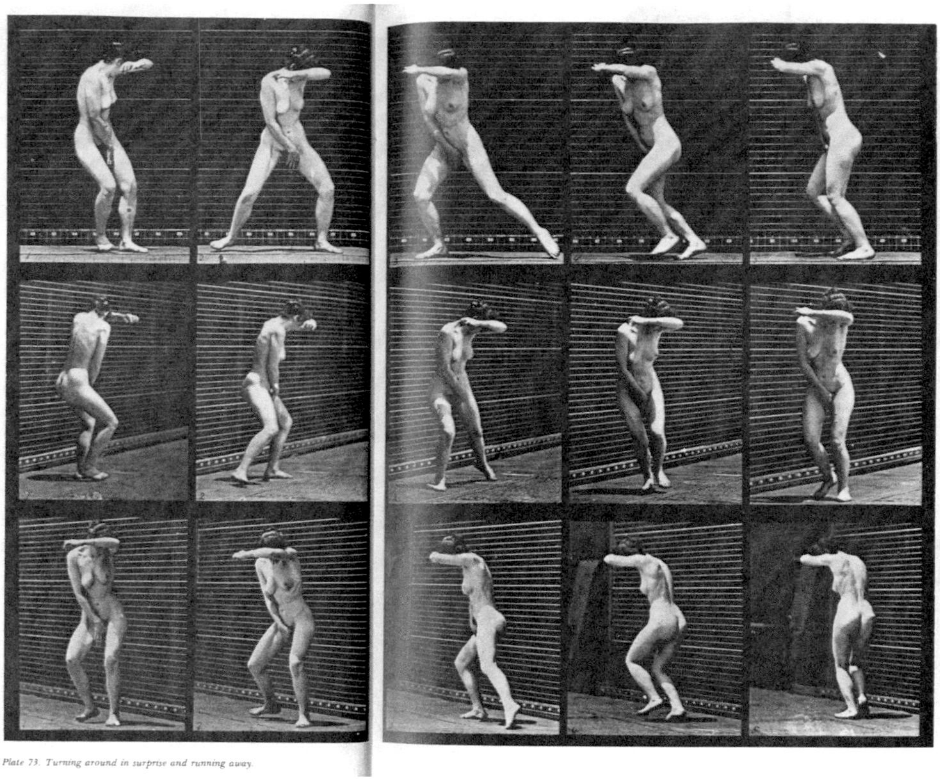

Fig. 6. Eadweard Muybridge, *Animal Locomotion*, Plate 73.

On Nostalgia (and Homer)

JAN SÖFFNER

1. A dog's *noesis*

> Thus they [Odysseus and the swineherd Eumaeus, who has not yet recognized him] spoke to one another. And a hound that lay there raised his head and pricked up his ears, Argos, the hound of Odysseus, of the steadfast heart, whom of old he had himself bred, but had no joy of him, for ere that he went to sacred [or damned] Ilios. [...N]ow he lay neglected, his master gone, in the deep dung of mules and cattle, which lay in heaps before the doors, till the slaves of Odysseus should take it away to dung his wide lands. There lay the hound Argos full of vermin; yet even now, when he marked [enóêsen] Odysseus standing near, he wagged his tail and dropped both his ears, but nearer to his master he had no longer strength to move. Then Odysseus looked aside and wiped away a tear, easily hiding from Eumaeus what he did; and straightway he questioned him, and said: "Eumaeus, verily it is strange that this hound lies here in the dung. He is fine of form, but I do not clearly know whether he has speed of foot to match this beauty or whether he is merely as table dogs are, which their masters keep for show."
>
> To him then, swineherd Eumaeus, didst thou make answer and say: "Aye, verily this is the hound of a man that has died in a far land. If he were but in form and in action such as he was when Odysseus left him and went to Troy, thou wouldest soon be amazed at seeing his speed and his strength [...]." (17,290ff Translation A.T. Murray)

This is the last moment of Argos' life. The aged dog dies in front of his master, who has been missing for the past twenty years. This master, however, is just as pitiable as the aged hound. And he denies the dog in front of Eumaeus – thereby denying the first one who recognizes him.

That Odysseus is recognized is important. When he arrives on Ithaca, he does not recognize his home, and his home does not recognize him. This first happens because of a mist sent by Athena, which hinders recognition in both directions. The mist, though, seems to be symbolic for what is to come too. Athena gives Odysseus an old man's body, thereby making him unrecognizable – even for Penelope (13, 189–193). And Athena still has to tell him where he is. Lifting the mist is not enough: Ithaca has changed too. Upon this information, though, Odysseus will nevertheless be able to meet up with his past in his environment, and encounter memory in sensuality, as is described thereafter. However, this is only half of the arrival. Up to this point he has not yet been recognized by anything or anyone.

Argos is the first to do so. But unlike humans recognizing Odysseus, he just sensually and emotionally revives the shared past and thereby *recognizes* Odysseus in both senses of the word: discerning him and accepting him. The verb for Argos' cognition is *noeo*. It is derived from the word for spirit and thought: *nous* – a word which, in the present psychological and philosophical tradition, is usually translated with 'mind'. In Homer, though, it does not yet have this precise meaning. Indeed, in the Odyssey, embodied action, feelings, thoughts and the mind are not yet separable. Thoughts take *on* and move *through* space. Like bird-signs, demons, personified dreams and the "winged" words of which Homer speaks so often: thoughts can be thought of as flying. And moreover they are not quite as personal as one would currently think of a mind and its thoughts. Homer's mind is plural. The instrumental intelligence for which Odysseus is famous competes with many other forms of comprehension. Odysseus lives in a time in which it is still difficult to be intelligent, as Roberto Bazlen once put it.[1]

On the other hand, there are the noetic abilities of dogs. These are emotional and enactive.[2] In understanding, Argos lets his ears hang and wags his tail. Different from the *Iliad*, where Achilles' divine horses weep for Patroclus, Argos' cognition is not based on human emotions but only on canine emotions. However, Homer positions canine and human emotional understanding on the very same level. Argos and Odysseus recognize each other by *sharing* physical motion. They recognize each other in a form of "second person interaction" – to use Shaun Gallagher's and Dan Zahavi's term.[3] They turn homecoming into a shared, emotional event.

However, there is still a difference between human and canine cognition. Odysseus can hide his emotions; he can secretly wipe away his tears and disavow his arrival. In Homer this ability is a complex and problematic fact. Feelings simply do not exist with Homer as long as they are not embodied, and thus, Odysseus' ability to hide his tears usually requires detailed explanation. Homer, indeed, uses the scene here not only for this kind of explanation, but also to distinguish the contrast between human intelligence and canine comprehension – both of which have their specific strength. On the one hand, Odysseus can, yes, easily hide his emotions from humans – but neither his cunningness nor Athena's disguise can help against the *noesis* of a dog. Conversely, though, there is something which Argos' form of cognition cannot convey either. In recognizing Odysseus, he can do *nothing but* take part in the shared event of homecoming. His emotions do not differentiate between "being" and "seeming": they are not familiar with "as if". And this is why Argos is unable both to deny *Odysseus* and to recognize Odysseus' denial of *himself*. He cannot abandon a situation in which

1 Bazlen: *Note senza testo*, p. 96.

2 I am using this term in the sense once established by Varela / Thompson / Rosch: *The Embodied Mind.* For a more recent discussion, see Menary: *Radical Enactivism*, and Thompson: *Mind in Life*.

3 See: Gallagher / Zahavi: *The Phenomenological Mind.*

he feels *with* him and where everything is a shared arrival. Odysseus can. He also knows a level where dog and master are two discrete and distinct bodies that can become opaque to one another. And this is especially why he is able to arrive at the idea to hide his emotions from Eumaeus: he can do so only on the strength of the chance of such opacity.

Hence, there are two forms of cognition. On the one hand, there is the sharing of an arrival, where Odysseus encounters Argos on a level on which the bodies are disclosed in reciprocal accordance. And, on the other hand, there is an intersubjective understanding based on discrete bodies with a surface and something hidden beneath this surface or expressed by it. And this fact allows for a state of disguise and ruse – for which Odysseus is famous, and which Argos, on the other hand, cannot understand.

Both forms of cognition, though, also imply their own emotionality. On the one hand, there is a kind of sym-pathy in the etymological sense: a feeling-with. This sympathy may be one of intercorporal communication as is the case with Odysseus and Argos. But it may also concern a stance towards the whole environment. Then it shows several affinities to Matthew Ratcliffe's concept of "existential feelings" – i.e. "feelings in the body, which are experienced as one's relationship with the world as a whole."[4] On the other hand, though, Odysseus is

4 Cf. Ratcliffe: *Feelings of Being*, p. 2. When considering the relation of an emotional habitus and an emotional habitat, existential feelings, indeed, play a key role. The existential relation of these feelings as action-related and cognition-driving orientations of a living human body in the world, indeed, coincides with the relation of emotional habitus and emotional habitat from the very moment when one considers habituations: Seen from this angle, existential feelings can make the culturally developed habitus and the culturally shaped form and meaningfulness of the habitat meet. The emotional meaning of a relation like this thereby does not consist in a merely inner or personal emotionality formed by culturally shaped experience 'referring' to a reality of culturally constructed meanings. It rather consists in the participation of the emotions in the world.
Ratcliffe, indeed defines existential feelings as "both feelings of the body and ways of finding oneself in the world" (ibid., p. 2). And – contrary to a concept of inner feelings – he describes them as "a sense of belonging to the world" (ibid., p. 55). Leaving behind concepts of emotional embodiment focused on the discrete body and its emotional prorioception (the self-perception of emotional states of these discrete bodies) Ratcliffe focuses on "feelings [which] are not of the world in isolation from the body or of the body in isolation from the world" (ibid., p. 35). The feeling body is described as a relation, not as a discrete unity. Moreover, it is a decisive feature of the existential feelings that they do not concern discrete 'outer' entities either. They are "not directed at specific objects or situations" (p. 2, cf. also p. 38). The concept shares decisive traits with Martin Heidegger's theory of moods (*Stimmungen* – cf. Martin Heidegger: *Sein und Zeit*, p. 130–148 = § 28–31), and the major difference is just that Ratcliffe does not aim at a fundamental ontology of existential feelings, but that he is rather more precise about the concrete embodiment. Ratcliffe defines them as feelings "through which experience as a whole is structured" (p. 2). This means: The manifest plurality is faced with a latent holism, which, though, might utter itself exactly in the existential feeling of a plural and incoherent world. A subliminal holism of meaning, hence, can be granted even under the condition of a plural and fractal constitution of cultural meanings. Subliminal existential feel-

known for taking an emotional *distance* from the world too. And, what I want to say in this paper is that his reflexive distance follows his emotional stance, which implies its own existential feeling.

Indeed, two emotional forms of distance emerge in this little episode. On the one hand there is the emotionality of Irony. Odysseus conceals himself astutely from Eumaeus behind an *ironic* discourse about "table dogs" – and thereby distances himself from both the swine-herd and from what he shares with the dog. On the other hand, Odysseus is the hero from *afar* who, upon arrival, still suffers from being *afar* in the sense that, yes, he is present physically – but neither emotionally nor symbolically: For everybody else it is just as if he were not there; and hence, on the other hand, even for him it is as if he were not there, because he cannot share in the acts and emotions that would be the habitat into which his habitus has to fit in order to make him feel like at home (which would be an existential feeling). He cannot yet assume his old attitudes – because the changed situation, the changed situatedness does not yet allow for that. The power of the suitors still requires ruse. And hence, when meeting Argos, he still suffers from nostalgia, while having arrived at home.

Nostalgia creates a different emotional distance than does irony. Nevertheless, both produce a lack of shared emotions. The question about what the others feel arises – and to answer this question, empathy is required – instead of sympathy: Feeling into, instead of feeling with, simulating a distinct other, instead of sharing in an emotional event. Hence the problem of emotions confronts Odysseus in a threefold manner. The scene *at the same time* shapes the coincidence of an emotionality of taking (ironic) distance, of overcoming distance by empathy hidden and one of sympathetic sharing.

2. Odysseus' nostos

The Odyssey tells a story of *overcoming* distance. The plot develops the process of homecoming, until the hero arrives in his complete and brilliant presence. The Greek word for homecoming is *nostos*. The word nostalgia is derived from it – the pain (*algos*) that has to do with (the impossibility of) *nostos*. The word was first introduced into the medical discourse in 1688 by Johannes Hofer – apparently with Homer in mind.[5] Today 'nostalgia' describes in English and German the pain of a temporal distance: one where the place has changed to such an extent that it no longer feels like home – or where oneself has changed, and desires for

ing is thereby an essential ground for the establishment of a cultural meaning as a relation between habitus and habitat as a whole – even if single meanings are coherent.

5 Hofer: *Dissertatio medica de nostalgia oder heimwehe.*

long-lost youth. Both are reminiscent of Odysseus and Argos. Furthermore, in the Romance languages the word 'nostalgia' also describes *spatial* homesickness.

This is even more important in Homer. Odysseus is introduced as someone who looks out upon sea, or rather beyond it (5,158). The nymph Calypso has fashioned a comfortable environment for him on the island of Ogygia. The idyllic charm of this island is apt to amaze even the gods (5,74). However, Odysseus submits to this world only at night, when he shares Calypso's bed – sometimes with pleasure (5,227), other times with reluctance (5,17f). The inconsistency of this relationship shows that, in Homer, feelings do not follow subjective coherence. Rather they are determined by the situation. What makes up something coherent in the Odyssey's culture is not the unity of experience granted by a *subjective* consciousness. It is *that which* slowly comes to *shared* manifestation in a continuum of shared latencies. So does Odysseus' *nostos* – which is first announced by bird signs, then by his hidden arrival, and finally in his regained presence on Ithaca. Likewise *emotional* coherence, too, is not established by the inner self. It rather follows the storyline bringing some trans-individually shared latent options to manifestation.

Against this logic, Odysseus' homesickness seems, yes, to be something personal and context-resistant – something he cannot share with Calypso. But following this logic and seen from a broader angle of view, Odysseus' perseverance in his homesickness on Ogygia proves to be the prevailing feeling after all – and this triumph of nostalgia is part of the *nostos* announced by the bird signs and dreams and thoughts and the words of the seers: Nostalgia is an enactive existential feeling, and it drives his actions, leading the plot to evolve and change latent nostalgia into manifest *nostos*. And as such it even relates to fate, or rather *is* part of this very fate. It is one of the early manifestations of what – in most aspects – is still latent.

Seen from this angle of view, the nostalgic reluctance of Odysseus is not simply a consequence or result of a "mismatch" of habitus and habitat. Indeed, it cannot be that difficult for a man like Odysseus to adjust if even the gods are amazed by the surrounding idyll. And in the beginning it wasn't. Odysseus was able to share in the beauty of both the nymph and the surrounding. In addition he says himself that Calypso is even more beautiful than Penelope. And she offers him much more – namely luxury and eternal youth. The mismatch, though it may be passively suffered by Odysseus, is also produced by the amalgam of fate and his personal habitus. Homesickness will be homesickness: it cultivates context-resistant identities, generates loyalty for those not present, creates habits such as weeping out over the sea; habits that perpetuate and cultivate the mismatch into an emotional habitus, holding absent Ithaca present, making the distant place the real home. On the strength of homesickness, Odysseus turns the idyll into something foreign; and he turns the woman whose bed he shared for seven years (longer than with Penelope herself) into a stranger. Homesickness is not simply a consequence but is also the cause of emotional alterity; and thereby it even blocks shared understanding and – instead – comes through only to (partially wrong) theories and simulations of opaque others:[6] Odysseus lives with Calypso for seven years – but still does not come to understand how much she is sacrificing herself for him, when he decides to leave. He even suspects a trap when she finally lets him go and helps him in doing so. By producing alterity, nostalgia also produces a mediated stance towards others as opaque surfaces: Calypso's love is something inner, some emotional stance now hidden to Odysseus' eyes, instead of something shared by their bodies.

To say it again: Not only the storyline produces emotional coherence. Emotional perseverance also produces the coherent storyline. Wandering and emotion are no longer separable. The Odyssey is in this respect just as much an epic of *nostos* as it is an epic of the *emotion* of *nostalgia.* To understand this, one must know that the Greek concept of emotion often did not clearly separate an emotion from its cause, nor from its consequences or its expression. In order to sing the wrath of one single person, one had to perform the entire *Iliad.* The *Odyssey* is similar. If Achilles' *emotion* is his wrath, Odysseus' *emotion* is homecoming and its obstacles: It is nostalgia.

However, it is not as symmetrical as this: The first sentence of the Odyssey does not begin with "nostos sing me" as the *Iliad* begins with "wrath sing me." The Odyssey rather begins with the word "man" – and only afterwards does Homer mention the suffering of the many ways this man had to go. Thus, the emotion of *nostos* functions differently than Achilles' wrath. In the *Iliad*, wrath is, in a way, the protagonist. As Arbogast Schmitt has argued, this emotion is not opposed to intelligence or moral conflicts – nor is it to Achilles' heroic personality. Achilles' wrath is rather embodied by the hero. And – in symbiosis with his excellence – it cannot be just blind rage. It rather has its own balanced reasoning.[7] In the Odyssey, though, the hero's intelligence and his emotion are split. The hero in his ruse often takes an ironic stance upon his existential feelings and even gains a proto-intellectual attitude on his own emotion, which is also his path.

But this very distance can also be understood as a specific feature of nostalgia itself. Indeed, nostalgia is about having a place 'where the emotion is located' that is different from the place, where the body is situated – and this very doubled existence can be understood as parallel to the emotionality in irony and ruse, that also divides the embodied expression of the situated body on the one hand and the concealed feeling on the other. Both are about giving the emotion a location that is somewhat 'elsewhere'. This very fact can be seen by his tears while with Calypso. Odysseus is not only where *he* happens to be at the moment as a person. He is also there, where he is not. Or, to put it the other way around: Odysseus' *existential feeling* holds present what is absent.

6 Cf. Gallagher / Zahavi: *The Phenomenological Mind.*

7 Arbogast Schmitt: "HOMER, ILIAS. – ein Meisterwerk der Literatur?".

I would like to describe nostalgia as this paradox – i.e. as the creation of absence as presence. Or – to say it in terms of Hans Ulrich Gumbrecht: I wish to think of it as a *Production of Presence*.[8] But the presence produced is the presence of an existential feeling that deals with the production of an *existential feeling* concerned with absence. Indeed, as the decisive feature of an existential feeling, absence cannot be described as the absence of one particular object or person. If one tries to focus on its condition, it appears to be highly unspecified. But, on the other hand, as an existential feeling, it is highly nuanced and takes part in very specific actions and attitudes. The difference between this specificity on the one hand and the lack of specificity on the other, though, is a problem of the difference between representational knowledge *about* something – and non-representational, enactive knowledge on the other.[9] The absence concerned here is non-representational. Its meaning is not a meaning *referred to* by specific signifiers. It is intrinsic to the habituated feeling and acting.

Nostalgia, thereby, is a paradox existential feeling. It, yes, consists in the production of an emotional and enactive background orientation, in a world as presence. But this latent, emotional presence is the feeling of a lack of encountering an intrinsically meaningful world in one's actions and sensual experience. Its non-representational meaning thereby is the very lack of any other non-representational meanings. It is a sense of now belonging to a world one does not really belong to, a sense of inadequacy and of difference.

8 Gumbrecht: *Production of Presence*.

9 Non-representational considerations are indeed becoming more and more prominent in current discussions about embodiment – especially in the 'enactivist' theory in the tradition of the influential work by Varela, Thompson and Rosch: *The Embodied Mind*. Indeed, one of the most challenging developments in the Cognitive Sciences and related disciplines is the fact that subjective reflection and subjective production of mental representation is becoming less and less convincing as a model for conceiving of both the construction of realities and theories of human understanding. William M. Ramsey (cf. *Representation Reconsidered*) recently even went as far as to challenge the whole concept of mental representation.
As a background orientation, Ratcliffe's concept of existential feelings, indeed, has a strong non-representational claim too. These structure actions and experiences not by building models referring to reality, but by being part of the constellations. Ratcliffe thereby also focuses on realms traditionally described as part of a cognitive or social 'framing' (i.e. a metaphor working from 'outside') to an enactive emotionality working from inside. He thereby makes emotionality the decisive feature of a practical life in multiple realities (cf. Schutz, A.: "On Multiple Realities") and claims a subliminal background orientation to be the basis for this. The subliminal thereby gains importance as a felt meaning intrinsic in action and feeling. It thereby shares important traits with what Mark Johnson has called the *Meaning of the Body* (2007) as non-representational. The still highly influential concept of cognitive frames organizing realities (cf. e.g. Goffman, *E. Frame Analysis*) thereby becomes problematic. Emotion and action do not just follow a model of reality. The enactivist approach and the theory of existential feelings reverses this constellation. Realities and frames would only become manifest when the enactive appropriateness and meaningfulness fail – and the same would be true for models of reality.

Homesickness as an existential feeling thereby also implies a paradox of identity and alterity. As a non-representational kind of meaning, it does not differentiate self and other, own and foreign: It shares and participates. But since this sharing and participating faces its own impossibility, the subliminal background orientation leads to representational modeling of self and others, of one's own habitual relation with a world and a strange form of this, of identity and alterity. It is a background orientation producing a difference between a habitus experienced as one's 'own' and a habitat experienced as inadequate and thereby other. Homesickness, thereby, figures as one of the key feelings to produce identity and alterity – and their representation.

Pathology of nostos

Still today – perhaps again – homesickness is an important and paradox *existential feeling*. It is, indeed a challenge for all too neat distinctions between short-term embodied emotions, long-term subliminal moods, cognitively indirect feelings, personal habits, social behavior and perception. It is about all of that.

The psychological literature addresses some traits of this figuration.[10] Nostalgia is said to consider maladaptive coping, absent-mindedness, insecure interpersonal attitudes, and the perseveration of negative moods. Homesickness is at once dependent on an environmental relation and, at the same time, it is accompanied by the refusal of the novel environment. And thereby it is also a kind of withdrawal. By producing alterity, it also produces inwardness.

On the base of this, still (or again) 'Homeric' discussion, I wish to consider homesickness and nostalgia as threshold phenomena. They are positioned between that which is experienced as an embodied environmental relation, and a denial of both sympathy and empathy, between a sense of sharedness and non-representational, intrinsic meaningfulness and a *per se* meaningless immanent world, which has to be deciphered (with regards to absent features or 'inner' feelings) in order *to give* it its meaning.

I would like to delve a bit deeper into the emotionality of this threshold. Indeed, Helmuth Plessner,[11] one of the rare theorists on weeping, positions his great theory at a similar constellation. According to him, the human *is* not just a body – s/he also *has* this body. Thus, for Plessner, the human being is *eccentric*. One has an external stance on what one *is* as a body at the same time. One is not only – *centrically* – identical with one's body, but one can also use it instrumentally, thereby getting a stance on this center. By using what one *is* as a means – one can act and *express* oneself, thereby establishing a referential meaning: a meaning *about* oneself.

10 Jaspers: *Allgemeine Psychopathologie*, pp. 324–327; Thurber: "The Phenomenology of Homesickness in Boys"; Martin: "Nostalgia", esp. p. 100f.

11 Plessner: *Lachen und Weinen*; Plessner: "Zur Anthropologie des Schauspielers".

The same evidently goes for Odysseus hiding his identity from the Ithacans, eccentrically using his body as a means of simulation and dissimulation and thereby expressing thoughts to those for whom they are opaque. Expression brings about the ability to lie – and Odysseus is the most prominent liar in Greek mythology. The relation with Argos, though, can be described as centric: Here Odysseus shares his embodied actions with Argos to whom he cannot hide his identity, or better: his body. Odysseus, too, is placed at the threshold between a centric and an eccentric position.

Now, for Plessner weeping occurs when physical procedures and articulations emancipate themselves and centric corporality assumes power. Thus, weeping takes place in a state of letting-go, giving-oneself-over-to-the-centric-body. It is triggered in the face of an overpowering force, which compels to resigned self-abandonment.

When one thinks about Odysseus' fight to control his tears, it all makes sense – also and especially when compared to Argos' tail-wagging. The dog's emotions are merely centric. And it also makes sense when, on the other hand, thinking about the eccentric option of hiding one's tears, and hence of communicating *by means of* a body. Indeed, Odysseus' weeping seems to stand between a centric and an eccentric positionality.

The psychological basis of Plessner and Homer is, however, fundamentally different. For Plessner, human feeling is mediated: a fact he calls "mediated immediacy"[12]. According to him, one does not feel simply *as* a body, but *by means* of a body. Plessner accordingly writes: "There can only be a heart where there is also understanding. Animals sense desire and pain, they are often closely bound to familiar situations or environments – and as such, attached. But they do not feel […] loyalty or faithfulness (Treue)."[13] In other words: Their habitual emotions and their specific habitat *can* refer to each other, but animals do *not* have 'feelings' about this relation, since they do not find an excentric position. And Plessner regards this very eccentric position as a precondition for the existential *feeling* of loyalty.

That dogs do not feel loyalty, though, is a bold assumption. Especially when it is put forth by someone who is not a dog. As seen, Homer does not answer the question so counter-intuitively. The major difference is that Homeric beings are not distinct bodies; they are bodies-in-relation. And if one proceeds with this, then Homer even had an empirical reason to assume that loyalty can be canine too. According to these premises, the phenomenology of feeling loyalty is *not* a question of *what a dog feels* (or what it is like to be a dog – to say it using Thomas Nagel's terms).[14] It is a question of how one feels *with* dogs, of what emotions one shares with them. And, indeed, it is not just *possible* for humans to

12 Plessner: *Die Stufen des Organischen und der Mensch*, p. 417.

13 Plessner: *Lachen und Weinen*, p. 349.

14 Nagel: "What Is It Like to Be a Bat?".

actually share loyalty *with* dogs. It is even rather essential for the feeling of loyalty to be shared: Loyalty is a feeling as a relation, not a feeling for and by oneself.

This fact makes clear, though, that the concept of existential feelings also changes the notion of a centric body: The body-in-relation has no center within the discrete corpus. It develops intercorporeal events as *shared* centers, such as the shared arrival of Argos and Odysseus. The centric is therefore not just where the body is. It is where it participates in its environment: Where habitus and habitat can meet in a shared space of emotion and action.

But what does all this have to do with nostalgia? As seen above, nostalgia is, itself, a threshold phenomenon between a shared centric position and an eccentric distance: As an existential feeling and hence as a background orientation in the world and with the world, it is centric. But since it is a background orientation implying absence, it is also on the verge of an eccentric position, or – to be more precise – it is an existential feeling of a blocked centric position, a production of the presence of absence. Thereby it is one of the very background orientations on the verge of producing a structure absence and thereby of referential meaning to be expressed.

This does not mean that it does not work as an existential feeling any more. On the contrary: Feelings such as loyalty even prove to be very strong if they can be described as existential feelings of absence – and to experience this, one only has to share in the feelings of a dog waiting in front of a supermarket (just to avoid misunderstandings: In saying this I am not claiming to know what a dog feels – I am only referring to a feeling a human can share that shares loyalty with another human).

Moreover, there is a good point about this shared centricity as a production of absence concerning weeping. Even today (perhaps again?) many people are able to gaze upon the corpse of a loved one without shedding a tear and begin to cry only after they come across the objects that were part of the dead person's environment. Sometimes, there seems to be more of the dead to be found in what the body has enactively shared, than in the body itself. The emotional *centric* in this case seems to be built upon embodied relations – not upon discrete bodies. And again, it becomes present as an absence. What is now missing is the embodied and embedded and emotional relation of the loved one dealing with the objects around – but as soon as this latent fact becomes manifest, it implies the first step into an experience, when these objects begin to just stand for her in her absence.

The same seems to be true for Odysseus' arrival with Argos. It makes present the *impossibility* of a life as dog and master. Indeed, in sharing the arrival both Odysseus and Argos are held back: Odysseus by prudence, Argos by old age. Sharing an arrival with a dog without the dog jumping up at one's body means to share a tragically subliminal feeling of loyalty instead of sharing manifest joy.

There is a much more famous Episode in the Odyssey modeling a similar constellation of sharing while being held back from sharing. And it also shows how eccentric and exiled emotions are interrelated, if the centric is a shared one. To sail by the Sirens, bound and mesmerized, clearly shows this eccentric position: *seira* means rope in Greek, and *Seirênes* are the sirens. They bind and captivate through their song – just as the ropes bind Odysseus to the course of the ship; and like the ropes of the goddesses of fate bind him to his arrival. He is thus brought into an eccentric position by a physical double- or triple-bind acting upon his body. These bindings meet him on the ship – but they also meet him where the ship could go: on the Siren's Island, and on his home island as well. It is by physical binding that Odysseus becomes a *discrete*, i.e. a centric body that does *not share* this very center intercorporally. Therefore he can use (or "have", to say it in Plessner's terms) his body in order to listen to the song of the Sirens from an 'ironic' distance. He can experience it as merely esthetic, instead of being lead by an enactive sensuality and emotionality driving him into ruin.

Weeping on Ogygia works analogously: If Odysseus refuses environmental participation, then he is no longer just there where he is. As emotionally bound to his *nostos*, he dwells as much in the absence of Ithaca and Penelope as he dwells in the presence of Ogygia and Calypso. And thereby he gets the option to form the centric relation to what is *not* there. Ithaca becomes the 'more real' home, and hence Odysseus' body does not share Ogygia, which thereby becomes a strange land. An eccentric stance is also related to concealment and lies – for which Odysseus is known. It becomes a fact of disloyalty (as seen in the denial of Argos and the refusal of Calypso). More than this: Refusing to share in situations with people easily leads to concealing emotions – which thereby become inner ones. And it leads to communicating and expressing emotions, which are opaque to the others.

To sum up: Nostalgia, as a threshold between centric and eccentric position, thereby makes Odysseus both the man who "suffered many things" (*polutlas*) and the man who "thinks about many things in a prudent way" (*polumêtis*) – as Homer tells us over and over in his epitheta. The interrelation of suffering and thinking might even be the reason why "man", not "nostos" is the first word of the Odyssey.

Conclusions

The threshold of weeping, in Homer, seems to be also related to the *production* – and not only to the *overcoming* of the eccentric position, especially when related to homesickness. It is obvious that such a stepping-out can also happen with tears. It can be, after all, accompanied by the loss of a self-evident intimacy and sympathy.

Plessner's own examples lead us to suspect that this could still hold meaning too. He writes, "The child weeps because s/he does not get what s/he wants; because s/he must do what s/he is told; because s/he is hurt or left alone"[15]. Plessner sees superior powers in play to which the child is forced to capitulate. When seen from a Homeric point of view, all of these scenes are also examples of a mismatch in a sympathetic relationship with the parents and the world. This also coincides with more recent findings on weeping.[16] Painful weeping is placed especially in the context of phenomena of loss, rejection, helplessness, and even inadequacy. Hence one may assume that weeping can also be found where an eccentric position is *developed* – and not only where one must abandon it. And all of this is also about a lost existential feeling of – in a way – being 'at home' in one's environment.

Also the more plessnarian direction of passing the threshold from the eccentric to the centric can relate to a similar feeling of being 'at home'. As you know (and as also has been shown in recent studies), tears even today flow at unions and reunions. They accompany weddings as much as funerals. And weeping with Argos, too, partially marks the *return* from the exiled condition into a shared centric one – where habitat and habitus match again.

Actually in Homer weeping marks the threshold in both directions. While being a fact of a reunion, it still marks the production of the impossibility of this match – and hence of being dog and master. It still produces the emotional presence of *absence*. This does not mean, though, that Homer's eccentric position has nothing to do with the eccentric position Plessner conceives of. On the contrary, Odysseus hiding his tears shows how much he knows how to use his body as a *means* of communication – and thus to *have* it. And Odysseus traveling by the Sirens also uses his body – this time for a kind of mediated immediacy, an esthetic form of sensing and feeling.

I do not want to claim that this is the anthropological 'truth' about homesickness. One should not forget that there was not even a word for it until Hofer coined one – and one should also consider that, once it *was* coined, for a further 90 years it was thought of as only concerning Swiss people who missed the special climate of their mountains. What I do want to claim, though, is that home-

15 Plessner: *Lachen und Weinen*, p. 356.

16 Vingerhoets / Heck / Becht: *Adult Crying*.

sickness can be linked to a phenomenological characteristic that – at least – can be discussed as anthropological: a centric and excentric positionality concerning a relation with the world. Moreover it seems to be a powerful figuration of an emotional habituation concerning the production of identity and alterity. The influence of Homer on this figuration seems to be still very strong, at least in Western cultures. Nevertheless, of course, it is not the only important text to consider. Perhaps it is no coincidence that both influential, Western traditions of transcendence, understood as large "emotional communities", to say it in the same way as Barbara Rosenwein,[17] model homesickness, too – but instead relate to unknown or otherworldly places as truer homes. This ultimately applies to the exodus out of Egypt as well as to Plato's myth of a home in the realm of the ideas. "Wo gehen wir denn hin?" asked Novalis' character Heinrich von Ofterdingen – and he answered: "Immer nach Hause."[18] And wherever this may be: It is the place where habitus and habitat fit.

References

Bazlen, Roberto: *Note senza testo*, Milan (Adelphi) 1970.

Thompson, Evan: *Mind in Life: Biology, Phenomenology, and the Sciences of Mind*, Cambridge, Mass. & London (Harvard University Press) 2009.

Gallagher, Shaun / Dan Zahavi: *The Phenomenological Mind*, London (Routledge) 2007.

Goffman, E.: *Frame Analysis. An Essay on the Organization of Experience*, New York (Harper and Row) 1974.

Gumbrecht, Hans Ulrich: *Production of Presence – What Meaning Cannot Convey*, Stanford (Stanford University Press) 2004.

Heidegger, Martin: *Sein und Zeit* [1927], reprint: Tübingen (Max-Niemeyer) 1993.

Hofer, Johannes, *Dissertatio medica de nostalgia oder heimwehe*. (Diss. Basel 1688).

Jaspers, Karl: *Allgemeine Psychopathologie*, Berlin / Heidelberg (Springer) 1923.

Johnson, Mark: *The Meaning of the Body. Aesthetics of Human Understanding*, Chicago (University of Chicago Press) 2007.

Martin, Alexander R.: "Nostalgia", in: *The American Journal of Psychoanalysis*, 16 (1954), pp. 93–104.

17 Rosenwein: *Emotional Communities in the Early Middle Ages*.

18 Novalis: *Heinrich von Ofterdingen*, p. 325.

Menary, Richard: *Radical Enactivism: Intentionality, Phenomenology, and Narrative. Focus on the Philosophy of Dan Hutto*, Amsterdam / Philadelphia (PA) (John Benjamins) 2006.

Novalis: *Heinrich von Ofterdingen*, in: Paul Kluckhohn / Richard Samuel (eds.) *Novalis Schriften. Die Werke Friedrich von Hardenbergs*, Bd. 1/IV, Stuttgart (Kohlhammer) 1960–1977.

Plessner, H.: "Die Stufen des Organischen und der Mensch. Einleitung in die philosophische Anthropologie" (1928), in: *Gesammelte Schriften*, Frankfurt am Main (Suhrkamp) 1981, Vol. 4, p. 417.

Plessner, H.: *Lachen und Weinen*, Bern (Francke) 1941.

Plessner, H.: "Zur Anthropologie des Schauspielers" (1948), in: G. Dux / O. Marquard / E. Ströker (eds.): *Gesammelte Schriften*, Frankfurt am Main (Suhrkamp) 1982, Vol. 7: *Ausdruck und menschliche Natur*, pp. 399–418.

Ratcliffe, Matthew: *Feelings of Being: Phenomenology, Psychiatry and the Sense of Reality*, Oxford (Oxford University Press) 2008.

Rosenwein, Barbara H.: *Emotional Communities in the Early Middle Ages*, Ithaca, N.Y., and London (Cornell University Press), 2006.

Schmitt, Arbogast: "HOMER, ILIAS. – ein Meisterwerk der Literatur?", in: Reinhardt Brandt (ed.): *Meisterwerke der Literatur von Homer bis Musil*, Leipzig (Reclam) 2001, pp. 9–52.

Schutz, A.: "On Multiple Realities", in: M. Natanson / Martinus Nijhoff (eds.), *Collected Papers of Alfred Schutz*, vol. 1, The Hague (Nijhoff) 1973.

Thomas Nagel: "What Is It Like to Be a Bat?", in: *Philosophical Review*, 83 4 (October 1974), pp. 435–450.

Thurber, Christopher A: "The Phenomenology of Homesickness in Boys", *Journal of Abnormal Child Psychology* 27 (1999), 125–139.

Varela, Francisco J. / Evan Thompson / Eleanor Rosch: *The Embodied Mind: Cognitive Science and Human Experience*, Cambridge (MA) (MIT Press) 1991.

Vingerhoets, J. J. M., Randolph Cornelius, Guus L, and Van Heck and Marleen C. Becht: "Adult Crying: A Model and Review of the Literature", in: *Review of General Psychology* 4 (2000), pp. 354–377.

Expressivity and Interaction

Situation and Motion
The Art of Expression in Fiedler and Freud

ERIK PORATH

Introduction

The interpretation of bodily motion as a phenomenon of expression and the concrete determination of its expressive value constitute a continuous problem that has been repeatedly raised by attempts at systematization. Be that as it may, approaches from the fields of physiognomy, histrionics, and (criminal) anthropology are part of an ongoing critical debate about the range, accuracy and reliability of the recommended strategies for decoding. Repertoires of expression or tables of gestures have been criticized for the changing contexts of their appearance. In this view, determining meaning means contextualizing any phenomenon of expression. Konrad Fiedler's and Sigmund Freud's writings can contribute to a theoretical approach designed to interpret expression situationally. This paper aims at a theoretical framework rather than the interpretation of specific expressions like gestures (shaking the head, handshake, pointing etc.) or mimic (laughing, smiling, weeping etc.).

This outlines the program of my text, which consists largely of reflections on methodology, concerning the small oeuvre of the art theorist Conrad Fiedler from the 19th century and Sigmund Freud's *The Moses of Michelangelo*[1] published in 1914. I begin with Freud, whose study I would like to classify using several central concepts from his reflections on the theory of art that are relevant to the question of the context in art, and in particular for the interpretation of the gestures, facial expressions, and body postures it depicts: "Subject-matter" and "effect"; "total impression" and detail; "transference" or "reading expression"; "emotional attitude" ("Affektlage"), "mental constellation" and the artist's "impetus" as "another source", which in the strict sense of psychoanalytical understanding could be taken as "source of the other", as I will refer to later.

In the course of doing so, I will pay particular attention to the points where Freud articulates an inadequacy in traditional art historical studies but also in his own ideas–an inadequacy that results from the problem of context and situation in any art. I would like to connect this inadequacy with several basic ideas from

1 German: *Der Moses des Michelangelo*.

Fiedler's writings *Über die Beurteilung von Werken der bildenden Kunst*[2] (1876) and *Über den Ursprung der künstlerischen Tätigkeit*[3] (1887; to be translated as "On the origin of artistic activity") – works that Freud probably did not know, or at least did not mention.

This should suffice as a first sketch of a horizon of problems that connects issues of expression, of constituting expression, and understanding expression to the complex contexts from which phenomena of expression emerge. In addition, these phenomena and their corresponding framework in Freud and in Fiedler will be explored with regard to their range of application to the visual arts and their specific *Ausdrucksbewegungen*, or "expressive movements" – a term I will address in a moment.

1. Freud

Subjectivity and Effect

Right at the beginning of *The Moses of Michelangelo*, Freud emphasizes the subjective experience of a "powerful effect" of works of art on him – that is to say, the author, Freud, speaks of himself in a way that he might not have been able to do as a psychoanalyst, who insists on professional distance and discretion. At the same time, this personal admission is negated in two ways. First, Freud emphasizes that he is "no connoisseur," and certainly not a recognized academic art historian. Moreover, Freud does not identify himself as a psychoanalyst either, but rather as someone who has heard of psychoanalysis and psychoanalytic insights. Hiding behind the mask of anonymity when the text was first published, Freud, as he indicates, was concerned with art itself: the status that Freud claims in the opening of his text for himself, as an 'eternal' layman, as Sigrid Weigel[4] has analysed it, is characterized as being dominated by an interest in the subject matter and detachment with regard to formal and technical qualities. Nevertheless, or precisely for that reason, he feels that works of art occasion him "to spend a long time before them" in order to "apprehend" them in his own way and explain to himself "what their effect is due to." (Freud 1914, SE XIII, p. 211)

2 In: Fiedler: *Schriften zur Kunst I*, Vol. I, pp. 1–48.
3 In: ibid., Vol. I, pp. 111–220.
4 Weigel: "Freuds Schriften zu Kunst und Literatur", pp. 41–61, particularly 55–61.

"Total Impression" and Detail

When Freud later speaks of the "analysis of the motivation of the movements of the figure" – i.e., of Moses carved in stone – (Freud 1914, StA X, p. 206), he emphasizes that the point is not simply to give in to the total impression but to assess the meaning of the details and draw conclusions from this with respect to interpretation. A certain hesitation[5] in judgment is required in order to arrive at a persuasive interpretation. To that end, the immediate effect of the work of art must be suspended if not completely eliminated. Effect and interpretation are, however, not mutually exclusive antitheses, since Freud explains as follows the "extraordinarily attractive […] attempts at an interpretation" art historians such as Justi and Knapp have made of Michelangelo's sculpture of Moses: "This is because they do not stop short at the general effect of the figure, but are based on separate features in it; these we usually fail to notice, being overcome by the total impression of the statue and as if were paralysed by it." (Freud 1914, SE XIII, p. 219) It is the stimulating effect on the analytical mind that Freud values. And it must be precisely this aspect that causes Freud to miss something, even though a seemingly cogent interpretation has been offered by some art historians. What he misses is an even deeper analysis of particular aspects, a specific working through of details and secondary matters that at first seem insignificant, since that alone could lead Freud to recognize a successful interpretation – as well as challenging him to carry out mental activity himself. Hence his maxim could be stated thus: the total impression easily obscures the individual facts; the whole distracts from the details, even though they are what constitutes it. Freud's hesitation results not just from uncertainty of judgment but also from a dissatisfaction with not having analyzed with sufficient precision and detail.[6] The hesitation of the figure of Moses he describes – being torn between various motives and impulses: anger erupting and passions inhibited, a need for revenge and a fidelity to the law – is thus repeated in the figure of the interpreter of the work of art, who vacillates between conclusive interpretation and unexplained details, between a homogeneous overview and contradictory tendencies of expression, searching for a better, more satisfying solution. In Freud's perspective only hesitation opens up the horizon to inquiry, to new reflections and interpretations: "The Moses of

5 It is not just a topic of the subject matter of the piece of art Freud relates to (the hesitation of Moses by Michelangelo) but a mode of temper in the author's perspective looking at the artwork (Freud's sceptical method of consideration). I will come back to the role of hesitation in the following parts of the text.

6 This also gives a reason for the interpretation of Freud's attempt to deny his position as an expert of art at first, but later on to reclaim his authority from the position of psychoanalysis, even against the art historian's expertise. Although he declared his little Moses study from 1914 as a "non-analytical child" ["nicht-analytisches Kind"] and thus rejected the affiliation at first, he "legitimized" this product of his interest in art and acknowledges his authorship years later (see letter to Edoardo Weiss from 12th April 1933; and Weigel: "Freuds Schriften zu Kunst und Literatur").

legend and tradition had a hasty temper and was subject to fits of passion ["Aufwallungen der Leidenschaft"]. It was in a transport of divine wrath of this kind that he slew an Egyptian who was maltreating an Israelite [...]; and it was a similar passion ["Affektausbruch"] that he broke the Tables of the Law, inscribed by God Himself. Tradition, in recording such a characteristic, is unbiased, and preserves the impression of a great personality who once lived. But Michelangelo has placed a different Moses on the tomb of the Pope [...]; he does not let Moses break [the Tables] in his wrath, but causes him to be influenced by the danger [in German: "Drohung", which means: "threat"] that they will be broken and makes him calm the wrath, or at any rate prevent it from becoming an act. In this way he has added something new and more than human ["Übermenschliches"] to the figure of Moses; so that the giant frame with its tremendous physical power becomes only a concrete expression of the highest mental achievement[7] that is possible in a man, that of struggling successfully against an inward passion for the sake of a cause to which he has devoted himself. ["und die gewaltige Körpermasse und kraftstrotzende Muskulatur der Gestalt wird nun zum leiblichen Ausdrucksmittel für die höchste psychische Leistung, die einem Menschen möglich ist, für das Niederringen der eigenen Leidenschaft zugunsten und im Auftrage einer Bestimmung, der man sich geweiht hat."]" (Freud 1914, SE XIII, 233/StA X, p. 217)

The Unconscious as a Condition of (the Aesthetics of) Effect

Freud associates with the "grandest and most overwhelming creations of art" like Michelangelo's Moses the "paradoxical fact" that what most "awes" us are "still unsolved riddles to our understanding." (Freud 1914, SE XIII, p. 211) Indeed, Freud considers whether "this state of intellectual bewilderment [could be] a necessary condition when a work of art is to achieve its great effects." (Freud 1914, SE XIII, p. 211–12) That is how he interprets the possibility of unconscious effects. He notes, however, that not everyone could be presumed to be "convinced of the existence of the unconscious," not even all "connoisseurs and lovers of art," however many words they might find "with which to praise such objects to us." (Freud 1914, SE XIII, p. 212) Freud initially adopts a sceptical tone towards the unconscious and speaks with restraint of a "conditional" lack of understanding that might have to be considered "necessary" and of a "state of intellectual bewilderment" on which the effectiveness of art may depend: "It would be only with the greatest reluctance that I could bring myself to believe in

7 This phrase of the "highest mental achievement" is closely related to the "advancement of intellectuality" (or spirituality) ("Fortschritt in der Geistigkeit") which Freud stated in his latest text on the biblical Moses (Sigmund Freud: *Der Mann Moses und die monotheistische Religion*, StA (= Standardausgabe) Vol. IX, p. 573; Engl. *Moses and monotheism*, in: The Standard Edition, Vol. XXIII, p. 128.

any such necessity." (Freud 1914, SE XIII, p. 212). What Freud, in the mask of a psychoanalytical layman, tries to fabricate and then reject is the possibility that the power of aesthetic phenomena to affect us lies precisely in a lack of understanding and hence is essential due to an unconscious effect.

On the other hand, Freud acknowledges without further ado the effectiveness of art, its powerful "impression," though perhaps in the way that Kant acknowledged necessary illusion, which could arise for a perceptive consciousness despite better, enlightened knowledge about deluding, deceptive conditions and principles. Freud ventured the "hope" that the "effect of the work will undergo no diminution after we have succeeded in thus analysing it." (Freud 1914, SE XIII, p. 212) This insight touches on Freud's clinical experience that an interpretation of the subject at an inopportune moment will fail in its analysis in that the subjective conditions and possibilities of understanding do not yet or no longer exist. Hence Freud wants both: an analytic comprehension of the work of art with an effect that continues. But on what level could these two aspects ever intersect?

Can the "unpretending admirer" (Freud 1914, SE XIII, p. 212) be reached at all by the many beautiful, sometimes apt "words" of "connoisseurs and lovers of art"? No, since the opinions expressed about works of art are too diverse to be convincing when taken as a whole: their contradictions with one another undermine their persuasiveness individually. But even beyond this inconsistency of opinion, clearly the *one* is lacking that would be suitable for the "admirer." Why is that? Because even admirers are not so "unpretending" as Freud initially suggests, because they want to *know*. And *what* do they want to know? The explanation of the mystery, or in Freud's terms: the solution of the riddle.

Art as Communication and/or Transference?

The path to Freud's response to the question of the powerful effect of art seems at first to lead to a traditional three-step model of communication between producer and recipient by way of art, going from (1) "the artist's intention" to (2) "expressing [himself] in his work" and then (3) "getting us to understand it." (Freud 1914, SE XIII, p. 212) The idea that the viewer understands art in a purely rationalist or intentionalist way – that is, limited to conscious understanding – is rejected by Freud: "I realize that this cannot be merely a matter of *intellectual* comprehension; what he [the artist] aims at is to awaken in us the same emotional attitude, the same mental constellation as that which in him produced the impetus to create." (Freud 1914, SE XIII, p. 212) Neither a conscious act of will nor a precise notion or an idea that can be clearly formulated is identified here with "the artist's intention." Rather, it is about an entire "mental constellation," which also includes an "emotional attitude" and "impetus." That is the further goal of awe-inspiring, overwhelming art, its true intention to affect, not the superficial subject matter or formal knowhow with which artistic activity seems to be concerned at first sight. This does not lead, as one might think, to a psychoanalysis of the artist, since the viewer is always confronted with the work of art and nothing else: "The product itself after all must admit of such an analysis, if it really is an effective expression of the intentions and emotional activities of the artist." (Freud 1914, SE XIII, p. 212)

Here, as so often in Freud, what matters is neither the psychology of the artist nor the *understanding* of the work of art but rather its specific effect on the viewer, which Freud described on the basis of his own experience. Moreover, the "effective expression" with which Freud begins refers both to the artist's "intentions" and to his other "emotional activities," which are, famously, anything but consciously controllable. And this effectiveness is intertwined in a process of transference that the "emotional attitude" – indeed, the entire "mental constellation" of the artist is in a position to produce or "awaken" again in the viewer. However, because this effect does not enable the viewer to understand, what is depicted in the work of art first has to be analyzed: "To discover [the artist's] intention, though, I must first find out the *meaning* and *content* of what is represented in his work; I must, in other words, be able to *interpret* it." (Freud 1914, SE XIII, p. 212) It is neither possible to address the artist's intention directly – it has to be "discovered," specifically, after analyzing the work of art – nor sufficient to determine "what is represented in his work." Rather, what matters is its "*meaning* and *content*," which escape direct observation and demonstrable perception. What matters is thus "interpretation" ["Deutung"].

The Interpretation of (the Effect of) Art as (the Enjoyment of) the Art of Interpretation

Freud here thus adopts one of those positions concerning art that postulate that it must be interpreted, as Arnold Gehlen[8] and Theodor W. Adorno[9] asserted for avant-garde modernism in particular: "It is possible, therefore, that a work of art of this kind needs interpretation, and that until I have accomplished that interpretation I cannot come to know why I have been so powerfully affected." (Freud 1914, SE XIII, p. 212) Thus it is not a commentary that merely repeats and doubles what has already been said (as Michel Foucault[10] says of the classical model for the hermeneutics of texts), since in the case of works of visual art it is not about something said but rather about, on the one hand, what preceded the work of art (the artist's "emotional attitude," "mental constellation," "impetus"), and, on the other hand, what is concomitant with the work of art but is not itself depicted ("meaning and content," which result only from the "interpretation"). When, in the next sentence, Freud "ventures" the "hope" that the effect will not

8 Cf. Gehlen: *Zeit-Bilder*.

9 Cf. Adorno: *Ästhetische Theorie*.

10 Foucault: *The Order of Things*, Chapter IV.1: Critique and Commentary.

be diminished by interpretation, it is clear now only that Freud knows that a considerable pleasure can be derived from this effect but also that he intends to cling to this pleasure, even if his desire is focused on analysis, of which "successful" interpretation is a necessary element. And this "vacillation" – the interim state of procrastination to which Joseph Vogl[11] recently devoted a study – finds its here in Freud's very next sentence: "Let us consider *Hamlet*," where it was only after psychoanalysis had traced its material back "to the Oedipus theme that the mystery of its effect was at last explained." (Freud 1914, SE XIII, p. 212) Freud's camouflaged self-praise underscores the achievement of the psychoanalytical view of having put a stop to multiple interpretations. But, on closer inspection, Freud's verdict is directed at the "mass of differing and contradictory interpretative attempts" and laments especially that they no longer affect us today: "And how many of these interpretations leave us cold! – so cold that they do nothing to explain the effect of the play." (Freud 1914, SE XIII, p. 212/213)

"Impressive Thoughts", the "Splendour of Language", and the Undiscovered "Source"

Just as Freud does not find immediate pleasure in the work of art and does not abandon himself to its effect, he does not trust an explanation based solely on language and aesthetics: When "opinions about the hero's character and the dramatist's intentions" remain unsatisfying, since they "do nothing to explain the effect of the play" but "rather incline us to the view that its magical appeal rests solely upon the impressive thoughts in it and the splendour of its language" (Freud 1914, SE XIII, p. 213), it seems to be precisely this dependence on language and ideas that makes Freud skeptical: "And yet, do not those very endeavours speak for the fact that we feel the need of discovering in it some source of power beyond them alone?" (Freud 1914, SE XIII, p. 213) Clearly, Freud considered a disinterested reflection on art and a contemplative, distanced view of works to be completely dissatisfying – indeed, a self-deception of the connoisseur. Failing to recognize the "source" of dissatisfaction in the interpretation of art also means failing to recognize the true forces, the "other sources" that are brought out in the effect of works of art and thus also characterize the artist's work.

The difficulties of interpreting works of art in general and Michelangelo's statue of Moses in particular do not lead Freud to conjure up a solution by sleight of hand, but rather to define strategies for dealing with the unexplained and perhaps unexplainable remains of an interpretation. That is the moment when Freud, after summoning up all his proof, abandons the paradigm of evidence and enters the field of "construction" and "interpretation" ["Konstruktion" und "Deutung"][12].

11 Vogl: *Über das Zaudern.*
12 See Freud: *Construction in Analysis.*

In the case of his interpretation of the expression of the figure of Moses, he mobilized possible knowledge of the context – that is, he tries to place the gestures, facial expressions, and body posture in the context of a narrative of actions and motivations in order to determine from its logic the meaning of the individual expressive gestures crystallized in the work of art and make them plausible. Furthermore, Freud brings his own experience as a viewer of the work of art into play when he recalls his visit to "the Church of S. Pietro in Vincoli in Rome", standing in front of the "gigantic tomb", and describes his own experience as a "stronger impression." This is not the place to get into the details of these two possibilities – namely, on the one hand, an autobiographical, psychoanalytical consideration of Freud the author as a viewer before the statue of Moses at a given time and, on the other hand, an "analysis of the motivation of the movements of the figure" of Moses ["Analyse der Bewegungsmotive der Gestalt"] – but they can be understood as strategies for "displacement" [Verschiebung] and for dealing with the irreducible "remnant" (as in *The Interpretation of Dreams*, where Freud found an image for the remnant that cannot be resolved by the analysis of a dream: the "dream's navel"). Despite the general interest of psychoanalytic theory in general laws of culture and the specifics of life of the mind, especially the structural circumstances of the *conditio humana*, Freud's strategy for intepretation [Deutung] makes it clear that it aims at radical individualization (1) by asserting that the meaning of the expressive gestures (in this case, of the statue of Moses) can only be determined in the context of a sequence of actions, a story or history, and (2) by tying the question of effect to the context of a unique biographical situation of the interpreter with its specific motives and motivations.

2. Fiedler

Conrad Fiedler's approach to observing works of art and the activity of artists inquires urgently after the unique characteristic of art: What is art able to attain that cannot be attained along other paths? What is the artist's genuine starting point and specific way of working, the actual field of his activity?

If one characterizes Fiedler's approach to the theory of art as one based on formal analysis and tied to the work, it in no way follows that Fiedler ignored all other aspects on which a consideration of art could be based, or that he regarded them as fundamentally unimportant or even wrong, or that he excluded them categorically. Quite the contrary, Fiedler viewed all of these interests in art as entirely legitimate. He merely considered such aspects as philosophical ethics, aesthetics, and epistemology to be external to art and artistic activity, brought in from elsewhere, and not within art's innermost impulse. Artistic activity, in Fiedler's view, feels no obligation to a social mission or an aesthetic norm of beauty.

Thus these aspects cannot contribute to the explanation of the specific achievement of art, that which can be attained only by and through artistic application. These aspects are simply in a different field. At the same time, Fiedler does not stylize art into a purely formal phenomenon empty of content, since art deals with, and is always realized through, concrete, situation-dependent materials and possibilities. Fiedler seeks to establish the field on which the genuinely artistic approach is brought to bear.

I quote Fiedler's thesis that "men owe the development of visual images to higher levels of existence to precisely one activity, the activity through which visibly demonstrable structures are brought forth, and this activity can be none other than artistic activity." (Fiedler 1887, I, p. 145) To put it another way: Regardless of themes or content, the way in which the artist goes about producing his work lies – for a visual artist – within the field of visibility. The artist seeks a creative realization of a visible design, the implementation of one possible shaping of the visible world.

In Fiedler's view, something central to artistic work is the connection between eye and hand, which is a main element in the sense perception of the overall, psychophysiologically determined human organism. He conceives visibility as something exceptional, to be sure, but not isolated from any of the other intellectual abilities or from corporeality. Instead, the possibility of shaping the visible world in and through art must be regarded as characteristic of humanity's fundamentally linguistic nature (that humans have language, are *zoon logon echon*): For Fiedler, there is not only access to the world through word-based language, interpreted in concepts and judgments, but, alongside this, the artistic approach to the world, which is directly related to visual perception and understood by Fiedler as a form of language. For Fiedler, this assimilation of the world through art, with nothing subordinate or secondary to words, concepts, or reason, ranks equally alongside the use of the word-based language in which poetry and the sciences are expressed. Visual art, poetry, music, and science each have a world-constitutive function that, in its particularity, is irreducible, unmistakable, irreplaceable, and inexhaustible.

Taking as a point of departure the visual perception that arises in the sphere of the senses, the artist's formative ability generates possibilities of depiction that are not foreseeable, nor can they even be derived from what is given. Rather, what the artistic impulse seeks is precisely the establishment of such possibilities for shaping the visible in ways that have not yet been presented to the senses. The process of giving form and depicting is thus itself the sphere in which artistic activity is realized without ever arriving at an impassable, exhaustive end. For Fiedler, each artistic production is distinguished by occurring only once and with unique characteristics, and is thus unsurpassable in its way; the underlying artistic activity, however, can be approached anew at any time and lead to different outcomes. In the context of such design processes, Fiedler often speaks of "development" (Entwicklung), which is not intended in a historical or Darwinian way (evolution); rather, it refers to a formation and transformation in a specific way and direction: from mere noise to well-formed tones and sound, to words or music; from the visible, approximate impression to the shaped form, the clear drawing, the painted image; from the physical movement, the reflexive twitch, to the specific gesture; in any case, from the sensation to the form of expression – and all by means of "expressive movement," as he describes this transition, borrowing the term from Wilhelm Wundt.

Not only does the "essence of expressive movement" lie in being "externally perceptible and understandable by another intelligent being" (Fiedler 1887, I, p. 115) but it is also in expressive movements that "a mental form that did not previously exist emerges in the first place." (Fiedler 1887, I, p. 117; cf. Boehm 1991, p. XIV)

Fiedler (following Wilhelm von Humboldt, Hermann Steinthal, and Wilhelm Wundt) studied "expressive movement," which is fundamental to all phenomena of expression, from gesture and facial expression by way of language and discourse organized conceptually to all forms of articulation (drawing, painting, architecture, music, literature, and so on). Fiedler believed that this concept of "expressive movement," which is so central to the relation between motion and emotion, overcame the traditional antitheses of inside and outside, mind and body, form and content, process and product, since none of these terms can be made absolute, can stand alone, can get by without its supposed counterpart.

Fiedler demonstrates the self-referentiality of this procedure – in which perception and expression, movement and emotion can be related to each other, thus resulting in continuous feedback between them, even though cause and effect cannot be clearly attributed between them – using the example of the hand and the eye. It is not always the eye that first sees and thus guides the hand; sometimes the movement of the hand contributes to the development of the design on paper, thus arriving at forms that the eye could never have achieved based on its own powers and perception. With this view from the 1870s, Fiedler anticipated the whole discussion that would characterize the arts in the twentieth century: the rise of abstraction, the no-longer-fine arts, and the performative character of the arts.

The finding of a form by the artist can just as well be described as an invention of form: in that sense, it is about the development of forms, about creative design of the visible, about "unprecedented achievement" ("vorbildlose Leistung", as Freud once called it)[13], even when the artist was inspired by a specific model such as something from nature or another work of art. The artist's task, according to Fiedler, is not simply to repeat or copy (though these are possible, even necessary activities of human life) but to provide an original solution to a given problem, to see, even create, a new design of traditional ways of seeing.

13 Freud: *Das Unbehagen in der Kultur*: StA Vol. IX, here: p. 221; English: *Civilization and its Discontents*, The Standard Edition, Vol. XXI, here: p. 90.

Fiedler thus liberated art from any attempt to put it in the service of any interests other than its own. But that raises the question what purpose this artistic effort serves? Does it have a purpose that can be generalized further? Or does artistic activity satisfy only itself, does its objective lie within itself? Fiedler's reply for the visual arts is: Artistic activity is dedicated to the visible design of the visible world. It is self-referential in that sense, but precisely because it pursues the urge for individuality that is immanent to art and cannot and does not wish to be satisfied with what already exists, artistic activity realizes unsuspected possibilities of the visible, and is thus analogous to a cognitive act. This cognitive act is to place the world before our eyes in a new perspective and to depict unfamiliar forms that have not existed as such previously in order to draw attention to visibility as such, to the possibility of making things visible. In the process, art makes an essential contribution to the philosophy of visibility and offers an opportunity to reflect on the conditions of the possibility of depicting the world. Art's aforementioned opening up of new possibilities for depiction signifies for philosophy that the activity of visual art is a fundamental approach to the world that deserves its place as an equal of literature and science.

How can this self-referential definition of art – art as the visible designing of the visible world – be connected to the fact that Fiedler attributes to it a fundamentally cultural character which lies precisely in the fact that it is part of a highly complex set of meanings determined by society, business, economics, and religion? To Fiedler's way of thinking, we should not see this as a mutually exclusive antithesis but rather emphasize that a self-referential or formal-aesthetic conception of art opens it up for concrete contexts in the first place. For, despite a widespread reproach of formalism that it treats the individual case according to general standards, Fiedler would have emphasized that a formal-aesthetic definition of art has no prejudices in terms of subject matter and hence is suitable to allow the specifics of the individual work of art to emerge. Such an approach to the particular can never be determined in advance by general theoretical premises but requires a knowledge of context. In Fiedler's words, this means: "The task of such [i.e., art historical] studies is to understand a work of art as a product and element of the entire cultural life." (Fiedler 1876, I, p. 14)

3. Summary

Artistic phenomena can be defined within the triangle of poiesis, work, and effect – in other words, production, product, and reception. Correspondingly, we can distinguish between three fundamentally different approaches to dealing with artistic phenomena: the technical aspects of production, the analysis of form and matter of the work itself, and the aesthetics of reception. Conrad Fiedler wanted to concentrate the effort to come to terms with art on the true concerns of art – namely, on the essence of artistic activity – and thus advocated an approach based on the analysis of form. Sigmund Freud was concerned, on the one hand, with the effect on the viewer and the subjective conditions of the perception of works of art and, on the other hand, with the conditions and conditional nature of production as they are crystallized in the personality of the artist as a historical individual. If Freud admits that he has no sense for or particular interest in the formal aspects of art – and hence could not really contribute anything to aesthetics in the stricter sense of a theory of the artistic principles for creating works – it seems appropriate to view Fiedler's essays on the "origin of artistic activity" as the missing piece that connects an aesthetics of production with an aesthetics of reception by offering an analysis of the artistic process itself and of the essence of the work of art.

It would, of course, be a mistake to imply or to try to construct a simple continuity between these approaches, since nothing could be further from Fiedler's intentions than reading his contribution to the theory of art as one element in a complete canon of aesthetics. His enterprise is sharply distinguished from any philosophically inspired aesthetics, since the artist moves in the sphere of visual perception, either in direct reaction to the material provided by the senses or by creatively producing not only the design for the work of art but also the material with which the work of art is produced. By that logic, any reaction, however modest, is not purely passive but also a creative act in Fiedler's sense. That is why any mimetic conception of art falls short. Rather, it is about the points of view that art can communicate by creating them in the first place, and not so much about the subject matter or objectives of art, even though they can be connected to art as well. So what makes art truly art? In Fiedler's view, because it is the creative design of the visible world.

Freud, by contrast, sought the explanation for art's effect in the structural, conflict-ridden commonalities of the *conditio humana*, which determine both the artist's work and every common viewer, since they share human nature. From a psychoanalytical perspective, therefore, it is about fundamental patterns of relationships such as the relationship to one's mother and father, to one's own body and those of others, to the symbolic and to the law, and, of course, to birth and death. The artist has merely found a way to depict them in his or her own way and thus make a contribution to their processing and refining – that is, to their sublimation – that the viewer is not in a position to make on his or her own but can nevertheless partake of its solution since he or she fundamentally shares premises with the artist, since they are both subject to the *conditio humana*. But these existential conditions do have their historical index. They form a specific constellation of social, linguistic, economic and technical determinations which have to be taken into account for the understanding and interpretation of any human articulation, be it an incidental action in everyday life or an elaborated piece of art.

For Fiedler all these points of view – specific historical situation, social standing, or conceptual understanding – are external to the artistic process, since the work of the artist is concerned with nothing other than a way to design the visible world – all subject matter and all moral or ethic, aesthetic, and discursive ambitions are secondary. It is not that they were not always present as well, but they do not represent the true specificity of the artistic interest, which is contributing something to the design of the visible world that has not yet been seen in that form.

References

Adorno, Theodor W.: "Ästhetische Theorie", in: Gretel Adorno / Rolf Tiedemann (eds.): *Gesammelte Schriften, Bd. 7*, Frankfurt am Main (Suhrkamp) 1970.

Fiedler, Konrad: *Schriften zur Kunst I*, ed. by and with an introduction (VII–XCVII) by Gottfried Boehm, Munich (Fink) 1912; first translated as *On Judging Works of Visual Art*, Berkeley (University of California Press) 1957.

Foucault, Michel: *Les Mots et les Choses* (1966); Engl. *The Order of Things. An Archaeology of the Human Sciences*, London (Routledge) 2001.

Freud, Sigmund: "Der Mann Moses und die monotheistische Religion" [1934–38]; Engl. "Moses and monotheism", in: *The Standard Edition of the Complete Works of Sigmund Freud*, London (The Hogarth Press) 1953–74, Vol. XXIII.

Freud, Sigmund: "Construction in Analysis" (1937), in: *The Standard Edition of the Complete Works of Sigmund Freud*, London (The Hogarth Press) 1953–74, Vol. XXIII, pp. 255–269.

Freud, Sigmund: "The Interpretation of Dreams" (1900), in: *The Standard Edition of the Complete Works of Sigmund Freud*, London (The Hogarth Press) 1953–74, Vol. IV.

Freud, Sigmund: "Das Unbehagen in der Kultur" (1930), Engl. "Civilization and its Discontents" in: *The Standard Edition of the Complete Works of Sigmund Freud*, London (The Hogarth Press) 1953–74, Vol. XXI, p. 57–145.

Gehlen, Arnold: *Zeit-Bilder. Zur Soziologie und Ästhetik der modernen Malerei* (1960), Frankfurt am Main (Athenäum) 1986.

Vogl, Joseph: *Über das Zaudern*, Zürich/Berlin (Diaphanes) 2007.

Weigel, Sigrid: "Freuds Schriften zu Kunst und Literatur zwischen Rätsellösung, Deutung und Lektüre. Die Studien zur Gradiva und zur Mosesstatue", in: Birgit R. Erdle / Sigrid Weigel (eds.): *Mimesis, Bild und Schrift. Ähnlichkeit und Entstellung im Verhältnis der Künste,* Köln/Weimar/Wien (Böhlau) 1996, pp. 41–61.

Affected by the Other
On Emotion in Psychoanalysis

CHRISTINE KIRCHHOFF

Introduction

When you look for a theory of affects in Freud you won't find much: As such there isn't any explicit theory of affects in Freud's work, which is no accident, although affects do matter in psychoanalysis. Affects do matter because of the well-known fact that remembering the past in a psychoanalytical setting does not have any effect if it is just remembered in the rational sense of the word: It has to be remembered with all related affection. However, affects are linked to the body. This means that the body, which is always more or less involved in the symptoms, also has to be involved in the process of remembering. This relationship also incorporates dimension of time: It is the affect belonging to the past but experienced in the present which links the past to present and to a possible future without the symptoms which made it necessary to remember their history.

I will use the terms affect and emotion more or less synonymously because there is no established, clear distinction between affect, emotion and – importantly – the German expression "Gefühl" in Psychoanalysis. The meaning depends on context and author. As you will see, Freud prefers affect, while Bion, for example, mostly uses emotion. I prefer to use the term affect, because the concept of affects in Freud is more complex and more interesting than his use of emotion.[1] Mai Wegener points out that Freud does not make precise distinctions between "Wahrnehmung" (perception) and "Empfindung" (sensation/sentiment): When he talks of feelings (German: Gefühl) he merges both phenomena by using the expression "Empfindungswahrnehmung" (perception of sensation).[2]

I would like to present three psychoanalytical theories that provide an interesting way to approach the topic of this anthology. All the theories chosen deal with the constitution of affects in a more or less implicit way, but all refer to the body's excitements and motions. I have chosen the theories of Sigmund Freud, Jean Laplanche and Wilfred Bion. From a wide range of psychoanalytical theories I have picked these three, because they share certain aspects which are in my

1 See Wegener: "Warum die Psychoanalyse keine Gefühlstheorie hat", p. 158; see also Freud: *Vorlesungen zur Einführung in die Psychoanalyse*, p. 410.

2 See Wegener: "Warum die Psychoanalyse keine Gefühlstheorie hat", p. 159.

opinion important to make a distinction between genuine psychoanalytical theories and other approaches to human psyche:

First, all these theories deal with the constitution of psyche and subjectivity from their very beginning without assuming given entities such as 'me and the other', 'inside and outside' or 'reality and fantasy'. In Freud, Laplanche and Bion all these oppositions have to be built up during ontogeny. They don't exist for the subject-in-spe from its very beginning.

Second, they all present a special kind of theory that was coined by Freud as "Witch"[3]. This common field of theory is also called Metapsychology. When Freud describes Metapsychology as a witch, he emphasizes the fact that its status cannot be defined easily: Metapsychological concepts do not deal with psychological phenomena, but with structures and dynamics that build up psyche. Dynamics and structures described by metapsychological concepts cannot be observed directly, but only through their effects. Apart from the unconscious there is another good example of such a concept. It had already been described by Freud in his early writings: the pleasure principle from the *Project for a Scientific Psychology*.[4] We are not aware of unconscious wishes other than experiencing them through their effects: symptoms, dreams, Freudian slips and so on. When this relation is taken seriously, psychoanalysis in fact will not be seen as psychology because psychoanalysis is not primarily a theory of phenomena of the psyche that can be observed in an experimental setting.

And third, in every chosen theory somebody, somebody as a person or someone's body, is affected by something that can be called "the other". In every case this process takes place in a different way.

1. Sigmund Freud (1856–1939) and the Constitution of Psyche

In the *Project for a Scientific Psychology* (1895) Freud not only constructed a model of the developed psychological apparatus. He also constructed a theory of the constitution of this apparatus, which means a theory of constitution of psyche and subjectivity, a fact which has been somewhat overlooked in recent times.

At the very beginning of Freud's construction there is an apparatus that avoids any excitation. It functions like a reflex apparatus: Every excitement coming in will be dispensed with immediately. Homoeostasis is the apparatus' one and only aim.[5] The apparatus functioning like that is affected by what Freud calls "Not des Lebens"[6], an expression which is difficult to translate. In the *Project* it

3 Freud: *Die endliche und die unendliche Analyse.*
4 See Freud: *Entwurf einer Psychologie.*
5 Freud: *Entwurf einer Psychologie*, p. 410.
6 Ibid.

means the fundamental needs of life, but if you follow it through Freud's work, you will find it has a far more complex meaning.[7] All of these meanings are concerned with claims from outside, from reality, which are first of all the claims of the body; or, as Mai Wegener calls it, claims coming from an "inner outside"[8]. The apparatus introduced by Freud cannot literally feed itself, so it needs somebody else, an "experienced individual", as Freud calls it, to get back to the level of zero energy.[9] During the primal scene of first breast-feeding ("Befriedigungserlebnis") Freud changes course by clearly using new terminology, and thereby moves towards psychology: the apparatus turns into a baby. This baby is not only fed, but something else, something very important, emerges from this process. Freud calls it the "secondary function of understanding and/or communication"[10]: Because the "experienced individual" has the ability to understand what the baby is demanding by crying and floundering, the baby's attempts to get rid of excitement attain a meaning.

This scene can also be seen as the primal scene of affection, because the experienced other is affected by the actions of the baby – and this affects the baby too. All the actions and motions of the baby start to gain a meaning because they do matter: They matter because adults – normally – react as if the baby's actions already had a meaning for the baby. In this way the baby is affected by the other, too. This scene can be seen as a general model of the origin of affects and meaning in Freudian psychoanalysis: Because the movements of excitement of the body have a meaning for the adults, they become meaningful in a psychological sense for the child too. Afterwards, it seems as if the actions of the body always had their special affective meaning.

The most important prefix in psychoanalysis is "re": remembering, representation, reminiscence, regression, reconstruction and so on. This implies a certain form of temporality, the temporality of German 'Nachträglichkeit'. Nachträglichkeit was roughly translated by Strachey, who translated Freud for the English Standard Edition, as 'deferred action'. Laplanche, on the other hand, suggested 'afterwardsness': The temporality of afterwardsness means that we never deal with immediate, first-hand issues, but always with whatever is being represented or remembered: whatever has been reconstructed in the present only "seems" as if it had always been like that. This, of course, means that the gap between a "thing" and its representations remains.

7 See also: Kirchhoff: *Das psychoanalytische Konzept der Nachträglichkeit*, p. 39ff.

8 Wegener: *Neuronen und Neurosen.*

9 See Freud: *Entwurf einer Psychologie*, p. 410.

10 In German: "*Sekundärfunktion der Verständigung*". See Freud: *Entwurf einer Psychologie*, p. 410.

2. Jean Laplanche and the generalized seduction by the other

Jean Laplanche, who was born in 1924, is a French psychoanalyst and a disciple of Jacques Lacan. Laplanche is best known for his attempts to generalize the early Freudian Theory of Seduction: Until 1897 Freud was of the opinion that every hysteric symptom must be caused by a real sexual event between the child and – usually – its father. Freud gave up this opinion and the whole theory, not only because of the empirical implausibility but also because of his newly gained insight that there is no "index of reality" in the unconscious.[11] In the early 1980s Laplanche started discussing Freud's Theory of Seduction again, which was in his opinion abandoned wrongly by Freud himself as well as by former psychoanalysts:

> By discussing the Seduction Theory we are doing justice to Freud, perhaps more than what he did to himself. He forgot the importance of his theory, and its very meaning, which was not only the importance of external events.[12]

In his "General Theory of Seduction"[13] Laplanche generalises the fact that children are seduced by adults. He makes the assumption of a "primal situation" in which "a new-born child, an infant in the etymological sense of the word (infans: speechless) is confronted with the adult world"[14] which "lies beyond the mother-child relationship".[15] We also know this primal scene or the "adult-child situation"[16] from Freud. But Laplanche stresses another aspect, the aspect of the message given by the adult: As "at the level of self-preservation the channel goes from child to parent [the child/apparatus doesn't even know at first, according to Freud – Ch.K.] whereas the reverse is true in the sexual domain"[17]. For Laplanche the primal relationship, therefore, is established as a two-fold register:

> We have both, a vital, open and reciprocal relationship, which can truly be said to be interactive, and a relationship which is implicitly sexual, where there is no interaction because the two partners are not equal.[18]

11 In a letter to his Berlin friend Wilhelm Fließ, Freud wrote on 21 September 1897 that he was now sure "that there is no sign of reality in the unconscious." (Freud: *Briefe an Wilhelm Fließ*).

12 *An Interview with Jean Laplanche.*

13 Laplanche's "General Theory of Seduction" was published in French in 1987, in German in 1989 and in English in 1989. I use the English version. See footnote 14 below.

14 Laplanche: *New Foundations for Psychoanalysis*, p. 89f.

15 Ibid., p. 92.

16 Ibid.

17 Ibid., p. 99.

18 Ibid, p. 103.

The infant is confronted with messages from the adult that are both conscious and unconscious, on the level of self-preservation and on the level of sexuality. And this means, of course, that the adult's messages are full of affection. According to Laplanche these messages create a basic necessity of translation for the child. It has to translate those messages. Because all actions of the adult incorporate unconscious aspects, and of course in Laplanche's work unconscious means dynamic, sexual and repressed, the child not only consumes milk, which it needs, but also all these unconscious, sexual, emotional meanings passed by the adult. This is how, according to Laplanche, the process of a child's sexual unconscious begins. It is affected by the unconscious of the other.

3. Wilfred Bion and the need for a containing other

Wilfred Bion, who was born in 1897 and died in 1979, was a British psychoanalyst who is well known for his work on group psychoanalysis, which he developed in association with the "Tavistock Group". As this text pertains to affects, it is more important that Bion is also one of the most significant followers of the psychoanalyst Melanie Klein, who was one of his teachers. Klein was primarily a child analyst, and her Object Relations Theory deals with early childhood, especially the period which, according to Freudian Psychoanalysis, is pre-oedipal.

Bion created a theory of thinking published during the 1960s in "Learning from Experiences" (1962), "Elements of Psychoanalysis" (1963) and "Transformations" (1965).[19] It is based on the hypothesis of the need to change what he calls beta elements (un-metabolized psyche/soma/affective experience) into alpha elements (thoughts that can be thought by the thinker).[20] To convert beta elements into alpha elements the child needs an adult, who is able to function as a container in which the elements are converted. Bion constructs his theory using the Kleinian concept of the good and the bad breast as a source:[21] Children experience the frustration of absence of the "good breast" as presence of a "bad breast". This means that children at first are not able to experience absence of something good, something they desperately need, as a temporal loss of an object they wish to be there, but as the presence of a persecutive object which has to be kept away and has to be expelled in the bodily sense of the word. For Bion, the presence of persecutive objects is significant for the experience of psychotic patients.

19 Bion: *Lernen durch Erfahrung*; Bion: *Elemente der Psychoanalyse*; Bion: *Transformationen.*
20 See Bion: *Lernen durch Erfahrung*, p. 53ff.
21 See Bion: *Lernen durch Erfahrung*, p. 55f, p. 110ff.

However, thinking requires what Bion calls – while using Keats as reference – the "negative capability": To be able to be unsure and insecure about an object.[22] Only a child who is able to withstand the absence of the good breast, which also means wondering how and when and why it will come back, can build thoughts like 'no object/no breast'.

Bion's language is quite abstract. He claims that our common language, even the more sophisticated academic or psychological language, is too full of meanings. This is why it is somehow incapable of describing those processes that are beyond thinking. In other words: In our common language we miss beta elements because when we do become aware of them they have already been converted into alpha elements.

In our days it is more relevant for us to bear in mind that Bion constructed his theory of alpha and beta elements, and hence to prove his theory of emotion he did not take any neuro-physiological elements into consideration. He developed these models of the elementary functions of the psyche from experiences gained from his work with psychotic patients. This kind of clinical work requires special concepts. The malfunction of elementary psychic processes led him to the normal psychological process of thinking: Like Freud, he not only reconstructed the normal based on the pathological, but as a state of being in which pathology is always present as a potentiality. For Bion, the psychotic way of thinking is always present, even in non-psychotic individuals. This is in line with Melanie Klein, who did not speak of stages of development, but of positions. Hence we all have to deal with positions of the past that co-exist in the present.

Bion claims that "emotional experiences" come before thinking.[23] The emotional experience of a "good breast" and the emotional experience of a "bad breast" are taken as being concrete and real like the milk, but at first, according to Bion, the child is not able to make a distinction: Being able to distinguish between different qualities of emotional experiences means being able to distinguish psychological qualities. Therefore the child needs the mother, who is able to "think" the beta elements coming from the baby and to give them back to the baby after turning them into alpha elements.

According to Bion, emotions/affects are at first "raw" sensations, more bodily than psychological. They have to be converted or metabolized in order to be experienced as someone's own discrete affects/emotions. The mother has to function as a "container" that "contains" the beta elements coming from the baby, converting them by a so-called alpha function into alpha elements which will be given back to the baby. This process could also be described as a process of stomaching, as Bion uses the digestive system as a model/basis for the psychological apparatus.[24] Bion's theory shows the urgent need for representation, as

22 See Bion: *Attention and interpretation.*
23 See Bion: *Lernen durch Erfahrung,* p. 105ff.
24 Ibid, p. 114.

the only way to get rid of the body's immediacy: There is no psyche without representation.

We can trace this figure back to Freud's "Vorlesungen zur Einführung in die Psychoanalyse" ("Complete Introductory Lectures on Psychoanalysis"). In the lecture concerning anxiety, Freud claims affects to be "sehr zusammengesetzt" (very composed)[25] – which does not make much sense, either in English or in German. Being composed of something is somehow difficult to compare, something which is presupposed by Freud's use of "very". Freud did not clarify this any further, but perhaps by using the word "very" he wanted to highlight the fact that he understands affects, in any form we can be aware of them as discrete and belonging to us, as being the result of psychological processes, and not as entities given by nature.

Conclusion

In Freud the primal scene of breast-feeding is the origin of understanding/communication, because the experienced other is affected by the baby and vice versa. In this scene the movement of the apparatus is converted into the meaningful actions of a baby, which is affected by the other, too, because its actions definitely matter. Physiological demands are transformed into psychological needs, which cannot be experienced without their meanings, both individual and cultural.

In Laplanche we can see that the sexual unconscious begins with the infant being affected by the other's unconscious. The infant is seduced by the conscious-unconscious messages coming from the adults to translate these messages.

In Bion we can see that discrete affects are a result of transformations. If they are not transformed they cannot be handled, and, more importantly in this context, they cannot be experienced as discrete states of affection.

All these attempts can be seen as psychoanalytical theories of embodiment which were developed a long time before the term "embodiment" started to gain any significance as a scientific concept.

Freud wrote that it is not possible to become psychologically aware of affects if they are not linked to what he calls a "Vorstellungsinhalt", a meaningful representation or conception.[26] If the intensity and character of an affect does not match the conception it belongs to, we enter the field of psychoanalysis. Our "waches

25 Freud asks himself "Was ist nun im dynamischen Sinne ein Affekt?" (What is an affect in the dynamic sense?) and begins his answer with the following statement: "Auf jeden Fall etwas sehr Zusammengesetztes" (In any case something which is very composed). Freud: *Vorlesungen zur Einführung in die Psychoanalyse*, p. 410.

26 "...weil wir einen Affekt nicht anders psychisch zu würdigen verstehen als in der Verknüpfung mit einem Vorstellungsinhalt." Freud: *Die Traumdeutung*.

Bewusstsein" as Freud calls it, goes crazy.[27] That means, as Mai Wegener puts it, that affects are not natural.[28] They are not natural because every affect is linked to its psychological representation, but this link is not fixed permanently or given by nature: "Between affect and presentation in humans there is the chain of signifiers, a network of different elements, which have to be treated by the unconscious."[29] When it comes to repression, the affect is separated from the representation.[30]

Affects do matter in psychoanalysis, but as I have tried to outline, it is not an accident that psychoanalysis is not at first a theory of affects. As the German philosopher Marie-Luise Angerer pointed out in her 2007 book "The Desire for Affects"[31] psychoanalytical theory belongs to those 20th century theories which claim an ontological difference: Humans are distinct from animals because of language.

In other words: The subject of psychoanalysis is founded in language, sexuality and – of course – the unconscious.[32] These dimensions, which are constitutive for each other, as Angerer claims, are attacked by what she calls desire for affects:

> The fact that today a version of human is preferred which claims the ontological difference to be closed can't be ignored. By preferring the affects an untroubled, undivided relationship between the ego and the world is suggested. Neurobiology, Brain Research, Theories of Arts and Culture work on this project together.[33]

Angerer asks whether the interest for affects can be seen as a passage or transition towards a "radical formation of organic bodies" which do not need any subjectivity:

> Can we understand euphoria about emotions and affects in Neurosciences and cognitive Psychology in a way that now human(s) can be put in line with animals and intelligent machines? Can we dismiss the psychological dimension, in which the 20th century was so interested in, for giving up the responsibility to a vitalistic force of motivation?[34]

The answer is: No, we cannot, unless we want to ignore the human dimension. This human dimension is inherent when psychoanalysis deals with affects in its theory and practice.

27 "Passen Affekt und Vorstellung der Art und Intensität nach nicht zueinander, so wird unser waches Urteil irre", ibid.

28 Wegener: "Warum die Psychoanalyse keine Gefühlstheorie hat", p. 148.

29 "Zwischen Affekt und Vorstellung läuft beim Menschen die Kette der Signifikanten, dieses Netz differentieller Elemente, die der unbewussten Bearbeitung anheimgegeben sind.", ibid.

30 Freud: *Das Unbewusste*, p. 278f.

31 Angerer: *Vom Begehren nach dem Affekt*.

32 See Angerer: *Vom Begehren nach dem Affekt*, p. 57: "Sprache, Sexualität und Unbewusstes sind die drei Dimensionen, die sich in dieser ontologischen Differenz artikulieren. Ihr Zusammenspiel, ihre gegenseitige Konstituierung wird vom *Begehren nach dem Affekt* attackiert, verworfen und letztlich gelöscht."

33 Angerer: *Vom Begehren nach dem Affekt*, p. 61.

34 Angerer: *Vom Begehren nach dem Affekt*, p. 119.

Bibliography

Angerer, Marie-Luise: *Vom Begehren nach dem Affekt*, Zurich (Diaphanes) 2007.

Bion, Wilfred R.: *Attention and Interpretation*, London (Tavistock Publications) 1970.

Bion, Wilfred R.: *Lernen durch Erfahrung* (1962), Frankfurt am Main (Suhrkamp) 1992a.

Bion, Wilfred R.: *Elemente der Psychoanalyse* (1963), Frankfurt am Main (Suhrkamp) 1992b.

Bion, Wilfred R.: *Transformationen* (1965), Frankfurt am Main (Suhrkamp) 1997.

Caruth, Cathy: *An Interview with Jean Laplanche* <http://www3.iath.virginia.edu/pmc/text-only/issue.101/11.2caruth.txt>, Emory University 2001, called up on November 21 2005.

Freud, Sigmund: "Die Traumdeutung" (1900), in: *Gesammelte Werke,* Vols. II/III, Frankfurt (Fischer) 1998.

Freud, Sigmund: "Das Unbewusste", in: *Gesammelte Werke,* Vol. X, Frankfurt am Main (Fischer) 1915, p. 278f.

Freud, Sigmund: "Vorlesungen zur Einführung in die Psychoanalyse", in: *Gesammelte Werke,* Vol. XI, Frankfurt am Main (Fischer), 1916–17, p. 410.

Freud, Sigmund: "Die endliche und die unendliche Analyse", in: *Gesammelte Werke,* Vol. XVI, Frankfurt am Main (Fischer) 1937.

Freud, Sigmund: "Entwurf einer Psychologie", in: *Gesammelte Werke, Nachtragsband*, Frankfurt am Main (Fischer) 1950.

Freud, Sigmund: *Briefe an Wilhelm Fließ. 1887–1904*, ed. by Michael Schröter, Frankfurt am Main (Fischer) 1985.

Kirchhoff, Christine: *Das psychoanalytische Konzept der Nachträglichkeit. Zeit, Bedeutung und die Anfänge des Psychischen*, Gießen (Psychosozial-Verlag) 2009, p. 39ff.

Laplanche, Jean: *New Foundations for Psychoanalysis*, Oxford/Cambridge (Basil Blackwell) 1989.

Wegener, Mai: *Neuronen und Neurosen,* Munich (Fink) 2004.

Wegener, Mai: "Warum die Psychoanalyse keine Gefühlstheorie hat", in: Johannes Fehr / Gerd Folkers (eds.): *Gefühle zeigen. Manifestationsformen emotionaler Prozesse. Edition Collegium Helveticum 5*, Zurich (Chronos) 2009, p. 158.

Shame and Grace.
The Paradox of the "Beautiful Soul" in the 18th Century

BURKHARD MEYER-SICKENDIEK

Ever since ancient times, the ideal of female beauty has been embodied by Aphrodite, as her ideal nude form emerges from the foam. The three Charites accompany her: Aglaea (splendor), Euphrosyne (mirth) and Thalia (bloom), gracing the ideal goddess with charm and mankind with good cheer. The image has become famous not least by its inclusion in Schiller's aesthetic reflections "On Grace and Dignity";[1] Schiller refers to a Roman depiction, choosing Venus instead of Aphrodite and the Graces, not the Charites, for her company. It is one special opposition that Schiller focuses on: Venus' beauty on the one hand, and the Graces' charm or 'grace' – 'Anmut' is his German term – on the other. Schiller distinguishes between these two as between scenes of two double arguments: The myth of Venus appears in the context of Schiller's proof against Kant that beauty is an objective quality, whereas his interpretation of the Graces amounts to an attempt at telling apart the realms of sensuality and of morals, of nature and of reason, of duty and of inclination, and then to balance these two sides by means of a concept of grace.[2] The latter, then, is no "excluding prerogative of beauty, but might pass to the less, or not, beautiful".[3] Emphasising this difference, Schiller uses a definition of grace known since Moses Mendelssohn: "beauty in movement",[4] but reinterprets that phrase in a characteristic and by no means trivial way: Grace is now defined as a kind of moveable beauty, that "can develop on a subject by chance and cease by chance",[5] so that no necessary connection exists between the quality and its carrier. It is only in another step that a movement will acquire grace, namely by being an "expression of moral sentiments",[6] an expression of "soul". This differentiates Venus' beauty – an objective and somewhat natural beauty – from that 'Anmut' or grace, for the latter is "a beauty not endowed by nature, but produced by the subject itself." So that which is expressed by grace as opposed to beauty is not "architectonic", but rather a moral beauty that lies at the core of the concept of the "beautiful soul": "It is the beauti-

1 Schiller: Über Anmut und Würde.
2 Cf. Brittnacher: "Über Anmut und Würde", pp. 587–609.
3 Schiller: Über Anmut und Würde, p. 434.
4 Cf. Knab: Ästhetik der Anmut.
5 Schiller: op. cit, p. 434.
6 Ibid., p. 436.

ful soul in which sensuality and reason, duty and inclination are in harmony, and grace is its expression in appearance."[7] The paradox here seems to be this: Schiller is not just harmonizing two spheres that were separate, but is circumventing the very distinction of objective beauty and subjective grace that was the only basis for his interpretation of the ancient myth! Indeed, Schiller saw that this paradox was the greatest problem for his treatise:

> But if the ultimate foundation of that movement that speaks of morals is outside, whilst the ultimate foundation of beauty must be inside the sensual realm, then grace, which is supposed to connect the two, seems to be faced with an obvious contradiction. To solve this, one must assume that the moral foundation within the mind that is the basis of grace, will by necessity produce in the beauty that depends on it that same state which includes in itself the natural conditions of beauty.[8]

That Schiller would anticipate and undo a rebuttal based on this contradiction is of course a result of his study in Immanuel Kant's transcendental philosophy. But according to that philosophy, the *a priori* ideas of reason – the concept of freedom, the ideas of God and of immortality – have no counterparts in the phenomenal realm. Schiller's reflections on beauty are immediately opposed to this assumption. Depicting the ideas of pure reason in empirical reality is impossible according to Kant, "because absolutely no intuition adequate to them can be given."[9] It is only by way of analogy that an indirect depiction becomes possible, resulting in Kant's famous formula of beauty: "Beauty as the Symbol of Morality."[10] As early as in his Kallias letters, Schiller voices the central opposition against this proposition in his own formula: "Beauty is Freedom in Appearance."[11] Freedom, as Kant determines its idealistic meaning, is the subject's freedom of heteronomy; according to Schiller, the same self-determination emerges in the autonomy of art, which seems to follow no exterior purpose in its harmony, but only its inner rule. While Kant basically determined beauty from the beholding subject's point of view, Schiller focuses on a characteristic of the object itself, which he regards as the actual foundation for any experience of beauty (thereby straining Kant's terms to their limit). Schiller's concept of grace as an "expression of moral sentiment", as expression of a "soul" – "Grace is a beauty not endowed by nature but produced by the subject itself"[12] – mediates the antagonism of nature and reason, of the sensual and the moral realm: Beauty cannot be conceived of without a sensual appearance, at the same time not *a priori* and necessarily included in the sensual material, but only if in correspondence with the idea of reason. The notion of the beautiful soul that Schiller develops at this

7 Ibid., p. 468f.
8 Ibid., p. 459.
9 Kant: *The Critique of Judgement*, p. 169.
10 Ibid.
11 Schiller: "Kallias", p. 400.
12 Schiller: "Über Anmut und Würde", p. 437.

point marks the internalisation of the moral law. For while Kant understood this moral law to be independent from any subjective inclination, as a "moral legislation" for mankind, Schiller again disagrees: It is not reasonable agreement to the demands of duty but a natural action emerging from the character's morality that results in the beauty of expression *in actu*. This is the mark of the "beautiful soul": that "sensuality and reason, duty and inclination are in harmony, and grace is its expression in appearance." So in a beautiful soul Kant's moral law, which places duty above inclination, intuitively controls the action:

> We speak of a beautiful soul when the moral feeling of all sentiments has ensured itself of the human up to a degree at which it can leave the rule of the will to the affect without hesitation and will never risk conflict with its decisions.[13]

This definition of an affectual control of affections that characterises Schiller's notion of the beautiful soul allows us to go beyond the confines of this text: What 'On Grace and Dignity' describes is very similar to that form of moral affect that Norbert Elias described in his famous "The Civilising Process". Elias asks (and answers): How were those civilisational affects and habits developed that are regarded as typical for occidental civilised mankind? Three affects are central to his argument: The emotions of shame, embarrassment and disgust. They can be regarded as civilisational affects, although this concept has been convincingly rebutted by Hans Peter Duerr and is viewed as obsolete. Elias showed that "the conditioning or fashioning of human behaviour is a process of developing societal standards that culminates in the internalisation of behavioural norms, proscribed by manuals on courtesy and the like as late as the renaissance. What emerges is a tendency towards controlling affects, developing taboos and delineating an intimate sphere, which explains among others the invention of the towel, the handkerchief or the separate toilet:

> It is for the very reason that the societal rule against nudity applies to all humans now and is in this form forced on the child, that the adult perceives it as a law internal to himself and that it becomes a more or less total and automatic form of self-coercion.[14]

This aspect of self-coercion is doubtless intolerable in Schiller's view, his affectual control of affects not being forced, but ruled by inclination and therefore by freedom. This is obvious in Schiller's analogies of political rule that illustrate the affectual control: They deal with the relation of sensuality and reason outlined above, which Schiller differentiates in three essential models: The rule of sensuality over the reason (ochlocracy), the rule of reason over sensuality (monarchy) and the harmony of the two (liberal government). In the first two cases, one side exerts force on the other, only the third state provides the basis "on

13 Ibid., p. 468.
14 Elias: *Über den Prozeß der Zivilisation,* p. 189.

which the beauty of play" becomes possible: only if reason and sensuality "match". So while Elias focuses on the aspect of self-coercion, Schiller describes the ease of internalised morality with a notion that he used as early as in his "Letters Upon the Aesthetic Education of Man" to describe the central category of freely developed subjectivity. It is the notion of *play*:

> For if neither reason ruling sensuality nor sensuality ruling reason will tolerate the beauty of expression, that state of the mind in which reason and sensuality – duty and inclination – match is the basis on which the beauty of play takes place.[15]

This passage is Schiller's explication of the phenomenon of grace. What follows is a discourse on the essence of dignity: "As grace is the expression of a beautiful soul, dignity is the expression of a sublime disposition." Such dignity will appear only in extreme situations, in which the laws that govern human properties are in crass conflict with those of nature and in which man, provided he is able to do so, delegates his will to reason and gains freedom from nature and its eternal laws: "Though man is in her [nature's] hand, his will is his own." So in the concept of the sublime, the affects oppose the moral law, which is why the character's morality in such a case cannot reveal itself other than in opposition to the affects. This model corresponds to the gendered distinction of grace and dignity – "One will find, on the whole, grace more likely in the female" – an adscription that is not least explained by the affects that Schiller associates with grace.[16]

In "On Grace and Dignity" the concept of grace is also identified as a kind of "sign language" (Gebärdensprache), which appears in "a gracious smile and a lovely blushing". Especially the concept of blushing gives us a hint that is essential for the following reflections. For Schiller combines two discourses in his essay, and their implicit proximity is indeed worthy of some attention: The concept of grace and the concept of shame and its connection to natural loveliness. While the motif of play made it possible to regard the combination as a harmonious one for a while, 17 years after "Grace and Dignity" the concepts seem irreconcilable. The point of comparison is the tale of the Fall of Man, which first created the affect of shame according to biblical tradition – "And the eyes of them both were opened, and they knew that they were naked; and they sewed fig leaves together, and made themselves aprons." – and which first introduced self-consciousness and thereby took away natural grace. In this reasoning, shame and grace oppose each other: man cannot be "natural", because the Fall has burdened him with shame and – in its wake – with "prudery", estranging him from nature for all time. This, at least, is the argument put forth in the Berliner Abendblätter in four episodes from the 12th to the 15th of December 1810 in Heinrich von Kleist's tale "The Marionette Theater". The main topic of this narrative is the endan-

15 Schiller: "Über Anmut und Würde", p. 463.

16 This stereotype of the "beautiful soul" as being female is analyzed by Konersmann: "Seelenschönheit als Weiblichkeitsideal", pp. 94–109.

germent of 'Anmut' or 'grace' by the reflections of conscious thought, that ability for self-knowledge that was created in the Fall. Returning to Paradise by a simple negation of that consciousness is impossible according to Kleist; innocence and grace become two modalities of an identical phenomenon: The marionette possesses grace both in the way of a special kind of beauty and of that grace which is innocence of knowledge, a lack of self-consciousness. But that lack is what man has lost, and a reconciliation of grace and shame is possible only once "awareness has virtually passed through an infinity". It is a paradoxical kind of awkwardness that we find in the tale of the boy who loses his former grace in an attempt to imitate before a mirror the gesture of an antique statue in the pose of pulling a thorn from its foot. This is why the Roman statue is considered as being graceful: Kleist's youth from the anecdote fails, when he tries to imitate the grace of the statue, not least out of shame: "He blushed, and raised his foot a second time to show me, but the attempt, as might easily be foreseen, was unsuccessful."[17] For the ideal graceful movement is marked (according to Kleist) by its thoughtlessness, almost unconsciousness *in actu*. This is why that Roman statue embodies grace: Kleist's boy must fail in his attempt at imitation. So the purest appearance of grace is "in that human body whose consciousness is either non-existent or infinite, that is in the puppet, or in God."[18]

In this tale, Kleist breaks away from the aesthetic tradition of the 18th century; the notions of grace or 'Anmut' were central its concepts. Removing them from the sphere of human appearance leaves a curious list of persons to whom Kleist grants the capacity for grace: a machinist's puppet, an animal innocent of all tactic or feint (the fighting bear), man before he was banished from paradise, and God characterised by his infinite consciousness. This enumeration is surprising, strange and contradictory, avoiding all mention of humane and cultivated man, as opposed to the philosophers of the 18th century who branded the term 'Anmut' or grace with aesthetic and moral implication: Winckelmann, Wieland, Lessing, Schiller and Goethe. It is not least that central motif of the discourse on grace that is categorically excluded from Kleist's reflections: namely, the 'beautiful soul'.[19] Is the reason for this omission the concept of shame as an affect resulting from Kleist's interpretation of the Fall of Man?[20] Does grace disappear from aesthetic study in the 19th century (as opposed to its career in virtually all styles of the 18th century, in rococo, in gallant and in Anacreontic poetry, and in sentimentalism) because of some kind of civilising process? In other words, is Schiller's internalised morality as the basis for grace the very point at which we find the beginning of the end? Meaning that the playful conception of affectuality, homogenous to contemporary

17 Kleist: "Über das Marionettentheater", p. 343.
18 Ibid., p. 345.
19 See also: Hart: "Anmut's Gender", pp. 83–95.
20 For the concept of shame in Kleist's tales see also: Benthien: "Gesichtsverlust und Gewaltsamkeit", pp. 128–143.

mores and therefore graceful to the beholder, capsizes and turns into a form of affectuality that lacks all grace because it hinders itself?

There is another prominent witness that argues against Schiller's ideal of the "beautiful soul" and refers to a kind of internality that comes close to Kleist's self-blockade as a result of self-consciousness: Georg Wilhelm Friedrich Hegel identifies the beautiful soul as ultimately not viable: "What they call the beautiful soul is noble subjectivity dying away in the vanity of all objectivity, in the unreality of its self." In this way Hegel draws the conclusion which he prepared in the "Phenomenology of the Mind" in 1806, which included a vast array of objections to that concept. Thought along the lines of a beauty of the soul is characterised as naïve, amorphous, paradoxical, childish, even pathological or even (though Hegel did not use the term) narcissistic. Although Hegel misunderstood the idea of the beautiful soul as a romantic concept and focused his criticism on early romantic authors such as Novalis or Friedrich Schlegel – though he missed the true inventors of the beautiful soul in the 18th century: Rousseau, Shaftesbury, Wieland, Schiller and Goethe[21] – the criticism he voices in the Phenomenology of the mind is nonetheless fundamental. For in the relevant chapter on morality – c) Conscience, the Beautiful Soul, Evil and Forgiveness – Hegel refers to Kant's theory of morality, which is central to the argument in "On Grace and Dignity". This chapter, besides some polemic, revolves around the fundamental problem of the "moral world-view" which is the context to Friedrich Schiller's theory of the "beautiful soul". It is in this world-view that Hegel discovers a paradox of self-consciousness that remains in two separate parts: one 'Ansich' (in-itself) and one self, or rather: one general, pure duty and one individual, natural morality. Hegel overcomes this contradiction – not unlike Schiller – by introducing the notion of "conscience" to complement that of the moral world-view.[22] This re-establishes the correct order, in it the mind is "sure of itself", i.e. it is not for the sake of duty, but duty is for its sake. But at the same time the individual isolates itself, up to the self-reflection of the "beautiful soul" which Hegel critically identifies with the notion of the "unhappy consciousness":

> It [the unhappy consciousness] lacks the power of realisation, the power to render itself a thing and bear its own being. It lives in fear of losing its immaculate inner by acting and being; and in order to preserve the purity of its heart, it flees from the touch of reality and insists on its stubborn powerlessness to deny its won being (sharpened to the height of abstraction) and to allow itself substantiality or change its thought into being and trust itself to the absolute difference – in that transparent purity of its moments an unhappy so-called beautiful soul, dying in itself and fading as an amorphous haze dissolving into air.[23]

21 Cf. Norton: *The Beautiful Soul.*

22 Cf. Well: *Die 'schöne Seele' und ihre 'sittliche Wirklichkeit'*, pp. 80ff.

23 Hegel: *Phänomenologie des Geistes. Werke 3*, pp. 483f.

The point is that Hegel conceives of the beautiful soul as a thesis – not a synthesis as Schiller did –, confronting its antithesis, evil. The beautiful soul proves unable to overcome this conflict, and its self-reflectivity and self-importance ends in a convulsion of self-ness. In short: Self-reflection, a lack of worldliness, inability to grasp evil, insubstantiality, i.e. empirically: desire and self-blockade are the characteristics of the beautiful soul. As a possible form for the mind it has failed Hegel, representing only an empty, unmediated abstraction. It is the gestalt not of an acting, but rather of a "spontaneously pure conscience", turning from action to language, to an expression in words" – i.e. its own inner convictions – "according to which it can never act for fear of losing its purity and generalness." This conscience is completely turned in on itself, it drowns in the I=I, in which that I is all essence and existence, the concept of itself. "Cleared to that purity, consciousness is its poorest form, and the poverty that is its only possession, is itself a fading; that absolute certainty into which substance has dissolved is the absolute lack of knowledge, collapsing upon itself; it is absolute self-consciousness, in which consciousness drowns." That 'absolute certainty of its self', originally acclaimed so forcefully, which pretended to overcome the problems of the moral world-view – 'pure duty on the one hand, manifold duties or special reality' on the other hand – is thus decrepit, a consciousness void of the power for realisation, to render itself a thing and bear its own being.

> The reality-less beautiful soul, in its contradiction of pure self and the necessity of the same to realise itself in a being and turn into a reality, in the immediacy of this sustained contradiction,… is therefore shattered in the consciousness of this contradiction in its unreconciled immediacy to the point of madness and dwindles in wistful consumption[24]

These sketches from Hegel and Kleist mark the borders of a discussion that revolves around the problem of grace as an expression of a harmony of reason and sensuality, as a mark of the soul's beauty. While Schiller in 'Grace and Dignity' was able to use the category of play as an ultimately anthropological reflection to realise that concept, the same concept is done away with no more than a generation later: This demonstrates a process that ends in a new view of the subject's self-understanding – its self-consciousness – seen in the light of a new problem: that of the self-blockade, which hinders the freedom of the body's movement for Kleist, and that of the mind's movement, of thought, for Hegel. But what Hegel regarded as an unsolvable contradiction of the beautiful soul – to realise itself and turn into a reality – seems to be no more than a prejudice when seen in the context of the history of this motif. The reason is that Hegel did not grasp the concept of the beautiful soul the way the 18th century had intended it: as an element of the art of living, led by an idea of sociality and interaction.[25]

24 Ibid., p. 491.
25 Cf. Adam: "Geselligkeit und Anakreontik", pp. 31–54.

Even Schiller's view is still connected to this tradition, for it is an expression of a feeling of ease that is characteristic of large parts of the 18th century. We see this with one glance at the anacreontic poetry of the 18th century, dominated by stereotypical motifs like the power of love, praise for the beloved, praise for wine and the shepherd's idyll, all of them understood as an expression of natural grace in which the niceties of external-sensual joy are coupled with grace and wit. As much as the joy of life in a lovely (amoenous) setting was no more than a wishful image and as much as the wine- and love-drunk poet's pose is an act[26], this imagination of free life, love and singing has an explosive power, realised most beautifully perhaps in Wieland's epos "Musarion" in 1768. A beautiful soul – the title's "Musarion" – is the protagonist, and grace is a philosophical disposition towards a certain art of living. The scene of the gay and playful story is a utopian Arcadian Greece, an antique artful landscape. Following a quarrel with his friend Musarion, the young dreamer Phanias has secluded himself in his villa near Athens in order to devote himself to serious, non-sensualist studies and strict meditation. When Musarion tries to reconcile herself with her old friend, she finds him turned into a cold rationalist who has joined "the joyless guild of swollen stoics". In order to resist the temptation poised by his former companion, Phanias hides behind philosophical phrases. However, Musarion deviously uses her attractive features and an arranged feast to dissolve the misogynist philosophical mood. Phanias' friends, the Stoic Kleanth and the Pythagorean Theophron submit to heavy drinking, until finally the reclusive Kleanth is snoring in the stables and the sensual-transcendental Theophron enjoys himself with Musarion's maid Chloë. Meanwhile Phanias, disappointed by the obscene deviations of his two mentors, who now seem "not quite as wise as their system", sneaks away to Musarion, rejects his former ascetic way of life, most of all his misogynism, shows remorse and makes peace with his old friend.[27] After this "mastered hardship", the couple has become "more able / For a wiser use, a lovelier joy / Of happiness." They remain at Phanias' manor and proceed to live a life in which "serious thought often couples with easy jest" and in which philosophy is no longer a fanaticism, but a gracious endeavour:

> Lovely philosophy,
> That, what nature and our lot allow,
> Enjoys delight, and does without the rest;
> That likes to see in these world's things
> Their beauty; that will submit to destiny
> And needs not know what all that means
> Which Zeus, by his good grace, in night
> And riddles has hid from us.[28]

26 Cf. Nägele: *Das Imaginäre und das Symbolische*, pp. 45–63.
27 Cf. Rickes: *Führerin und Geführter*.
28 Wieland: *Sämmtliche Werke*. Neunter Band, p. 99.

No doubt: It still might be questionable to what extent we can compare the mythological protagonists of Wieland's epic poem with those concepts as they are previously mentioned in texts of Schiller, Hegel, and Kleist. But Wieland, Schiller, Kleist, Hegel all treat a central theme of Goethe's time – the grace – and they all document the process of the "loss of grace". Although this process has often been mentioned in the research, up to now this loss has never been explained in a whole theorem. Norbert Elias's "process of civilization" is a model that allows us – due to its theory of an affectual control of affects – to explain this loss. This is because Elias focuses on the other side of that morality, which is characteristic of the "beautiful soul" and its inherent natural grace: the shame, which ultimately leads to the loss of this natural grace.

Bibliography

Adam, Wolfgang: "Geselligkeit und Anakreontik", in: Ernst Rohmer / Theodor Verweyen (eds.): *Dichter und Bürger in der Provinz. Johann Peter Uz und die Aufklärung in Ansbach*, Tübingen (Niemeyer) 1998, pp. 31–54.

Benthien, Claudia: "Gesichtsverlust und Gewaltsamkeit: zur Psychodynamik von Scham und Schuld in Kleists 'Familie Schroffenstein'", in: *Kleist-Jahrbuch* 1999, pp. 128–143.

Brittnacher, Hans Richard: "Über Anmut und Würde", in: Helmut Koopmann (ed.): *Schiller-Handbuch*, Stuttgart (Kröner) 1998, pp. 587–609.

Elias, Norbert: *Über den Prozeß der Zivilisation. Soziogenetische Untersuchungen. Erster Band. Wandlungen des Verhaltens in den weltlichen Oberschichten des Abendlandes*, Frankfurt am Main (Suhrkamp) 1992.

Hart, Gail K.: "Anmut's Gender: The 'Marionettentheater' and Kleist's Revision of 'Anmut und Würde'", in: *Women in German Yearbook* 10 (1994), pp. 83–95.

Hegel, Georg Wilhelm Friedrich: "Phänomenologie des Geistes", in: Moldenhauer, Eva / Karl Markus Michel (eds.), *Werke,* Vol. 3, Frankfurt am Main (Suhrkamp) 1986.

Kant, Immanuel: *The Critique of Judgement* (1781), trans. by James Creed Meredith, Oxford (Oxford University Press) 2008.

Kleist, Heinrich von: "Über das Marionettentheater", in: Helmut Sembdner (ed.): *Sämtliche Werke und Briefe. Band 2*, München (Hanser) 1984.

Knab, Janina: *Ästhetik der Anmut. Studien zur "Schönheit in der Bewegung" im achtzehnten Jahrhundert*, Frankfurt am Main and Berlin, 1996.

Konersmann, Ralf: "Seelenschönheit als Weiblichkeitsideal. Versuch, ein Missverständnis aufzuklären", in: *Psychologie und Geschichte* 5 (1993), pp. 94–109.

Nägele, Rainer: "Das Imaginäre und das Symbolische. Von der Anakreontik zum Schleiersymbol", in: Hofmeister, Gerhart (ed.): *Goethezeit: Studien zur Er-*

kenntnis und Rezeption Goethes und seiner Zeitgenossen, Bern, München (Francke) 1981, pp. 45–63.

Norton, Robert E.: *The Beautiful Soul: Aesthetic Morality in the Eighteenth Century*, Ithaca and London (Cornell University Press) 1995.

Rickes, Joachim: *Führerin und Geführter. Zur Ausgestaltung eines literarischen Motivs in Christoph Martin Wielands 'Musarion oder die Philosophie der Grazien'*, Frankfurt, Bern, New York (Peter Lang) 1989.

Schiller, Friedrich: "Kallias oder über die Schönheit", in: *Sämtliche Werke*, Band 5, München (Hanser) 1962, pp. 394–433.

Schiller, Friedrich: "Über Anmut und Würde", in: *Sämtliche Werke*, Band 5, München (Hanser) 1962, pp. 433–489.

Well, Karlheinz: *Die 'schöne Seele' und ihre 'sittliche Wirklichkeit'. Überlegungen zum Verhältnis von Kunst und Staat bei Hegel, Münchener Studien zur literarischen Kultur in Deutschland,* Vol. 1, Frankfurt am Main, Bern, New York (Peter Lang) 1986.

Wieland, Christoph Martin: *Sämmtliche Werke* (Leipzig: 1795) [Reprint: Hamburg {Greno} 1984].

The Body and its Representation in the Brain

ARNO VILLRINGER

I Introduction

Each part of the human body is equipped with peripheral nerves which transmit information to the brain. Information which is communicated can be classified according to (i) the 'type' of information, i.e. tension of a tendon, touch of the skin, or heat/cold on the skin etc., (ii) the type of nerve fibres which transmit this information (typically ordered by their thickness), or (iii) the location within the body from which this 'information' originates, such as skin / muscles at different locations, bowel, liver, etc.

Each of these general 'classes of events' based within the body, are reflected in 'classes of events' within the brain and the interrelationship between the two is frequently operationalized in a terminology which regards 'events in the brain' as 'representations' of 'corresponding events in the body'. The most well known visualization of such representations is the so called homunculus. Here, a map of the body is superimposed on parts of the brain following the correspondence of sensory events in the respective body part and localized evoked neural activity in the brain ('somatosensory homunculus') or the correspondence of elicited activity in areas of the motor cortex and subsequent movements of different parts of the body ('motor homunculus'). For many years it was thought that this kind of correspondence is the result of a 'hard-wired' connection between (pre-) specified brain areas and body sites, i.e. a static relationship. Recently, however, it has been shown that this relationship is extremely dynamic. There is no one-to-one relationship between a neuron / or a brain region and a body part, but rather patterns of activity in the former reflect certain events in the latter. E.g. macroscopically, light versus strong touch of the same skin area is reflected in different amplitudes of brain activity and different sizes of this brain area which becomes active. On a cellular as well as macroscopic level, during continuous stimulation, there is habituation of the cortical response, i.e. the area of activity becomes less active and smaller despite the same continuous stimulation. Furthermore, the brain continuously changes its functional (and structural) properties while adapting to internal and external events and associated peripheral stimuli. 'We never use the brain twice'. This process of brain plasticity can range from subtle to dramatic. E.g., after damage to peripheral nerves or after lesions in the central nervous system, very pronounced shifts in representational areas occur. For example, if a finger nerve is damaged (or a finger is amputated), the representations of adjacent fingers / nerves 'moves' into the brain area which previously 'represented' the now lost finger.

In summary, what has previously been regarded as static representations of the body in the brain is now regarded as a dynamic interplay which is continuously adapting to changes in environmental inputs, the body, the brain, and the connection between these. Our group is studying these events for the human somatosensory system. We are interested in (i) 'Normal functioning of the somatensory system', (ii) its adaption to lesions to the body/peripheral nervous system and to the central nervous system, (iii) recovery of function after such focal lesions.

II Physiology of somatosensory system

Somatosensory homunculus

While traditional homunculus maps were based on invasive/intraoperative stimulation studies of the brain cortex, in series of experiments, we attempted to establish a new operational definition of human somatosensory homunculus based on non-invasive functional magnetic resonance imaging (fMRI)[1] during stimulation of body parts. Specifically, we were able to show clear-cut finger somatotopy[2] in primary somatosensory cortex which followed a medio-lateral sequence. In a second study, we demonstrated that – consistently with studies in nonhuman primates – somatosensory representation in human subjects does not just consist of 'one map', but even in primary somatosensory cortex there seem to be a least four maps which are located in Brodmann areas 3a, 3b, 1, and 2, respectively.[3] Finally, we were able to show that there is not only a medio-lateral somatotopy, but also a proximal distal somatotopy along the finger and hand and that with respect to this proximal-distal somatotopy a 'mirror-reversal' can be observed with a inflection point at the border between the different subregions (3a,b,1,2).[4] Furthermore, we were able to show that along processing pathways in the somatosensory system, somatotopy is still present, however somewhat less fine-

1 See Kwong et al.: "Dynamic Magnetic Resonance Imaging of Human Brain Activity"; Ogawa et al.: "Intrinsic Signal Changes Accompanying Sensory Stimulation"; Bandettini et al.: "Time Course EPI of Human Brain Function During Task Activation"; Frahm et al.: "Dynamic MR Imaging of Human Brain Oxygenation During Rest and Photic Stimulation".

2 Kurth et al.: "fMRI Assessment of Somatotopy in Human Brodmann Area 3b".

3 Kurth et al.: "fMRI Shows Multiple Somatotopic Digit Representations in Human Primary Somatosensory Cortex".

4 Blankenburg et al.: "Evidence for a Rostral-to-Caudal Somatotopic Organization in Human Primary Somatosensory Cortex".

grained.[5] While these studies at first sight seem to confirm a traditional 'naïve' 'homunculus' picture, a notable difference to previous (invasive electrophysiological) studies is a remarkable overlap between 'adjacent' representational areas. This seems to indicate that these 'representations' are not independent of each other, rather there must be some kind of interaction which should become evident when different body parts are stimulated simultaneously.

Interaction

Indeed, when two fingers are stimulated simultaneously, the resulting cortical activation is not a mere sum of the two stimulations. Rather, we noted a mutual interaction in such a situation.[6] This phenomenon might be related to the electrophysiological finding of lateral inhibition which is well known for the visual system and which has also been shown in the whisker barrel of the rat. Most likely, such lateral inhibition helps to sharpen somatosensory detection. Interesting, in our studies, the mutual interaction does not only occur between adjacent fingers, but also – albeit weaker – between non-adjacent fingers. Recently, we have been able to show that mutual interaction / inhibition may also occur even between the hemispheres: In an EEG-experiment in which we recorded somatosensory evoked potential upon median nerve stimulation, attenuation of early components of the evoked potential was observed when the contralateral median nerve was stimulated between 20 to 25 ms before.[7] We conclude that – most likely – all somatosensory processing from reflecting adjacent or distant body parts is mutually interactive, and this is reflected in mutual influence on cortical activation patterns upon stimulation. A mutual inhibitory interaction may also explain why stimulation of one body part may suppress completely the conscious experience of stimulation of another body part ('masking').

Conscious versus unconscious somatosensory processing

Many sensory events which happen either in the environment or inside the body do not become conscious experiences. It is poorly understood, however, whether and if so how unconscious processing occurs in the brain. We investigated one model of non-conscious somatosensory stimulation of fingers for which there have been controversial discussions previously. During electrical finger nerve stimulation below the amplitude threshold for conscious detection, Libet et al. have reported an evoked cortical potential based on invasive recordings of human

5 Ruben et al.: "Subarea-Specific Suppressive Inter-Action in the BOLD-Responses.

6 Krause et al.: "Representational Overlap"; Ruben et al.: "Subarea-Specific Suppressive Inter-Action in the BOLD-Responses

7 Ragert et al. (in revision).

subjects.[8] While only Ray et al. 1999 have been able to show a similar finding, again based on invasive recordings, however, in non-invasive recordings this has not been reproduced. We used fMRI during subliminal finger nerve stimulation and were able to clearly show that this leads to a deactivation of the somatosensory network.[9] This deactivation seems to be associated with functional inhibition of the somatosensory system of the same as well as adjacent finger.[10] Furthermore, we have recently been able to record an evoked potential to subliminal stimulation based on the averaging across many subjects.[11] In the same study, we were able to show that subliminal stimulation seems to enhance cortical background rhythms in the alpha frequency range. This is consistent with the notion that these background rhythms are inversely related to the activity of the respective sensory system which is supported by the result of our EEG-fMRI studies.[12] Whether spontaneous modulations of these background rhythms indeed have functional significance we tested in a making experiment: Here a relatively weak but clearly detectable stimulus was applied to the right/left index finger (test stimulus). When x ms later a strong stimulus was applied to the contralateral index finger, the test stimulus was detected only in about half of the trials. In such an experiment one can retrospectively sort the trials according to whether the stimulation to the finger was consciously perceived or not. When contrasting the evoked potentials perceived vs. not perceived later ('cognitive') components of the evoked potential differed. Interestingly, this contrast also resulted in a difference in the strength of the prestimulus pericentral alpha rhythm. In those trials, in which the stimulus was NOT detected, the power of the prestimulus alpha rhythm was stronger, i.e. again a confirmation of an inverse relationship between the strength of a background rhythm and the activity of the respective system. Recent results by other authors indicate now that this inverse relationship probably refers to a certain range of alpha powers and that – considered over a wider range of alpha power strength – the relationship has an inverted U-shape (Jensen, Palva).

8 Libet et al.: "Responses of Human Somatosensory Cortex".

9 Blankenburg et al.: "Imperceptible Stimuli and Sensory Processing Impediment".

10 Blankenburg et al.: "Imperceptible Stimuli and Sensory Processing Impediment"; Taskin et al.: "Inhibitory Impact of Subliminal Electrical Finger Stimulation".

11 Nierhaus et al.: "Background and Evoked Activity".

12 Moosmann et al.: "Correlates of Alpha Rhythm in Functional Magnetic Resonance Imaging and Near Infrared Spectroscopy" 2003, Ritter et al.: "Rolandic Alpha and Beta EEG Rhythms' Strengths".

Plasticity in the somatosensory system due to lesions

a) Peripheral Lesions

While the results of studies mentioned above have shown that there is a complex spatio-temporal relationship between events on the body and those in the brain, other studies have shown that this relationship is not constant, but is adapting continuously. The first indication for this plasticity was obtained in studies in which peripheral nerves were damaged e.g., due to amputation. In these studies the relationship between events on the body and those in the brain was dramatically altered (Merzenich Review). Specifically, in studies of peripheral deafferentiation, the representations of now amputated limbs would be 'taken over' by representations of adjacent body areas. While early studies relied on invasive recordings in animals, with the advent of functional brain imaging, similar studies can be performed non-invasively. While these non-invasive studies in principle confirmed the above mentioned results from invasive recordings, the non-invasive approach allows new types of issues to be investigated. For example, it is well-known that amputees frequently experience the lost limb as still present, i.e. phantom sensation. In some cases these experiences are accompanied by severe pain (phantom pain). Using fMRI during induction of phantom sensations, we have been able to demonstrate that phantom sensation are accompanied by activation of those cortical areas which formerly represented the amputated limb (A. Villringer et al., unpublished results). Most likely, the deafferentiated cortical areas are activated via subcortical pathways which are upregulated due to the amputation.

b) Lesions in the central nervous system

Lesions in the central nervous system, i.e. the brain or the spinal cord can lead to pronounced disturbances of somatosensory function. Traditionally, it is assumed that the neurological symptom which is associated with a lesion depends entirely on the site of the lesion. Given recent studies which indicate that the brain is organized following small world principles, it is plausible that the 'connectivity role' (node versus non-node of network) also plays a major role. Recently, data have been shown which indicate that brain damage to nodes indeed affects neuronal function more severely than damage to less connected brain regions. In addition to the location of a lesion within the network, the reaction of the network to the lesion also seems to play an important role. Functional neuroimaging studies in patients after stroke to the motor or language network indicate that there is a time-dependent pattern of down/up regulation of an entire network after the lesion.

We studied a group of six patients in all of whom lesions had occurred in the ventro-posterolateral nucleus (VPL) of the thalamus and who all had disturbance of somatosensory function (hemihypaesthesia). When electrical stimulation of the affected hand was performed in these subjects, a pronounced down-regulation of SI activity was observed, while SII activity seemed relatively upregulated.[13]

Learning and the somatosensory system in health and after focal lesions

It is possible to improve the functioning of the somatosensory system by learning, and this applies to healthy subjects as well as patients after focal lesions. A rather classical 'test' of somatosensory function is the ability of two-point discrimination. In healthy subjects, recently, it has been studied how learning-induced improved somatosensory function is reflected in non-invasive neuroimaging signals. In an experimental setting, learning (improvement of two-point discrimination on a finger) was induced by a learning approach which followed a Hebbian idea, i.e. simultaneous excitation of adjacent neurons ('co-activation'). When such a co-activation protocol was applied to a finger tip, a transient increase in the somatosensory discrimination property was measured (Dinse). It was subsequently shown that this functional improvement is accompanied by changes in cortical activation patterns (fMRI) upon sensory stimulation. Furthermore, it was shown that glutamatergic neurotransmission plays a major role in this kind of learning, i.e. it was attenuated by the NMDA antagonist memantine. Amphetamine, on the other hand, led to enhanced learning in this paradigm. Another approach modeled according to Hebbian principles uses transcranial stimulation (either transcranial magnetic stimulation: TMS or transcranial direct current stimulation: TDCS) to improve brain function. Transient improvement of somatosensory function was also demonstrated for such central stimulation. Recently, it was shown that combination with a procedural learning paradigm leads to improvement of somatosensory function.

It will be interesting whether this kind of stimulation-induced learning can be used for recovery of function after focal lesions, e.g., after a stroke. First data indicate that this may indeed be the case, however, so far the improvements are transient. Approaches to make improve function permanently include repetitive stimulation, combination with learning, and combination with drugs. Obviously these non-invasive approaches are limited in their accessibility to regions throughout the brain. However, should proof of principle of the efficacy of brain stimulation in recovery from brain lesion be obtained, the idea could be transferred to a deep brain stimulation approach which offers (albeit invasively) access to almost all brain regions.

13 Taskin et al.: "Preserved Responsiveness of Secondary Somatosensory Cortex".

Bibliography

Bandettini P. A. / E. C. Wong / R.S. Hinks et al.: "Time Course EPI of Human Brain Function During Task Activation", in: *Magn Reson Med* 25 (1992), pp. 390–397.

Blankenburg, F. / J. Ruben / R. Meyer et al.: "Evidence for a Rostral-to-Caudal Somatotopic Organization in Human Primary Somatosensory Cortex with Mirror-Reversal in Areas 3b and 1", in: *Cereb Cortex*, 13 (2003), pp. 987–993.

Blankenburg, F. / B. Taskin / J. Ruben et al.: "Imperceptible Stimuli and Sensory Processing Impediment", in: *Science* 299 (2003), p. 1864.

Deuchert, M. / J. Ruben / J. Schwiemann et al.: "Event-Related fMRI of the Somatosensory System Using Electrical Finger Stimulation", in: *Neuroreport* 13 (2002), pp. 365–369.

Frahm, J. / H. Bruhn / K. D. Merboldt et al.: "Dynamic MR Imaging of Human Brain Oxygenation During Rest and Photic Stimulation", in: *J Magn Reson Imaging 2* (1992), pp. 501–505.

Freyer, F. / R. Becker / K. Anami et al: "Ultrahigh-Frequency EEG During fMRI: Pushing the Limits of Imaging-Artifact Correction", in: *Neuroimage* 48 (2009), pp. 94–108.

Krause, T. / Kurth R. / J. Ruben et al.: "Representational Overlap of Adjacent Fingers in Multiple Areas of Human Primary Somatosensory Cortex Depends on Electrical Stimulus Intensity: An fMRI Study", *Brain Res* 899 (2001), pp. 36–46.

Kurth, R. / K. Villringer / B. M. Mackert et al.: "fMRI Assessment of Somatotopy in Human Brodmann Area 3b by Electrical Finger Stimulation", in: *Neuroreport*, 9 (1998), pp. 207–212.

Kurth, R. / K. Villringer / G. Curio et al.: "fMRI Shows Multiple Somatotopic Digit Representations in Human Primary Somatosensory Cortex", in: *Neuroreport* 11 (2000), pp. 1487–1491.

Kwong K. K. / J. W. Belliveau / D. A. Chesler et al.: "Dynamic Magnetic Resonance Imaging of Human Brain Activity During Primary Sensory Stimulation", in: *Proc Nadl Acad Sci* 89 (1992), pp. 5675–5679.

Libet, B. / W. W. Alberts / E. W. Wright Jr. et al.: "Responses of Human Somatosensory Cortex to Stimuli Below Threshold for Conscious Sensation", in: *Science* 158 (1967), pp. 1597–600.

Moosmann, M. / P. Ritter / I. Krastel et al.: "Correlates of Alpha Rhythm in Functional Magnetic Resonance Imaging and Near Infrared Spectroscopy", in: *Neuroimage* 20 (2003), pp. 145–158.

Nierhaus, T. / T. Schön / R. Becker et al.: "Background and Evoked Activity and Their Interaction in the Human Brain", in: *Magn Reson Imaging* 27 (2009), pp. 1140–1150.

Ogawa, S. / D. W. Tank / R. Menon et al.: "Intrinsic Signal Changes Accompanying Sensory Stimulation: Functional Brain Mapping With Magnetic Resonance

Imaging", in: *Proc Natl Acad Sci U S A*. 1992 Jul 1;89 (1992), 13: pp. 5951–5955.

Preuschhof, C. / H. Heekeren / B. Taskin: "Neural Correlates of Vibrotactile Working Memory in the Human Brain", in: *J Neurosci*, 26 (2006), pp. 13231–13239.

Preuschhof, C. / T. Schubert / A. Villringer et al.: "Prior Information Biases Stimulus Representations During Vibrotactile Decision Making", in: *J Cogn Neurosci*, 2010 May; 22 (2010) 5, pp. 875–887.

Ray, P.G. / K. J. Meador / J. R. Smith et al.: "Physiology of Perception: Cortical Stimulation and Recording in Humans", in: *Neurology* 52 (1999), pp. 1044–1049.

Reinacher, M. / R. Becker / A. Villringer et al.: "Oscillatory Brain States Interact with Late Cognitive Components of the Somatosensory Evoked Potential", in: *J Neurosci Methods* 183 (2009), pp. 49–56.

Ritter, P. / M. Moosmann / A. Villringer: "Rolandic Alpha and Beta EEG Rhythms' Strengths are Inversely Related to fMRI-BOLD Signal in Primary Somatosensory and Motor Cortex", in: *Hum Brain Mapp* 30 (2009), pp. 1168–1187.

Ruben, J. / J. Schwiemann / M. Deuchert et al.: "Somatotopic Organization of Human Secondary Somatosensory Cortex", in: *Cereb Cortex* 11 (2001), pp. 463–473.

Ruben, J. / T. Krause / B. Taskin et al.: "Subarea-Specific Suppressive Inter-Action in the BOLD-Responses to Simultaneous Finger Stimulation in Human Primary Somatosensory Cortex: Evidence for Increasing Rostro-to-Caudal Convergence", in: *Cereb Cortex*, 16 (2006), pp. 819–826.

Schubert, R. / P. Ritter / T. Wüstenberg et al.: "Spatial Attention Related SEP Amplitude Modulations Covary with BOLD Signal in S1 – A Simultaneous EEG-fMRI Study", in: *Cereb Cortex*, 18 (2008), pp. 2686–2700.

Schubert, R. / F. Blankenburg / S. Lemm: "Now You Feel It – Now You Don't: ERP Correlates of Somatosensory Awareness", in: *Psychophysiology*, 43 (2006), pp. 31–40.

Schubert, R. / S. Haufe / F. Blankenburg et al.: "Now You'll Feel It, Now You Won't: EEG Rhythms Predict the Effectiveness of Perceptual Masking", in: *J Cogn Neurosci* 21 (2009), pp. 2407–24119.

Taskin, B. / G.J. Jungehulsing / J. Ruben et al.: "Preserved Responsiveness of Secondary Somatosensory Cortex in Patients with Thalamic Stroke", in: *Cereb Cortex*, 16 (2006), pp. 1431–1439.

Taskin, B. / S. Holtze / T. Krause et al.: "Inhibitory Impact of Subliminal Electrical Finger Stimulation on SI Representation and Perceptual Sensitivity of an Adjacent Finger", in: *Neuroimage* 39 (2008), pp. 1307–1313.

Thees, S. / F. Blankenburg / B. Taskin et al.: "Source Localisation and fMRI of Simultaneously Recorded Data During Somatosensory Categorisation", in: *NeuroImage*, 18 (2003), pp. 707–719.

The Arts Embodied

The Glass Veil
An Installation at the Medizinhistorisches Museum der Charité by Suzanne Anker in conjunction with *Habitus in Habitat*.

INTERVIEW: SUZANNE ANKER AND SABINE FLACH

I

Enshrouded in glass, and once again in glass vitrines, specimens for a scientist are stark reminders of life's material code. Suspended in time and put on display, the corporeal flesh becomes a relic of its own history. In a nether world reminiscent of sleep, yet without the degradation of time, the specimen floats in a pathos of insufficient sustenance: a neither here nor there but yet encased in liquids preserving its displaced existence. For a body or its tissue or organ or cell, scripted by performative unfolding, this once living matter is akin to a homeless refugee, whose sustenance relies on the kindness of strangers. In the mutability through time, such specimens speak simultaneously to ravishment and uniqueness as their failures to exist shift them into the domain of mortal countenance.

In zones of ambiguity, bodies and their parts float anonymously as mementos marking historical time. In an ocular joust, the observer assumes a pose, as details of his gaze achieve focus. Thoughts of definition enter and exit the viewer's consciousness until some determination of meaning, however tentative, is arrived at. What questions are provoked by this once living matter enclosed in a glass veil? To go behind a veil is to transgress a hidden boundary. At the same time veils become mirrors of our concealed selves, as we peek behind the curtain of inscrutable worlds.

The Glass Veil is an installation comprised of several elements, including large-scale photographs mounted on sintra, nylon parachutes, silver-leafed plumb bobs and elastic bungee cords. Installed in the Charité's Ruine, the work denotes its space as an historical vessel of messages. From World War II, to anomalies of nature and disease, to the ruin as an architectural metaphor of loss, the installation presents specimens in a familiar, yet unrecognizable, form. Through enlarged scale shifts and reduced hues, the installation takes on the character of water related life forms. From free-floating squid shapes to in-utero sacs, these works tend not towards morbidity, but towards reverence for the complexities of life encapsulated in death. As part of Sabine Flach's *Habitus in Habitat*, the works address notions of embodiment and the spatial compass of human perception.

SF: Would you please describe the way you choose topics for your photographs?
SA: My interest in photography is as a drawing medium, a means to work with light: to abstract, compound, alter and reframe my thoughts concerning nature. The infinitesimal complexity of natural processes, such as reproduction, regeneration and replication keep wonder in tact. My topics range from plants and animals to body parts and wax models, to laboratory and museum sites. The chosen icons describe historical, epistemological and political residue of technoscientific cultures.

SF: What relevance do the sizes of the images have? And the colors?
SA: The scale of the photographs for *The Glass Veil* range in size from very large to very small: for example, 8' x 10', 6'x 8', 24" x 36" and even as little as 8" x 10". By reducing or enlarging the dimensions of specimens beyond their standard ratios, alternative readings of the image emerge. Taken out of context, scale is an indicator configuring the internalized mind/body axis. The muted color effects of the lens' recording is the result of the chromatic arrays available through extant indoor light. In these works, color is not altered or manipulated. The delicate hues are arrived at in part by the double glass vitrines surrounding the specimens. Nothing has been modified or revised through Photoshop or other software.

SF: What is your perspective regarding these objects while taking photographs?
SA: With careful observation of the specimens I search for ways in which the glass vessel frames its subject. The distortions in glass, such as the multiplicities and silhouetting are what interest me, as well as the lighting conditions affecting the phenomenon itself.

Each one of these formal elements constructs the alternative meanings in the subject, *i.e.*, color and its chromatic coordinates alter signification through our perceptive faculties. Variety in chroma, for example, can range from tinting to saturating, rendering each choice a signifier of meaning and emotional response. Color intensity in these works speaks to the transparency and translucency of light and carries with it distinctions between sharpness, form and focus. Each of these characteristics is also an attribute interlocked in memory: fuzzy, clear, foggy, etc. The interplay between the colors and the forms are generated by chance in concert with availability of light sources. In shooting these works, I did not employ an "applied vision" as one would have if one were a photographer recording for a client. My process involves exploration, observation and somatic response.

Taxonomy or typology plays a role in determining what can be grouped in a final presentation. Sometimes the images are grouped according to iconography, or color, or even metaphor. Emotion always plays a role even if one is not aware of its underlying presence. When reviewing the contact sheets, editing becomes the next task. With regard to anticipating the viewer's emotional reaction, there is no set standard by which emotion can be pre-empted. Since each viewer brings to the work variegated knowledge streams and participatory practices, the range of emotions from empathy to shock are embedded in these images. Intent is not always clear, even for artists. The ambiguity of images themselves and their conjunction with "fetal forms" is labyrinthine at the get go.

SF: What role do the parachutes play? How did you make the decision to bring them into the installation?
SA: The Ruine is such a dramatic architectural, historical space. It is quite overwhelming in and of itself. I chose to articulate the spatial aspect of the site by adding an element that is historically related. The parachutes, transformed into squid-like, jelly-fish-like entities act in concert with the aquarium-like presence of the photographs. The transparent nylon (reminiscent of a fetal veil) is a memory marker of what had occurred during the horrific aerial bombardment of Berlin. Photography and installation, although separate genres, interact with one another in such ways as to reinforce the transitory nature of recombination and chance. Environmental factors also engage and disturb ready-made codes. The content of these photographs, that is, fragments of body parts or fetuses, are examples of the "ready-made" altered by cultural suppositions. In the case of the photographs, exterior phenomenon, such as the presence of diffuse light act upon the depicted specimens. In the case of the parachutes, external potency is generated by their unusual configurations. In each case expectation is circumvented.

SF: Could you please describe the interaction of the installation with this environment? Meaning: what role does the space play? Are there necessary conditions in choosing a space?
SA: After working in a variety of spaces: from white cubes to outdoor parks, from museums and their terraces, to funky alternative galleries, each sort of location dictates underlying solutions. Ranging from wall works to floor pieces to ceiling pieces, to work affected directly by the environment, each space is unique, requiring a site-specific solution. In this installation, particular attention is paid to the environment and its empathetic considerations. Both the subjects and the space are given such deliberation so that the viewer experiences a reverence for lost lives and failed agendas. From human diseases to congenital malformations to vengeful political orders, I was keenly aware of the loaded nature of all these remnants.

Therefore great care needed to be paid to the deceased, on all sides.

The electric fan in the space added a bit of performativity, gently swaying the parachutes, like one rocks a cradle.

SF: Would you say that The Glass Veil is mostly a work relevant to photography or would you say that it is an installation? Is it a site-specific work of art?
SA: Yes, both a site-specific work and relevant to both photography and installations. The works operate in tandem with one other, reinforcing an overall image base as a field of aquatic memories.

SF: Are your photographs related to iconographic codes from art history? If so, which ones? If not, what kind of other symbols and iconography do you have in mind?

SA: The images I make relate to many and various art historical references, particularly the *wunderkammer* and the more current critiques of museum studies. If an image or object is recontexualized (as in the Duchampian strategy) it is to render the ordinary into art. My concerns, however, are to expand hidden messages encapsulated in form. Whether utilitarian, as in the case of parachutes, or scientific, as in the exemplars of specimens, in every occasion, visual transactions achieved through framing provide correspondences that would otherwise pass unnoticed. The concept of the *wunderkammer* has been theorized up to the present by Barbara Maria Stafford and Francis Terpak in their exhibition *Devices of Wonder: From the World in a Box to Images on a Screen* held at the J.P. Getty Museum in 2001. The idea of wonder, going beyond the ordinary, is in a sense an aspect of our own consciousness in which revelation is sought after by careful observation, unexpected circumstance and novel technologies. Christopher Knight, art critic for the LA Times, comments that this exhibition and catalogue is an instance in which "sight connects with insight" and "images are themselves ideas." The wunderkammer, coming into existence the 17th century, was an opportunity to bring together knowledge garnered through many disciplines: geology, biology, early investigations into automata, and works of art. Its configuration is the creation of an encyclopediac vision encapsulating man-made objects and natural entities. My interest in the contemporary *wunderkammer* spans natural history, botany, medical history and includes a current blurring between the natural and the manmade. Although taxonomic structure of classification of knowledge permeates many disciplines, natural history is my central concern. What happens when oddball man-made mutations swerve and bend the natural order in enormous proportions?

SF: In the fall of 2008 while we were working on The Glass Veil, one of my favorite pieces was a photo depicting a subject from behind. The subject appears to turn towards a bright light, a figure standing out as itself through your staging. Later on you titled the piece Lonely Planet. The same goes for the pink embryo in uterus; meaning was also displaced and shifted to something else. Your staging of light converted a medical object into the auratic presence of a fresco. Would you please explain your working process for this shift?

SA: Transformation of any kind is a subtle, fragile process. It is ethereal, ephemeral, and unpredictable. It requires novel ways of looking, circumventing expectation, and going beyond the obvious. It also entails grace, which cannot be predetermined. The word *transformation* has myriad usages: from mathematics to genetics to linguistics. What I am concerned with in this work is how medical specimens can in fact be pictured as being qualifiedly changed. Such modification is obviously indebted to photography and the manners in which an image is perceived. However, other aspects of this process are imbued with intentionality, reframing and conversion.

SF: Have you any specific interest in cognitive and neurosciences and if so, which ones? Do these works play a role for your art? Assuming yes, which one?
SA: Yes, but I haven't as of yet fully articulated a satisfactory engagement with this area. I am working with images extracted from neuroanatomy's brain scans. I have also created an animation of flapping butterfly wings superimposed onto MRI scans which create perceptual illusions. In this work, a transparent, yet identical butterfly is superimposed over a unique inkblot, which in turn is overlaid on one of the brain's distinct ventricles. Because of the butterfly's transparency, its composition appears and reappears as if it is morphing. In addition, this "real-time" device engaging the temporal is a metaphor for the way in which thought or consciousness is in constant flux.

II

SF: Would you describe the role the viewer plays in your artworks? Would you say that he has a constituent role already in your plan? Assuming yes, what kind of part?
SA: Yes, a viewer is made aware of the fact that his gaze may not have recognized all there was to observe in his initial scanning of the object. His subjectivity of seeing is enhanced by the conditions created by the lighting, reflections, scale shifts and the like.

I embrace the temporal attributes of seeing as a way to reveal vision as a process. Jonathan Crary's *Techniques of the Observer* has influenced the way I think about observation. Observation, although rooted in empiricism, also carries with it degrees of subjectivity, and it is this subjective means of seeing, a somatic gaze, which pivots a medical specimen into an ambiguous, and sometimes fleeting, image.

SF: Does the number of spectators visiting your installation affect the manner of experiencing of the piece?
SA: In the case of the installation at La Charité, the setting is so immense. The number of people seeing the installation is dwarfed by comparison. The kinesthetic experience of the place itself diminishes the viewer in all cases.

SF: Would you say that planning your installation would evoke in the viewer the feelings of being part of a social or cultural group? How is space, that is, environment in a larger sense considered a subjective experience?
SA: The architectural space and the subject matter of the photographs alternate between inclinations of loneliness and melancholy, as they address loss. Feelings

of lost lives, exhausted history and frozen reflection float through time and space anonymously becoming an embedded narrative in these works. From the harvesting of body parts to the stationary Ruine as a center for discourse, the viewer is suspended between wonder and the politics of the real.

SF: What differences between the social and subjective do you interweave in your installation?
SA: Of course, the social is omnipresent in this installation, seizing an historical narrative of time and place. The fact that the Ruine was employed by scientists and physicians as a lecture hall for examining pathological case studies is quite ironic when we convert individual pathology to political pathology. The metaphor drives itself. When I think about the subjective, symbolist nature of this work, I come to realize correspondences between language and materials. The amniotic sac, visible in the *Hand-Mirror*, is a corresponding material to the parachutes. When I consider translucence I think of an ether world, neither light nor dark, but a combination of both, a transcendent sense of light with positive associations.

SF: The parachutes are constantly moving. What relevance does movement have in The Glass Veil? Is there a link between the movement of the parachutes, a moving spectator, and an inner movement of recognition?
SA: The movement of the parachutes interacts with nature's (and history's) ongoing flux. This operational view of nature recalls agency as posited in Bergson's *Creative Evolution*. Whereas the specimens are static and require the viewer's gaze to animate them through their glass veil, the parachutes move and in turn are moved through by the force of air or wind. The link between the movement of the parachutes, a moving spectator and an inner movement of recognition comes down to a philosophical argument in which the spectator is presented with several options simultaneously. Holding inconsistent meanings concurrently is also an attribute of a work of art.

SF: How would you describe these different interacting kinds of movement?
SA: The parachutes sway in slight alternating directions, while a viewer completes a path, by advancing up and down stairways or gazing straight ahead to fully realize the installation. Looking up, looking down, looking straight ahead, the physical repose of the viewer is spatially and kinesthetically directed towards shifting perspectives. There are no fixed directives, no correct angles of viewing. Through discovery, the viewer is escorted through various fields of perception.

SF: What role do such movements play in your piece? Your text speaks about 'zones of ambiguity' – could you please explain this further?
SA: I refer to zones of ambiguity as images that recall an unimaginable presence. What does it feel like for a viewer to be confronted by a brain or a fetus floating in fluids on display? How does one address personhood issues with regard to these images? Dead, but yet still animated by the reflected light. Akin to looking

into an aquarium, viewers are confronted with the anthropomorphic nature of these fragments cum beings. Although these "cuttings" remain dead, they still perform a function in the living world.

SF: Is there an ongoing exchange between inner and outer forms of representation in your work that 'creates' emotions?
SA: Yes, emotions of course are slippery states of being with shifting personas, intensities and durations. Closely aligned to the concept of time, deep time, emotions are conjured up within the domain of art as one of its telltale signs. Walt Whitman's "A Hand Mirror" from his *Leaves of Grass* (1900) summons a poetic parallel to the work:

> Hold it up sternly – see this it sends back, (who is it? is it you?)
> Outside fair costume, within ashes and filth,
> No more a flashing eye, no more a sonorous voice or springy step,
> Now some slave's eye, voice, hands, step,
> A drunkard's breath, unwholesome eater's face, venerealee's flesh,
> Lungs rotting away piecemeal, stomach sour and cankerous,
> Joints rheumatic, bowels clogged with abomination,
> Blood circulating dark and poisonous streams,
> Words babble, hearing and touch callous,
> No brain, no heart left, no magnetism of sex;
> Such from one look in this looking glass ere you go hence,
> Such a result so soon – and from such a beginning!

III

SF: Would you agree that your installation creates an environment in which bodies are reframed by their habitat? And if so – how? What is your intention?
SA: As the glass vitrines frame the specimens, so too are we circumscribed by our container. As space is displaced by a body in its environment, a mutable boundary is marked and can be traced through locomotion and gesture. Our path outlines an alternative architecture, a neuroarchitecture created by movement. Francisco Varela and Humberto Maturana's theories of Autopoesis, come to mind to describe this phenomenon. In such a system, change is self-directed and cannot be distinguished from its structure. It is a continuous trajectory in which the medium and its environment form a feedback loop in which one is continuous with another, resembling the cognitive apparatus of sensory-motor dynamics.

SF: How would you describe "photographic transference" from the specimens to the photographs to the spectator? What role does the space play?
SA: We are accustomed to seeing photography in books or on computer screens. However, when we are confronted with large-scale photographic installations

they produce a kineaesthetic jolt. Situated within the Ruine's space is a photographic image garnered from a specimen in another wing of the medical museum. After viewing the museum's collection and then experiencing these specimens as images, a mental refashioning occurs. One administrator, who has observed the museum's collection of objects numerous times, was nevertheless upset when she was confronted with a large-scale version of one particular specimen. Do we see or understand images more clearly than objects?

SF: Would you describe the relation between vision, motion and emotion? How are embodied emotions brought into visibility?
SA: This is a really good question. I'll take a cue from Varela's concept of "embodied" philosophy as a way to experience the body in both its phenomenological sense and its biological sense. Sense perception electrifies thought and emotion as one moves in space. Akin to dance, intuitive movements frame experience to form mental pictures which in turn can be retrieved at an alternate time from the brain's data bank. The recovery of images, as receptacles of meaning, restates propositions inherent in my exhibition. Viewing the container and the contained, through a glass veil, is not a static experience.

SF: Could you describe the process of encoding and decoding as being part of the emotional process in your work?
SA: The body and its parts are iconic images calling into question identity, natural history, longevity and disease as well as fashion. As forms of what could be called "the dark sublime", the images generate a range of emotions from terror to awe. Sometimes perceived as beautiful, these images partake in the aesthetic dimension, even though their source is wedded to a clinical telos. Bodies in pain, or in the sense represented here, fragments of bodies, stripped of identifying data, for the viewer, can be very emotional, even disturbing. At once grotesque and beautiful, these images oscillate back and forth between these domains of vision and thought as indicators of lived experience.

SF: Could you describe the relation between cognition and sensory-motor aspects of emotions, and their relation to the imaginary as well as proprioception in 'The Glass Veil'?
SA: Our senses drench and filter us with data, providing access to an external world. The internal world operates in a more covert way. Accessing the world through an unconscious nervous system brings into play the connecting loop between body and mind.

The nervous system, operating autonomically, expands our ability to multitask and self-regulate. The mind also relays with the body through cognition, but the body's physical stance, such as muscle tension or complex motions are carried out under the body's radar. Muscle memory and the repetition of movements act as a GPS, maintaining the body's awareness in its proprietary space. Thus, as in Varela's theories of *The Gesture of Awareness* how does a spectator perceive phenomenon while suspending belief? How does the spectator's autonomic nervous system get recharged by aesthetic enchantment or stimuli? Questions addressing the relationship between the imagination and cognition and the sensory-motor circuit are brought to bear once again by way of aesthetic experience, particularly sculpture and architecture. As an embedded visitor to the artist's construction of fictive space, the viewer must for a moment suspend his rational mind to allow for wandering. In this sense, the slow articulation of messages to be gleaned from works of art is fostered by moving through space, referencing angles of perception and accessing nodes of memory markers. *The Glass Veil*, situated in Charité's Ruine, transforms an historical stage into a living one.

References

Crary, Jonathan: *Techniques of the Observer: On Vision and Modernity in the Nineteenth Century,* Cambridge, MA (MIT Press) 1990.

Varela, F. / N. Depraz / P. Vermersch: "The gesture of awareness: An account of its structural dynamics", in: M. Velmans (ed.): *Investigating Phenomenal Consciousness*, Amsterdam (Benjamin Publishers) 2000.

Whitman, Walt: *Leaves of Grass*, Philadelphia (David McKay) c. 1900.

Figures

(See following pages)

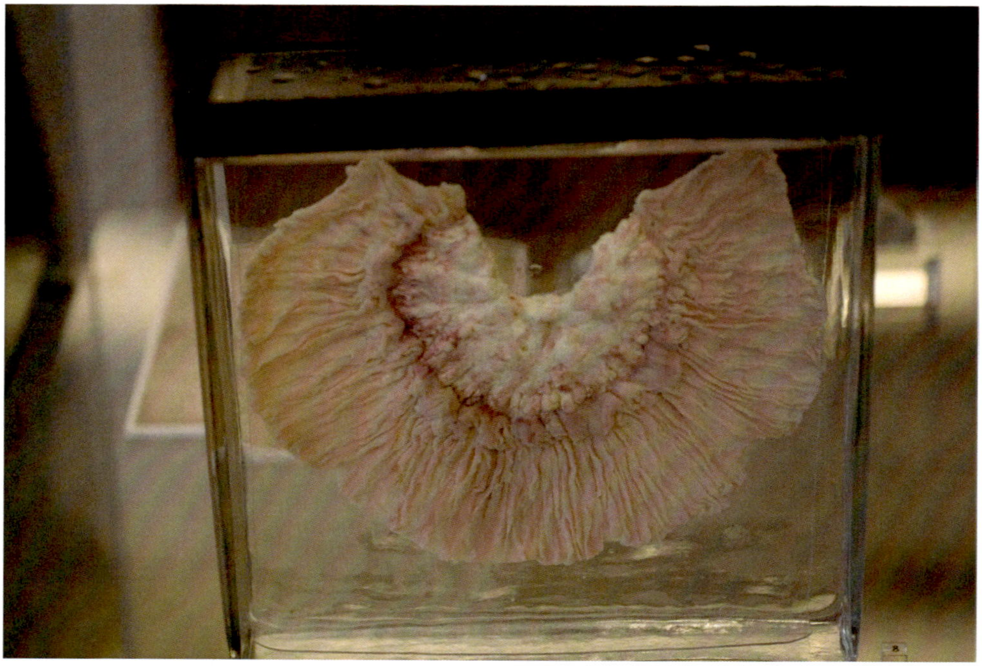

Fig. 1: *The Glass Veil (Crimp)*, 2009, Digital print on watercolor paper, 8"x10"/ 20.3cm x 25.4cm.

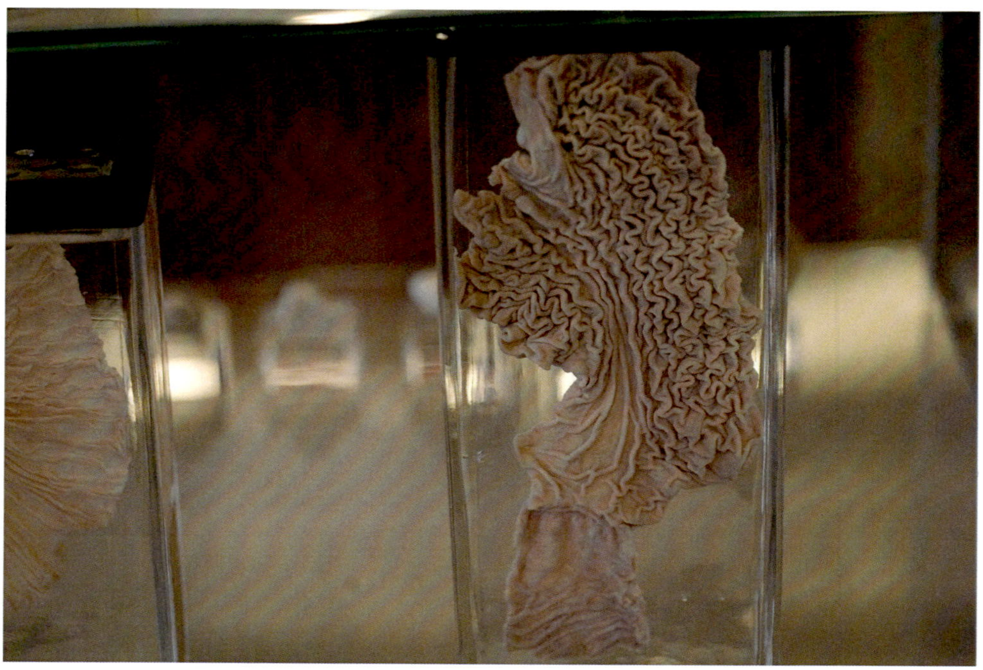

Fig. 2: *The Glass Veil (Crimp II)*, 2009, Digital print on watercolor paper, 8"x10"/ 20.3cm x 25.4cm.

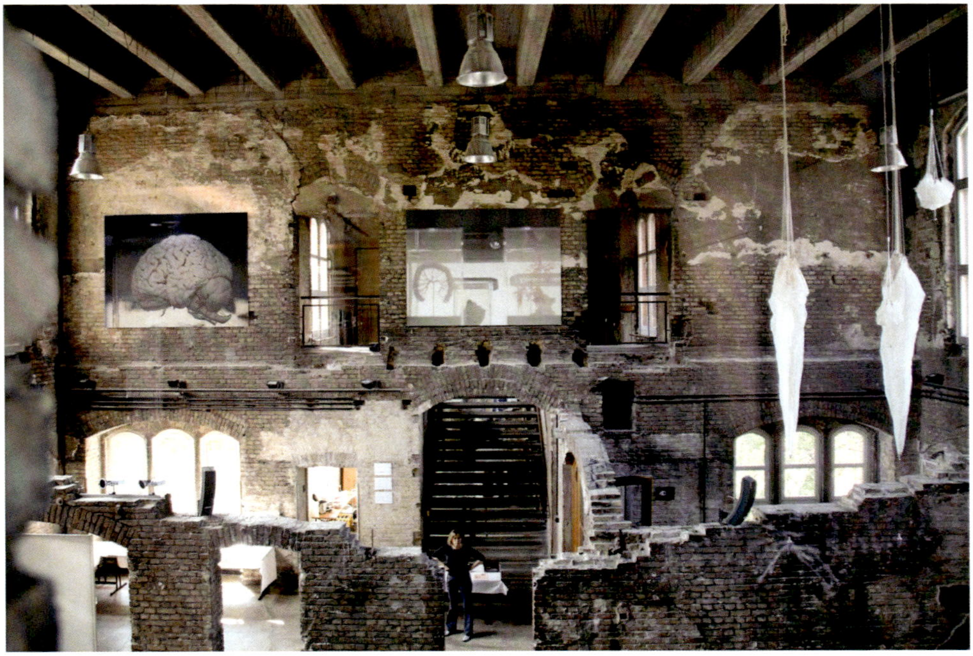

Fig. 3: *The Glass Veil, (White Light)*, and *The Glass Veil*, 2009, digital prints mounted on sintra, 9"x120"/ 243.8cm x 304.8cm each. *The Glass Veil (The Center of Gravity)*, (Installation Berliner Medizinhistorisches Museum der Charité, Berlin, Germany), 2009, nylon, bungee cord, silver leaf, lead and brass, dimensions variable.

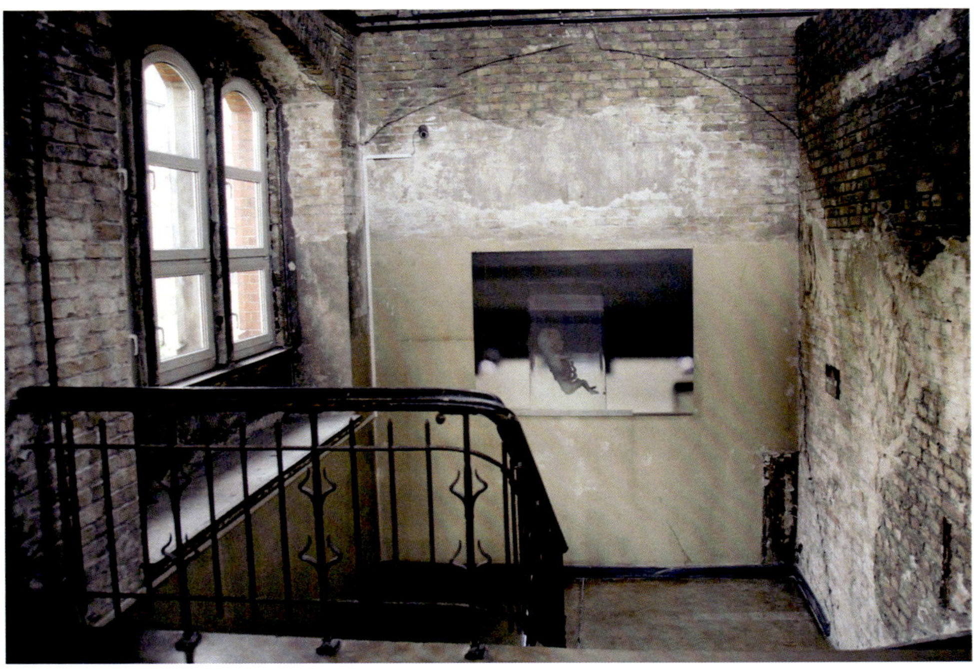

Fig. 4: *The Glass Veil (In and Out of Time),* (Installation Berliner Medizinhistorisches Museum der Charité, Berlin, Germany), 2009, digital print mounted on sintra, 76"x 96" / 193cm x 243.8cm.

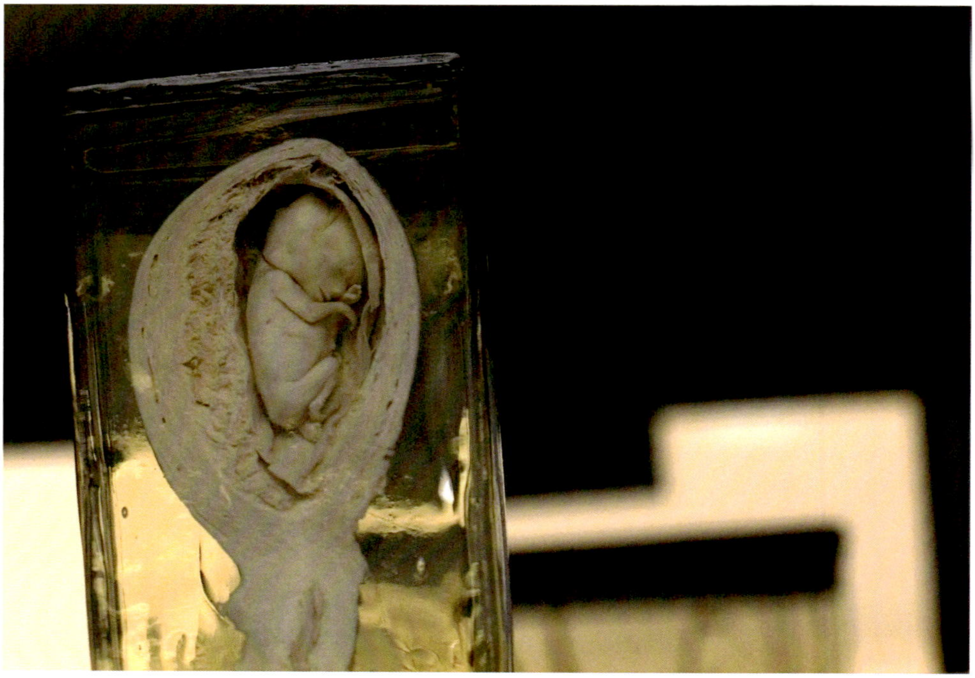

Fig. 5: *The Glass Veil (Spoon)*, 2009, Digital print on watercolor paper, 24"x 36" / 61cm x 91.4cm.

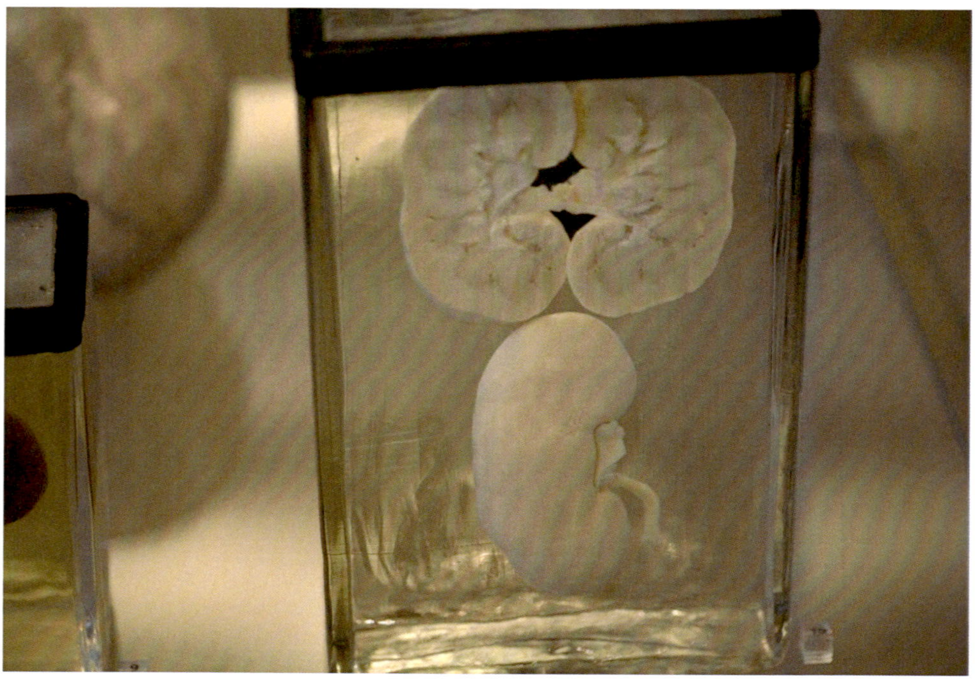

Fig. 6: *The Glass Veil (Kidney)*, 2009, Digital print on watercolor paper, 24"x36" / 61cm x 91.4cm.

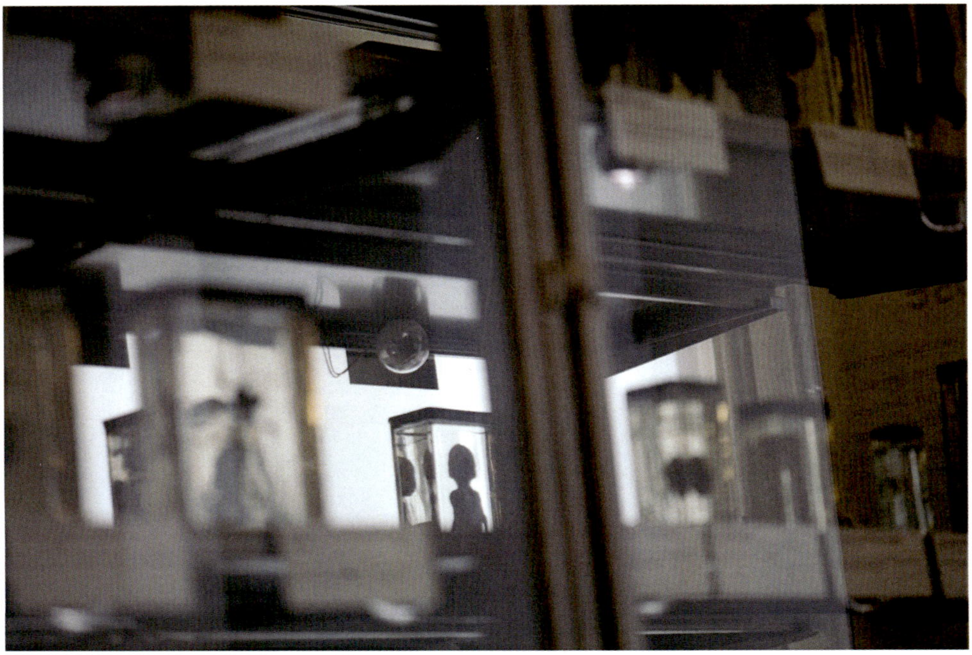

Fig. 7: *The Glass Veil (Lonely Planet)*, 2009, Digital print on watercolor paper, 24" x 36" / 61cm x 91.4cm.

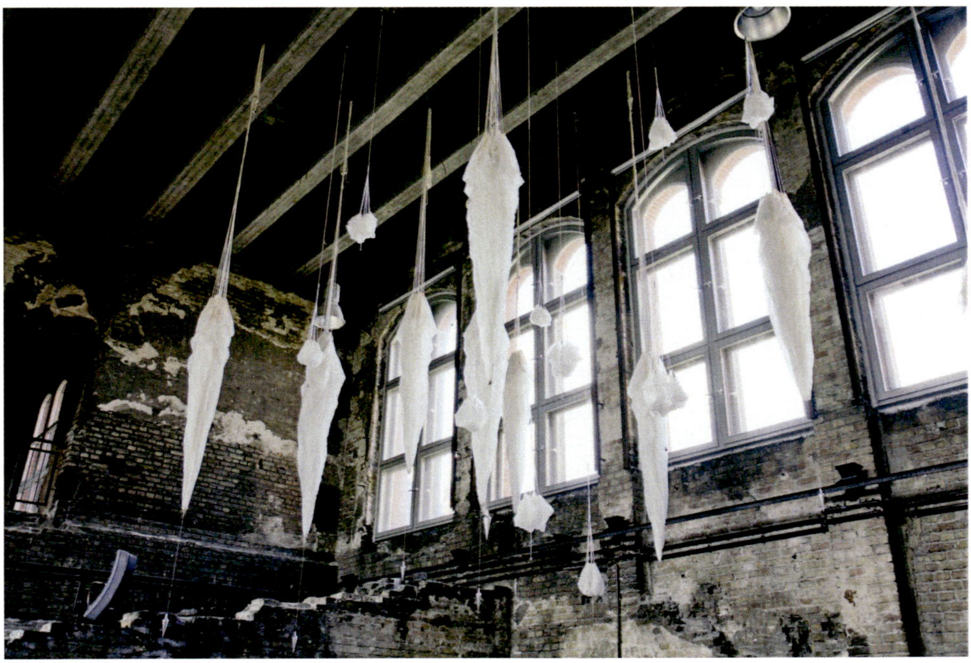

Fig. 8: *The Glass Veil (The Center of Gravity)*, (Installation Berliner Medizinhistorisches Museum der Charité, Berlin, Germany), nylon, bungee cord, silver leaf, lead and brass, dimensions variable.

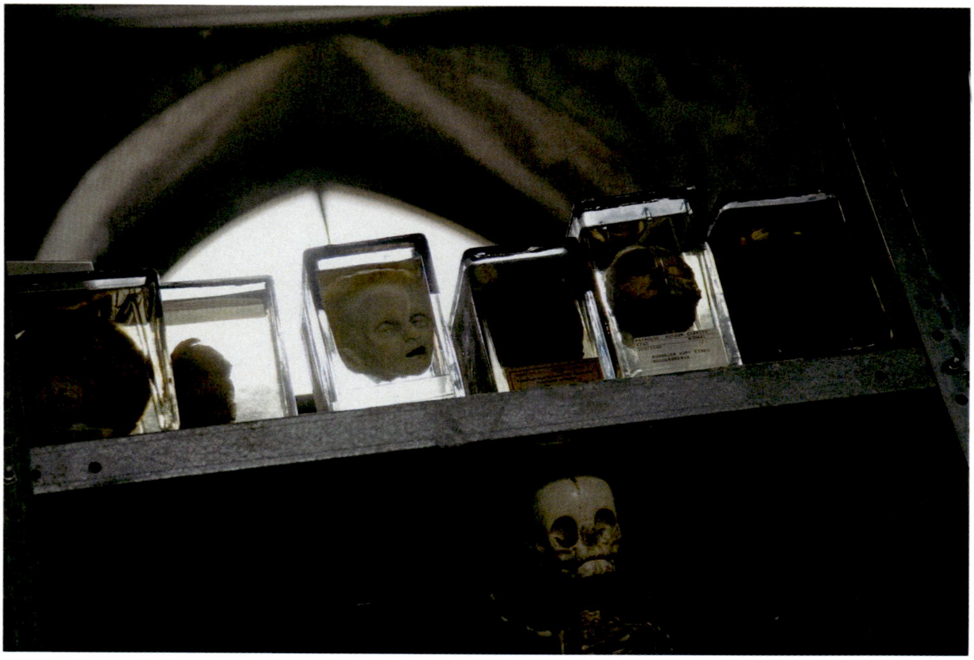

Fig. 9: *The Glass Veil (Shelly's Dream)*, 2009, Digital print on watercolor paper, 24" x 36" / 61cm x 91.4cm.

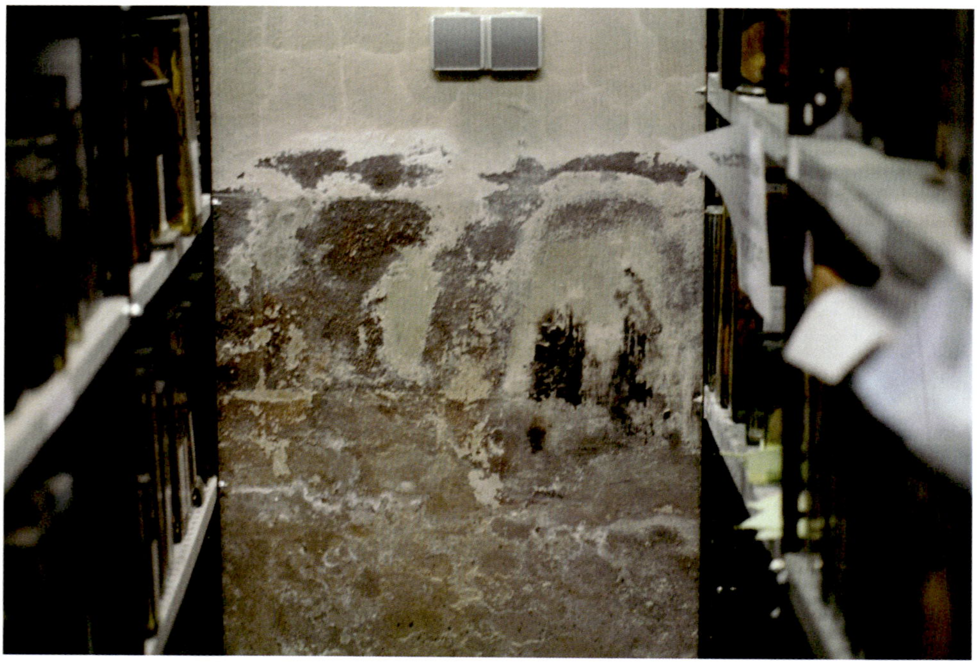

Fig. 10: *The Glass Veil (Deep Storage)*, 2009, Digital print on watercolor paper, 24"x36" / 61cm x 91.4cm.

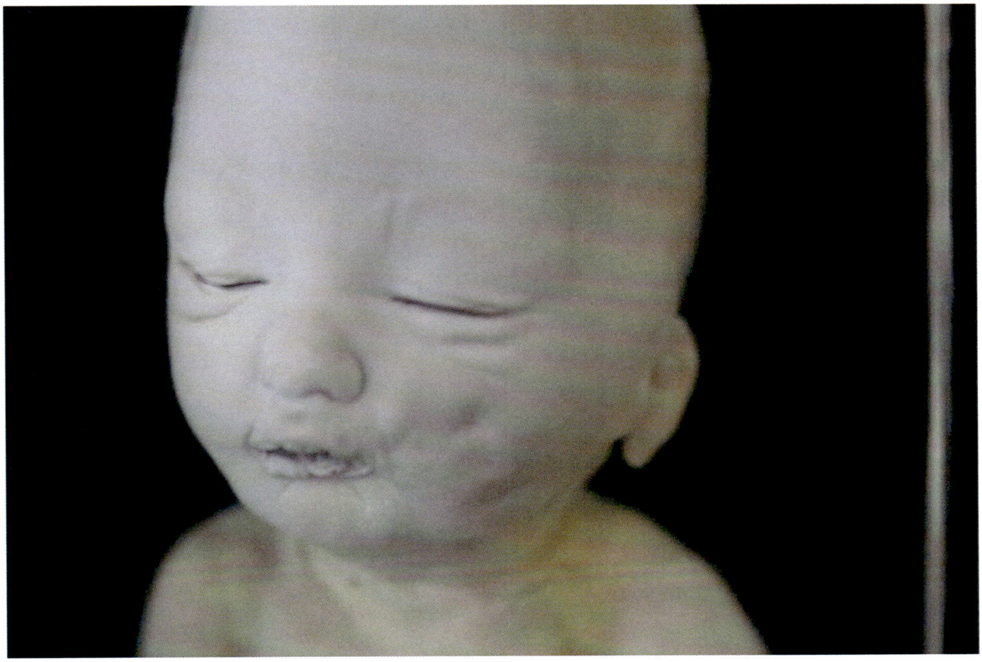

Fig. 11: *The Glass Veil (Sleep)*, 2009, Digital print on watercolor paper, 24"x36" / 61cm x 91.4cm.

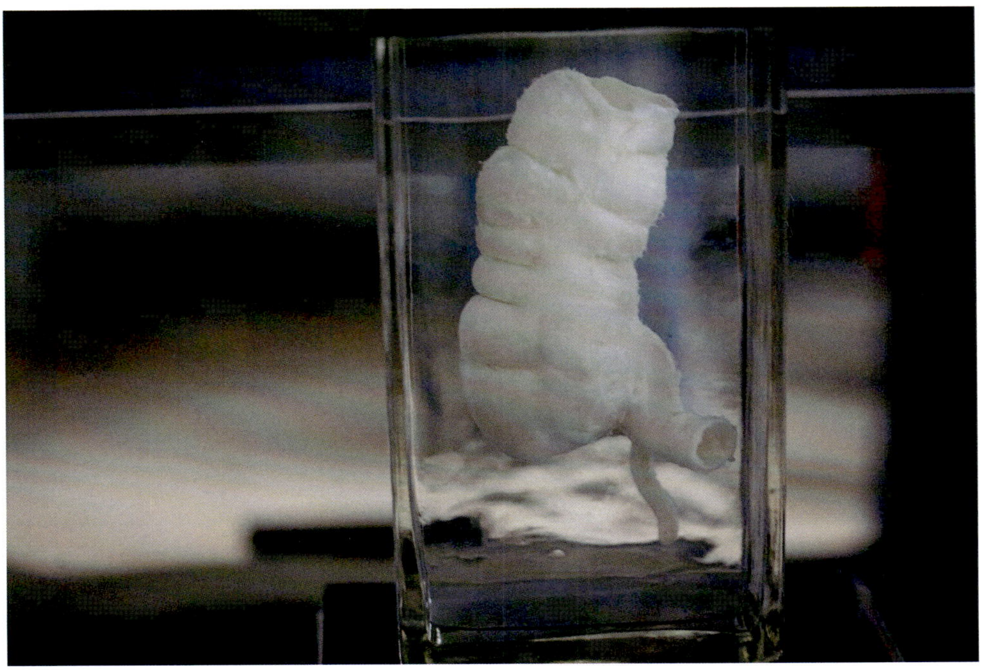

Fig. 12: *The Glass Veil (Tunnel)*, 2009, Digital print on watercolor paper, 24"x36" / 61cm x 91.4cm.

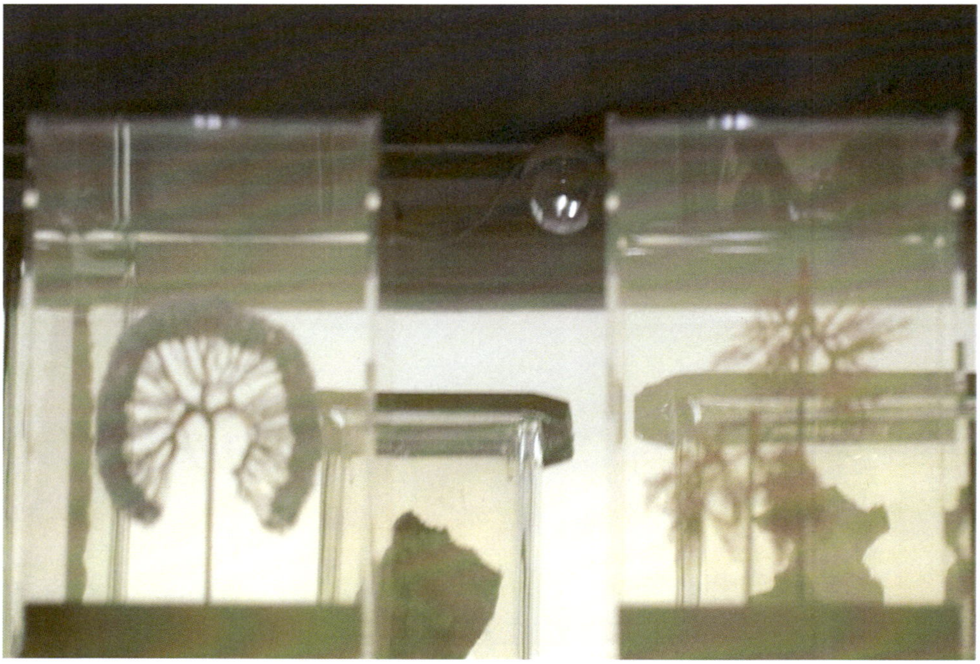

Fig. 13: *The Glass Veil (White Light)*, 2009, digital print mounted on sintra, 96"x120" / 243.8cm x 304.8cm.

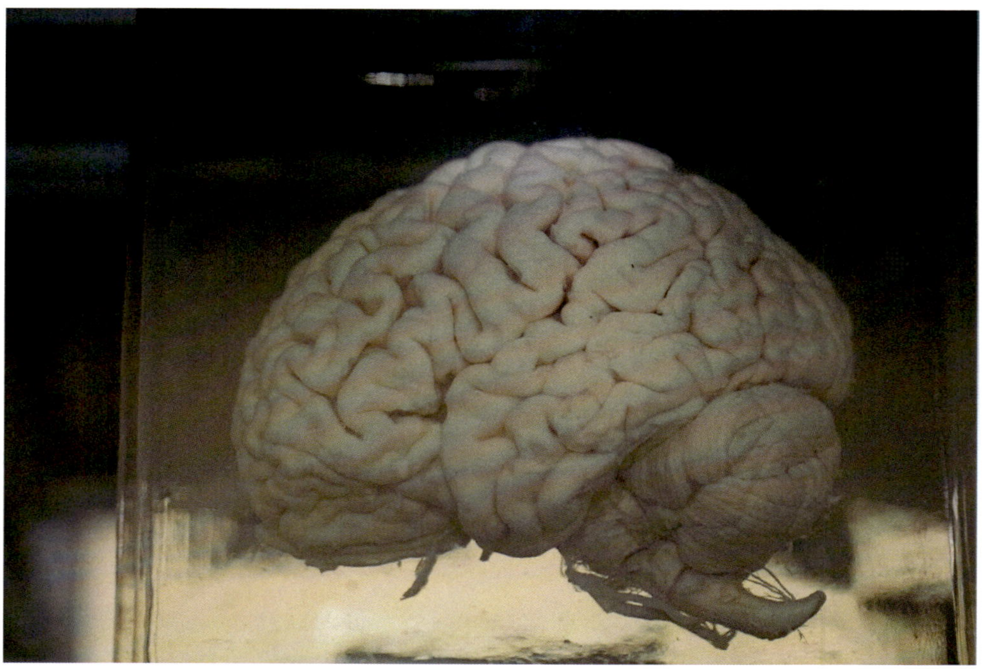

Fig. 14: *The Glass Veil*, 2009, digital print mounted on sintra, 96"x120" / 243.8cm x 304.8cm.

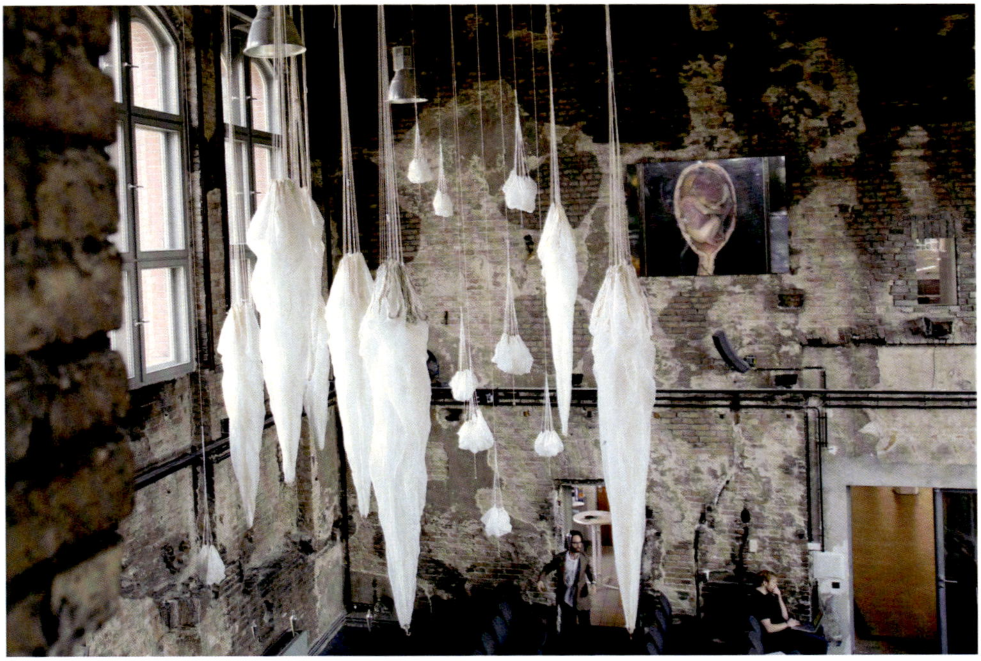

Fig. 15: *The Glass Veil (The Center of Gravity)*, (Installation Berliner Medizinhistorisches Museum der Charité, Berlin, Germany), 2009, nylon, bungee cord, silver leaf, lead and brass, dimensions variable. *The Glass Veil (The Hand-Mirror)*, 2009, digital print mounted on sintra, 76"x 96" / 193cm x 243.8cm.

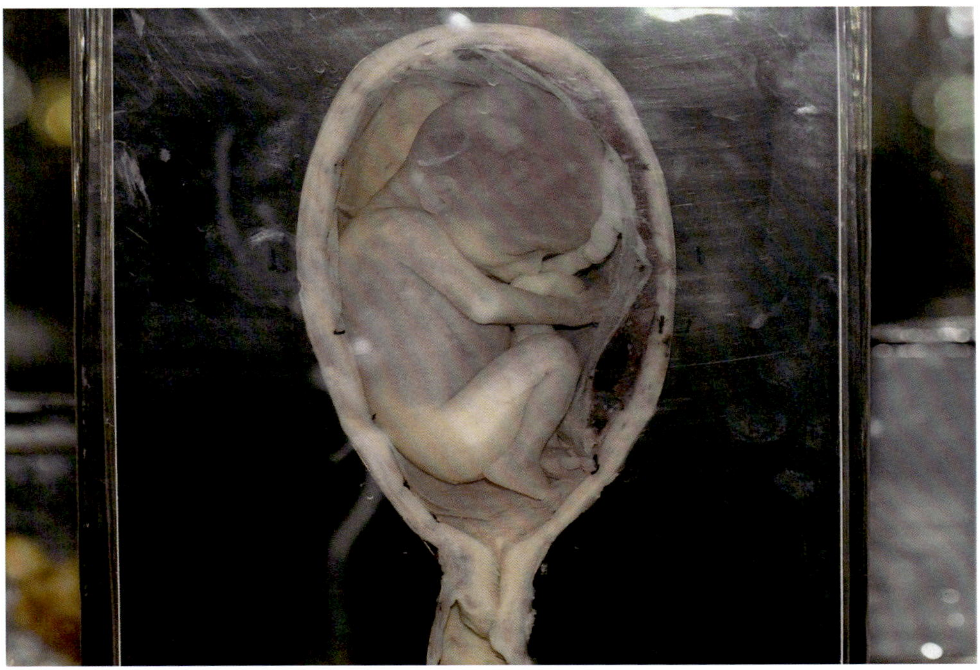

Fig. 16: *The Glass Veil (The Hand-Mirror)*, 2009, digital print mounted on sintra, 76"x 96" / 193cm x 243.8cm.

Experiencing Emotion in Depictions
Being Moved without Motion?

JOHN MICHAEL KROIS

I

Pictures can seem to be alive. Rubens' drawing of "Daniel in the Lion's Den" (Fig. 1) seems animated and not simply made of chalk and paper. This fact has attracted relatively little attention in the history of philosophy[1] – unlike other aspects of depiction such as epistemological questions about truth in pictures or aesthetic topics such as the objectivity of beauty and judgments of taste. Kant was particularly concerned with these issues, stressing that aesthetic judgments required disinterestedness if they were to be objectively valid, meaning that they could not be based either upon sensuous pleasure or practical, utilitarian concerns. Things appear beautiful (or not) to a disinterested spectator because they possess the appearance of "purposiveness without purpose". This meant that beauty exists for its own sake, and later thinkers, influenced by Kant, largely thought the same about art. But neither such beauty nor the humbling or exhilarating feeling of the sublime as Kant understood them can explain the animated character of pictures.

Kant does not deal with this issue, but he noticed something similar. Certain concepts, he pointed out,[2] circulate universally, yet we are at a loss to justify or explain their existence either on the basis of experience or reason. As examples he mentions "luck" and "fate" (Glück, Schicksal). Kant called such concepts "usurpatory", for although they are generally employed, they have, as he puts it, "no clear legal entitlement" to circulate as they do. So, too, the perception of emotion and animation in pictures is similarly widespread, yet philosophy is hard-pressed to explain how this is possible.

1 The capacity of pictures to express emotions and moods has been investigated in detail by art historians. A classic study is Freedberg: *The Power of Images*. Cf. also James Elkins: *Pictures and Tears*. This topic is discussed in detail in the forthcoming book by Horst Bredekamp: *Theorie des Bildaktes*.

2 "Es gibt indessen auch usurpierte Begriffe, wie etwa Glück, Schicksal, die zwar mit fast allgemeiner Nachsicht herumlaufen, aber doch bisweilen durch die Frage: quid juris, in Anspruch genommen werden, da man alsdann wegen der Deduktion derselben in nicht geringe Verlegenheit gerät, indem man keinen deutlichen Rechtsgrund weder aus der Erfahrung, noch der Vernunft anführen kann, dadurch die Befugnis seines Gebrauchs deutlich würde". (Kant: *Kritik der reinen Vernunft*, A 84-85.)

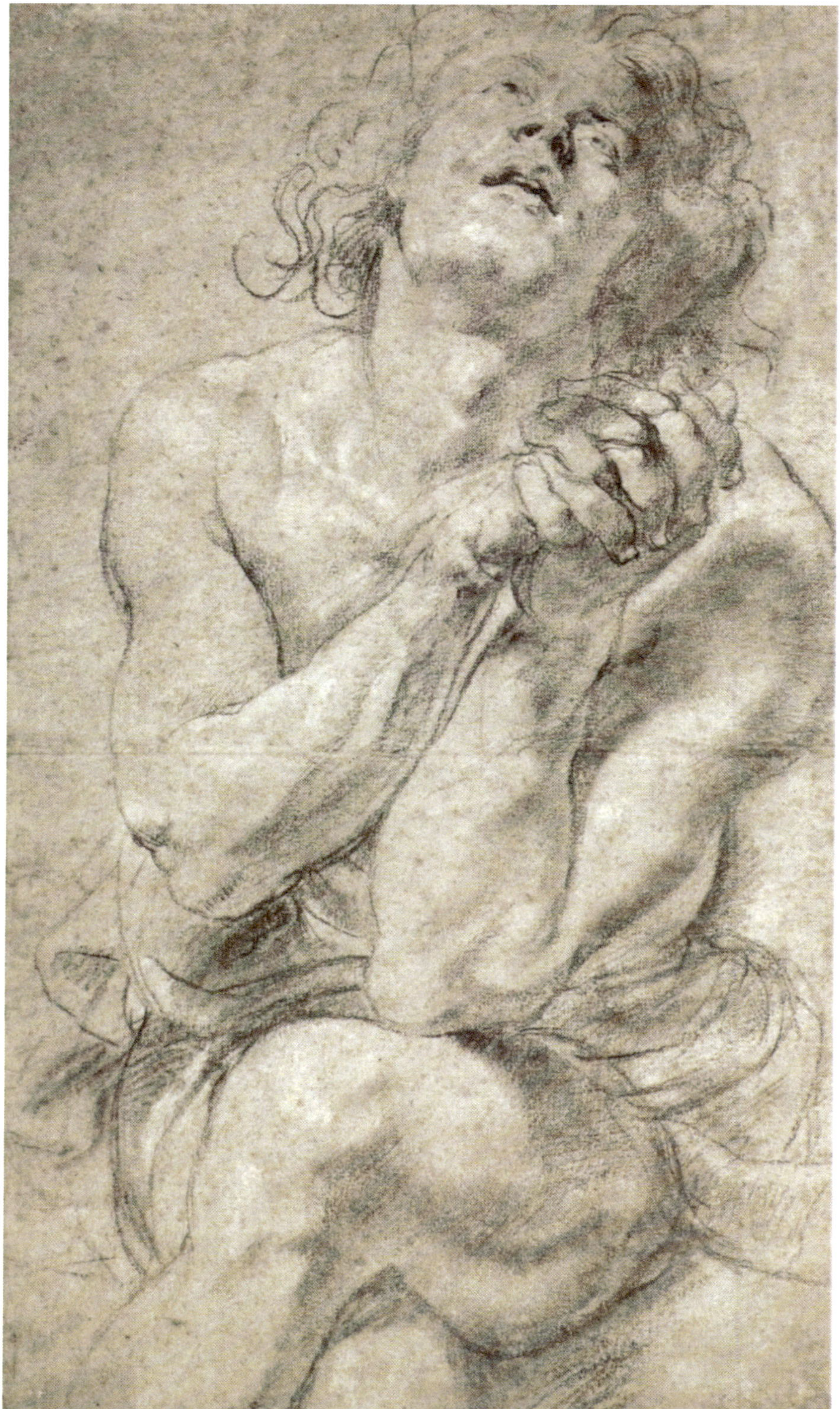

Fig. 1: Peter Paul Rubens, Daniel in the Lion's Den, ca. 1620.

Some thinkers acknowledge this usurpatory character in pictures (E. Cassirer, J.-L. Nancy, W. J. T. Mitchell), accepting it as a phenomenological fact or even toying with animism,[3] but the alternative perspective, widely held today, is rather that this feature of pictures is the result of human psychology. The mind projects affective meaning onto pictures. Hence, on this view, pictures possess no affective meanings themselves, but exist only in the mind of the artist and viewer, while the picture is just a material thing – black and white chalk, and light gray paper.

Sticking with Kant's philosophy for the moment, this is in line with his claim that "Thoughts without perceptual contents are empty, perceptions without concepts are blind."[4] In order for our perception of pictures to possess an affective, animated character, the mind must organize them somehow, not by concepts, but by giving pictures meanings which they do not possess in themselves.

At the beginning of the last century psychologists and aestheticians investigated the psychological capacity that they believed was responsible for the ability to lend animation to pictures, a process they termed "Einfühlung" or "empathy". For the philosopher Theodor Lipps, empathy was the ability to feel as if your experience was occurring in another person or object. During empathy the "other" is experienced as possessing feelings.[5] Unlike empathy with another person in a social situation, requiring practical or moral action, aesthetic empathy occurs during pure contemplation "reine ästhetische Betrachtung". It was unclear, however, what was going on when the viewer entered imaginatively into what is seen in this dreamlike way, without practical bearing.[6]

This conception of empathy was regarded with skepticism by many philosophers,[7] especially by followers of Kant, because it was based upon individual psychological inclinations and so lacked objectivity.[8] For Kant, the aesthetic attitude was not characterized by psychological considerations at all, but by the

3 Cassirer called the phenomenon of expressive meaning an "Urphänomen", incapable of further explanation. Mitchell: *What do Pictures Want?* goes further in affirming the autonomy of pictures.

4 "Gedanken ohne Inhalt sind leer, Anschauungen ohne Begriffe sind blind." (Kant: *Kritik der reinen Vernunft*, B75, A51.)

5 Lipps: *Ästhetik*, 2:1.

6 "Wir versetzen uns also gleichsam mit unserem eigenen Körper in (eine) Linie und tun so, als hätte sie ebenfalls einen Körper" [bis hin zu der] "Einfühlung in die sinnliche Erscheinung lebender Wesen" – Lipps: "Ästhetik", 1:6, pp. 355–359; also cf. *Ästhetik: Psychologie des Schönen und der Kunst*, vols. 1–2 (Hamburg/Leipzig: Voss, 1903–1906).

7 Goldie / Coplan (eds): *An Empathic Eye, Empathy.*

8 Darwin speculated that singing was connected with mating. See Darwin: *The Descent of Man* p. 138: "When we treat of sexual selection we shall see that primeval man, or rather some early progenitor of man, probably first used his voice in producing true musical cadences, that is, in singing ... this power would have been especially exerted during the courtship of the sexes..." The perception of expressive forms goes back to the ability to recognize whether something is benign or threatening, but the survival benefits of the capacity to recognize expression does not explain why humans make and understand pictures, and knowing what caused this would not explain how the depiction of affect works in pictures.

perception of the form of "purposiveness" in things without regard to any personal desires or feelings. But this left the animated character of pictures unaccounted for.

II

Today, the idea of the "emotional brain" has gradually gained acceptance, and it is widely assumed that the affective character of experience carries over somehow from ordinary perception to the perception of pictures. As the neurophysiologist Alain Berthoz asserts categorically: "there is no perception of space or movement, no vertigo or loss of balance, … no sound heard or uttered, no gesture of capture or grasping that is not accompanied by emotion or induced by it".[9] This agrees with the findings of developmental psychology, according to which the most elementary forms of perception are affective. As Kurt Koffka once put it: the perception of friendliness or unfriendliness is primitive, more primitive than a "blue patch"[10]. Perceptually, an emotional tone or mood is recognized before the identity of an object. Lewis Carroll's fanciful description of the Cheshire cat which disappeared leaving behind only its grin had its basis in fact: the perception of expression or affect is the most basic element in perception, so, logically, it should also be the last to disappear.

But unlike affective meanings experienced in real life, an immobile picture lacks the means to transport expression in a kinetic manner. Pictures express emotion without motion. This is why attempts to explain the affective character of pictures have centred upon viewers' active projection of feelings, not on the pictures themselves.

Today this phenomenon is no longer believed to originate "from above", through intellectual interpretation, but to come "from below," as Fechner put it, from somatic sources. The discovery of mirror neurons in the 1990s has revitalized research on the topic of empathy[11] and has played an important role in the attempt to develop a "neuroaesthetics". Instead of arguing top-down from mental capacities, neuroaesthetics seeks to uncover the neurological processes that make aesthetic perception possible.

A good example of this approach is Gallese and Freedberg's publication "Motion, emotion and empathy in esthetic experience" in which they discuss

9 Berthoz: *The Brain's Sense of Movement*, p. 7.

10 Koffka: *Die Grundlagen der psychischen Entwicklung*, pp. 94 ff.

11 This assessment is found in the introduction ("Einführung in die Einfühlung") to Curtis: *Einfühlung*, p. 14. It remains to be seen if Ramachandan's prediction that the discovery of mirror neurons will do for psychology what DNA did for biology. See Ramachandran, "Mirror Neurons and Imitation Learning".

among other examples Caravaggio's "Incredulity of St Thomas"[12] (Fig. 2). According to their conception, mirror neurons enable a viewer who sees someone actually touching somebody in this way as well as a viewer seeing this picture of a touching action to automatically experience in both cases what it is like to do the touching oneself, since in both cases the same cortical network of areas is activated that is normally involved in the actual activity of touching. But a problem arises here, for this conception does not address the difference between the perception of affective meaning in real life – seeing somebody touch something – and seeing this depicted in different artificial media. A theory of aesthetic response is not per se a theory of depiction.

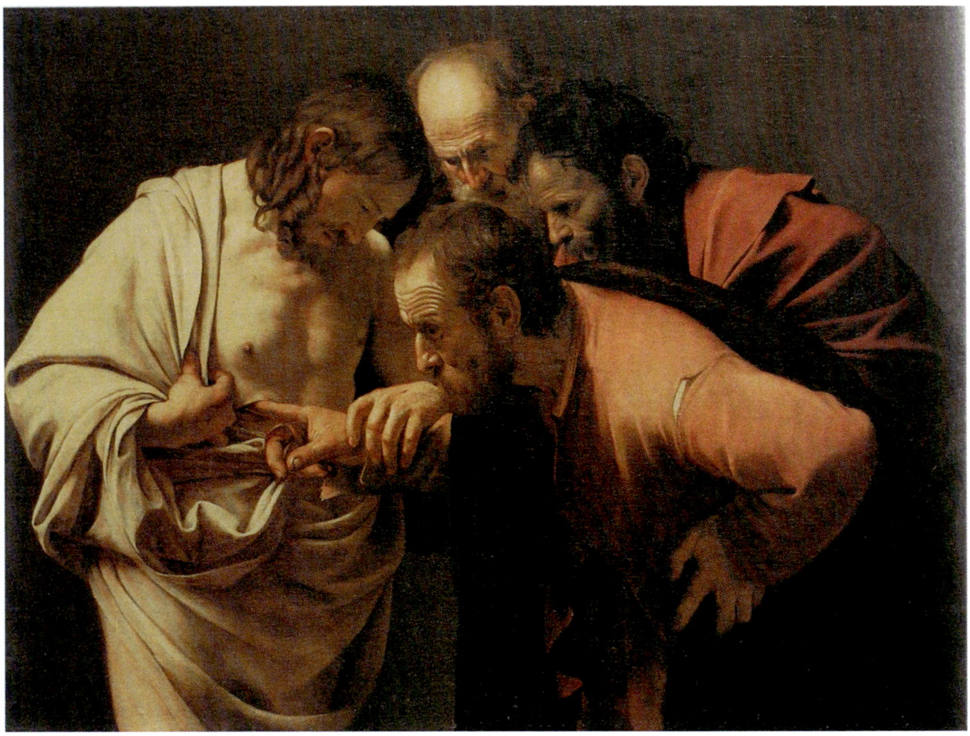

Fig. 2: Michelangelo Merisi da Caravaggio, Incredulity of St. Thomas, 1601/02.

Perception is a psychological and biological process, but depiction is a symbolic and cultural one. Symbolism has long been a topic in the theory of art, especially regarding its cognitive content,[13] but it is not immediately clear how the depiction of feelings is symbolic. It was assumed that, to be symbolic, pictures had to be "read" like a text.

12 See Gallese / Freedberg: "Motion, Emotion and Empathy in Esthetic Experience", p. 411.

13 Iconography and allegory and representational techniques such as the use of lines to stand for edges and rules for the depiction of spatial organization all involve some kind of representational processes.

Nelson Goodman's symbolic theory of art enjoyed a widespread reception since its publication in the 1970s because it offered a way to interpret the depiction of expressive qualities in a different, proto-linguistic way. Goodman framed the analogy between experiencing a picture and reading a text in terms of the phenomenon of labeling. A picture, Goodman says, may *possess* the *property* of, for example, being grey, but it can thereby *exemplify* the *label* "sad" metaphorically. Looking at pictures is like looking at labels, albeit non-verbal ones, which exemplify feelings metaphorically by signifying them in a non-verbal way. The color grey is a non-verbal metaphor for sad. A picture may undeniably possesses certain properties such as being grey, on Goodman's view, but "sadness" is not one of them: it is a metaphor based upon symbolic conventions that are brought to the color grey.

Goodman's claim that pictures exemplify expressive meanings by non-verbal metaphor needs to be distinguished from his explanation of it. The notion of "labeling" shifts attention away from the phenomenon of expressive meaning to the perception and classification of objects and reduces the phenomenon to be explained (the emotional content in pictures) to the cognitive activity of understanding labels.

The claim that the expressive character of pictures results from particular cultural conventions also conflicts with the findings of classic experiments on the perception of expression. Wolfgang Köhler's tests dealing with the cross-modular matching of nonsense words such as "Takete" and "Maluma" with abstract drawings[14] showed a high correlation whenever subjects were asked to match them. The result, often known as the kiki-bouba-effect, is irreconcilable with the claim that the depiction of expression is based upon cultural convention. Further experiments have reconfirmed the non-conventional character of expression. Metaphorical pictures such as these (Fig. 3) were used by John M. Kennedy to determine the ability of test persons to understand pictorial metaphors. These depictions show numbness in a thumb, a thumb in pain as well as thumbs moving differently. These drawings were identified by many subjects with a high degree of agreement. These experiments were conducted with both blind and seeing subjects. The blind were presented with tactile raised line drawings of the same images. The correlations were nearly the same except that the distinction between the two kinds of movement was slightly less well recognized by the blind. The visual metaphor of the broken line to represent an absence of feeling or numbness, the lines radiating from the thumb like the feeling of a pain radiating out from a location, and the motion lines all have one thing in common: they relate directly to experience of the human body and do not depend upon cultural convention. It is no coincidence that Goodman focused on the example of the color grey to explain his theory of expression rather a picture like Caravaggio's "Doubting Thomas," for in Goodman's conception of symbolism the body as the seat of feeling and emotion has been bracketed out.

14 Köhler: *Gestalt Psychology*.

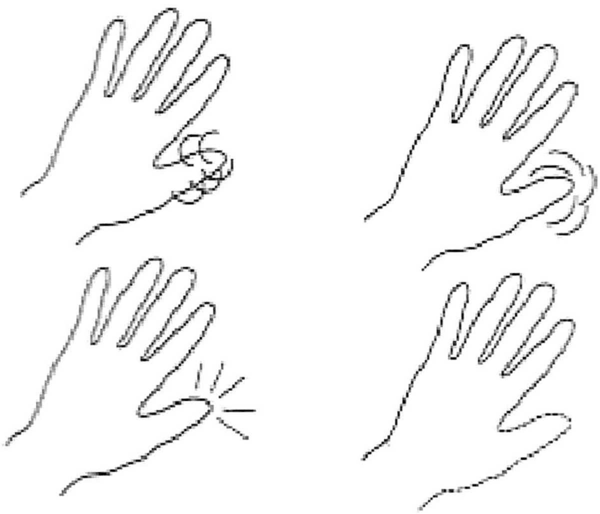

Fig. 3: J. M. Kennedy, *Drawing & the Blind: Pictures to Touch*, 1993.

Goodman's symbolic theory of depiction is an extreme instance of the tendency to ignore the somatic senses and embodiment in the theory of depiction. Depiction is usually considered to be purely a matter of visuality and the viewer just a spectator – although phenomenology and neurological research both show that this is not the case.[15]

Lucio Fontana's various cut and puncture pictures focus on the feeling of touch. Their impact depends upon the fact that human viewers can be wounded and know what it is like to be cut. Traditionally, philosophers have been skeptical about the objectivity of claims regarding somatic feelings for, like all first person phenomena, they were taken to be private. On this conception, the visual appearance of a work by Fontana (Fig. 4) is intersubjectively accessible, but not the perception of its expressive qualities, since the feeling of what it is like to be cut is private.[16] Yet this epistemological claim about the senses seems to be contradicted by the experience of Fontana's works and countless other depictions of feelings and emotion. How is that possible?

15 The perception of the identity of objects and of expressive character involve different kinds of neural processing. See, e.g., Fox / Iaria / Duchaine et al.: "Behavioral and fMRI Studies of Identity and Expression Perception".

16 There are exceptions to this rule. Peirce's essay "The Law of Mind" famously argues that feelings are extended. Wittgenstein once said, "Das 'Innere' ist eine Täuschung" (*Last Writings: The Inner and the Outer*, Volume II, p. 84) whereby he did not question the veridicality of the inner but its supposed privacy.

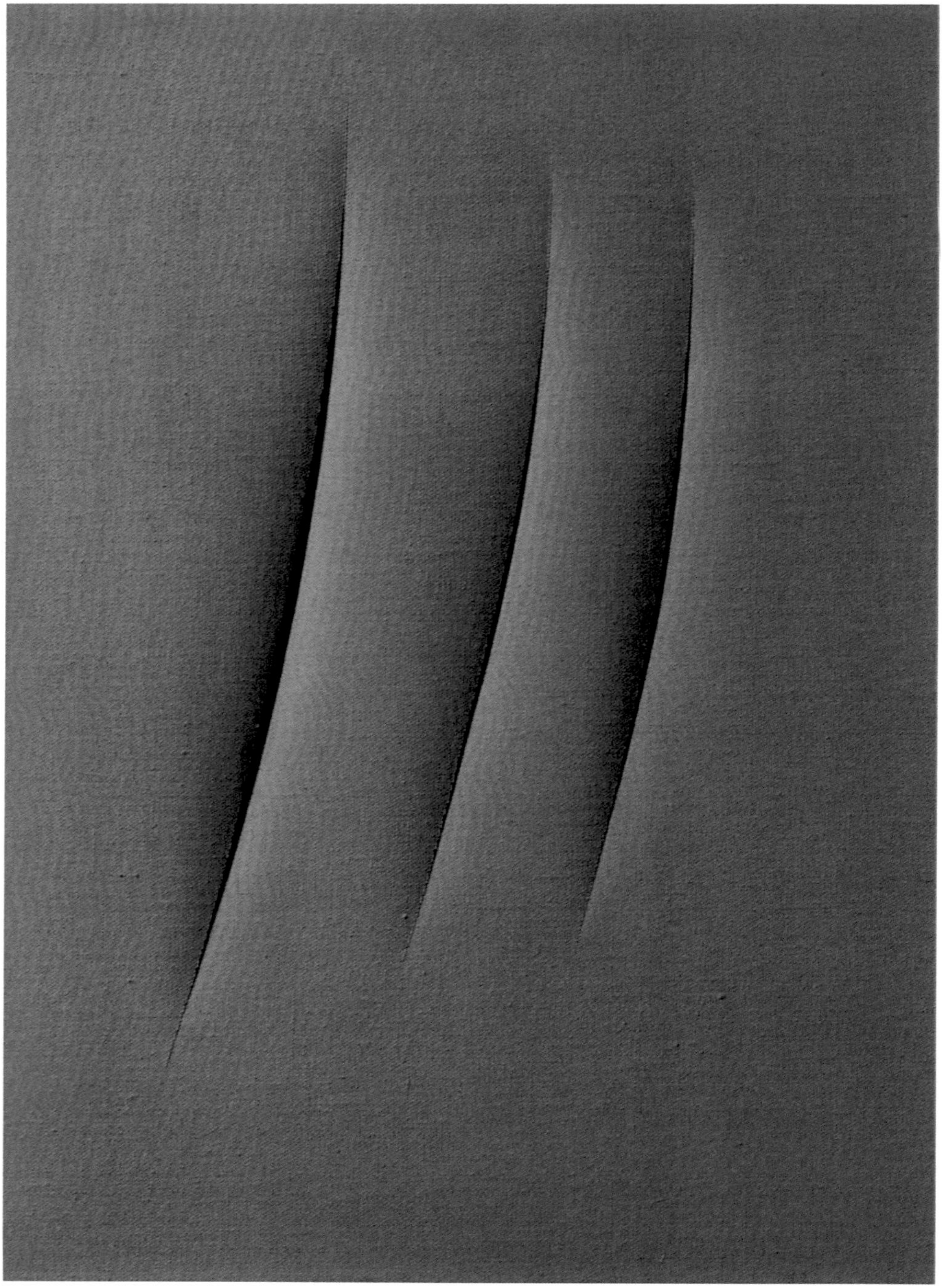

Fig. 4: Lucio Fontana, Concetto spaziale: Attese, 1961.

III

William James claimed that emotions are nothing but the feeling of bodily processes. As he put it, we can be sure that someone who is exhibiting shallow breathing, trembling lips, weakened limbs, gooseflesh, visceral stirrings, flushing of the face, dilatation of the nostrils, and the clenching of teeth, is in a highly emotional state.[17] James suggests that there is no real gap between emotion and its display, so depicting emotion would be like depicting anything else.

But human emotions and the affective meanings in pictures are usually subtler and less obvious than what James describes and usually less brutal than in Fontana's cut and puncture pictures.

For example, Bruegel's depiction of the fall of Icarus (Fig. 5), whose death is seen only in his remaining raised limb, contrasts with the rest of the world, which is unaffected. This stoic attitude towards human finitude contrasts with Turner's painting "Slave Ship throwing overboard the Dead and Dying captives with a Typhoon Coming On" (Fig. 6), which uses a similar composition, showing the shackled leg of one of the drowning captives in the foreground.[18] Knowledge is required in both cases in order to understand what is being shown in these pictures and to bring out the moral sentiments expressed in them. This does not falsify James' conception of the bodily basis of emotion, but shows that affective meaning in pictures may require the understanding of historical contexts in order to link the viewer's world and the world in which the picture was created. In the final version of James' theory of emotion he refined his conception to include the situation in which an emotion was experienced. Emotional states, he then claimed, do not arise simply because of the proximity of an object or person in thought or in fact, but due to the entire situation. James, who liked to hike in the wilderness, gave the example of encountering a bear in the wild, which results in considerable emotionality, yet not when this sudden close proximity occurs in a zoo. This means that the perception of place and the location of the body, and not just feeling, is an inherent part of emotion.

17 James: "What Is an Emotion?", p. 193.

18 Icarus was a fable, but Turner depicted an actual event. The crew of the British ship "Zong" sailing from Liverpool to Jamaica in 1781 threw 133 slaves overboard in order to collect insurance money.

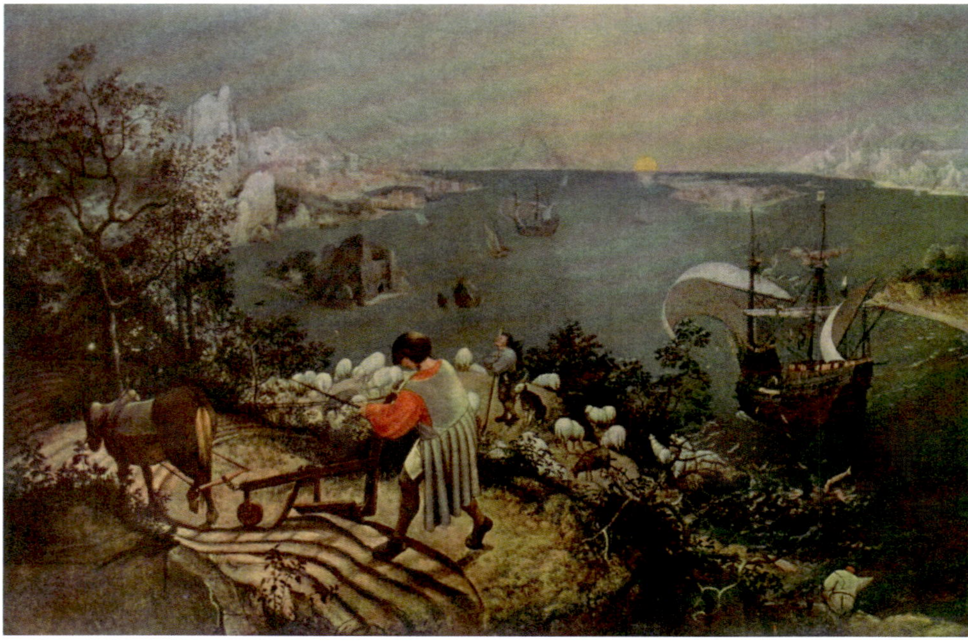

Fig. 5: Pieter Bruegel the Elder, Landscape with the Fall of Icarus, ca. 1558.

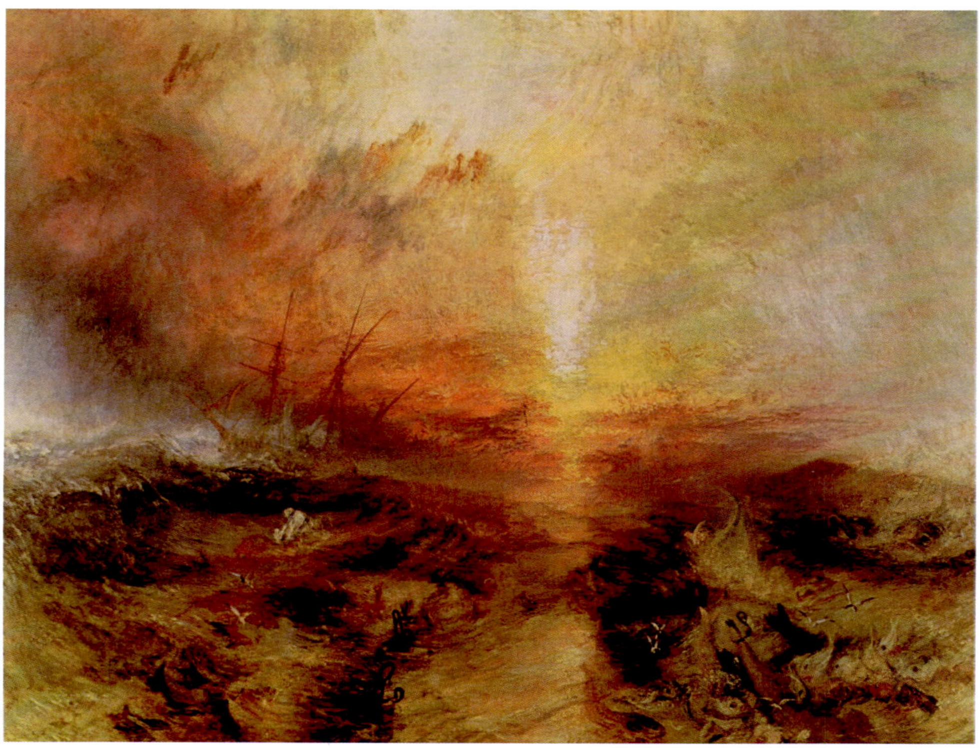

Fig. 6: William Turner, Slave Ship throwing overboard the Dead and Dying captives with a Typhon Coming On, 1840.

IV

Spatial embodiment is an integral aspect of depiction. In the 19th century fad of cycloramic paintings[19] that surrounded the visitor, the actual space of viewer's body was incorporated into works of art. This practice has been revived in today's digital immersion art in which the audience engages physically in an interactive way with what is seen. The viewer's spatial embodiment was also explicitly addressed in classical Chinese painting (Fig. 7). These paintings favored the landscape as the subject matter, through which the viewer was supposed to take an imaginary journey, along a path traversed by a wandering scholar. (Such paintings even applied aesthetic principles employed in traditional Chinese gardens.)[20]

Panoramic pictures naturally guide the viewer imaginatively through a scene. This picture (Fig. 8) depicts a large beach area in Australia on a sultry day. This is a tactile picture, drawn by a blind person, using raised lines that can be felt as well as seen. The wavy lines transversing it depict the path taken past different activities, cooking food, people talking, and walking by the water. The artist told the psychologist John M. Kennedy that it depicts not only things we can recognize, the activity and crowds in the foreground and the beach in the back, but also her changing mood as she moved through the crowded scene with her husband. These mood shifts are seen in the wavy lines' different spiked peaks. This picture focuses on the fact that we experience in a sensorimotor and affective way and not as passive observers.

There are other examples of pictures that depict the emotional reactions to a place like the mape of the city of Greenwich in England.[21] It was generated by computer, using inputs from over 1500 people over four years, showing their emotional reactions. Participants were outfitted with devices that measured their Galvanic Skin Response and heartbeats. The values were picked up by sensors made for this purpose and installed throughout the city. The result is a picture of the places eliciting the greatest emotional response on the populace. The resulting picture is an emotional map of the city. The emotionality is located but not what kind – the loud and dangerous busy intersection and the yacht club bar at the harbor both incite emotions in many people, but only the excitement is marked, not its positive or negative character – as in the drawing of the beach scene before. To recognize the character of the emotion requires knowing what the concrete situation is like.

19 For example, the battles of Atlanta and of Gettysburg are shown in diaramas, as was the German "peasants' war" (Tübke's *Bauernkrieg* in Bad Frankenhausen).

20 This technique was preserved even when the motion picture was first introduced into China. See Hongxun, *The Classical Gardens of China*, p. 70. Cf. Pang: "Walking into and out of the Spectacle".

21 See the "Greenwich Emotion Map", Christian Nold – Oct. 2005–March 2006. http://www.emotionmap.net/download.htm. *Last accessed 01.02.2010.* I am indebted to Viktor Bedö for bringing this work to my attention.

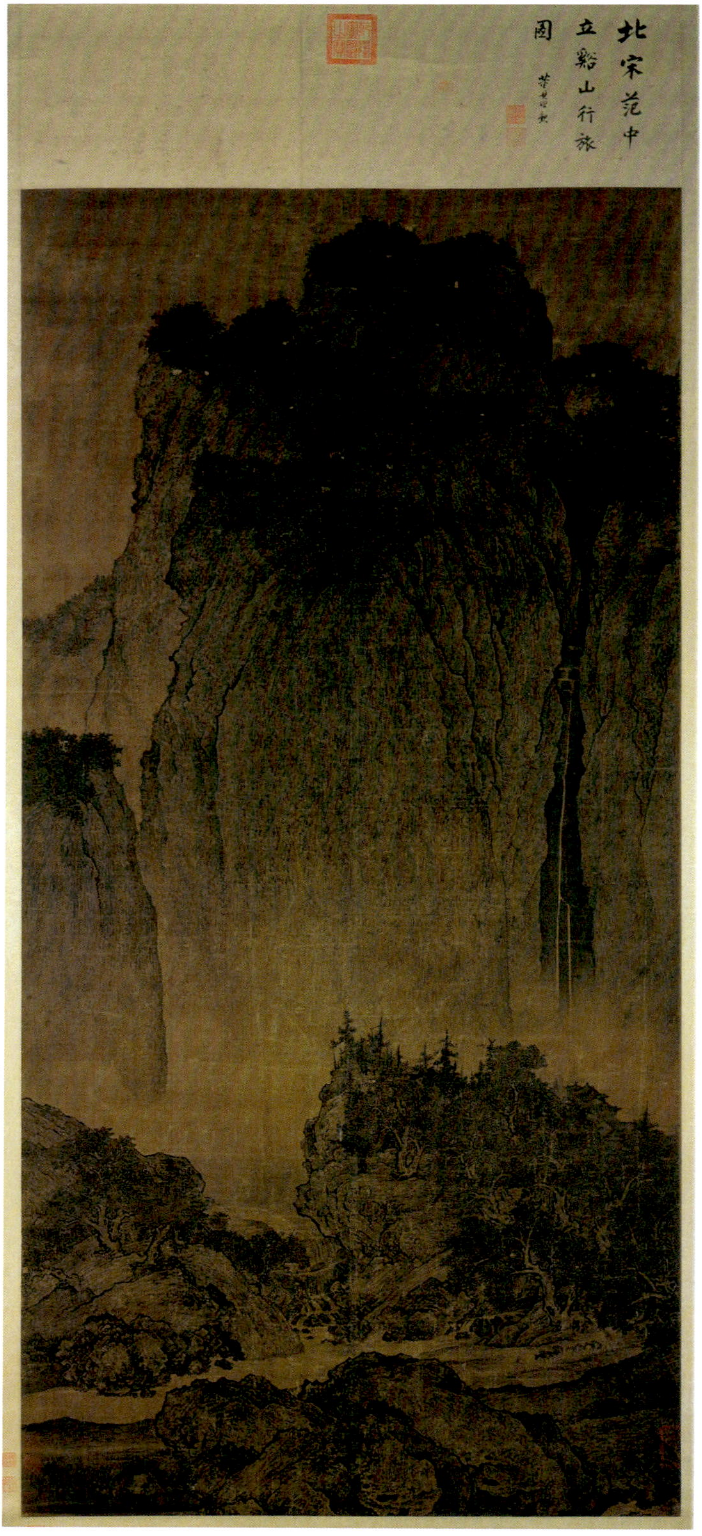

Fig. 7: Fan Kuan, Travelers Among Mountains and Streams, 10th Century.

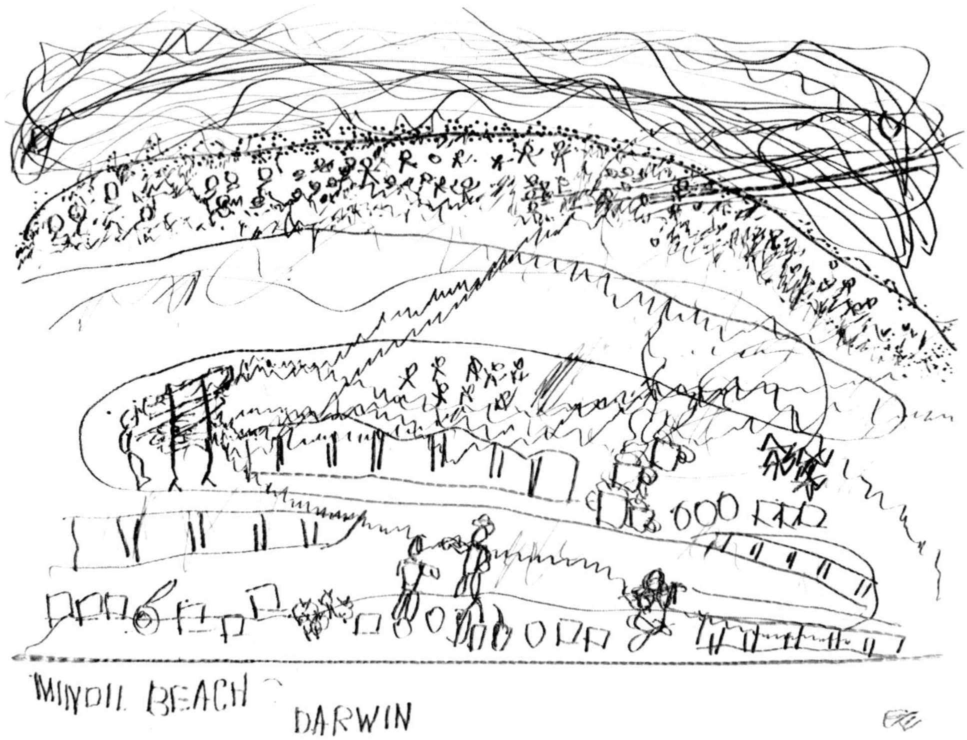

Fig. 8: J. M. Kennedy. "Outline, Mental States, and Drawings by a Blind Woman", 2009.

The world is navigated by the body, and the ability to move imaginatively into a picture derives from this fact. Empathic understanding of pictures derives from the embodied, sensorimotor character of experience and not from a mental or psychological capacity.

Even abstract pictures involve this dimension. A spatial organization can appear to embodied viewers as a map or something to climb on. A painting with a rugged opaque surface seems to embody a tactile experience.[22] A smooth monochrome surface is a fog that we could enter into without being able to find our way.[23] This metaphorical way of putting things deliberately underlines the importance of proprioception – a sense normally ignored in discussions of depiction. It has been suggested[24] that proprioception needs to be taken into account in expla-

22 A viewer described Mark Rothko's paintings (later in the Rothko chapel): "I felt as if my eyes had fingertips moving across the brushed textures of the canvases," adding: "The paint was not flat like a wall: you could look into it, and it had a kind of watery motion." (Elkins: *Pictures and Tears*, p. 2f.)

23 This was recently expounded upon in Stjernfelt: *Diagrammatology*, esp. in the section on Pictural Accessibility, pp. 306–319.

24 Montero, *Proprioception as an Aesthetic Sense*, in pp. 231–242.

nations of the aesthetic enjoyment derived from viewing dance performances, but this is true of static depictions as well.

This fits with the claims made by Gallese and Freedberg, and others who contend that mirror neurons play a role in the perception of emotion in static pictures. These claims gain in plausibility to the degree that pictures can be shown to exhibit the kind of extended bodily activity in space that mirror neurons respond to.

V

The affective content in pictures cannot be the result of the viewer's projections or deliberate acts of empathy. Neurologists explain that it is not possible to tickle yourself because the brain distinguishes expected from unexpected sensations, canceling out the incoming redundant information.[25] Similarly, you cannot consciously scare yourself by making a sudden loud noise. But a picture can surprise even the one who made it. The myth of Pygmalion in all its variations plays upon this fact.

Affective meaning in pictures is a kind of "gestalt" effect: a whole that is more than the sum of its parts. Pictures consist of more than the sum of the results of the individual steps that enter into their production.[26] This is true both of the 'identity' of the objects that emerge from the sequence of individual steps, and, even more remarkably, the new entity can seem to be alive.

The mistaken assumption behind most explanations of this phenomenon is the belief that pictures are purely visual phenomena. For example, the affective appearance of a color, as Goodman understood it, involves only vision and symbolic convention: It has no bodily basis. This conception fits with a cultural color category such as "royal blue," which makes sense only if the institution of royalty exists, but not with the notion of a "cold blue." This derives from sensory intermodality and the experience of water. Human intervention is required for the production of pictorial objects, but these exhibit both conventional and non-conventional meanings, as in these two kinds of blue.

The most extensive examinations of expressive meaning in art undertaken by a philosopher so far stem from Susanne Langer. Like Cassirer, whose work Langer continued, she was convinced that affective contents in art were a kind of symbolism, completely different, however, from the conventional signs that concerned semioticians in the tradition of Saussure. Neither language nor vision were of primary importance to Langer, but what she termed "feeling". Feeling is

25 Blakemore / Wolpert / Frith: "Central Cancellation of Self-Produced Tickle Sensation".

26 For a *tour de force* presentation of this phenomenon see Stjernfelt: *Diagrammatology*.

meaningful but not referential. Instead of reference, feeling has "import", namely the pattern, as she puts it, of "sentience – the pattern of life itself as it is felt and directly known."[27] Patterns of sentience occur in every sense modality. In the artifacts we call "works of art" an analogy or parallel exists between the course of human feelings – taking "feeling" to mean sentience of any kind – and the form of the artifact. Such artifacts possess what Langer called "presentational" symbolism. Her claim that "Art is the creation of forms symbolic of human feeling" has nothing to do with linguistics. The symbolic character of art derives from the fact that it exhibits the artist's knowledge of human feeling, ranging from bodily sentience to moral sentiments.[28] This presentational meaning, she says, "does not rest on convention, but motivates and dictates convention."[29] Langer built her theory upon an interdisciplinary study of art, biology, and the psychology of feeling, but her thinking was guided by her lifelong interest in music. This meant, however, that her conception of feeling focused upon the temporal and the psychological rather than on spatial structures or human embodiment, so her conception of presentational symbolism did not necessarily involve the spatial coordinates that are constitutive of human embodiment[30] – up/down, front/back, left/right, in/out, and other such invariants. These coordinates are also fundamental in depictions – upward or downward, symmetry and non-symmetry, balance and imbalance, inversions, and spatial oppositions of all kinds are the elements of composition.

In the 1980s cognitive scientists developed a theory of these schematic forms from – ironically – the study of language. Linguists searching for a conceptual basis for metaphor hit upon the concept of "image schemas".[31] An image schema is defined as "a recurrent pattern, shape, and regularity in ongoing activities at the level of our bodily movements through space, our manipulation of objects, and our perceptual interactions."[32] Typical image schemas include: compulsion, containment, balance schemas, blockage (Fig. 9), removal of restraint, and many more, which can be combined to create blends such as "source-path-goal". Image-schemas are not bound to any particular sense modality, such as vision, nor are they concrete perceptual images. They are types, not tokens. Image-schema theory permitted linguists to explore metaphor in a new systematic way. For example, the word "permitted" in the last sentence exemplifies the "Removal of Restraint" schema, just as the word "explore" is also image-schematic, transfer-

27 Langer: *Feeling and Form*, p. 31.

28 Like Panofsky's notion of "pre-iconographic" meaning, Langer's conception of non-referential (presentational) symbolism concerns what is found in vital experience.

29 Langer: *Feeling and Form*, p. 22.

30 With the proliferation since the 1980s of theories of embodied cognition, sensorimotor skills have increasingly become a topic of concern in the theory of perception.

31 Lakoff / Johnson: *Metaphors We Live By*. Cf. Johnson: *The Meaning of the Body*; Lakoff: "The Neuroscience of Form in Art".

32 Johnson: *The Body in the Mind*, p. 29.

ring the notion of a physical search to intellectual space. One of the founders of image-schema theory, Mark Johnson, claimed that since the spatial organization of image schemas is purely structural, their "geometrical" character does not involve affective meaning.[33] By contrast, Langer's theory focuses upon the opposite perspective: "feelings" considered independently of spatial structure.

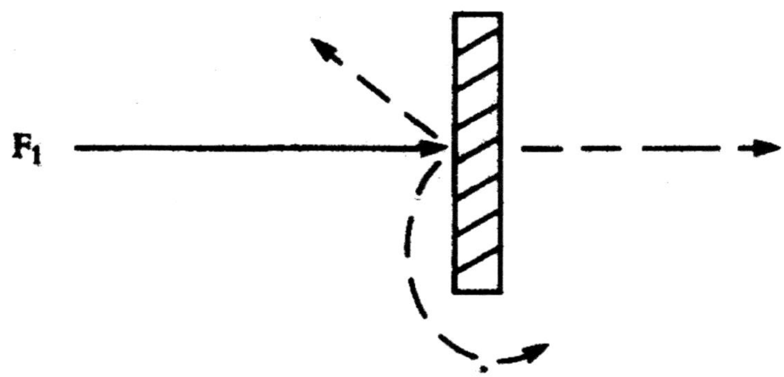

Fig. 9: Mark Johnson: *The Body in the Mind*, p. 46: Example of the image schema 'blockage'.

Both perspectives overlook the affective dimension of the human body's instantiations of image-schemas. The container schema characterizes the human body's internal-external organization, marked off by its border: the skin. So two different bodily activities instantiate the different image-schemas that characterize the organization of motion: force relations and balance. But in an actual situation these possess an affective character.[34]

The metaphorical relationship between structure and emotion was already apparent to the art historian Heinrich Wölfflin in his "Prolegomena to a Psychology of Architecture" of 1896. Wölfflin began with the claim that "Our bodily organization is the form, under which we understand everything bodily."[35] As he explained: "If we were able only to perceive optically, then an aesthetic judgment of the world of bodies would be denied to us. As humans with a body which teaches us what heaviness, contraction, force, and so on are, we collect the experiences that enable us to sympathize with the states of other bodies."[36] Bodily

33 Johnson: "The Philosophical Significance of Image Schemas".

34 Image schema theory first found application in aesthetics in the study of performance art. See esp. Fischer-Lichte: *Ästhetik des Performativen* and Johnson: *The Meaning of the Body*, which deals mostly with music.

35 Wölfflin: *Prolegomena zu einer Psychologie der Architektur*.

36 Wölfflin: *Prolegomena*, p. 119–120: "Wären wir bloß optisch auffassende Wesen, so müßte uns eine ästhetische Beurteilung der Körperwelt stets versagt bleiben. Als Menschen mit einem Leibe, der uns kennen lehrt, was Schwere, Kontraktion, Kraft, usw., ist, sammeln wir an

states involve – in addition to "feelings" – dynamic spatial forms: weight is downward, contraction pulls together, force is compulsion in a direction. These are image-schematic forms.

Wölfflin claimed that the organization of the human body provides the objective basis for the expressive character of architecture, but this thesis can be extended to depiction generally. Doing so makes it possible to give up the belief that affective content in pictures derives from the viewer's mental acts. Rather, the affective and expressive meaning in pictures depends upon knowing what it feels like to engage in bodily activity. This permits an understanding of force, weight, and apparent motion – not only in architecture, but also the balance, upward and falling directions present in any pictorial form.

But a gap still remains: The theory of image schemas explicates meaning in the third person perspective, in terms of dynamic geometrical forms, while movement and affect are experienced in the first person. Here a neurological concept offers a way to close the gap between first person and third person perspectives: the body schema. "Body schema" was Henry Head's name for the constantly changing and constantly updated, largely unconscious model of our body's spatial disposition in movement and at rest, which is responsible for guiding our automatic movements[37] in contrast to our conscious picture of ourselves, the body "image."[38] As a neurological process the body schema functions largely unconsciously, but it can become conscious by paying attention to automatic movements in walking, sports or dancing – at the expense of appearing to act mechanically and perhaps even tripping. The body schema is innate and usually unconscious, but it is also the original iconic form that humans are exposed to: the organization of the body as a lived object. This is the continuous background of the varied forms of movement instantiated in the forms described in image-schema theory. The body schema is physiological,[39] whereas image-schemas are considered to be impersonal geometrical carriers of meaning. However, their instantiations in human movements are always accompanied by affect, since human movements are felt.[40]

The concept of the body schema offers a way to link the neurological processes involved in the bodily understanding of image-schemas in lived expe-

uns die Erfahrungen, die uns erst die Zustände fremder Gestalten mitzuempfinden befähigen."

37 Since Head's time the neurological conception has been considerably expanded. Alain Berthoz sees it distributed over four different systems in the central and peripheral nervous systems. Berthoz: *The Brain's Sense of Movement*, p. 229f.

38 The clarity of this distinction is due to the efforts of Shaun Gallagher, e.g. in *How the Body Shapes the Mind*, p. 24.

39 Berthoz admits that the concept of the body schema is, as he puts it, "a little woolly", but adds that "it turns out to be surprisingly useful." Among its surprising uses is the fact that it helps to explain the affective content in pictures (Berthoz: *The Brain's Sense of Movement*, p. 227).

40 See e.g. Cole / Montero: "Affective Proprioception".

rience with the affective content in pictures, for the latter depends upon the viewer's understanding what it is like to be embodied.

The scale and sensory and motor capacities of the organism in its surroundings dictates the kinds of forms it perceives and how it can respond to them.[41] This is not a matter of psychology and not merely a question of anatomy, but a question of spatial schemata as well – in/out, up/down, left/right, and so on, including the affective meanings that accrue to these forms. The action space and world negotiated by the embodied subject possesses various expressive qualities that are as important in depiction as they are for linguistic metaphors. The image-schematic metaphors discussed in linguistics, such as that "Up is good" and "being down is bad" or that "inside is good" and "being on the outside" is bad all have counterparts in depiction.[42]

The fact that pictorial objects embody feelings for an observer is not the product of the viewer's psychological acts or of cultural conventions. The emotive character of a direction such as "down" cannot be divorced from the feeling of gravity, which enters into depictions as do all the other force coordinates of embodied existence. These structural aspects of embodiment, like the peculiarities of color perception and the vulnerability of the body mentioned before, serve as the background for unlimited cultural variations in pictures. The usurpatory character of pictorial objects – the fact that they possess affective meanings independently of the artist's intentions and the viewer's deliberate interpretations – results from the fact that like the viewer, they too embody dynamic affective image-schemas. To better understand this, researchers in philosophy, art history, and cognitive neuroscience will have to work together.

41 Berthoz locates his research on the neurology of movement in the context of Jakob von Uexküll's notion of "Umwelt" or "surrounding world". For Uexküll, each organism has its own kind of Umwelt due to its particular anatomy, what Uexküll called its "Bauplan" (itself an architectural term), Berthoz pays particular attention to the aesthetics of architecture, arguing that 'perception is inseparable from action' and that our aesthetic response to architecture depends upon whether we experience merely straight lines and corners or more expressive forms. He reflects on a visit to a building under reconstruction and compares the new banister with the old one on the next floor: "The more recent one was square, as rigid as an insensitive person, sad and gloomy, going nowhere; the staircase that belonged to the old building had that marvelous curvature you see in Parisian bannisters … it showed the way without hesitation … The old banister was shape and movement; already I felt in the palm of my hand the rounded curves that embraced me as I got my spinal locomotor generator into gear. The banister was refinement itself, the lover of the craftsman who had created her." Berthoz: *The Brain's Sense of Movement*, p. 259.

42 See the explication of these universal terms in ancient Chinese by Li: "How Politeness Is Embodied Through Image Schemas".

References

Berthoz, Alain: *The Brain's Sense of Movement*, Cambridge MA (Harvard University Press) 2000.

Blakemore, S. J. / D. M. Wolpert / C. D. Frith: "Central Cancellation of Self-Produced Tickle Sensation", in: *Nature Neuroscience* 7 (1998), pp. 635–40.

Bredekamp, Horst: *Theorie des Bildaktes*, Frankfurt am Main (Suhrkamp) in press.

Cole, Jonathan and Barbara Montero: "Affective Proprioception", in: *Janus Head: Journal of Interdisciplinary Studies in Literature, Continental Philosophy, Phenomenological Psychology, and the Arts*, issue edited by Shaun Gallagher, 9 (2007), pp. 299–317.

Curtis, Robin (ed.): *Einfühlung: Zu Geschichte und Gegenwart eines ästhetischen Konzepts*, Munich (Fink) 2009.

Darwin, Charles: *The Descent of Man, and Selection in Relation to Sex*, London, 1871.

Elkins, James: *Pictures and Tears: A History of People Who Have Cried in Front of Paintings*, New York/London (Routledge) 2001.

Fischer-Lichte, Erika: *Ästhetik des Performativen*, Frankfurt am Main (Suhrkamp) 2004.

Fox, Christopher J. / Giuseppe Iaria / Bradley C. Duchaine et al.: "Behavioral and fMRI Studies of Identity and Expression Perception in Acquired Prosopagnosia", in: *The Journal of Vision* 8 (2008) 6.

Freedberg, David: *The Power of Images: Studies in the History and Theory of Response*, Chicago (University of Chicago Press) 1991.

Gallagher, Shaun: *How the Body Shapes the Mind*, Oxford (Oxford University Press) 2005.

Gallese, Vittorio / David Freedberg: "Motion, Emotion and Empathy in Esthetic Experience", in: *Trends in Cognitive Sciences*, 11 (2007) 5, pp. 197–203.

Goldie, Peter / Amy Coplan (eds.): *An Empathic Eye, Empathy: Philosophical and Psychological Perspectives*, Oxford (Oxford University Press) 2010.

James, William: "What is an Emotion", in: *Mind*, 9 (1884), pp. 188–205.

Johnson, Mark: *The Body in the Mind: The Bodily Basis of Meaning, Imagination, and Reason*, Chicago (University of Chicago Press) 1990.

Johnson, Mark: "The Philosophical Significance of Image Schemas", in: Beate Hampe (ed.): *From Perception to Meaning: Image Schemas in Cognitive Linguistics*, Berlin (Mouton de Gruyter) 2005, pp. 27–31.

Johnson, Mark: *The Meaning of the Body: Aesthetics of Human Understanding*, Chicago (University of Chicago) 2007.

Kant, Immanuel: *Kritik der reinen Vernunft* (1781), reprint Paderborn (Voltmedia) 2005.

Köhler, Wolfgang: *Gestalt Psychology*, New York (Liveright) 1929.

Koffka, Kurt: *Die Grundlagen der psychischen Entwicklung. Eine Einführung in die Kinderpsychologie*, Osterwieck am Harz (Zickfeldt) 1921.

Langer, Susanne K.: *Feeling and Form: A Theory of Art Developed from Philosophy in a New Key*, New York (Scribners) 1953.

Lakoff, George and Mark Johnson: *Metaphors We Live By*, Chicago (University of Chicago Press) 1985.

Lakoff, George: "The Neuroscience of Form in Art", in: Mark Turner (ed.): *The Artful Mind: Cognitive Science and the Riddle of Human Creativity*, New York (Oxford University Press) 2006.

Li, Thomas Fuyin: "How Politeness Is Embodied Through Image Schemas", presented at International Cognitive Linguistics Conference 11. (linguistics.berkeley.edu/~iclc/pdfs/a242.pdf), last accessed 01.02.2010.

Lipps, Theodor: *Ästhetik: Psychologie des Schönen und der Kunst*, Hamburg/Leipzig (Voss) 1903–1906.

Lipps, Theodor: "Ästhetik", in: Paul Hinneberg (ed.): *Die Kultur der Gegenwart: Ihre Entwicklung und ihre Ziele*, Teil 1, Abt. 6, Berlin/Leipzig (Teubner) 1907, pp. 355–359.

Mitchell, W. J. T.: *What Do Pictures Want? The Lives and Loves of Images*, Chicago (University of Chicago Press) 2005.

Montero, Barbara: "Proprioception as an Aesthetic Sense", in: *Aesthetics and Art Criticism*, 64 (2006) 2, pp. 231–242.

Ramachandran, V. S.: "Mirror Neurons and Imitation Learning as the Driving Force behind 'the Great Leap Forward' in Human Evolution", in: *The Third Culture* (http://www.edge.org/3rd_culture/ramachandran/ramachandran_p1.html), last accessed 2010.

Pang, Laikwan: "Walking Into and Out of the Spectacle: China's Earliest Film Scene", in: *Screen* 47 (2006), 1, pp. 66–80.

Peirce, Charles S.: "The Law of Mind" (1892), in: *The Monist* (1892). Reprinted in *The Philosophy of Peirce: Selected Writings*, New York (Dover) 1940, pp. 533–559.

Stjernfelt, Frederik: *Diagrammatology: An Investigation on the Borderlines of Phenomenology, Ontology, and Semiotics*, Dordrecht (Springer) 2007.

Wittgenstein: *Last Writings on the Philosophy of Psychology: The Inner and the Outer*, 1949–1951, Vol. II, Oxford (Blackwell) 1992.

Wölfflin, Heinrich: *Prolegomena zu einer Psychologie der Architektur* (1896), reprint: Berlin (Mann) 1999.

Yang Hongxun: *The Classical Gardens of China: History and Design Techniques*, New York (Van Nostrand Reinhold) 1982.

List of figures

Fig. 1 Peter Paul Rubens, Daniel in the Lion's Den, ca. 1620, Black Chalk on Grey Paper, The Pierpont Morgan Library, New York.

Fig. 2 Michelangelo Merisi da Caravaggio, Incredulity of St. Thomas, 1601/02, Oil on Canvas, Gemäldegalerie Potsdam.

Fig. 3 J. M. Kennedy: *Drawing & the Blind: Pictures to Touch* (New Haven & London: Yale University Press, 1993), Fig. 8.9., p. 280.

Fig. 4 Lucio Fontana, Concetto spaziale: Attese, 1961, Museum Ludwig, Cologne.

Fig. 5 Pieter Bruegel the Elder, Landscape with the Fall of Icarus, ca. 1558, The Royal Museums of Fine Arts of Belgium, Brussels.

Fig. 6 William Turner, Slave Ship throwing overboard the Dead and Dying captives with a Typhon Coming On, 1840, Museum of Fine Arts, Boston.

Fig. 7 Fan Kuan, Travelers Among Mountains and Streams, 10th Century, Ink and slight colour on silk, National Palace Museum Taipei.

Fig. 8 J. M. Kennedy. "Outline, Mental States, and Drawings by a Blind Woman." *Perception* 38,10 (2009): 1481–1496, Fig. 3, p. 1488.

Fig. 9 Example of an image schema: 'blockage'; Mark Johnson, *The Body in the Mind*: The Bodily Basis of Meaning, Imagination, and Reason (Chicago: University of Chicago Press, 1990), p. 46.

Lament in Contemporary Art

SABINE FLACH

1. "A Loss of Calm Contemplation"[1]

> She stands at the water's edge, turned to face leftward in strict profile, and holds out to Venus the wind-blown mantle that she grasps in her outstretched right hand above and in her left hand below. … Her gown ... clings to her body, clearly revealing the outlines of her legs. A fold curves gently downward to the right from the back of her left knee, fanning out in smaller folds below. Her narrow sleeves, puffed at the shoulders, are worn over a white undergarment of soft material. Most of her hair wafts back from her temples in long waves, but some has been made into a stiff braid that ends in a bunch of loose hair.

This is how Aby Warburg describes the birth of Sandro Botticelli's Venus. The figure does not appear as a stable entity, but seems to be born from a play of contradictory forces converging at the limit of the body's exterior, to use Aristotle's terms, and not in the self-manifestation of its immobile presence. The movement is described as an active dissociation between the fluttering contours of the figure and its mass, which seems to dissolve at the extremities, like a dance introducing disorder to its symmetry, shattering the measured equilibrium of the static apparition.[2]

And describing Sandro Botticelli's artistic approach, Warburg writes:

> Sandro Botticelli's eye and hand are the equipment of an early Renaissance Florentine artist, in all their natural freshness and keen precision; but in Sandro, the sense of reality that distinguishes his contemporary mentors – Fra Filippo, Verrocchino, Pollaiuolo – becomes more than a means to an end, that of expressing the whole cycle of human emotional life, from melancholy stillness to vehement agitation.[3]

With his emphasis on the "pathos formula", Aby Warburg did nothing less than redefine the manner in which art historians view human expression.

Winkelmann's work *Reflections on the Imitation of Greek Works in Painting and Sculpture* was a little-questioned canon of art theory in Warburg's age. In it the great scholar writes:

1 Warburg, quoted after Michaud: *Aby Warburg and the Image in Motion*, p. 70.
2 See Michaud: *Aby Warburg and the Image in Motion*, p. 71.
3 Warburg: *Sandro Botticelli*, p. 157.

> The general and most distinctive characteristics of the Greek masterpieces are, finally, a noble simplicity and quiet grandeur, both in posture and expression. Just as the depths of the sea always remain calm however much the surface may rage, so does the expression of the figures of the Greeks reveal a great and composed soul even in the midst of passion.[4]

Warburg not only cited and criticized this very passage at the end of a 1914 essay entitled "The Emergence of the Antique as a Stylistic Ideal in Early Renaissance Painting." He also developed a new method for art historians. In *Grundlegende Bruchstücke zu einer pragmatischen Ausdruckskunde* and *Grundlegende Bruchstücke zu einer Psychologie der Kunst*, both of which were written between 1888 and 1901, Warburg worked on a method that he intended to be more comprehensive and different from the canonical art theory of his day. His goal was nothing less than the establishment of an epistemology of art that endeavoured to explain physical gestures, emotions and movement. Warburg wanted to establish a "knowledge-movement of images" – a knowledge "in extensions, in associative relationships, in ever renewed montages, and no longer knowledge in straight lines, in a confined corpus, in stabilized typologies."[5]

It is precisely this "knowledge-movement of images" that makes Warburg's set of instruments highly relevant to current theory, which deals with the complex relationship between emotion and motion in images. That, in any case, is the fundamental idea and methodological approach underlying the following reflections.

2. Art as the moved mover[6]

From this perspective, it is not only the themes of the images that are of interest, but also their genuine, productive capabilities – in other words, the reality of the image beyond its function as mere representation of the world. After all, a "real" image is subject to special demands: it not only confirms what we already know, but is expected to bring added value in the form of an *increase in knowledge*.

This provides us with an important insight: the images that I will address in the following do not function as static mirrors that simply reproduce a reality that is always assumed to exist. These images are not doubles. As a result, they must be perceived in the mode in which they appear. This means that the nature of images is based on a difference. Since images cannot be viewed simply as parts of reality and the gaze must not become too caught up in the represented subject matter, we must perceive them as images. As such, images contain an inner ref-

4 Winkelmann: *Reflections on the Imitation of Greek Works*, p. 33.
5 Didi-Huberman: *Knowledge: Movement*, here p. 10.
6 This is an inversion of Aristoteles' 'Art as an unmoved mover'.

lection and address modes of perception. They are characterized by the tension between the medium of representation and the subject that is represented. [7] However, they also lay claim to a form of autonomy that the traditional representational relationship forfeits in order to make this structure more dynamic. Images are thus *processes* that do not reproduce reality, but *render it visible*.[8]

This visibility, which is always generated by a process, becomes all the more striking in contemporary artworks – or to be more precise, in the spaces of video installations (fig. 1, still image of an installation), which I will focus on in the following. When viewers enter such a space, the very first thing that the so-called *black box* does is provide a *concrete site* for the interaction between habitus and habitat. *Then, however*, this concrete installation space between the viewer and the image of the installation generates an *intermediate space*. Temporary, transitory, and unfolding in the interplay between perception, imagination, remembrance and feeling, this space defies any attempt to determine its location. On the contrary – it *marks out the space* in which gestures and emotions are first able to *occur*. Here, once again, gestures and emotions take on a double nature: they are present and are presented, i.e. they *show* themselves and *are shown*. In other words, the focus is always on giving gestures and emotions a *presence*.

Like video installations, media environments have many immersive qualities which form the basis of interaction with the viewer. A media space is always already a performative *scenario of an image*. These images do not show emotions; much more *they are* the emotion by the iconic itself. What all media installations have in common is that they create a *sense of being there*.[9] Nevertheless, being there not only raises the issue of presence but also calls upon us to recognise that a perceptual impression is formed in a very special way: the network of relations in a stimulus pattern – not its individual parts – is recognised as a structural whole, or gestalt. This is precisely how Rudolf Arnheim describes it in his study *Kunst und Sehen*: "The forces that identify the meaning of events also come to life within the viewer and result in that kind of excited participation that distinguishes artistic experience from the mere passive intake of information." [10] According to Arnheim, the structural framework of the artistic work, within which the theme of the action is expressed, triggers a corresponding play of forces in the viewer. In Arnheim's perspective the viewer *animates* what he sees. Arnheim examines this process, which he calls "isomorphic symbolism," in his study "Gestaltpsychologie und künstlerische Form": "This method is not dependent on the supposed associations of one object with another, but on the percep-

7 See Flach: *Körper-Szenarien*, and also Spielmann: "Schichtung und Verdichtung".

8 See Flach: "Meine Bilder sind klüger als ich", Flach: "Realfiktionen. Versuchsanordnungen von Olafur Eliasson", Flach: '*Körper-Szenarien*' and Boehm: "Die Wiederkehr der Bilder", here p. 33.

9 Carrie Heater: "Being There".

10 Arnheim: *Kunst und Sehen*, p. 15.

tual qualities of the visual form itself."[11] In this sense, expression and symbolic form are interchangeable for Arnheim. He regards every image as symbolic if it expresses a general truth through a concrete example perceptible by the senses.[12] In his model, form is the "source of spontaneous symbolism"[13], which goes back to *elementary* perceptual sensations and *physical* experiences. Here the viewer of the artwork has a function in the whole structure that differs from what is propagated by the traditional aesthetics of empathy: in contrast to the idea of an animating projection found there, Arnheim does not regard spontaneous symbolization as being rooted in mythical consciousness or Romantic tradition, but in the neurophysiological structures of the viewer![14] With this he creates a first link to current cognition and neuroscientific studies focusing on "embodiment" and the "embodied mind." Since this type of research also does not conceive of the mind as an autonomous entity that exists independently of the body, it is evident that every conclusion (in our case concerning gestures) is grounded in a body-based experience of the environment. However, the body is not reduced to its biological, physiological or neural functions. Of interest are social and cultural influences, as well as the interaction with the environment. This conception of the body focuses less on a pure subjective perception anchored in the senses and the body. The body in the concept of a Habitus in Habitat understands – on the basic structure of embodiment research – the body as a complex *structure* that encompasses cultural influences, subjective experiences, emotional stimuli and cognitive capabilities.

The point is thus to recognise that if we want to understand such works, we must link them constitutively to the act of physical movement. They not only depict movement but are, by nature, movement themselves. And since images have no body, but require a medium in which to be embodied,[15] every image is always a habitus of images – and every theory concerning the "knowledge of the motion of images" is thus a theory of an image *as a habitus in habitat*. This thesis informs my next set of reflections.

As suggested above, *this habitus of an image* is inextricably linked to a theory governing the way expressive gestures are shown. This is an additional argument in my reflections, and its purpose is to narrow the context down to emotion. The application of this *theory of showing*[16] uncovers correspondences to its sub-phenomena, to physiognomy, emotions, traces, *gestures* and *expres-*

11 Arnheim: *Gestaltpsychologie und künstlerische Form*, here p. 145.

12 See Arnheim: *Kunst und Sehen*, p. 461.

13 Arnheim: *Die Dynamik der architektonischen Form*, p. 215.

14 See Liptay: "Die geistigen Augen im Verbund mit den leiblichen", here p. 168–169.

15 See on this: Flach: '*Körper-Szenarien*'.

16 For the *Subphänomenen des Zeigens* see Boehm: *Wie Bilder Sinn erzeugen*. Boehm herein establishes a theory which is based on the deictic character of the image. This means that images show a something from within themselves. I, on the other hand, would like to point out the genuine meaning of the image, which is always more than mere deixis.

sions –all bodily phenomena whose content and sense are revealed by *image-generated* meaning.

The argument thus emerging is therefore always an *iconic*one in which the habitus of the *image* is inextricably linked to the *physical image act of showing*, which, on the one hand, refers to the production of a material image and, on the other, transforms the body into an image itself. But far beyond the deictic capacities of an image it is much more relevant to show the meaning of an image by itself, which means that an image could have deictic qualities but that this concept by no means explains the capacities of an image. Exactly this iconic potential reveals the importance of a theory of image acts. When asked what a similar theory constitutes, one could describe it as the opening of a space of possibilities for what will then have a concrete shape. The potential of what is indeterminate can thereby be exhibited in the act of opening up a space in which something is showing and determining itself.[17] This theory of an image act – and this means of the image itself – operates with transitions, with the absent, with indeterminancies, ambiguities, affective energies, the subliminal, with what is evident and with sensual issues. Thereby Emotions become manageable.[18]

However, body images as image scenarios are – and this is my next argument – always characterized by a fundamental oscillation between *nature* and *culture*, *imagination* and *imago*, *facticity and fictionality,* between *habitus, habitat and heredity* (which, through their interaction, account for the importance of *accessories*), and between *intentionality and non-intentionality*. This oscillation is key to understanding the connection between expression and emotion.

The body image thus unites *imagination* and *representation*, as expressed in the French term *représentation*. It forges a link to the neurosciences, which distinguish between *external (media)* and *internal (mental)* representation, primarily to explain the origin and meaning of emotions. However, a closer look shows that it makes little sense to define a strict opposition between internal and external images in an attempt to explain the capacity for emotional expression. Assuming that this emotional capacity can explained only if we recognise that it is constitutively linked to a subject's ability to produce images and even to be an image itself, we must see "the mental and material image as two aspects of the same process."[19]

In this case, though, it makes most sense to use the constitutive double meaning of *image* – i.e., the fundamental connection between internal and external image processes and generation – as the foundation to explain the relationship between neural and physical interaction and to gain *access* to the *processes* of perception and imagination. This makes it clear that internal representation as

17 Cf. Boehm: *Das Paradigma 'Bild'*, here p. 82. Gottfried Boehm exemplifies his theory of the deictic character of the image and its potential for producing visible evidence.

18 Flach and Söffner: *Emotionaler Habitus.*

19 Tisseron: *Y a-t-il un pilote dans l'image?* Here quoted from Belting: "Die Herausforderung der Bilder", p. 14.

a mode of image generation that is specific to the body has fluid borders with external representation – as expressed in the term *représentation*.

With this elementary double encoding process we can now study the way in which emotions, moods and feelings are shown. All are distinguished by the fact that they emerge from the fundamental link between internal and external images, between neuronal and visceral processes. An additional characteristic is that they create a space of sensory experience out of the surrounding environment.

I have now presented a methodological tableau that interweaves several approaches characterized by the interdependence of two fields:

Habitus and habitat on the one hand and hereditary on the other, which, through their interaction, account for the importance of accessories.

The interaction between imagination and imago, facticity and fictionality, and intentionality and non-intentionality.

In what follows I will devote my full attention to these approaches to emotion and attempt to explain them on the basis of the lament in art and two video installations.

For this, we need to keep in mind that images by themselves explore the appearance, the composedness (Verfasstheit) and the understanding of emotions, explicitly as *image*. But first of all they produce emotions, and this is relevant for my following arguments: images are by themselves the emotions, and these emotions are – on the other hand – the character of the image. If this is correct, then we need to understand that such an emotional Habitus – as environment – is not just created by an actively perceiving subject (meaning us) but much more and much more basically: Configurations of an image create our organisation of perception. Images are never just a mere reproduction (Abbild) of an already given reality but much more an ideal (Vor-Bild) in the double sense of the German word, relating both to attitudes and to regarding the visible world – this is what this means. Images are in this sense passions – they are always already a habitus that is always impassioned.

The point is then not to make the basically unquestioned assumption that lamentation is a form of cultural expression that is highly ritualistic. Rather, in the examples introduced here, including the moving image, we must examine how they have become this way in the first place and thus create a link between art research and neurological theory. In contrast to the anthropological research that regards lamentation, mourning, compassion and crying as fundamental conditions for what is generally human, Hellmuth Plessener shows in his philosophical anthropological works *Stufen des Organischen* and *Lachen und Weinen*[20] that we must attempt to understand the creative, "artificial" practices of human beings on the basis of their physical constitution. Plessener uses the term "exzentrische Positionalität," or excentric positionality, to describe this process. Excen-

20 Plessner: *Stufen des Organischen*, and also *Lachen und Weinen*.

tric positionality means that a person does not simply exist, but that he can show that he has a body. He can step out of and enter into a relationship with himself. This "mediated immediacy" – which is, in itself, always a phenomenon involving distance – makes gestures possible, as it does imagination.[21]

Aby Warburg emphasized the process of empathy in order to guarantee not only the display of emotionality but a process of participation. Like Rudolf Arnheim after him, Warburg did not give his concept of empathy metaphysical and largely inaccessible underpinnings. Rather, he developed it on the basis of Robert Vischer's *On the Optical Sense of Form (Über das optische Formgefühl)*.[22] This and other of Vischer's writings examine various aspects of the interaction between neuronal processes, perception, emotion, and human powers of expression. For example, in his work *Das optische Feingefühl*, Vischer makes a distinction between sensations and feelings that is comparable to the current neuroscientific distinction between emotions and conscious feelings. Vischer writes that sensations – which inhabit a more basic level of the perceptual process – arise "intuitively" (to use his term) and take place before conscious feeling. Conscious feeling, in turn, precedes our empathetic capacity, which shows itself with and within the form and appearance of an object. According to Vischer, each of these states is related, on one hand, to what he calls the "motor nerve function" and, on the other, to the perceived form of an object in relation to one's own body form.[23]

Warburg used *this* definition of empathy as the foundation for his own concept. In his work, we also see that the gestures associated with emotion – in short, the pathos formulae – are not used merely to illustrate a story. Rather, the narrative function is kept to a minimum and does not lead to the immediate immersion of the viewer. Seen as such, the pathos formula is a means to create *distance*, which is supposed to produce a kind of emotional compensation and have both a stimulating and calming effect.[24] So the pathos formula has an entirely different function: it serves to *focus thought*.[25]

Using videos by the artists Sam Taylor-Wood and Bill Viola as examples, I would now like to discuss how this is shown in contemporary artwork. To introduce an additional thesis, this does not depict emotions, but *presents* them *without* offering an immediate interpretation of their meaning. Contemporary art explores their genesis, the way they are perceived and decoded.

21 See Wulf: *Der Performative Körper*, p. 214.
22 Vischer: "On the Optical Sense of Form".
23 See Freedberg: *Empathy, Motion and Emotion.*
24 See Krois: "Die Universalität der Pathosformel", p. 302.
25 Ibid., p. 303.

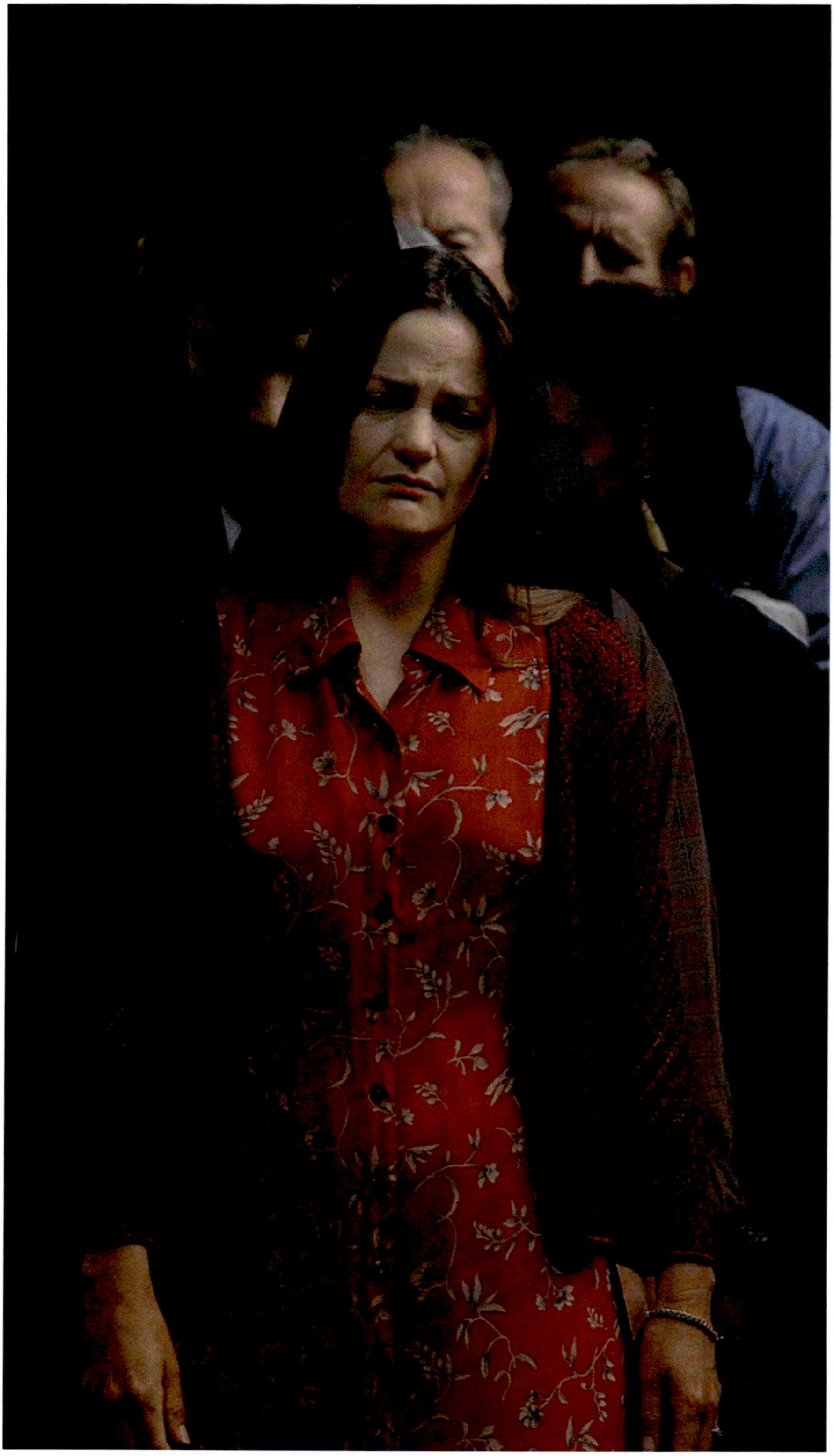

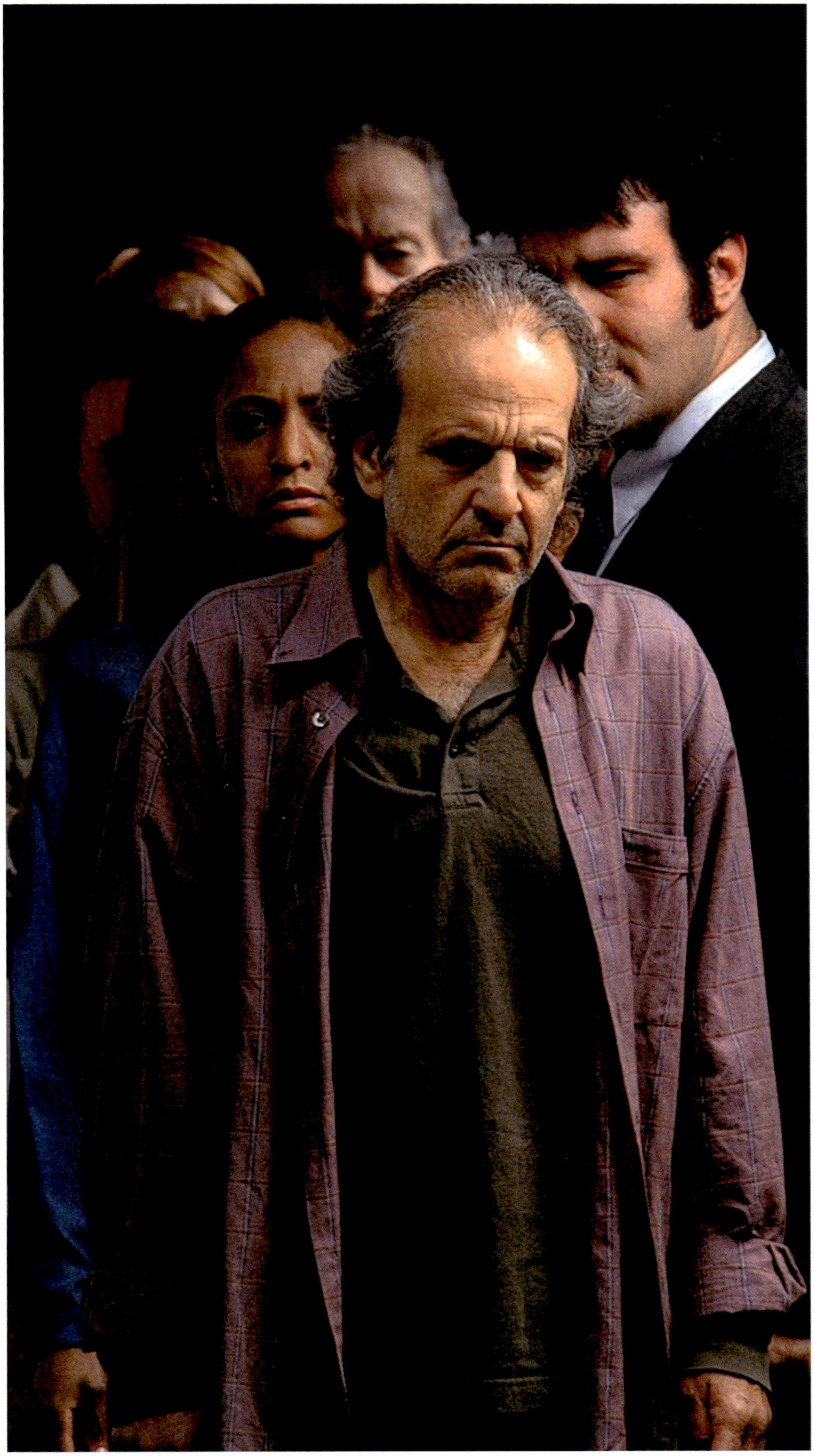

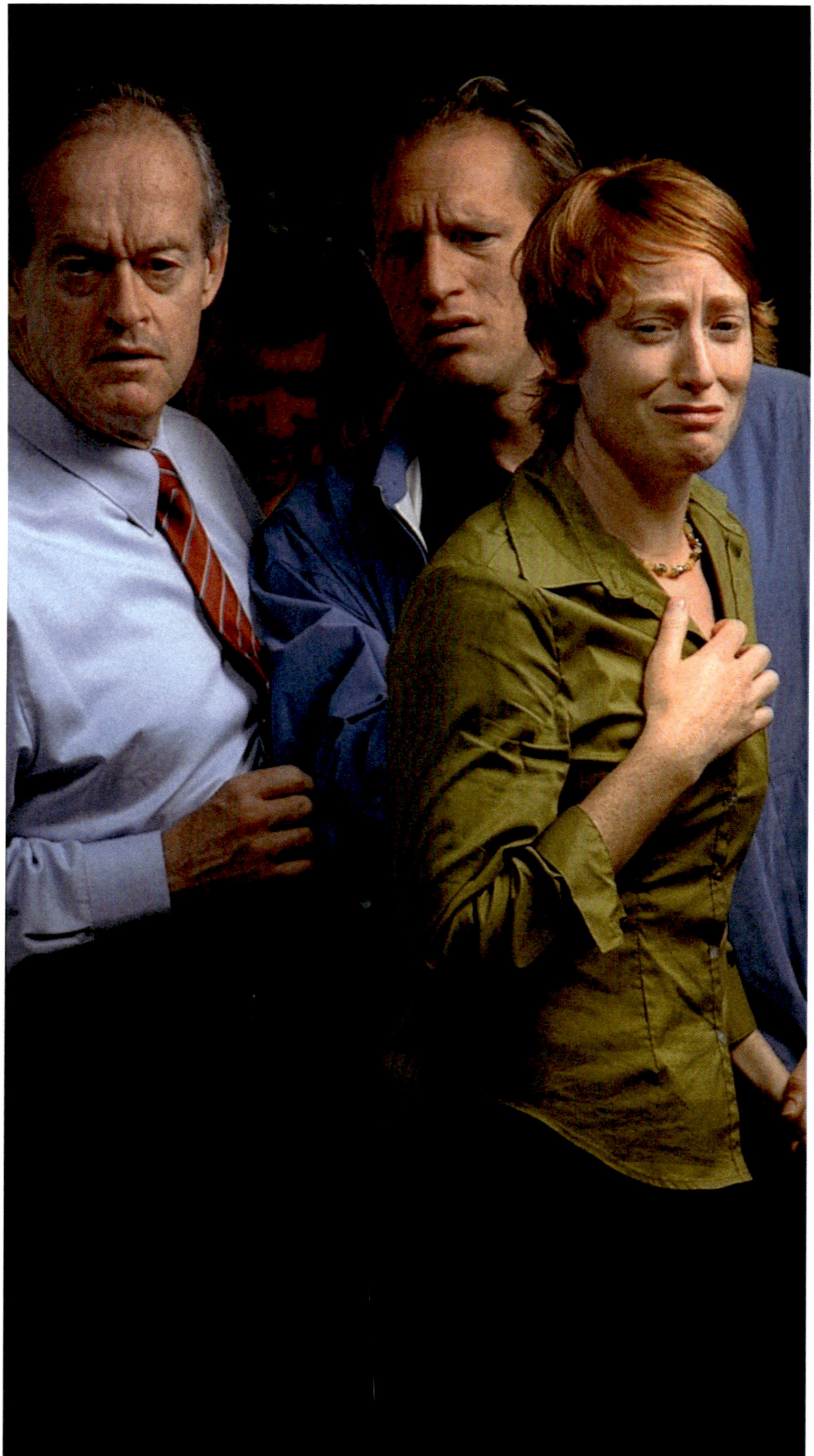

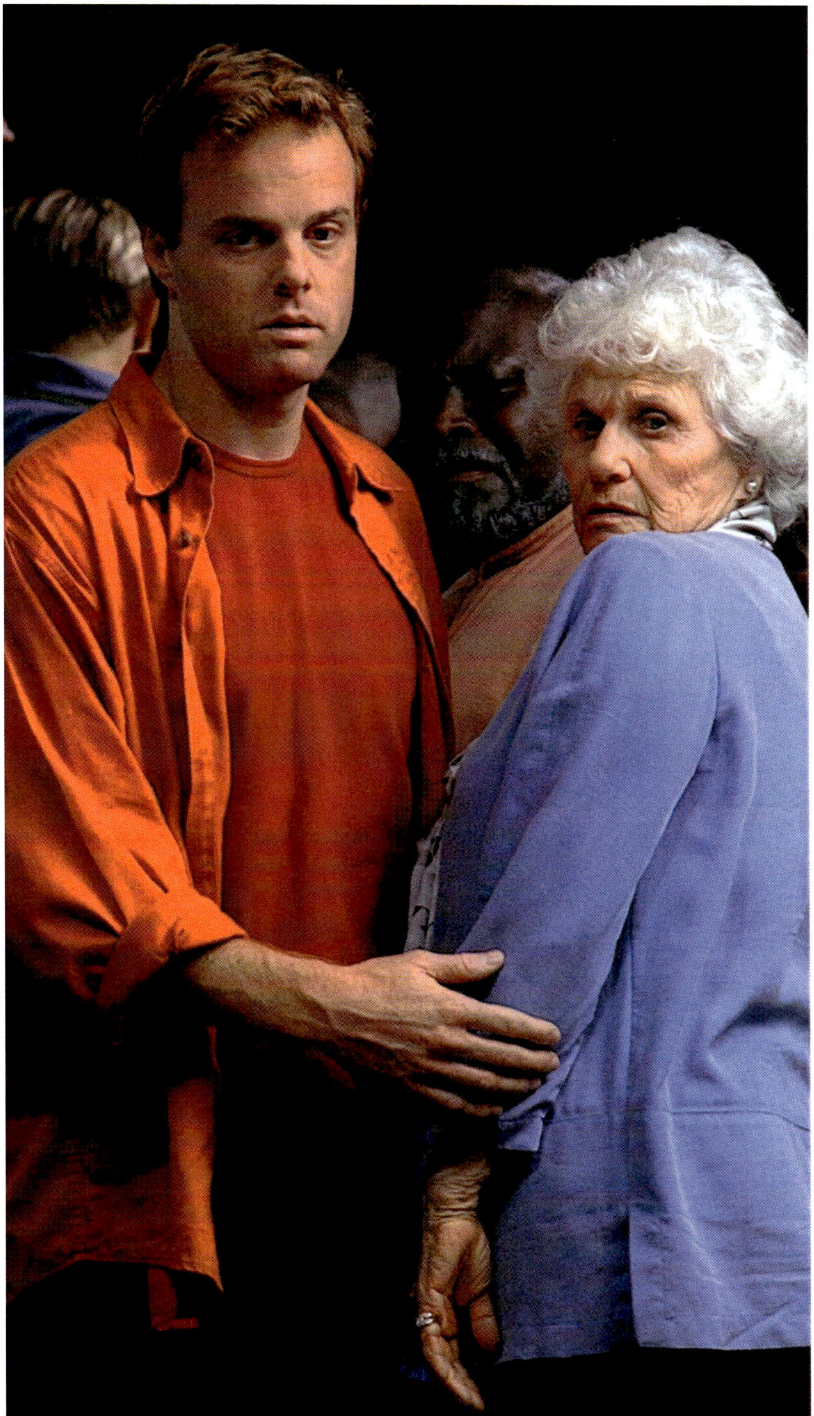

Fig. 1–4: Bill Viola. Observance. Video-Stills. Colour High Definition Video on Plasma Display mounted on wall. 120.7 x 72.4 x 10.2 cm. Edition of five. 2002

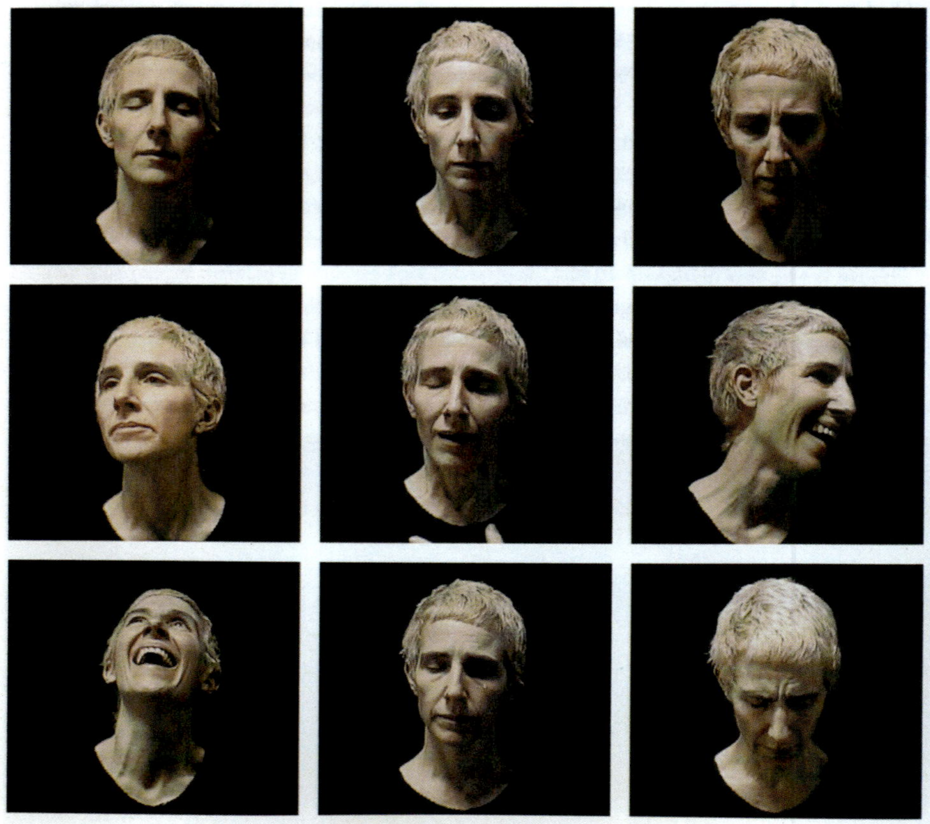

Fig. 5: Bill Viola. The Quintet of the Astonished. Video-Stills. February 2000.

3. Accessories as the interplay between habitus, habitat and heredity

The smallest of movements – called "accessories" by Charles Darwin – direct our attention to explicit questions of representation, as raised by accessories, appurtenances, auxiliary items and details.

What the viewer sees in Sam Taylor-Wood's Pent-Up is a darkened installation space that he must enter. There the viewer finds five screens that fill the entire wall and show five people in different stages of fear, tension, desperation and grieving. From the context it becomes clear that all the people have just been left by their partners.

Many things can be shown by seeing this video installation as an example of emotions research that draws its approaches from the arts. I would like to analyse the aspects of the work that are related to image theory, but I will also touch upon the question of verbal communication:

A prosodic analysis reveals that these five people do not communicate by language and that they do not have access to the spaces that each of them occupies. Nevertheless, the order of their monologues and above all the related gestures create the impression that they are part of a continuum. The crouching man seems to be responding in a cynical and latently aggressive fashion to the woman on his left, but the connection between the two immediately dissolves when the man on the right also seems ready to respond to the woman. It is only through the musical phrasing and choreography of the gestures that emotional communication is conveyed to the viewer. However, this communication is completely severed from place.

However, in terms of image-habitus theory, this video installation reveals two things: On the one hand, it is always the actors' *entire bodies* that express emotion. On the other, the artwork is not experienced by the eyes alone. It is always the entire body that perceives and is perceived. The image act staged here integrates the viewer into the installation. It illustrates that an emotion cannot be reduced to an external-internal schema and that the process generally has an interdependent structure. This interdependence allows us to see that the respective environment in which a body exists generates an arc of suspense (existing here between the viewer and image) that marks out the intermediate spatiality we know from the arts. This spatiality shows that every emotion can only be perceived in a surrounding space which the emotion habitualizes and by which it is itself habitualized. It is only in the habitat created in this way that a habitus becomes visible as embodied emotion. The installation produces this intermediate spatiality *ex negativo*. In other words, because the people so clearly seem unable to interact, interaction is created by the phenomena to which the work of art draws attention *in the first place*.

It is the smallest movements in the work of Sam Taylor-Wood – the raised shoulders, the outstretched index finger, the swinging of the legs and the *non-movement* of a collapsed figure – that provide us with information about events.

What is at stake here is therefore the connection between movement on the one hand and unimportant things, or "accessories," on the other. This concentration on quasi "infra-figurative graphemes"[26] supplies the optical codes of internal and external movement. They transfer the meaning of an expression, which arise between the concrete figurations to create a transitory moment. They remind us, if only in passing, of Walter Benjamin's optic unconscious.

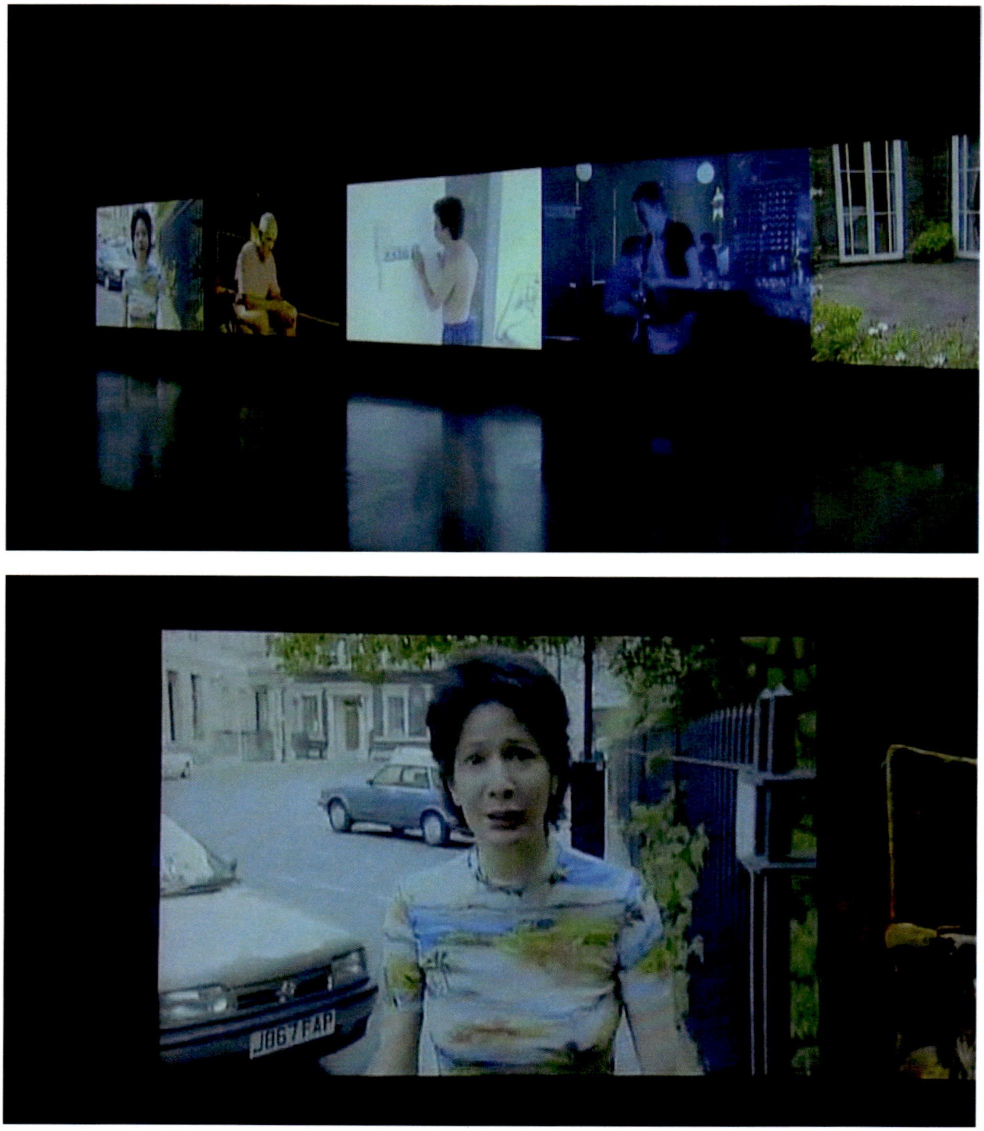

Fig. 6–7: Sam Taylor Wood: Pent-Up. Video-Stills of the Video Installation. 1996.

26 Raulff: *Wilde Energien*, p. 145.

As privileged figures in the representation of movement, accessories are movable and fluid in themselves, based on their internal spectrum of meaning.[27] The goal here is to study what Warburg called the *bewegtes Beiwerk*, the moving accessories that allow us to understand the visual codes of emotion and energy without allowing them to merge with the seeming unity of symbols. If, as Georges Didi-Huberman has shown, Warburg's primary concern "s'etait engagé sur une voie inverse: révéler, dans l'unité apparente des symboles, la schize structurelle des symptômes" – then this perspective can be expanded to include the present. What is at stake is exposing the structural tears in the symptoms themselves.[28]

The focus is always on two things: the comprehension of the intensity of internal *and* external movement, and thus the expression of both *motio* and *emotio*. Not only is the *bewegtes Beiwerk* a sign of movement, "accessories" serve as a method for deciphering "expressions" because accessories transmit the passionately excited representation.[29]

In his work *The Expression of the Emotion in Man and Animals,* Darwin explains the complexity and difficulty of decoding emotional powers of expression when he writes that this difficulty arises from the merging of "residual" and "associated" habits. Here Darwin refers to the possibility of an automatic or unconscious response as the result of a habitus and also to the fact that certain emotional states only emerge from a specific habitus.[30]

The question that now arises concerns the principle of habitualization. It is a question of just how much specific feelings, desires and sensations are associated with certain movements, whether this is useful or not, whether they are purely habitual, or whether they do not perhaps stem from a more complex system in which habit, spontaneous adaptation to the surrounding system and individuation merge into one.[31] Darwin concludes that "some physical change is produced in nerve cells or nerves which are habitually used" and that "this applies to the nerves of motion and sensation, as well as to those connected with the act of thinking." In a more precise statement, he writes: "When our minds are much affected so are the movements of our bodies."

But we must also consider the concept of engrams, which, in the natural sciences, refer to the traces left by a stimulus or experience in the central nervous system. In other words, an experience modifies the functional architecture of the

27 See Raulff: *Wilde Energien*, p. 145.

28 See Didi-Huberman: *L'image survivante*, p. 493.

29 At the same time, this kind of observation makes it possible to understand how accessory as a habitus is situated in the tension between habitat and heredity. I quote Darwin again: "Emotions are the hereditary effects on the mind, accompanying certain bodily action". This quotation shows not only the close relationship between neuronal and bodily connections, but also the necessity to understand a habitus in connection with a habitat – as the environment and the Heredity of a subject – and to analyse it exactly there.

30 Darwin uses constantly the words 'actions', 'movements' or 'expressions' as terms to explain manifestations of the nerve system as well as individual gestures.

31 Weigel: *Genea-Logik*.

brain, which allows us to recall this experience at a later point in time. The conditions that make this modification possible – the plasticity of the brain – also open up the possibility of reinterpreting experiences and giving them new meaning. However, engram always refers to an image of memory, particularly in cultural studies.

So here we also see a connection between the neurosciences and cultural studies, one that allows a model of thought to be established in which the body image seeks to systematically grasp[32] the concrete coherence or coexistence of pre- and post-images, past and present, authenticity and presentation. This connection shows that emotional processes always result from a complex interplay between brain and body, an interplay that in turn is constantly overlaid with ideas and images in the brain.

4. Interaction between imagination and imago, and facticity and fictionality

"Probably the loudest scream I have ever recorded is in the soundless work 'Silent Mountain.'" This is how Bill Viola describes his video installation – as a work informed by a soundless scream. But in what way does he manage to "embody" something that deliberately seeks to circumvent spoken language?

The experiential nature of the artwork and the virtuality of the image itself can be used to show that the work creates a *hypothetical space* in which the reality of the representation is constantly constructed and produced, and must be produced,[33] but that events can nevertheless be seen in the end.

Here the artist creates an observatory scenario in which the fleetingness of the moment is translated into a latent tension that illustrates the principle of movement. This latency is generated by the cramped fingers, the folding of the sweater, the tense muscles, the bending and stretching of the back – all physical phenomena that generate an image act.

It is these movements that make "expressions" visible as *agitation* by focusing on details. In the next step we must see this agitation as a means to analyze emotion.

The purpose is not to "lock in" or classify an emotional state, but to combine concepts from image aesthetics on the one hand and *elasticity* concepts from physiology on the other: it is through the immobility of tense expectation that the movement of the representation is conveyed.[34]

32 See: Krüger: "Das Bild als Palimpsest", p. 140.

33 See Flach: "It's not easy being green!"

34 See Strowick: *Ausdrucksbewegungen*.

In this significant representation of movement, the intent is not to show a mere movement in time, but to present a far more complex movement in space, which is stretched out by the process-oriented nature of the medium.

With this we also address what is relevant for the concept of an iconic episteme that examines the link between expression and emotion. The work also shows the internal proximity between imagination and imago, between invention and image. In this sense it is the "imaginary" itself that uses the internal meaning of the image to create external images.[35]

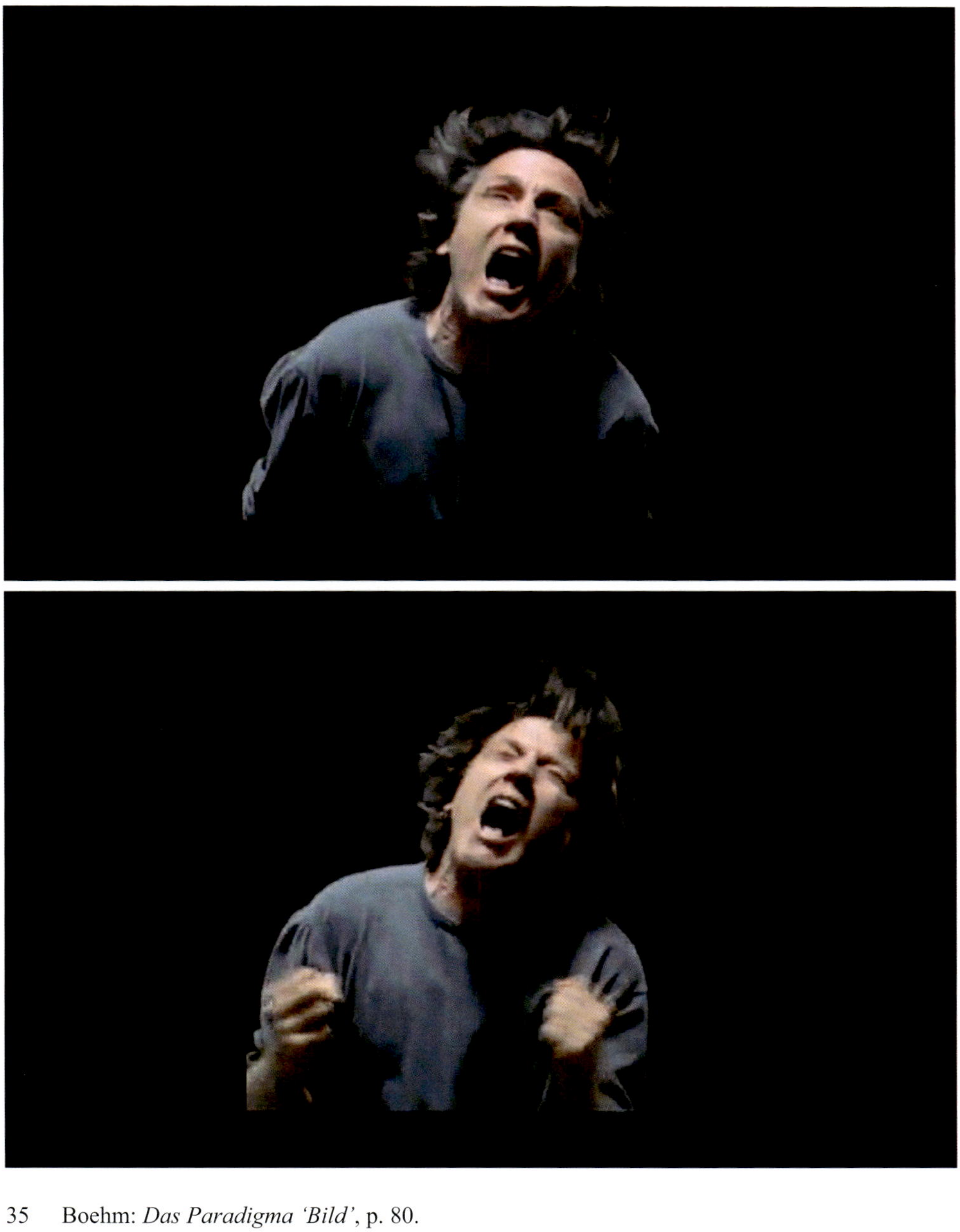

35 Boehm: *Das Paradigma 'Bild'*, p. 80.

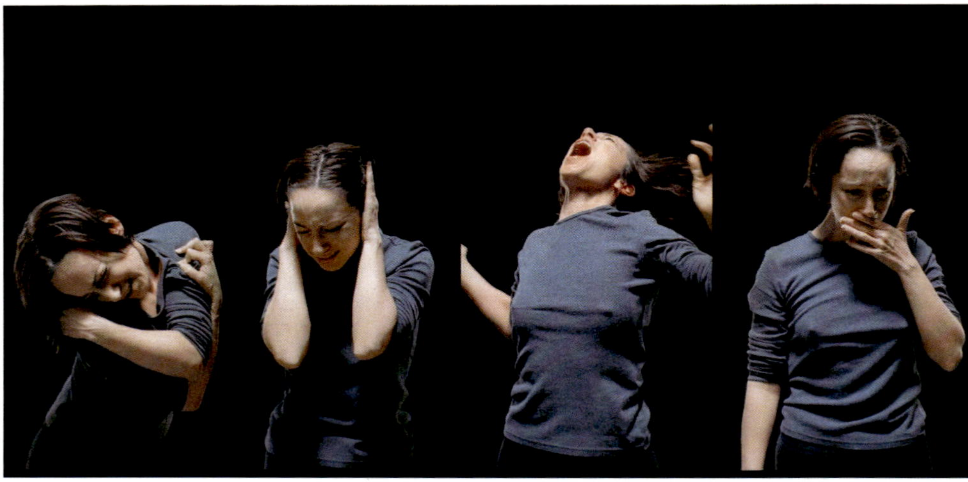

Fig. 8–10: Bill Viola. Silent Mountain. Video-Stills of the Video-Installations. Colour video diptych on two plasma displays mounted side-by-side on wall. 102.1 x 121.9 x 8.9 cm. Edition of five. 2001.

This use of images can be linked to such recent concepts as the discovery of the EBA, or extrastriate body area. The EBA is the neural system responsible for visual perception of the body. With the discovery of the EBA, researchers have been able show not only that people respond empathetically when they see other people in action (i.e. the principle of mirror neurons that is explicitly related to the moving organic body), but also that the same neural reaction occurs if subjects are shown an *image* of an expression.

This makes it clear that the accentuation and modification of images generates a state in the viewer in which he or she feels sympathy. The feeling of sympathy allows the viewer to empathize with what is shown, and this empathy, in turn, is a deep process-oriented feeling that adapts to the expression of emotion as a bodily process.

This interconnection between nature and culture in a representation illustrates a principle that is closely related to the idea of the imaginatio and imago: the principle governing the connection between facticity and fictionality, which is constitutive of the analysis of the relationship between "expression" and "emotion."

If an emotion, as a concrete physical sensation, can be interpreted by means of a form of "locking in" and "freezing," it can be semanticized by the classification of emotional states. Through this these states become factual. They are recognizable and decipherable.

Expressions, on the other hand, refer to two things: in the first place, they are a dynamic process of representation; in the second, knowledge of cultural meaning is contained in the specific represented movement. What is unique to an "expression" is a fleetingness that runs counter to the facticity of emotions: as a result of its movement and performativity, an expression is marked by a fictionality in which the cultural performance of expression, as reflective thought, can itself be depicted.

What is at stake here is the experience and identification of the interwoven nature of models of thought that seem to be mutually exclusive. Concerning the knowledge of internal connections between "expression" and "emotion," this means in concrete terms that the facticity of emotions is not inevitably antithetical to the fictionality of "expressions." Rather, both exert a mutual influence and are interrelated. This also means that one *cannot* experience the reality of an expression *without* an encounter with its fictionality. The result is a constant, distinct oscillation between nature and culture, imagination and imago, and facticity and fictionality. A pendulum movement is promoted that facilitates mutual definition. This relationship must be understood as a kind of echo chamber, in which the past, present and the future meet.

In other words, "expressions" experiment with the borders of visibility insofar as the primacy of visibility – namely, the display of a concrete, readable state – is suppressed in order to represent a fleetingness, which is given the *possibility* of becoming visible. Nevertheless, if "expressions" are seen as latently active graphemes, figurative symbols are removed, and we take what I see as a decisive step: we move from naturalistic representation to *abstraction*: to the abstract representation of an *expression in movement* and the *representation of a moving image*. This transforms the representation into an energy field, into a space in which movement is *momentarily* captured and frozen and can at any moment break free again.[36] What is shown is a *stance* in its constant ambiguity and interrelatedness.

In the process, a naturalistic representation breaks down and disintegrates into the atoms and morphemes forming it. From them a new *theory of showing* can be constructed that is oriented to abstract image and thought processes.

5. "Das Wissen von fremden Ichen – Knowledge of other egos"[37]

But what is the structure of the process in which we attribute convictions, wishes and intentions to other people in order to understand their behaviour? And how does the capacity to attribute mental states – including perceptions, thoughts, feelings – enable us to predict or at least explain their behaviour? What is the structure of the mentalizing process in which we attribute intentions, wishes and aims to others, such as when we respond to subtle, non-verbal signals in order to form a conscious or unconscious impression of other people's states of consciousness and to respond to them adequately?

36 Raulff: *Wilde Energien*, p. 43.
37 Lipps: "Das Wissen von fremdem Ichen".

How is lamentation presented to us in these artworks, and how do we respond as viewers? How are we able to know "other egos," to quote from Theodor Lipps's psychological studies? Lipps used the term "self-objectification" to describe the influence that personal involvement has on understanding social interaction.[38]

In his introduction to the pictorial atlas *Mnemosyne,*[39] Aby Warburg writes: "The creation of distance between oneself and the external world can be called a fundamental act of human civilization." The pathos formula is also a means to create distance.[40] However, this distance is *not* created by the theatrical aspect of catharsis in the image. Pathos formulae do not eliminate space in the sense of creating an empathy that involves no distance. Rather, they open up space, extend it and thereby give expression to emotion. After all, since image acts form the prodding energies, they cause the *immediate* space to be activated and neutralised, remembered and relinquished.[41]

Warburg calls such images "outlets for temperament" and speaks of the "aesthetic decontamination"[42] which they perform. "According to Warburg, works of art function as "compensatory products." [43] He states: "The consciousness of distance should become a permanent social function."[44]

But how can this distance be measured? If the focus is on the embodied meaning of a gesture that cannot be entirely attributed to the sphere of the subject or the sphere of the object, artworks always produce hybrid events. To return to the lament, such events do not show *what* a lament is in the sense of creating a system or a topology. Rather, they show how it appears in the sense of an image act. However, this image act is always released from intentionality and can initially be explained by its seeming opposite: non-intentionality.

After all, it is not the meaning behind the gesture of the lament that provokes interest and that only makes this gesture a plaintive one as it is performed. Rather, the gesture is what is analysed in the work of art in the first place. In Warburg's eyes, gestures were *symptoms* – not *signs* – and he went beyond the "iconographic" notion of the symptoms found, for example, in nineteenth-century mental hospitals. He understood that symptoms are not signs (the semeia of classical medicine) and that their temporalities, their clusters of instants and durations, their mysterious survivals, presuppose something like an "unconscious memory."[45] A symptom is understood as a movement in bodies. In this sense motion is not just a simple conveyance or narration from one point to another.

38 See: Vogeley / Schildbach: *Virtuelle Begegnungen.*

39 Warburg: *Bilderatlas Mnemosyne*, p. 3.

40 Krois: "Die Universalität der Pathosformel", p. 303.

41 See Warnke: "Der Leidschatz der Menschheit wird humaner Besitz", p. 141.

42 Ibid., p. 141.

43 Ibid., p. 141.

44 Ibid., p. 157

45 See Michaud: *Aby Warburg and the Image in Motion*, p. 16.

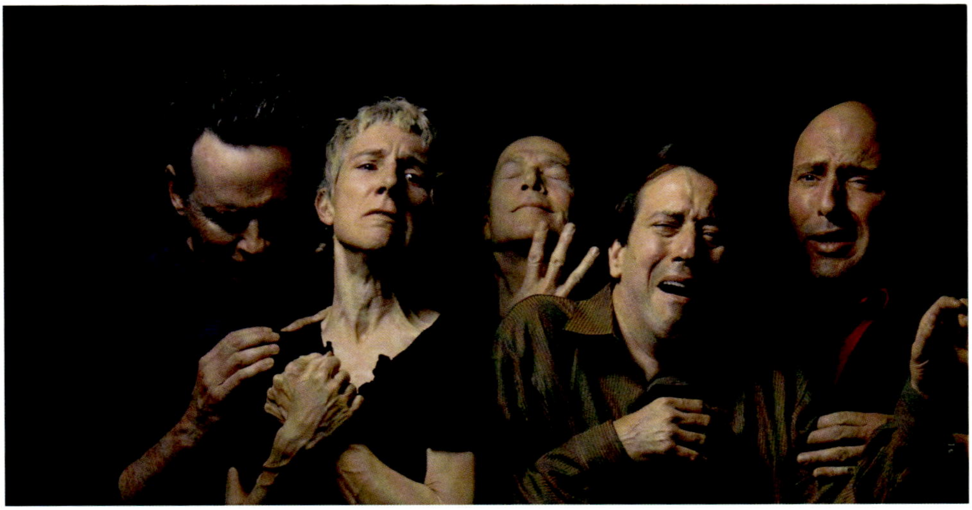

Fig. 11: Bill Viola. The Quintet of the Astonished. Video-Still. Colour video rear projection on screen mounted on wall in dark room. Projected image size: 1.4 x 2.4 m. Room dimensions variable. Edition of three. 2000.

But it includes much more jumps, cuts, montages, harrowing connections. Repetitions and differences: moments when the work of memory becomes corporeal, becomes a symptom in the continuity of events.[46]

So the focus for Warburg is non-intentionality, the display of movement itself, in which emotion is shown. Here I would like to quote from Warburg's notes, summarised under the heading of "Fragment" and dated 7 and 8 September 1890: "Wind movements of hair and clothing are signs of the person's heightened movement or - - - *of a strong wind*. Hence one can rightly infer the heightened activity of the person represented, while wrongly making this movement depend on the will of the person, and therefore inferring something personal *when nothing of the sort is there.*"[47] He continues: "With the introduction of the forward-moving figure, the spectator was constrained to exchange comparative for anthropomorphic observation. The question was no longer: 'What does this expression mean?' but: '*Where is it moving to?*'"[48]

46 Didi-Huberman: "Knowledge: Movement", p. 16.

47 Aby Warburg quoted after Michaud: *Aby Warburg and the Image in Motion*, p. 83 – my own italicization.

48 Aby Warburg quoted after Michaud: *Aby Warburg and the Image in Motion*, p. 82 – my own italicization.

Conclusion

Warburg's pathos formula not only explains the visual arts and their wild origins. The "kunstgestaltende Gebärdensprache" – or the "art-forming language of gestures" – offers a profound set of instruments for linking the image act to neurological, cognitive and biological findings. There is in fact a close interdependence between perceptual capacity and imagination, an interdependence that transforms the arts, in particular, into knowledge media for those wishing to understand the complex nature of emotion and motion. It becomes clear that they elude definition, that they are ambiguous. This is why, in an early series of images from 1926/27, Warburg deliberately provided explanations of gestures that elude symbolism in the sense of clear meaning. Examples are: "the defensive gesture of the downcast," "contemplative listening," "reaching for the head" and also the "lament".[49]

This kept the narrative form to a minimum. Pathos formulae provide emotional compensation by having a stimulating and calming effect.

For Warburg, the study of these issues represented a long-term project, one that apparently continues to the present. This led him to write: "The task of depicting human life in motion has not yet been achieved."[50]

References

Arnheim, Rudolf: *Die Dynamik der architektonischen Form*, Cologne (Dumont) 1980.

Arnheim, Rudolf: "Gestaltpsychologie und künstlerische Form" (1951), in: Dieter Heinrich / Wolfgang Iser (eds.): *Theorien der Kunst*, 3rd edition Frankfurt am Main (Suhrkamp) 1999, pp. 132–147.

Arnheim, Rudolf: *Kunst und Sehen. Eine Psychologie des schöpferischen Auges*, Berlin/New York (DeGruyter) 2000.

Belting, Hans: Bild-Anthropologie, Munich (Fink) 2001

Belting, Hans: "Die Herausforderung der Bilder. Ein Plädoyer und eine Einführung", in: Belting (ed.): *Bilderfragen. Die Bildwissenschaften im Aufbruch.* Munich (Fink) 2007, pp. 11–27.

Boehm, Gottfried: "Die Wiederkehr der Bilder", in Gottfried Boehm (ed.): *Was ist ein Bild?*, Munich (Fink) 1994, pp. 11–38.

49 See Krois: "Die Universalität der Pathosformel", p. 303.

50 Warburg quoted after Krois: "Die Universalität der Pathosformel", p. 303.

Boehm, Gottfried: *Wie Bilder Sinn erzeugen. Die Macht des Zeigens,* Berlin (Berlin University Press) 2007

Boehm, Gottfried: "Das Paradigma 'Bild'. Die Tragweite der ikonischen Episteme", in: Hans Belting (ed.): *Bilderfragen. Die Bildwissenschaft im Aufbruch*, Munich (Fink) 2007, pp. 77–83.

Didi-Huberman, Georges: *L'image survivante*, Paris (Minuit) 2002.

Didi-Huberman, Georges: "Knowledge: Movement (The Man Who Spoke to Butterflies)", in: Philippe-Alain Michaud (ed.): *Aby Warburg and the Image in Motion*, New York (Zone Books) 2007, pp. 7–21.

Flach, Sabine: *'Körper-Szenarien' Zum Verhältnis von Bild und Körper in Videoinstallationen*, Munich, 2003.

Flach, Sabine: *'Körper-Szenarien' Zum Verhältnis von Bild und Körper in Videoinstallationen*, Munich (Fink) 2003.

Flach, Sabine. "'It's not easy being green!' Schnittpunkte von Kunst, Medientechnik und Naturwissenschaften am Beispiel der Transgenic Art", in: Martina Heßler (ed.): *Das Technische Bild*, Munich (Fink) 2005.

Flach, Sabine: "Meine Bilder sind klüger als ich… Der Bilderatlas als Konfiguration des Wissens in der Gegenwartskunst", in: Sabine Flach / Inge Münz-Koenen / Marianne Streisand (eds.): *Der Bilderatlas im Wechsel der Künste und Medien*, Munich (Fink) 2005, pp. 45–71.

Flach, Sabine: "Realfiktionen. Versuchsanordnungen von Olafur Eliasson", in: Matthias Bruhn / Kai-Uwe Hemken (eds.): *Modernisierung des Sehens. Sehweisen zwischen Künsten und Medien*, Bielefeld (transkript) 2008, pp. 287–299.

Flach, Sabine / Jan Söffner: *Emotionaler Habitus. Verkörperte Sinnlichkeit zwischen Subjektivität und Umweltrelation*, Munich (Fink) 2011 (in preparation).

Freedberg, David: "Empathy, Motion and Emotion", in: Klaus Herding / Antje Krause-Wahl (eds.): *Wie sich Gefühle Ausdruck verschaffen. Emotionen in Nahsicht*, Taunusstein (Driesen) 2007, pp. 17–53.

Krois, John Michael: "Die Universalität der Pathosformel", in: Hans Belting / Dietmar Kamper / Martin Schulz (eds.): *Quel Corps? Eine Frage der Repräsentation*, Munich (Fink) 2002, pp. 295–309.

Krüger, Klaus: "Das Bild als Palimpsest", in: Hans Belting (ed.): *Bilderfragen. Die Bildwissenschaften im Aufbruch*, Munich (Fink) 2007, pp. 133–165.

Liptay, Fabienne: "Die geistigen Augen im Verbund mit den leiblichen", in: Matthias Bauer / Fabienne Liptay / Susanne Marschall (eds.): *Kunst und Kognition*, Munich (Fink) 2008, pp. 163–197.

Michaud, Philippe-Alain: *Aby Warburg and the Image in Motion*, New York (Zone Books) 2007.

Plessner, Helmuth: *Die Stufen des Organischen und der Mensch* (1928), reprint: Günter Dux et al. (eds.): *Gesammelte Schriften*, Vol. 4, Frankfurt am Main (Suhrkamp) 1981.

Plessner, Helmuth: *Lachen und Weinen*, Munich (Francke) 1941
Raulff, Ulrich: *Wilde Energien. Vier Versuche zu Aby Warburg*, Göttingen (Wallstein) 2003.
Spielmann, Yvonne: "Schichtung und Verdichtung im elektronischen Bild", in: Spielmann / Gundolf Winter (eds.): *Bild – Medium – Kunst*, Munich (Fink) 1999, pp. 59–77.
Strowick, Elisabeth: *Ausdrucksbewegungen. Zum Verhältnis von Poesie und Naturkunde bei Durs Grünbein, Ian McEwan und Charles Darwin*, Lecture, TU Berlin, Institut für Literaturwissenschaft, November 2007.
Theodor Lipps: "Das Wissen von fremdem Ichen", in: Lipps (ed.): *Psychologische Untersuchungen,* Vol. 1, Leipzig 1907, pp. 694–722.
Tisseron, Serge: *Y a-t-il un pilote dans l'image?* Paris (Aubier) 1998.
Vischer, Robert: "On the Optical Sense of Form" (Über das optische Formgefühl), Leipzig (Credner) 1872.
Vogeley, Kai / Leo Schildbach: "Virtuelle Begegnungen. Über die neurobiologische Grundlage des Erlebens von sozialer Präsenz", in: Matthias Bauer / Fabienne Liptay / Susanne Marschall (eds.): *Kunst und Kognition. Interdisziplinäre Studien zur Erzeugung von Bildsinn*, Munich (Fink) 2008, pp. 67–87.
Warburg, Aby: "Sandro Botticelli's Birth of Venus and Spring". In A. Warburg, G. Bing, F. Rougemont et al. (eds.): *The Renewal of Pagan Antiquity: Contributions to the Cultural History of the European Renaissance*, trans. by David Britt, Los Angeles (Getty Trust Publications) 1998, Vol. 1, pp. 89–156.
Warburg, Aby: *Bilderatlas Mnemosyne*, ed. by Manfred Warnke and Claudia Brink, Berlin (Akademie Verlag) 2000.
Warnke, Martin: "Der Leidschatz der Menschheit wird humaner Besitz", in: Werner Hofmann / Georg Syamken / Martin Warnke (eds.): *Die Menschenrechte des Auges. Über Aby Warburg*, Frankfurt am Main (Europäische Verlagsanstalt) 1980, pp. 113–187.
Weigel, Sigrid: *Genea-Logik. Generation, Tradition und Evolution zwischen Kultur- und Naturwissenschaften*, Munich (Fink) 2006.
Winkelmann, J. J.: *Reflections on the Imitation of Greek works in Painting and Sculpture*, translated by Elfriede Heyer / Roger C. Norton, La Salle, IL (Open Court) 1989.
Wulf, Christoph: "Der Performative Körper", in: Hans Belting / Dietmar Kamper / Martin Schulz (eds.): *Quel Corps? Eine Frage der Repräsentation*, Munich (Fink) 2002, pp. 207–219.

List of figures

The images of Bill Viola's art (except the stills of Silent Mountain) are taken from the exhibition catalogue: Bill Viola: *The Passion*. Los Angeles, 2003

The stills of Silent Mountain are taken from the Internet. Access: July 1st 2009

The Stills of Sam Taylor-Wood's Pent Up are taken from: Sam Taylor-Wood: Illuminations 2004, 2005. DVD Made in England.

Excentric Crucifixions circa 1500
On the Invention of Emotional Resonance in Painting and the Theories of Transfering Depicted Emotions to the Beholder

HEIKE SCHLIE

Since the 13th century, the imitation of Christ (*imitatio Christi*), in the sense of an "empathetic" participation in the Passion, belongs to the main cultural techniques of western Christianity. The principle remained essentially the same right up to the early modern period, even though the external forms and media of the *compassio* would experience modifications and new characteristics. In this respect, the opportunities that painting introduced would especially be explored. The Passion of Christ himself was the primary focus until concentration turned increasingly to the ancillary figures of the Crucifixion or the Entombment of Christ at the beginning of the 14th century. A parallel is found in the 13th century hymn *Stabat Mater*, which presents a dramaturgical portrayal of the 'Compassion' (*compassio*) of Mary at the cross up to the transference of the Passion of Christ through the *mediatrix* Mary to the invocator.[1]

The first two verses contain the description of Mary at the foot of the cross in third-person perspective. In the third verse, not only the perspective of the observer comes into play, but also the body of the observer himself and his emotions:

> Quis non posset contristari/
> Piam matrem contemplari/
> Dolentem cum filio?
> (Who would not have compassion/
> on beholding the devout mother/
> suffering with her Son?)

The verse which follows most clearly depicts Mary's perspective on the suffering of Christ:

> Vidit Jesum in tormentis/
> Et flagellis subditum./
> Vidit suum dulcem natum
> (She saw Jesus in torment/
> and subjected to the scourge/
> she saw her sweet Son)

1 On the interrelation of the Stabat Mater and the Visual Arts see also Sigrid Weigel: "Pietà und Mater Dolorosa".

In verse five, and continuing through verse ten, the invoking "I" begins a speech addressed to Mary in which the plea to be inundated with the pain of the *compassio* is made in various forms. In verse five, the "I" asks Mary to share her pain with him:

Me sentire vim doloris/
Fac ut tecum lugeam
(Make me feel the power of sorrow/
that I may grieve with you)

The central thought is found in verse six. Here, Mary herself becomes a medium of Christ's Passion which inflicts the invocator bodily with the pain and wounds:

Sancta mater, istud agas/
Crucifixi fige plagas/
Cordi meo valide
(Holy Mother, grant this of yours/
that the wounds of the Crucified be well-formed/
in my heart).

Verses eight and nine show that Mary is expected to act on the invocator, to change the status of his body and emotions actively:

Fac me tecum plangere/
Fac ut portem Christi mortem/
(Make me mourn with You/
Make me bear the death of Christ)
[...]
Fac me plagis vulnerari/
Cruce fac inebriari
(Hurt me with His wounds/
Make me bear His cross)

Verse seven states exactly how this transference of the *compassio* should come about: Mary places the invocator next to herself at the foot of the cross:

Iuxta crucem tecum stare/
Te libenter sociare/
In planctu desidero
(To stand beside the cross with you/
and for me to join you/
in mourning – this I desire).

The technique of joining the cross works by the means of the "Piam Mater Contemplari" in the third verse, which means that "seeing" or "beholding" is assigned a special status, either in the imagination or in the material picture. Essentially, the *Stabat Mater* is not only a prayer but also a theory of the visual transference of emotions for the *compassio*, which is, of course, decisive for the pictures. If the visualized or imagined picture of the *Stabat Mater* were to be materialized in a picture, Mary would be focused in the middle, since she is the center of attention; she is the only one who is described and addressed. She would stand at the foot of the cross, which would not have to be located at the pictorial center.

Such pictures do not exist at the time of the hymn's origination, and around 1300, Christ can only be conceived as at the center of a material picture. As early as here, however, posture, expression, and substantial signs of Mary's grief serve as concrete *exemplum* for imitation by the observer. The compassion of Mary and other ancillary figures is immediately evident through their gesture and expression. The gestures of mourning by Mary Magdalene in Duccio's Entombment of Christ (fig. 1) became an often-repeated formula of pathos,[2] and it is possible here to place Christ in the center, as well as the one who is the example of an emotional *compassio*. This manner of representation is joined with the idea that the *compassio* can also be expressed with one's own body. The movements of the body and the gestures of the limbs are not only an expression of grief but, in the process of imitation, also the originator of the emotion.

It is conspicuous that the artistic achievements of every art historical premodern period were also made fertile for this "function of transference". This applies to the so-called detail realism of the Early Netherlandish Masters, which attempts to exactly capture the physiognomies of emotional expression in the first half of the 15th century, as well as to the representation of space as an "emotions container" around 1500. First an example of early Netherlandish painting: Otto von Simson called attention to the representation of Mary in the Descent from the Cross by Rogier van der Weyden (fig. 2) and declared it as essentially a *compassio* motif.[3] This is indicated content-wise by her collapse at the foot of the cross, the expression of her pallid face and the tears clearly shown. Her compassion is indicated compositionally by the similarity of her body posture to the dead body of Christ, which has just been removed from the cross. The transference of suffering onto the body itself identifies Mary past a motif of grief to one of co-redeemer. Another example of *compassio* is Mary Magdalene, who wrings her hands over her head in a variation of Duccio-like pathos (see fig. 1). The observer's gaze wanders back and forth, alternating from the center to both examples of *compassio*. In contrast to the *Stabat Mater*, a picture composition that represents the one and dominant example cannot be spoken of here.

2 See also the gesture of Mary Magdalene in the *Entombment* by Simone Martini. On the iconography of these gestures see Büttner: *Imitatio Pietatis*.

3 Simson: "Compassio und Co-redemptio". On the concept of Mary as "mediatrix" see Aquinas: *Summa Theol.* 2 qu. 103, art. 4 ad 2. The analogy between the body of Christ and the body of Mary in Rogier's painting might refer to Aquinas' term of the "deiformitas" which is attributed to the Saints in general: *Summa Theologiae* 1, 12, 5.

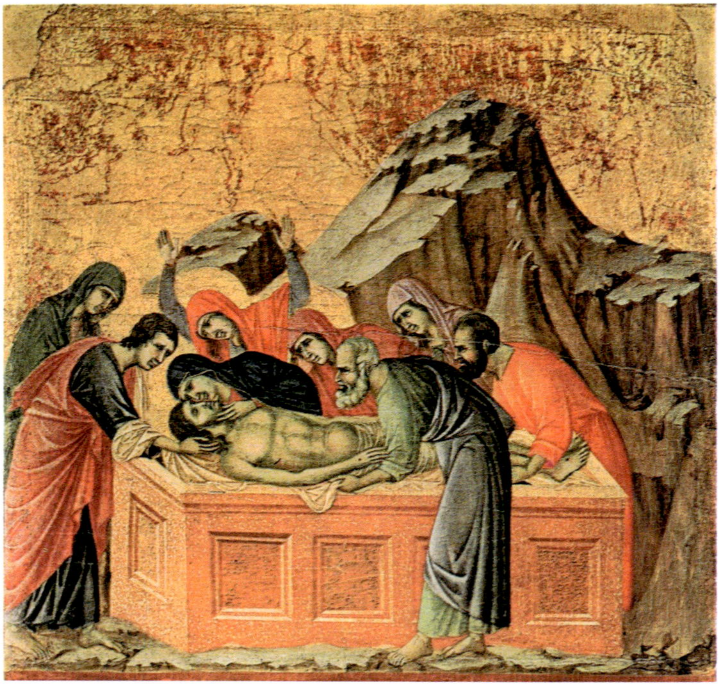

Fig. 1: Duccio di Buoninsegna, Lamentation/Entombment, 1308–11.

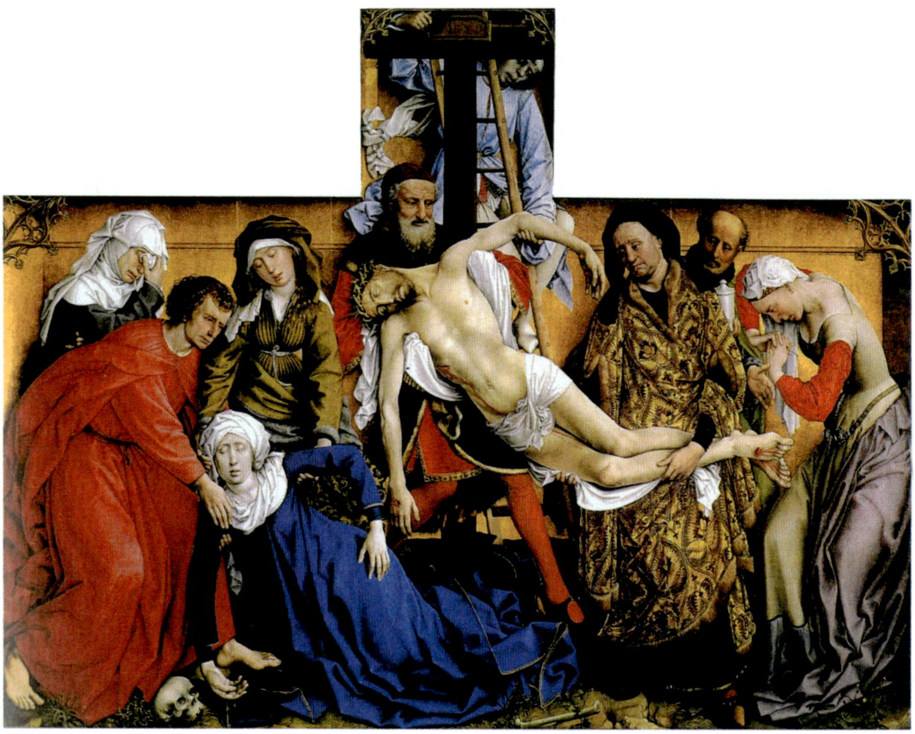

Fig. 2: Rogier van der Weyden, Descent from the Cross, 1435/40.

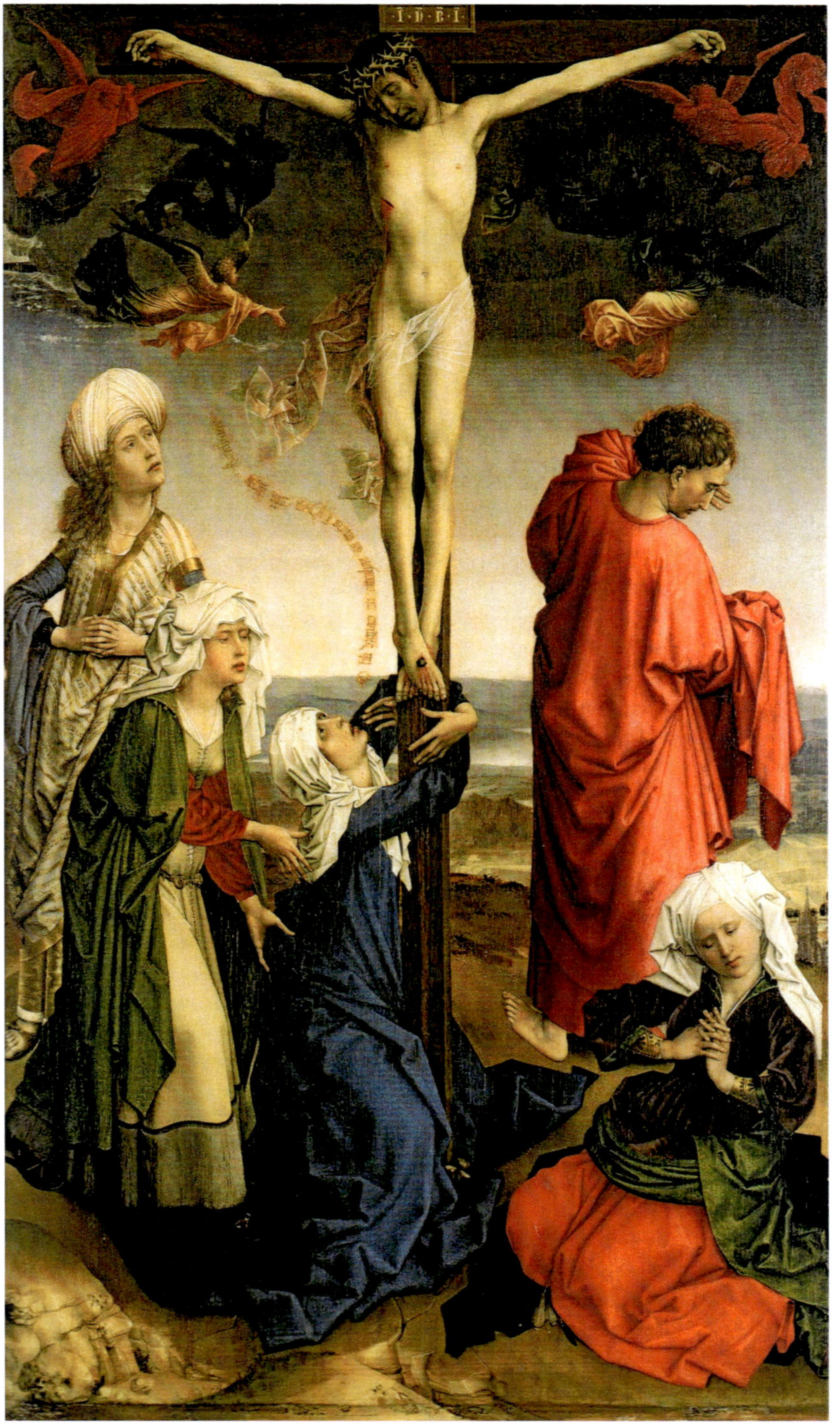

Fig. 3: Rogier van der Weyden (Workshop), Crucifixion, ca. 1430.

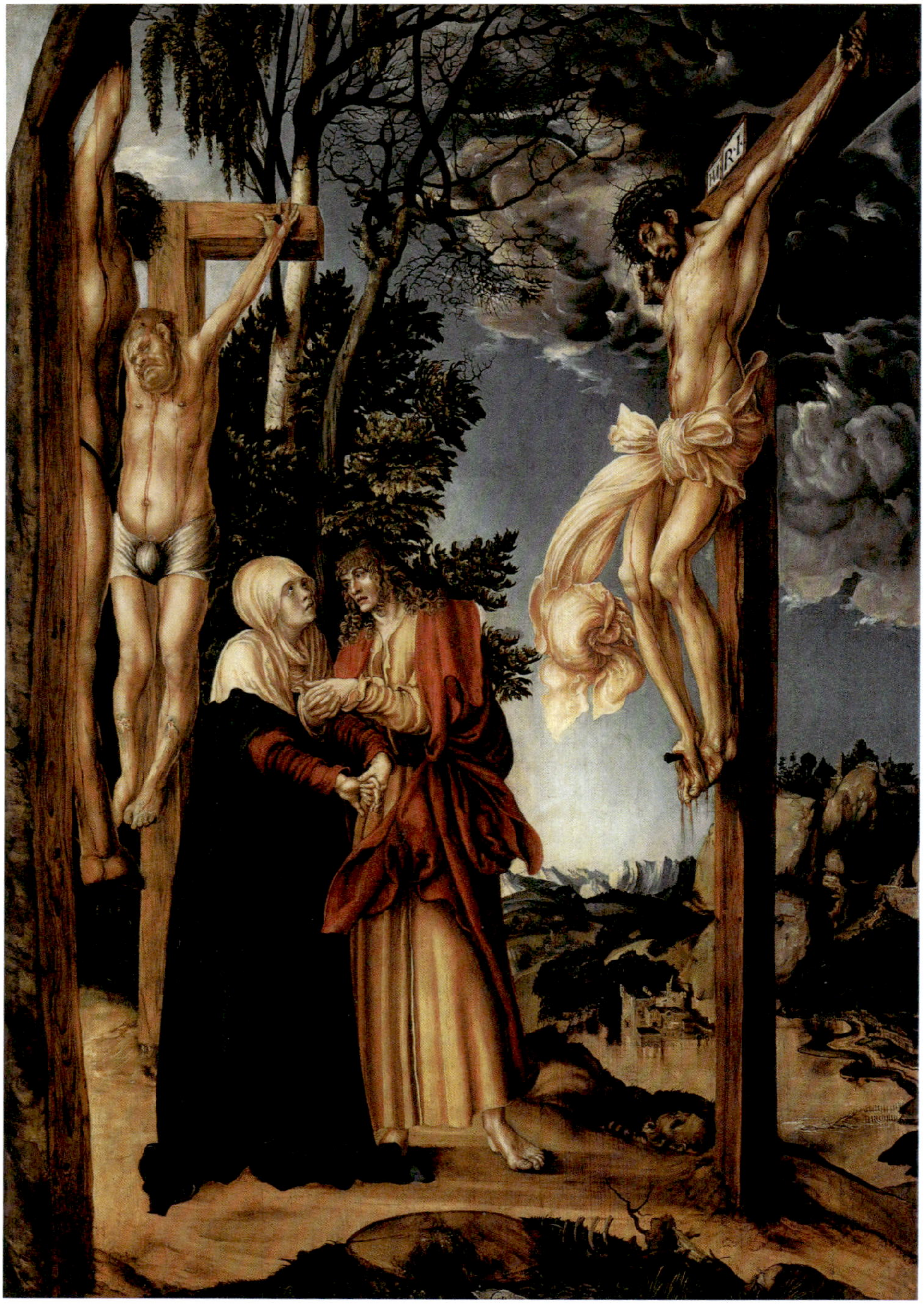

Fig. 4: Lucas Cranach the Elder, Crucifixion, 1503.

The same may be said for the *Crucifixion* by the workshop of Rogier van der Weyden in Berlin (fig. 3), in which all composition formulae of grief and mourning imaginable are called up in the sense of a rhetorically understood truth. In both paintings the pictorial space itself is not made fertile for the *compassio* motif and the *compassio* plea. On the contrary: in Rogier's *Descent of the Cross*, the life-size figures do not appear in a painted landscape but rather in a carved wooden shrine, resembling carved altarpieces. This is not only a theoretical reflection on the differentiation of mediation through painting and sculpture, but also evidence that painting can represent and seminally interlace everything, including the imitation of other media.[4] In my opinion, the entire picture does not only serve the purpose of transferring the *compassio* onto the observer but also as an explicit (even theoretical) demonstration of how the relationship between the movements of the body and the affections is represented in painting.

It is different with certain representations of the *Crucifixion* dated around 1500. In a very surprising way, these resemble the imaginary pictures of the *Stabat Mater* motif described above. Lucas Cranach's *Crucifixion of Schleißheim* (fig. 4), dated 1503, virtually sets up the invention of an emotionally laden pictorial space in which Christ himself moves to the periphery and relinquishes the center of the picture to the most important figures of the *compassio*, Mary and John. It is also a visual incitement in order to think about the question from which angles and perspectives Christ is 'seen' by the believer, which turned out to be one of the religious consequences of the invention of linear perspective with a central vanishing point.[5] In fact, Cranach unites two types of crucifixion scenes here: firstly, those of Cavalry, heavily populated with figures, including both thieves but also depicting the grieving women, along with henchmen who carry out the execution, and secondly, those with only John and Mary. He needs the thieves to create an inner space that is separated from the rest of the pictorial content and rhythmically arranged by the landscape setting. Cranach distributed the crosses in such a way that they spatially form a regular triangle, with the thieves creating a figurative unity in the planimeter of the picture surface on the left, while Christ towers over the distant landscape in three-quarter view to the right. The thief at the left picture margin is to some extent the counterpart to Christ: in his lost profile we see exactly that which we cannot see in the figure of Christ. The second thief, shown frontally, adapts perfectly to his contours. Mary and John are thus placed in the center, creating a comparably dense, planimetric figuration both in regard to pictorial composition and to semantic unity. As they are standing between the three crosses, they also form a closed group of figures. Mary, who is looking up to Christ, twists her hands not into a gesture of prayer but into a gesture of pain.[6] John, in turn, faces Mary and has brought his

4 See Schlie: *Bilder des Corpus Christi*, pp. 324ff.

5 See Vaisse: "A Propos de la Crucifixion", esp. p. 119.

6 An imitation of the gesture causes a disagreable feeling, even pain.

hands together in a gesture of prayer or grief; at the same time, his arms are intertwined with hers. This motif of a multiple, gestural knot corresponds to the pathos formula of Christ's billowing loincloth, whose fluttering pieces of fabric are similarly intertwined like the arms of the Compassion figures. The Passion's entire pathos, physically simulated by the crossed arms, is thus also concentrated in the loincloth's knot that is prominently set against the sky and against the long-distance landscape, while Christ hangs quietly on the cross, only his deformed feet emblemizing his suffering. Considering the relationship of the painted movements of the body and the affectations of the soul in his treatise *De Pictura* (1435), Leon Battista Alberti (1404–1472) also mentions the movements of the inanimate objects at the end of the respective passage of the text (which will be mentioned later in this study). These objects are the "Beiwerk" in a Warburgian sense, as hairs, branches, foliage and draperies. However, he argues against expressive and strong movements of the draperies, as they are caused by the wind, for example.[7] It is exactly this expressivity refuted by Alberti that is chosen and in a way valorized in terms of an art theoretical statement by Cranach, following the tradition of earlier German Masters. As in opposition to Alberti the "Beiwerk" follows merely the rules of the emotional *habitat*.

Mary leads the observer's gaze to Christ, while John inwardly corresponds to her exemplum; this means he has already received Christ's pain through the mirror of her compassion. While Mary is directly related to Christ, John has coalesced with her suffering through his act of prayer. We have a double-staged exemplum here. When the observer follows the exemplum of John, he is placed with the co-redeemer Mary at the foot of the cross and can ensure his participation in the Passion. The observer arrives at the cross only through the reflection of emotion, only through the process of similarity. The missing nimbus of the Saints is also owed to the spatiality of emotion.[8] But it is not just the posture, expression and gesture of the two pictorial *compassio* figures which are to be mimetically transferred to the body of the observer. The movement of the vegetation (as a pathos formula, as it were) takes part in the emotional *habitus* surrounding Christ. The movement of the trees, their slant towards the figure of Christ and the link to the dark clouds above their tops are all destined to be transferred to the observer as emotion, because no pictorial element here is contingent. [9] The emotion is understood spatially in two respects; firstly, by the sepa-

7 "Sed in hac venti pulsione illud caveatur ne ullei pannorum motus contra ventum surgant, neve nimium refracti, neve nimium porrecti sint." Leon Battista Alberti: *Das Standbild*, pp. 278–280 – "In this blowing of the wind the painter should pay attention that the drapery does not surge up against the wind and that it is not too buckled nor stretched too far." (Transl. H.S.).

8 Heiser: *Das Frühwerk Lucas Cranachs des Älteren*, p. 101; she speaks of a "great immediacy" and a "modern style" in comparison to Dürer's panel reredos of the Seven Sorrows in Dresden.

9 According to Heiser, the branches of the dead trees resemble the crown of thorns and emblemize the "pain that even encompasses nature". See Heiser: *Das Frühwerk Lucas Cranachs des Älteren*, p. 102. See also Behling: *Die Pflanze in der mittelalterlichen Tafelmalerei*, p. 119.

rated space between the crosses that is formed by the acting out of the *compassio*, and secondly, through the emotional feeling of the entire image space. With the *Stabat Mater*, one ended up at the foot of the cross by the offering of prayer in individual steps; with the picture serving as container of emotion, its content is transferred to the body of the observer as a vessel or bearer of internal and external *compassio*. This is clearly depicted with the skull of Adam, which is not actually a skull here. A monochrome painted head lies at the bottom of the cross, its eyes directed upwards. The ear can be recognized especially well, and the head is still attached to the spinal column which comes out of a hole in the muddy ground. The corrupt body of the one in need of redemption and in whom the Passion should be gathered is joined with the materiality of the picture itself. The painting with its colors and pigments which are gained from mineral substances similar to the 'mud' turns out to be the explicit bearer of the Passion and a container of emotion, and the body of the observer is also to become a vessel of the Passion transferred to it. In the so-called Lamentation of the Magdalena by Mathias Grünewald which has only survived as a copy,[10] Christ's cross is situated at the picture's margin in such a way so that we can see neither his face nor the wound in his side. In contrast to the beholder of the painting, Mary Magdalene, whose face is distorted with pain, sees the front of Christ's body and his face. She is the medium of Christ's Passion by mirroring his suffering through her *compassio*,[11] which is to be transferred from her to the observer of the picture. In this respect, her lamenting figure is also a metaphor for all the pictures which successfully achieve this.

How was this cultural method of emotional transference thought to be working; how – in the view of the contemporaries of the discussed paintings – does the body become a bearer of the Passion? In the 15th century, production of the textual, now vernacular *Lamentation of Mary* soared. It was spoken or sung by the faithful and personified for a single moment simply by this act. "It is always a body, a voice, which again lends form to the writing. Each reader was at the same time a listener to his own voice and experienced as such his body as an annexed medium."[12] The reader performed the emotions formulated within the text by using the modulation and intonation of his voice and his body as a medium of resonance. In addition, *The Lamentation of Mary* was part of the various pivotal, spiritual plays that were performed with increasingly complex created settings and stage directions, whereby a church or an entire city could become a resonating space of emotion. The main figures were especially Mary and John, sometimes Mary Magdalene, although these Lamentations usually had very large casts. Research based on an iconographical approach has already used the texts

10 See Lüdke: "Die 'Donaueschinger Magdalenenklage'".

11 Bushart: *Sehen und Erkennen*, p. 150.

12 "Stets ist es ein Körper, eine Stimme, die der Schrift wieder eine Gestalt verleiht. Jeder Leser war somit zugleich auch ein Hörer der eigenen Stimme und erfuhr somit seinen Körper als Aneignungsmedium", Elsner/Gumbrecht/Müller et al.: "Zur Kulturgeschichte der Medien", p. 171.

of the Lamentation of Mary as an explanation for the emergence of the excentric crucifixion. As so often, a primacy of the text is asserted: Kuhn, for example, assumed that the reception of Planctus texts – not the performances – led artists to change the composition.[13]

However, the pictures did not simply borrow a pattern or an iconography from the textual Lamentation of Mary,[14] but instead turned the body into an annexed medium by another method of transference. The emotionally laden pictorial composition entered the body through the eye, and it was thought to do so well in accord with contemporary physiological theory. Visual theory then held that elements perceived through the eye were internally embodied. With the asserted intromissions theory, it was assumed that the species, the likenesses or similitudes of the perceived agents (substance, matter, form, bodies) entered the body through the eye and impressed themselves into the soul like a seal onto wax.[15] Accordingly, the emotional figuration as perceived in the pictorial composition was also enacted within the body of the perceiver even without his or her voluntary performance. Just seeing an emotionally moved figure would equal the embodiment of the emotion. Roger Bacon (1214–1292/94), for instance, was convinced that all worldly entities emitted their own species' properties, which left behind material traces within the body of the perceiver.[16] Suzannah Biernoff, who studied medieval and early modern forms of the Imitatio Christi in regard to their relation with medieval theories of seeing and emotion, correctly notes that "affected" or "moved" originally just meant "perceived" in its Aristotelian sense: perception resulted in bodily change. "The medieval phenomenon of imitatio Christi shares a number of basic principles with Bacon's optics, most importantly the conviction that sight entails a physical transformation of the spectator. […] seeing was not only believing, but being assimilated with Christ's flesh and

13 Kuhn: *Cranachs Christus am Kreuz als Marienklage*, pp. 12–15.

14 Heiser refuted Kuhn and Schawe's description of Cranach's crucifixion as a "Lamentation of Mary", as she wanted to emphasize the autonomy of the inventio. See Heiser: *Das Frühwerk Lucas Cranachs des Älteren*, p. 108, note 29. Ascribing the shift of the cross to the periphery as a reaction to the situational description in the written version of the Lamentation of Mary would be to take a reductionist view of the picture. This approach would proceed from a "before" element of the writing that is only imitated by the picture. I would like to reconcile these two approaches to the effect that the picture should be understood as exemplary of the Lamentation of Mary; however, not as a transcription of the literary into a picture but rather as an alternative medium for a similar cultural model. I proceed from a standpoint of concurrency; this does not affect the artistic inventio, even when it is made seminal for the cultural technique already mentioned.

15 This goes back to Aristotle: *De Anima II*, 12,1.

16 See Lindberg: *Roger Bacon's Philosophie of Nature*, XV. See also Lindberg: *Roger Bacon and the Origins of Perspectiva in the Middle Ages*, p. LXVIII. See Biernoff: "Carnal Relations", here p. 42. Biernoff investigates the relationship between a "medieval theory of embodied vision" and the concept of Merleau-Ponty's "embodied vision" in his unfinished work "The Visible and the Invisible".

blood through a visual interaction."[17] Thus, the emotion of the perceived composition was firmly established in the body, without the observer having to do anything more than "beholding". The perception of an emotional figure had become a physical performance. In this respect, it is necessary to point out that the cultural practices of piety closely resembled contemporary scientific theory – a relation well noted already by Biernoff.

In the first half of the 15th century, written art theory turns the mediation of emotions into another scholarly subject. And it is not an accident that these reflect theories of seeing, Leon Battista Alberti, who developed the conception of the linear perspective with a central vanishing point on the basis of medieval theories of optics, also elaborated conceptual approaches to the transfer of emotions within pictorial compositions, approaches, moreover, that related the emotions and the movements of bodies intrapictorially.[18] Of course, he does not explicitly account for a theory of embodiment in a scientific manner, like a theory of the bodily impression of perceived emotion, but I am still convinced that he at least refers to some such theory and does not merely index quasi-cognitive, rhetorical concepts. Beyond the nagging questions about linear perspective, it remains a scholarly desideratum to reintegrate medieval theories of seeing into the research on medieval and early modern media, pictorial theory and history of emotions. It simply is no accident that Alberti dealt with both perspective and the transfer of emotions simultaneously, even though both aspects were covered in two different chapters of De Pictura. However, both reflect theories of seeing, of perception and of psychology that reach back to antiquity.

Approaches to an art theory that take visual theory into consideration (beyond the aspects of linear perspective with a central vanishing point) have already been developed. The idea to not only make use of the figures, their gestures and expression but also of the entire picture composition and of the image space for the visual transference of exemplary emotion means a quantum leap in painting that has consequences right up into the Baroque. Baroque image space is often compared with the theater and the tertium comparationis is, of course, the emotional resonance. This experienced a sharp acceleration around 1500 in the pictorial inventions already mentioned. The pictorial strategy encouraging prayer and devotion goes hand in hand with the artistic inventio and – if one considers

17 Biernoff: "Carnal Relations" p. 42. See above.

18 On the relationship between the affects and the movements of the body in a picture see Alberti: *Die Malkunst*, pp. 272/274. "Sunt namque motus alii animorum, quos docti affectiones nuncupant, ut ira, dolor, gaudium, timor, desiderium et eiusmodi. Sunt et alii corporum [...] Nos autem pictores, qui motibus membrorum volumus animos affectos exprimere, [...] de tantum eo motu referamus, quem tum factum dicunt, cum locus mutatus sit." – "In fact there exist movements of the soul on the one hand which are called 'affectiones' by the learned, as rage, grief, joy, fear, desire and so on; on the other hand there are the movements of the body. [...] As painters, who are involved with the expression of the affected souls through the movements of the limbs [...] we are concerned with the specific movement that is executed when the position has been changed." (Transl. H.S.)

the abundance of relevant examples – deals with mutual outdoing or surpassing, aemulatio. The motif of the cross placed at the picture margin is not an invention of Cranach's. In my opinion, however, he was the one who most consequently developed the link between image space as fully emotionally laden, as emotional resonance, and the inner being of the observer as a spiritual 'receptacle'. His idea began perhaps with a picture such as the St. Jerome in Penitence of 1502 (fig. 5), in which the Church Father does not clearly focus on the image of a crucifix but rather on a living representation of the same.[19] The use of light especially shifts the small crucifix deep into the background at an attempt to suggest life-size representation. The representation of the landscape leaves room for several points of view because the cross cannot clearly be located within the logic of spatial image. The crucifix represents Christ himself, his image, or Jerome's inner emotion. The whole painting resonates Jerome's gesture who is about to hurt himself with the stone in his hand, as a pathos of penitence. This picture shows without a doubt that the focus is on the emotion directed at Christ and that the landscape also plays a very important role.

The notion of the "holy space" and the 'topography of the sacred' (sakrale Topographie) within the research field of emotion is a highly complex topic because the image space is, of course, linked with actual space; for example with liturgical space but also with the sacred space of the holy sites, e.g. Jerusalem. Little has been investigated as to, for example, the correlation of the mental mapping of spiritual pilgrimage and the inner emotional comprehension of the Passion. The spiritual pilgrimage, meaning the mental exploration of holy sites, and the imitation of Christ through emotion, are two central culture methods that can only insufficiently be described by the term "imagination". Emotion and space have an alternately generative relationship. In the spiritual play it is the emotion of the participants which turns the church or city into Holy Jerusalem; it is the emotion which places the observer of Cranach's Crucifixion on Calvary, etc.

What type of relationship do the depicted emotions have to the performed rituals or to the "actual" (and basically and historically impalpable) expressions of feeling? In historical research, for example, it is assumed that the form of mourning and grief (which I understand as forms of ritual or paraliturgical *compassio*) shown in the pictures changes with the new codes of mourning found within a society.[20] In late 15th century Italy, certain erudite humanist groups propagated a reserved, disciplined mourning to replace an older form of lamentation which involved very loud and extreme expressions of emotion. In this context, the discussion would be of whether the pictures depicted existing practices and/or if they participated in the authoritative example of codification. Basically, the question is at which levels the *compassio* and the rituals of grief in the context of ordinary deaths can be aligned.

19 See Heiser: *Das Frühwerk Lucas Cranachs des Älteren*, p. 77.
20 Jussen: "Dolor und Memoria", here esp. 230ff.

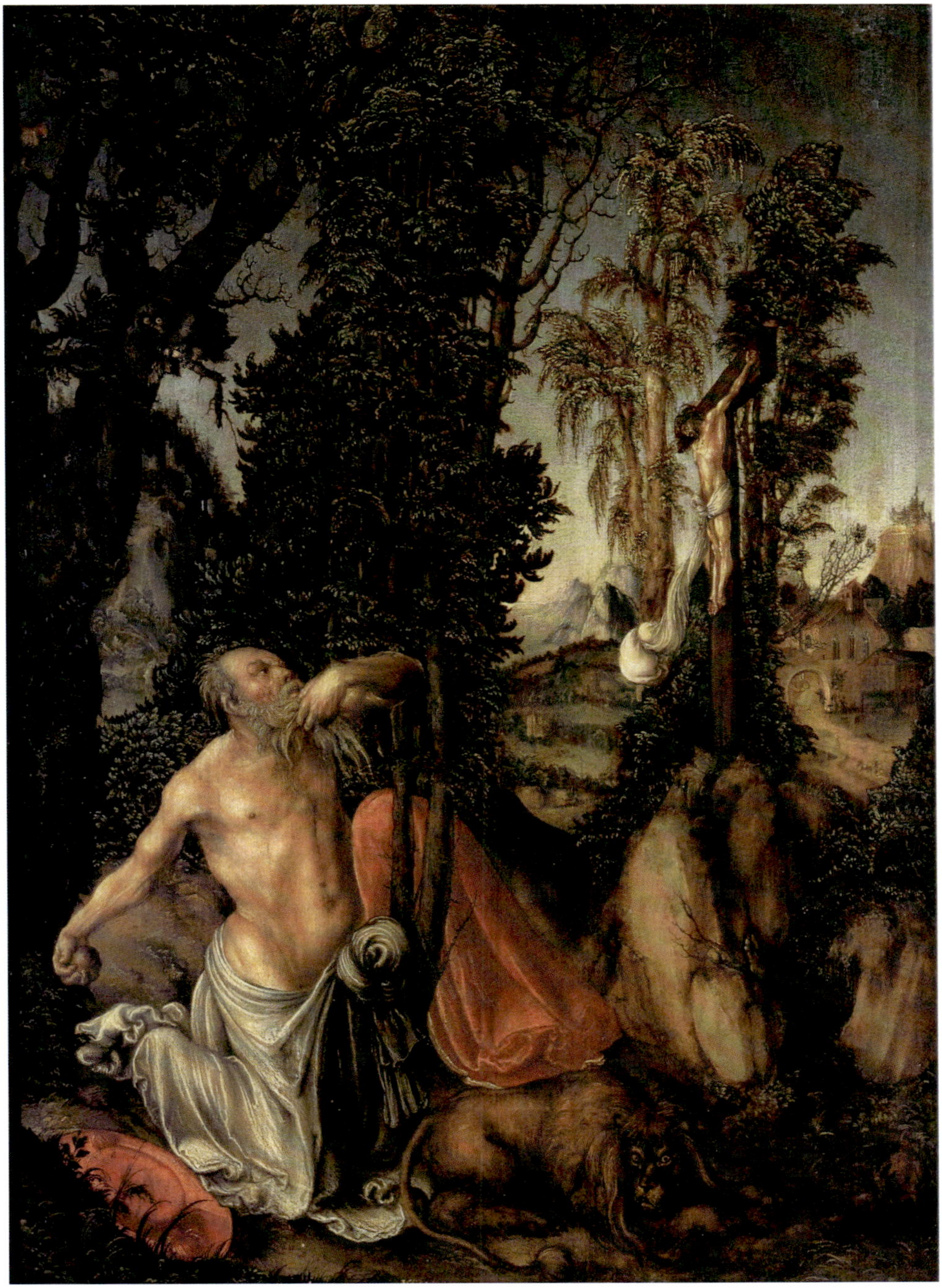

Fig. 5: Lucas Cranach the Elder, St. Jerome, 1502.

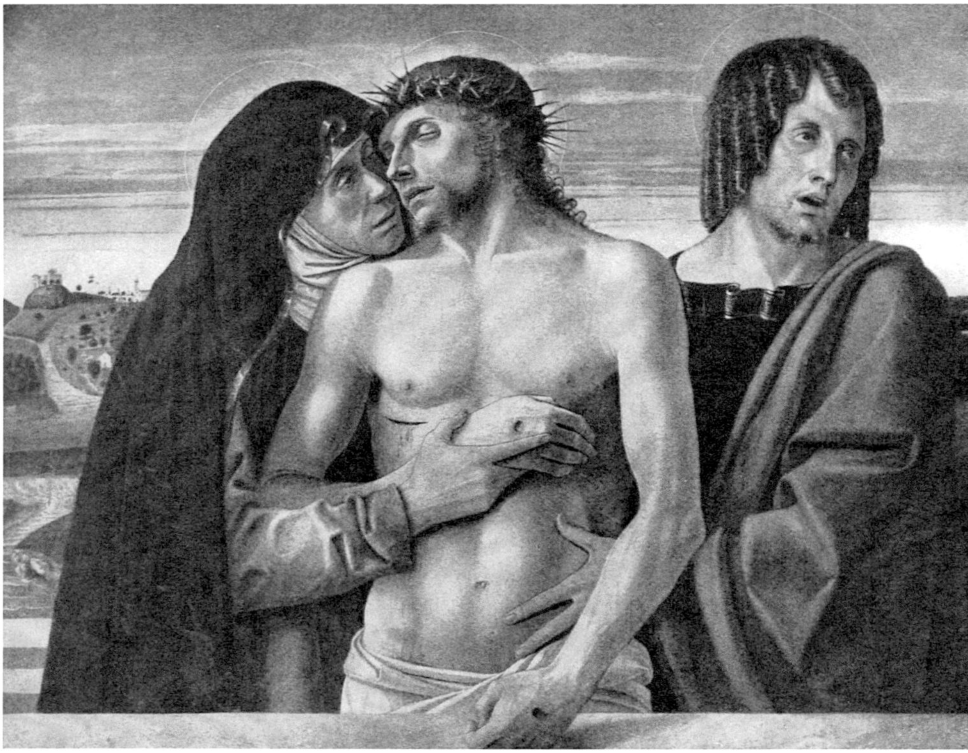

Fig. 6: Giovanni Bellini, Lamentation/Pietà, 1470.

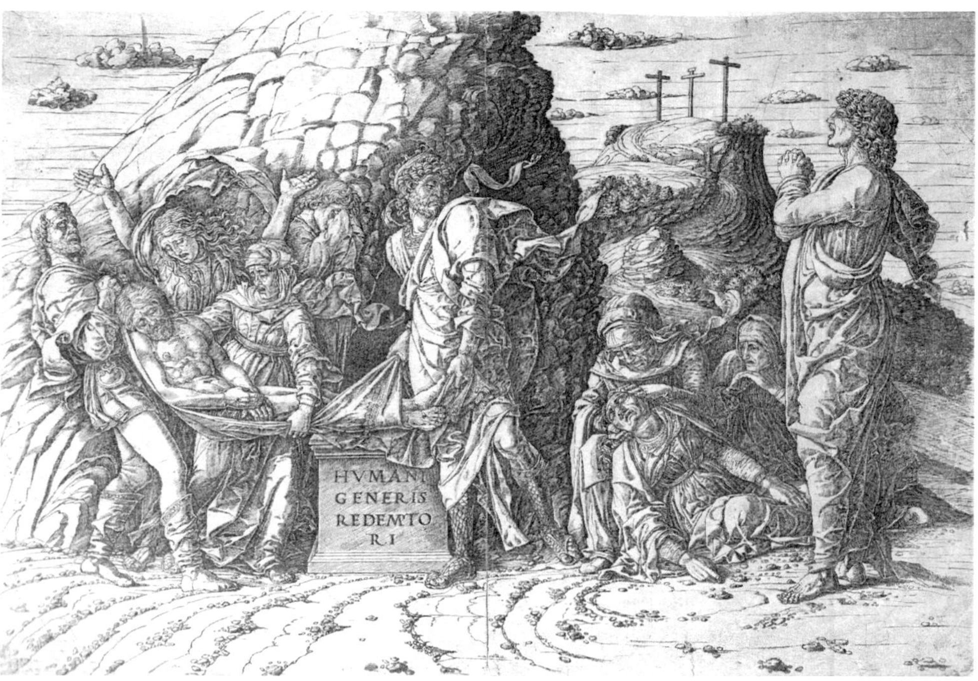

Fig 7: Andrea Mantegna, Lamentation, 1470–75.

The space of mourning for decedents is not the same performative space as that of the *compassio*.[21] This can only be aligned when the death of the deceased qualifies as an imitation of Christ's Passion, which essentially means the death of a martyr. This does not mean that sharing Christ's passion on the one hand and grief on the other have nothing to do with each other – pictures such as Rogier's Crucifixion (fig. 3) presumably also reveals aspects of actual, ordinary, mourning ritual – but the differentiated depicted modes of mourning on Christ's death most certainly had a function other than the coding of everyday grieving habits for decedents.

Hans Belting understood the difference between two Lamentation pictures by Bellini (fig. 6) and by Mantegna (fig. 7) as an art theoretical positioning of the artists: Mantegna made an artistic declaration for principles of representation relating to the emotional gestures and body formulas as depicted in the antique sarcophagi (fig. 7). In contrast, Bellini searched for a modern way to atmospherically unite the icon and the picture's narrative in the medium of painting (fig. 6).[22] The Cartellino with the Signature of Giovanni Bellini, inserted in his Pietà in Milan, says: "As soon as the swollen eyes burst into tears, the opus by Giovanni Bellini was able to cry."[23] The crying painting is not to be understood like a weeping cult image, but it weeps as a consequence of Bellini's art: he makes the painting cry, which makes the observer cry. The whole image, consisting of the three figures of Christ, Mary and John, is thought to make the observer suffer with the configuration of passion. The painting becomes a subject which is understood as having emotions, and as a subject it transfers the affect to the beholder. But in contrast to Cranach's crucifixion Bellini does not make use of the pictorial space for the emotional contagion; in his painting the affect is still bound to the bodies of the depicted persons.

Bernhard Jussen employed the comparison between the same two pictures in relation to Belting in order to demonstrate the concurrence of the loud sounds of mourning and those of the quiet and to trace the pictures back to the differences in the funeral rituals of mourning.[24] Basically, however, these pictures have to do with the theories and perceptions of emotion transference through the picture itself. With Mantegna, it is visually said that this works by the internal or external imitation of the single *compassio* figure – as cited pathos formulae borrowed from the sarcophagi imagery. With Bellini, it is less the individual pathos formulae and more the undertone of the painting's entire figuration that is destined to find its way directly into the observer's inner being. The goal may be the same but the theories of emotion transference are somewhat different. One theory assumes the transfer of emotion by physical mimesis from a particular body in the

21 See Küsters: *Maria Magdalena und die Legitimität der Trauer*, pp. 175–215.

22 Belting: *Giovanni Bellini, Pietà: Ikone und Bilderzählung in der venezianischen Malerei.*

23 "HAEC FERE QUUM [CUM] GEMITUS TURGENTIA LUMINA PROMANT/ BELLINI POTERAT FLERE JOANNIS OPUS". See Belting: *Bellini*, p. 35 (Transl. H. S.).

24 See Jussen: "Dolor und Memoria", (cf. Note 20).

painting to a single body in front of the painting, which means experiencing feelings directly through the depicted body's movement, and the second is a theory of an imagination of the whole picture as such within the soul. These two theories, which are basically also different notions in image theory, result in two diverse medial paths of the *compassio*. As far as the difference of mediality and an art theoretical background is concerned, I absolutely agree with Belting, but would like to stress the inseparable link between the art theoretical position of the artist and the religious function of the pictures.

But all this has nothing to do with replacing ordinary rituals with others. Funeral ritual is concerned with social communication, whereas with the *compassio* it is not necessarily a ritual of show in order to create a sense of community, but rather one of singular feeling and redemption for the individual.

While the above-mentioned problematic of coding pertains to ritual and its social and religious functions, my interest is directed toward the respective historical theories on emotion transference through the media. Information on the character, physiological conditions and techniques of this transference is offered by the paintings themselves, by medieval texts on the Imitation of Christ and by written art theory. In "De Pictura" of 1435 Alberti states that we cry with those who cry and laugh with those who laugh.[25] The art historian David Freedberg, author of "The Power of Images. Studies in the History and Theory of Response" which was published in 1989 and became a very relevant book for the moving power of images in the history of art, also refers to these texts. Freedberg spent several years intensively studying the neuroscientific discovery of mirror neurons and their meaning for emotion research related to painting. During a recent lecture in Berlin in 2009, Freedberg showed, among other things, Rogier's *Descent of the Cross* (fig. 2) and offered the hypothesis that these pictures exist because the observer, by the means of his mirror neurons, performs an imitation of Mary. Freedberg assumes a directly neuronal, non-cognitive reaction of the observer to the emotions embodied in the picture, whereby he would not exclude a culturally coded method of emotion transference. However, he assumes that a work of art primarily functions on the basis of a neurophysiological disposition.[26] That may be: perhaps we can only be affected by material images and depicted emotions for the reason that we have mirror neurons. However, this does not explain the cultural need for being affected or the various historical methods of pictorial strategies; it does not really explain why the images look as they actually look.

25 "Animos deinde spectantium movebit historia, cum qui aderunt picti homines suum animi motum maxime prae se ferent. Fit namque natura, qua nihil sui similium rapacius inveniri potest, ut lugentibus conlugeamus, ridentibus adrideamus, dolentibus condoleamus. Sed hi motus animi ex motibus corporis cognoscuntur." Alberti: *Malkunst*, p. 268: 'Furthermore, a 'historia' will move the souls of the beholders if the painted men show their affections very clearly. Nature who absorbs all which is similar to hers will achieve that we grieve with the grieving, that we laugh with the laughing and suffer with the suffering.' (Transl. H. S.)

26 See also Freedberg / Gallese: "Motion, Emotion, and Empathy in Esthetic Experience".

Let me give a very simple comparison: A hammer is an appropriate tool and can work because we have hands. This physiological or anatomical disposition does not explain exactly *how* a hammer as such works, what kind of different variations there are, exactly how the movement in the sense of its function and meaning must be carried out, etc. The physiological basic condition cannot explain the technical aspects, least of all their variations, such as those of the hammer head and the weight of its different parts. The pictures of emotion transference function on the basis of complex, cultural relations; they are positioned within a tradition familiar to the observer. They deal with knowledge and remembrance, with difference and similarity within the media themselves. However, the reception of natural scientific research on emotions and the physiological conditions of the brain can be quite insightful for the disciplines of the Humanities. The research on emotions in Neurophysiology provided general models for a reclamation of "feel" categories within a rational discourse of the Humanities at a time when emotions had been simply excluded as a subject from the respective disciplines. Furthermore, Freedberg as well as a number of other scholars in cultural studies who have researched physiological and neurophysiological models of emotional transfer have (voluntarily or involuntarily) reminded culture historical scholarship that the medieval and early modern periods had their own specific theories about the physiology of emotional transfer[27] and that they were an integral component of pictorial culture. These theories were decisive in choices concerning what kinds of picture were produced, what they had to look like, and how they had to be perceived.

Complementary to these findings, culture historical research has also sensitized us to the fact that even current neurophysiological models and pictures are also subject to – or at least interact with – cultural frames of attention, needs and codes. So there is an increasing demand for critical intervention by cultural studies within the field of emotion research – not only to "balance" the current methods of absorbing neurobiological concepts into the various disciplines of cultural study.

27 See Heinen: "Emotionales Bild-Erleben in der Frühen Neuzeit."

References

Alberti, Leon Battista: *Das Standbild, Die Malkunst, Grundlagen der Malerei*, ed. by Oskar Bätschmann, Darmstadt (Wissenschaftliche Buchgesellschaft) 2000.

Aquinas, Thomas: *Summa Theologica,* English: *The Summa Theologica of St. Thomas Aquinas,* Second and Revised Edition, translated by Fathers of the English Dominican Province, London (Burns Oates and Washbourne) 1920.

Aristotle: *De Anima*, in: Jonathan Barnes (ed.): *The Complete Works of Aristotle*, 2 vols., Princeton (Princeton University Press), 1984, 402a.

Behling, Lottlisa: *Die Pflanze in der mittelalterlichen Tafelmalerei*, Weimar (Böhlau) 1957.

Belting, Hans: *Giovanni Bellini: Pietà. Ikone und Bilderzählung in der venezianischen Malerei*, Frankfurt am Main (Fischer) 1988

Biernoff, Suzannah: "Carnal Relations. Embodied Sight in Merleau-Ponty, Roger Bacon and St. Francis", in: *Journal of Visual Culture* 4 (2005), pp. 39–52.

Bushart, Magdalena: *Sehen und Erkennen. Albrecht Altdorfers religiöse Bilder* (*Kunstwissenschaftliche Studien 117*), Munich/Berlin (Deutscher Kunstverlag) 2004.

Büttner, Frank O.: *Imitatio Pietatis. Motive der christlichen Ikonographie als Modelle der Verähnlichung*, Berlin (Mann) 1983.

Dietmar Lüdke, "Die 'Donaueschinger Magdalenenklage' der Sammlung Würth in Schwäbisch Hall" in: *Ausstellungskatalog Grünewald und seine Zeit*, Staatliche Kunsthalle Karlsruhe 2007/08, Munich/Berlin (Deutscher Kunstverlag) 2007, pp. 331–349.

Elsner, Monika / Hans Ulrich Gumbrecht / Thomas Müller, et al.: "Zur Kulturgeschichte der Medien", in: Klaus Merten / Siegfried J. Schmidt / Siegfried Weischenberg: *Die Wirklichkeit der Medien. Eine Einführung in die Kommunikationswissenschaft*, Opladen (Westdeutscher Verlag) 1994, pp. 163–187.

Freedberg, David / Vittorio Gallese: "Motion, Emotion, and Empathy in Esthetic Experience", in: *Trends in Cognitive Sciences* 11 (2007) 5, pp. 197–203.

Heinen, Ulrich: "Emotionales Bild-Erleben in der Frühen Neuzeit", in: Rüdiger Zynmer and Manfred Engel (eds.): *Anthropologie der Literatur. Poetogene Strukturen und ästhetisch-soziale Handlungsfelder*, Paderborn (mentis) 2004, pp. 356–383.

Heiser, Sabine: *Das Frühwerk Lucas Cranachs des Älteren. Wien um 1500 – Dresden um 1900*, Berlin (Deutscher Verlag für Kunstwissenschaft) 2002.

Jussen, Bernhard: "Dolor und Memoria. Trauerriten, gemalte Trauer und soziale Ordnungen im späten Mittelalter", in: Otto G. Oexle (ed.): *Memoria als Kultur*, Göttingen (Veröffentlichungen des Max-Planck-Instituts für Geschichte) 1995, pp. 207–252.

Kuhn, Rudolf: "Cranachs Christus am Kreuz als Marienklage", in: *Alte und Moderne Kunst* 123 (1972), pp. 12–15.

Küsters, Urban, "Maria Magdalena und die Legitimität der Trauer. Zu den mittelhochdeutschen Magdalenenklagen", in: Claudia Brinker et al. (eds.): *Contemplata aliis tradere. Studien zum Verhältnis von Literatur und Spiritualität*, Bern et al. (Peter Lang) 1995, pp. 175–215.

Lindberg, David C.: *Roger Bacon's Philosophy of Nature. A Critical Edition of De multiplicatione specierum and De speculis comburentibus*, Oxford (Clarendon) 1983.

Lindberg, David C.: *Roger Bacon and the Origins of Perspectiva in the Middle Ages. A Critical Edition and English Translation of Bacon's Perspectiva with Introduction and Notes*, Oxford (Oxford University Press) 1996.

Merleau-Ponty, Maurice: *The Visible and the Invisible*, Evanston, IL (Northwestern University Press), 1968.

Schlie, Heike: *Bilder des Corpus Christi. Sakramentaler Realismus von Jan van Eyck bis Rogier van der Weyden*, Berlin (Mann) 2002.

Simson, Otto von: "Compassio und Co-redemptio in Rogier von der Weyden's Descent from the Cross", in *The Art Bulletin* 35 (1953), 9–16.

Vaisse, Pierre: "A Propos de la Crucifixion vue de biais", in: Jean Richer (ed.): *La Gloire de Dürer*, Paris 1974, pp. 117–129.

Weigel, Sigrid: "Pietà und Mater Dolorosa – Trauer, (Selbst-)Mitleid und die Universalisierung der Opfer", in: Sigrid Weigel, *Märtyrer-Porträts. Von Opfertod, Blutzeugen und Heiligen Kriegern*, München (Fink) 2007, pp. 169–172.

List of figures

Through Stained Glass
Abstraction and Embodiment in Early Twentieth Century Avant-Garde Circles

BARBARA LARSON

The history of modern art in the twentieth century has given a privileged place to abstraction as the most radically innovative direction in the second decade of that century. Mondrian, Kupka, Delaunay, and Kandinsky – all of different nationalities – have been hailed as those breakthrough radical experimenters who painted the first non-representational paintings in the west at virtually the same moment, around 1912. Even today their canonization as initiators of abstraction positions them as so innovative in their outlook that their colorful works – tending towards the primaries – are primarily discussed against a backdrop of treatises in optical theory or occult interests popular around 1900, especially theosophy. Without denying those interpretive strategies, this essay positions these artists within a social and cultural milieu in which a number of their earliest abstractions had deep historical resonance, both for themselves and their viewers – namely churches and cathedrals, with their luminous, brightly colored stained glass windows. It offers suggestions regarding the relevance of familiar ritual spaces in terms of memory and community at a time when the church – Catholic and otherwise – was under increased pressure from growing secularity, and it connects early abstraction to the emerging field of sociology and to the recent field of the cognitive science of religion.

In Paris in 1912, where Delaunay, Mondrian, and Kupka were each in early but crucial transitional stages of their careers, Emile Durkheim published his central text *Les formes élémentaires de la vie religieuse*. At that time, he had been chair of education at the Sorbonne for ten years, a position which was now renamed chair of education and society. This early French sociologist had made religion a central concern of his scholarship in explicating a theory addressing a general breakdown of the western social fabric in the face of capitalism. According to Durkheim, social groups uphold unity through powerful shared emotions in group rituals and ceremonies. This occurs within a sacred sphere – utterly separate from the profane space and making use of sacred representations or objects, which express collective realities. And all religions, including Christianity, derive from the same basic mental functions and needs. Even time and space are in essence social and, therefore, at base religious. Time is based in the rhythms of society deriving from rites, festivals and so on, and spatial orientation and categories such as the weighted meaning of east or west are communally recognized as part of social organization. However, modern society in its recent secular phase – increasingly distanced from traditional rituals and symbols – was losing its social memory. Durkheim's work is foundational to the cognitive science of religion, secularization theory, and the sociology of religion.[1]

In the same year in Germany, where Kandinsky was living, Ferdinand Tönnies, Germany's first sociologist, reissued his well known *Gemeinschaft und Gesellschaft*, first published in 1887. Like Durkheim, he was concerned with societal breakdown in the face of the industrial present and the changing shape of time for those severed from *Gemeinschaft* or community. Community in Tönnies' terms was an organic, natural coming together of individuals who gained emotional sustenance from a communal sense of place, reverence for tradition, shared religious beliefs, and common rituals, with the individual being subordinate to the collective. The importance of communal sacred space to the integrity of human life was topical in these years.

In Paris in 1912, a number of canvases of Gothic cathedrals were exhibited by the most groundbreaking of modern artists, including Gleizes and Pierre Dumont. Gleizes's *Chartres Cathedral* (Sprengel Museum, Hanover) made the rose window a prominent feature, though it exhibits the neutral palette of Picasso or Braque. Both Gleizes and Dumont upheld the Gothic cathedral as a communally valid and even crucial subject. Robert Delaunay, an enthusiast of Gothic cathedrals and stained glass, painted Laon Cathedral in the same year. This was the first time he used colorful semi-transparent color patches throughout a painting, an approach he continued to explore in the window paintings and cosmic abstract works that quickly followed.[2] Though these planes still describe architecture, the idea for the bright, non-naturalistic colors may have come from the interior contrasts of stained glass. Indeed, Delaunay painted one of Laon's circular stained glass panels with its contrasting red and blue tones (Kunstmuseum, Berne). One year later in 1913, he painted a completely abstract disc of similar colors on the verso of this painting, part of his circular forms series. Delaunay's first true series paintings – from 1909 to 1910 – were of the interior of St.-Séverin in Paris. Here, he explored how refractions from stained glass distorted the columns of the ambulatory, in a way that implicates the relationship of the body itself with this sacred space as one visually traverses the narrow corridor. As pillars narrow one can imagine the solemn passage of one body after another. According to Sonia Delaunay, the two often visited together the cathedral St.-Germain l'Auxerrois at this time, which would remain a favorite haunt for both of them.[3] Though Chevreul is often cited as Delaunay's principal point of departure in his abstract

1 On secularization theory and the period under consideration see McLeod: *Secularization in Western Europe*.

2 On the dating of *The Towers of Laon* (Musée national d'Art Moderne, Paris) as immediately preceding the window series and abstractions, see Spate: *Orphism*, p. 182.

3 Buckberrough: *Sonia Delaunay: A Retrospective*, p. 23.

paintings of color contrasts, Delaunay had worked out a spiritual explanation for his interest in light and color, and believed that the soul's harmony corresponded to complementary color fields within light.[4] In an old-fashioned biblical sense, light brought meaning out of chaos. "Our eyes", he wrote, "are the essential intermediary between nature and our soul."[5] According to Delaunay, the soul exists in a state of harmony, and harmony is engendered through the simultaneity with which the measure and proportion of light enters the soul via the eye.[6] He would also agree with Kandinsky that color itself should provoke a vibration in the soul of the viewer.

The Czech artist Kupka also took on the conflation of architecture and colored light in the Gothic cathedral, and had been a long-time enthusiast of stained glass. In 1906, he installed a stained glass window in the corner of his studio, where it remained until his death. Kupka's preoccupation with light reflection and refraction in stained glass was paramount throughout his transitional period into abstraction. He claimed this source, along with music and general cosmological and biological forces, to be crucial for his explorations. As early as 1910, he began to create colored abstractions based on his experience with luminosity inside churches and cathedrals. Kupka scholar Margit Rowell attributes his abstract vertical paintings like *Arrangement of Verticals in Yellow* of 1910–11 (Musée National d'Art Moderne, Paris) to the massing of columns in a church interior and flickering stained glass – the dominant impression being an all-over pattern.[7] A Czech critic, upon interviewing Kupka at this time, came away with the summary statement that stained glass cathedral windows had inspired

4 On the soul and light in Delaunay, the most helpful references can be found in Apollinaire's notes from interviews with Delaunay. See Marchi: "Pure Painting in Berlin", pp. 157–58.

5 Quoted in Spate: *Orphism*, p. 189.

6 Ibid. Delaunay's interest in Viollet-le-Duc warrants investigation in this context. Viollet had written an important and influential treatise on stained glass, "Vitrail" (an entry in his *Dictionnaire raisonné de l'architecture française du XIe au XVIe siècle*, volume 9) in 1868, in which he discussed color contrasts. Delaunay's early window series (1912) with its color contrasts and visible medieval tower may be a kind of homage to the architect, whose writings on stained glass were considered authoritative in the first quarter of the twentieth century (Johnson, "The Stained Glass Theories of Viollet-le-Duc,", pp. 121–34). Delaunay's first "Gothic" painting (1908) was of Viollet's iron spire on Notre Dame in Paris. Delaunay drew the ribbed vaulting of the interior of St.-Séverin repeatedly in advance of his paintings of the church interior: Viollet's interest in Gothic architectural principles included its potential for new urban social structures to create "an authentic style of our own times." For example, in his *Entretiens sur l'architecture* (1863–72), he proposed an enormous public hall for 3,000 people, with a skeletal iron structure, making use of the vaulting principles of Gothic cathedrals. The Eiffel Tower (a favorite subject of Delaunay's), though it post-dates Viollet-le-Duc's death by a decade, was often discussed during the period of its construction in light of Gothic towers with renewed interest in Viollet-le-Duc's vision of the modern. The Eiffel Tower appears in one of the 1912 *fenêtre* paintings, beside the luminous medieval tower.

7 Kupka / Mladek / Rowell: *František Kupka*, p. 158.

Kupka's earliest abstractions.[8] The importance of embodied vision and reduction to linear effects is discussed in Kupka's *Creation and the Plastic Arts*, in which he wrote: "The different body positions; the voluntary or automatic movements that we make in the course of our life, are so many ways of situating ourselves in space. In an upright position, we place ourselves from top to bottom. In walking, we feel the height of the body following the balance of the limbs…The upright body is a vertical in relationship to the ground. The plastic arts are admirable in the way they offer a confirmation of these great lines of orientation, which followed point by point, can initiate us to the reality of space. To seize and to hold invisible lines, the artist must look for and find means of materializing abstraction."[9]

In the years before the war, Kupka took his students to Chartres Cathedral, where they studied the effects of light on the body through the mainly red and blue stained glass.[10] One result of these trips is *The Cathedral* of 1912–13 (figure 1, 3). Of such works Kupka suggested that what he was seeking might be better found by painting directly onto glass, something that Kandinsky did. The unification of columns and colors of certain Kupka paintings, like the St.-Séverin series by Delaunay, underscores the importance of the sacred architectural site and embodied vision to these artists.

Mondrian found himself in Paris during this period as well. A Protestant, and like Kupka a non-national, political meanings of the Gothic in France would have had little relevance for him. Just before leaving Paris for his native Holland at the outbreak of the war, he did studies based on the cathedral Notre Dame des Champs, followed in the Netherlands by his concentration on the façade of a church in Domburg. This would be his last recognizable series, along with studies of the ocean, before the abstractions that preoccupied him for the rest of his life.

The political vicissitudes of Holland had been such that many protestant churches originated as Catholic structures, the case with the fourteenth-century church in Domburg, which retained its Gothic windows. In Mondrian's highly abstracted drawings of the church done during the war years, Gothic arches are still visible among the scaffolding (figure 2). However, in a major oil painting based on the façade series, with its vertical and horizontal lines and yellow, blue, and pink patches, they have been removed (*Composition 1916*, Solomon R. Guggenheim Museum, New York). Of one of the drawings in the façade series, Mondrian wrote to van Doesburg in October of 1915: "As you [have seen], it is a composition of vertical and horizontal lines which in an abstract way is meant to express the idea of rising, of greatness. The same idea which was behind the building of cathedrals. I refrained from giving it a title. An abstract human mind will receive the intended impression."[11] In that year, Van Doesburg wrote the poem "Cathedral I" in response to Mondrian's work.

8 Ibid., p. 32.

9 Quoted in Andel / Kosinski: *Painting the Universe*, p. 68.

10 Kupka / Mladek / Rowell: *František Kupka,* p. 32.

11 Quoted in Joosten (ed.): *Piet Mondrian: Catalogue raisonné*, p. 247.

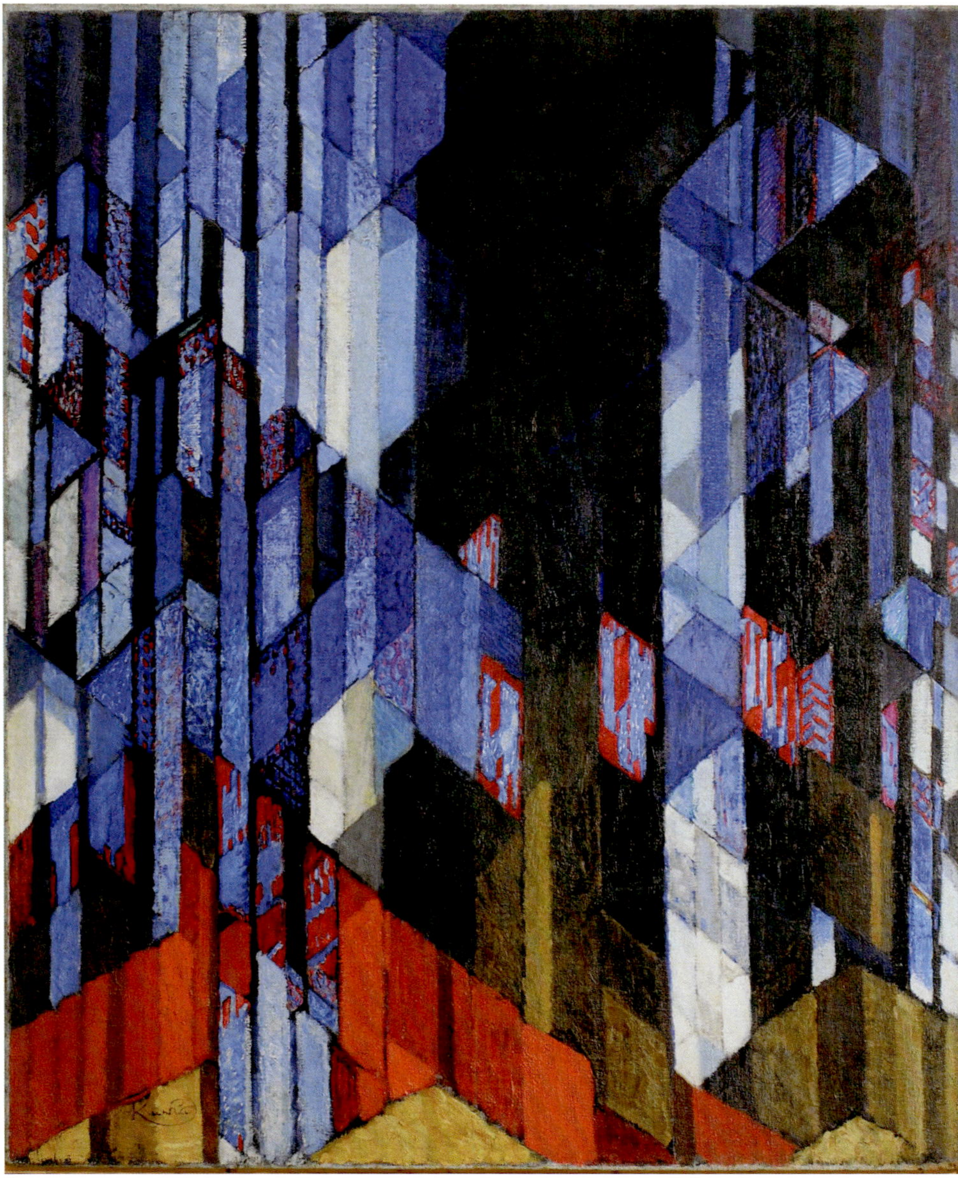

Fig. 1: František Kupka, *The Cathedral*, 1912–13.

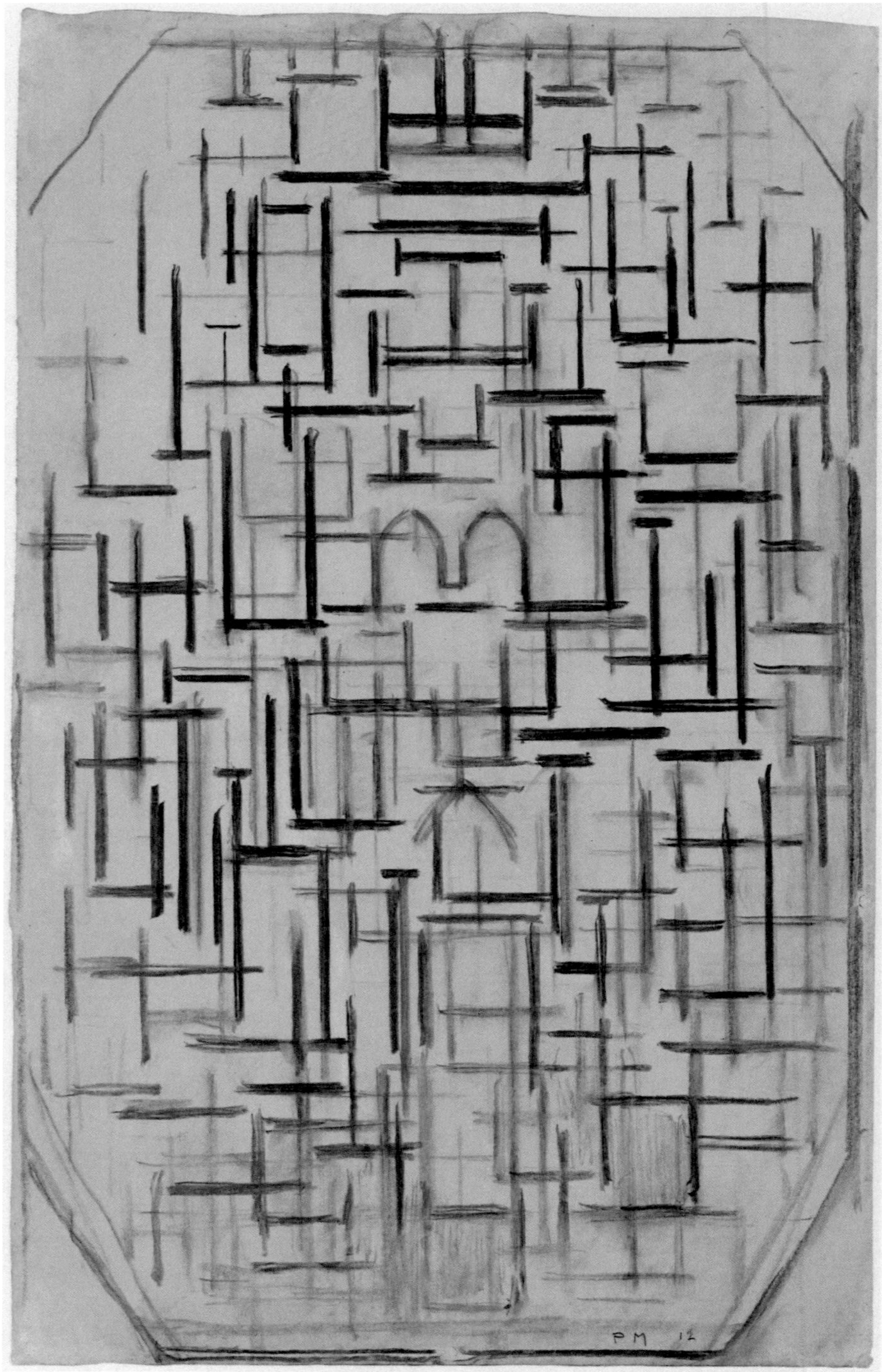

Fig. 2: Mondrian, Piet (1872–1944) © HCR International Church Facade. (1914) (inscribed 1912). Charcoal on paper, 39 x 25" (99.0 x 63.4 cm). The Joan and Lester Avnet Collection. The Museum of Modern Art, New York, NY, U.S.A. Digital Image
© The Museum of Modern Art / Licensed by SCALA / Art Resource, NY.

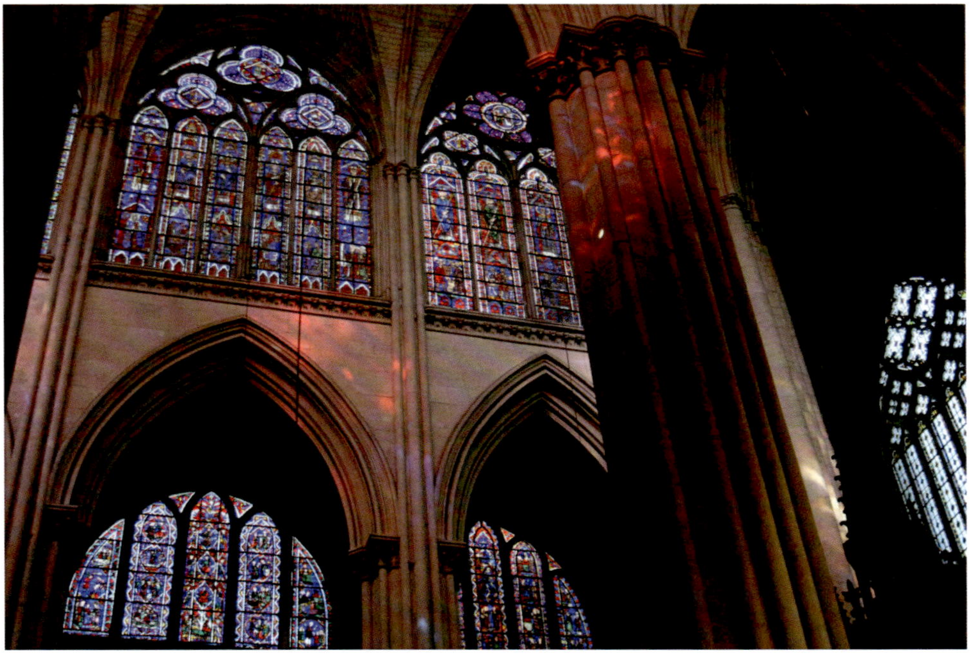

Fig. 3: Interior Chartres Cathedral.

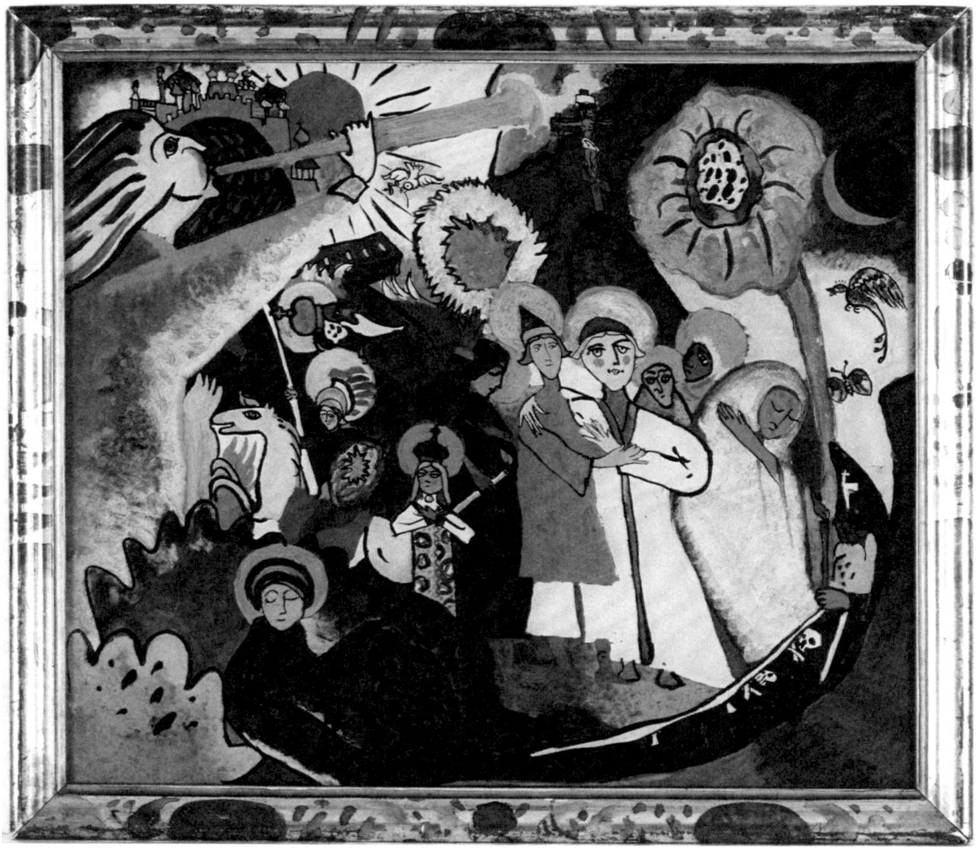

Fig. 4: Wassily Kandinsky, *All Saints* I, 191.

The church in Domburg had appealed to Mondrian earlier, and he had first painted it in 1909 when his work was more representational. Even at this early date, he associated churches with primary colors and painted the Domburg church in pink and blue patches. In Domburg, he communed with the Roman Catholic artist Toorop. Both artists were interested in the Gothic tower of nearby Westkapelle, a remnant of a cathedral, as a subject. For Mondrian, the near phallic depictions of the lone tower of 1909, also rendered in primaries, were part of his developing ideas of vertical elements referencing masculine principles – the complement being the horizontal as a feminine, balancing principle. Mondrian apparently agreed with the basic tenets of Catholicism, writing to a friend, "Toorop sees the Catholic faith as it was in its primeval period. I remain broadly in agreement with Toorop, and I could tell that he goes to the depths, and that he is searching for the spiritual."[12] During the early twentieth century in Holland, mystic Christianity was a popular trend: Mondrian was also close to the Catholic

12 Quoted in Blotkamp (ed.): *De Stijl: The Formative Years,* p. 8.

Schoenmaekers, a self-described "christographer", who combined religious references with mathematical principles and a preference for primary colors which he read symbolically.[13]

Along with the tower, churches and trees were also part of Mondrian's world of the masculine principle. His paintings of trees around 1912 were often likened to leaded stained glass by critics. Churches in combination with trees had featured in some of his earliest works, such as the Dutch reformed church, originally the fifteenth century Catholic St. James the Major, in *Village Church* of 1898 (Private collection, Amsterdam). The multiple peaks formed by the branches in this painting suggest popularized romantic ideas that Gothic structures were inspired by earlier believers worshipping in forests.

The fact that the Domburg Church was Mondrian's final meditation on an identified vertical motif finds important continuities in Mondrian's earliest abstractions. *Composition in Line*, of 1916, consisting of black verticals and horizontals on a white background was one of the first oils without a subject. It was exhibited in 1917 purposefully in between his first two paintings making use of floating rectangular color planes of red, yellow, and blue. Of this triptych grouping Mondrian wrote: "This work shows the religious so well…and placing the three next to one another is quite expressive."[14] Robert Welsh has connected the two color works to oil studies of Notre Dame des Champs.[15] Of the vertical and horizontal lines he continued to pursue, Mondrian invoked the biblical tale of Genesis in his later "Plastic Art and Pure Plastic Art" of 1936 in his discussion of Male (vertical) and Female (horizontal) principals. He wrote: "Adam in the Paradise story live[d] in perfect equilibrium", but since this state was seen to be unearned by God, Eve was created for "opposition".[16]

While Mondrian entered an experimental abstract period for a short time before adopting a linear scaffolding and a saturated primary palette around 1920, the mature formula may well reference both church architecture and stained glass. The inspiration also has a more immediate and modern point of inspiration. During this period, Mondrian was close to Bart van der Leck, along with Toorop part of Catholic revivalism in early twentieth-century Netherlands, and Theo van Doesburg. Both van der Leck and van Doesburg, along with Vilmos Huszar, all three of whom were associated with the emerging de Stijl movement, were working with stained glass and primary colors by 1916. Van der Leck had trained in stained glass ateliers in the 1890s and also painted on glass, writing a 23-page essay on the subject in 1905. During the war, when stained glass was expensive he created many painted glass pieces. Van der Leck, who used principally red, yellow, and blue, promoted these colors to Mondrian as those that embodied light

13 On Catholic mysticism in Holland during this period, see Blotkamp: "Annunciation of the New Mysticism", pp. 89–112.

14 Joosten: *Piet Mondrian*, p. 256.

15 Welsh: "Piet Mondrian: The Subject Matter of Abstraction", p. 53.

16 Quoted in Marc Cheetham: *The Rhetoric of Purity*, p. 42.

and also reduced his forms to verticals and horizontals. Just in advance of his considerable exploration of stained glass, Van Doesburg wrote in 1916: "In the medieval museum and at the St. Bavo church I found my task – a crystal atmosphere. I have a positive plan for creation and what I shall create now will top everything."[17] His stained glass *Composition IV* of 1917 (Stedelijk Museum, Leiden) is a triptych – a traditional Christian format – and makes use of primaries in the outside panels. This is not to say that the planar abstractions of this period are based on specific examples in cathedrals or spiritual iconographical signs, but they are his first contributions to Neo-Plasticism.

When the Russian artist Kandinsky organized the first Blaue Reiter exhibition in 1911, he invited Delaunay to show a couple of his St.-Séverin paintings. Kandinsky himself exhibited three glass paintings with religious imagery based on a folk technique he had learned in southern Germany, where he was living. At this time, he was working on the first issue of the Blaue Reiter almanac in which he had intended to publish "some reports on the Russian religious movement in which *all* classes participate" by Sergei Bulgakov, whom he called "….one of the greatest experts on religious life."[18] In paintings of this period, Kandinsky incorporated religious imagery including deluges, horsemen of the apocalypse, and saints, many of whom were based on Russian orthodox icons (figure 4). Increasingly, during the second decade of the century, many of these paintings would hide or veil imagery as Rose-Carol Washton Long has discussed, though the content was nevertheless implied.[19]

Despite the modernism and abstraction of these works, even some of the most avant-garde critics questioned the deeply conservative religious references that repeatedly suggested the Last Judgment. Kandinsky's messianic approach to the spiritual was encouraged by his exposure to Russian mystics such as philosopher Vladimir Soloviev or Russian writer Merezhkovsky, who opposed the materialism of the present and believed that the current moment signaled the third and final revelation, the revelation of the spirit. Even in later years, when Kandinsky's work had entered a geometric phase, he claimed that the Holy Spirit was at work in these forms.[20] Christian theosophist Rudolf Steiner, an influence on both Kandinsky and Mondrian, believed that the Revelation of St. John held the key to understanding the universe.

In her book *The Gothic Visionary Perspective*, Barbara Nolan addressed the later medieval visionary arts, focusing on narrative scenes of the apocalypse, emphasizing the journey of the pilgrim to "the new Jerusalem" and cathedral

17 Quoted in Blotkamp (ed.): *De Stijl: The Formative Years,* p. 11.
18 Quoted in Kandinsky and Marc (eds.): *The Blaue Reiter Almanac*, p. 17.
19 Long: "Kandinsky and Abstraction", pp. 42–50.
20 Sixten Ringbom discusses the history of Kandinsky's interest in apocalyptic imagery in *The Sounding Cosmos*, vol. 38, no. 7. See especially chapter five, "Apocalyptism and the Third Revelation".

programs that indicated a final age preceding the last judgment.[21] She argues that medieval vision was reorganized beginning in the twelfth century to emphasize revelation and the human nature of Christ. Throughout Western Europe thereafter, these themes were found in stained glass and sculptural programs in cathedrals. In France, Emile Mâle, popularizer of the history of medieval cathedrals in the early twentieth century and chair of art history at the Sorbonne in 1912, published *L'Art religieux du XIIIe siècle en France* in 1898 and *L'Art religieux de la fin du moyen âge en France. Etude sur l'iconographie du moyen âge et sur ses sources d'inspiration* in 1908, examples of well-known discussions on the medieval cathedral with its colorful stained glass as the symbolic heavenly Jerusalem in the modern period. However, medieval revivalism in general at the turn of the century had made cathedral programs and craft topical.

Spectacular programs of stained glass throughout medieval cathedrals from the twelfth century on were to suggest the bejeweled heavenly Jerusalem and the divine nature of light, bringing a foretaste of heaven to earth. Stained glass raised congregations from the material to the immaterial realm.[22] For Abbot Suger of St. Denis, who wrote a widely influential treatise on stained glass, once *lux* or natural, physical light, entered the cathedral through stained glass it became *lux nova,* symbolic, spiritual light; the stained glass was a sacred threshold, on one side was profane light, but on the other it was holy. For Suger, this sacred light was an important source of faith and divine inspiration, an agency of grace that fed the soul. When this light passed into the eye of the beholder it became *illumination* and elevated vision. Suger had initiated a program of color in stained glass that would be followed at Chartres and many other cathedrals, including Laon: the use of red referencing jasper and blue symbolizing sapphires. Allegories of color shifted in the medieval ages, and the abstract artists under discussion similarly had varying ideas about the meaning of the primaries, but red often referred to earthly passion – the body, while blue often referenced eternity and the heavenly realm, and gold frequently symbolized God, truth, or the sun. The idea of light through stained glass touching the soul was popularized again by the turn of the twentieth century and is found, for example, in the writings of Huysmans, such as in his novel *La cathédrale* of 1898.

Though unlike Delaunay, Mondrian, or Kupka, Kandinsky does not seem at first to allude to Christian ritual spaces, he wrote that he wanted the experience of his paintings to be as if one could enter the space and walk within them. On the similarity of entering cathedrals and being surrounded with the spectacle of brilliant color, he said of an early experience:

21 Nolan: *The Gothic Visionary Perspective.*

22 In Germany before the Great War, this vision affected avant-garde architecture, including that of Peter Scheerbart and Bruno Taut. Here the "crystal", ultimately deriving from St. John's description of the new Jerusalem as "clear as glass" and the river of life "as bright as a crystal", was a point of reference. See Whyte: "The Expressionist Sublime", pp. 118–37.

> "Colorful houses of the Vologda taught me to *move in the picture*, to live in the picture. I still remember how I entered a room [in the Vologda] for the first time and stopped short on the threshold before the unexpected sight. The table, the benches the oven...and every object were painted with bright-colored, large-figured decorations. The beautiful corner thickly and completely covered with painted and printed pictures of saints....I felt myself surrounded on all sides by painting, into which I had thus penetrated. The same feeling slumbered within me, unconsciously up to that moment, when I was in churches in Moscow and especially in the great cathedral of the Kremlin. On my next visit to this church after my return from the trip, this feeling revived in me perfectly clearly. Later I often had the same experience in Bavarian and Tyrolean chapels. The impression was differently colored each time, being formed by different constituents. Church! Russian Church! Chapel! Catholic Chapel!"[23]

The type of memory Kandinsky is describing is episodic memory. In this case, a powerful memory, often laid down because of its attachment to a strong emotion or impression, is jarred because of a stimulus that has certain similar components (pictures of saints, brilliant colors, a total environment in the case of Kandinsky). Episodic memory is one of the principal avenues of investigation in the recent field of the cognitive science of religion.[24] The original memory is not a snapshot in the brain, but is formed by a network of neurons connecting at nodes that come from different centers of the brain – areas that are responsible for visual, spatial or auditory experiences, for example. The neurons in question were not originally connected, but became that way because of experiences and impressions that took place. Thus, the specific neurons that fired together during the original experience (childhood days in a cathedral) become sensitized to one another and tend to fire together again – repeated exposure to the same stimulus strengthens the connections. At a later time, an experience with similar components will spark those memories, making us think we have retrieved a "snapshot." Describing this type of memory in relationship to Kandinsky's developing ideas is relevant not only where his painting is concerned in regard to all its spiritual complexity and Russian orthodox history, but because Kandinsky's generation – the generation of artists under discussion – grew up during a tumultuous time for the church that would bring memory and spiritual meaning to center stage. Their parents' generation was more generally steeped in traditional patterns and habits of belief, affecting childhood experiences of the sacred sphere. Together these generations witnessed the breakdown of a deeply rooted social

23 Kandinsky: "Reminiscences". In a 1918 Russian publication of "Reminiscences", Kandinsky added "...especially the Cathedral of the Assumption and the Church of St. Basil the Blessed."

24 Harvey Whitehouse has connected "imagistic" religion with episodic memory and doctrinal religion with semantic memory. Of the "two modes of religion" see his *Arguments and Icons: Divergent Modes of Religiosity* and *Modes of Religiosity: A Cognitive Theory of Religious Transmission*. For more nuanced responses and a further discussion of episodic memory and religion where one does not necessarily replace the other, see Whitehouse / McCauley (eds.): *Mind and Religion*. For more on the formation of neuronal connections in childhood see Damasio: *Descartes' Error*, pp. 108–13.

institution – that also experienced a certain though by no means complete resurgence. For example, when Delaunay was seventeen, he witnessed the moment when all religious communities were expelled from a traditionally Catholic France, much the case of Germany. In France, this was followed by the trauma of separation of church and state when Delaunay was twenty, with an immediate neo-Catholic backlash, circumscribed but prominent, at the time he painted his St.-Séverin series. Additional government repression was then taking place, including state ownership of churches. For his part, Kupka had originally chosen to study with late Nazarene artists, including the religious painter František Sequens. Kandinsky always held onto his Russian orthodox faith. In the Netherlands, Mondrian grew up in a religious Calvanist family. But in the late nineteenth century there was also a strong Catholic revival there and much cathedral building. Mondrian himself, when young, joined a branch of the Dutch reformed church that believed the world was soon drawing to a close.

Embodied and situated cognition theory is useful in examining the "religious" nature of early abstraction. It posits a joint environmentally, historically, and culturally related relationship with an organic basis between artist and viewer.[25] Memories of a sacred sphere and communal emotions raised in a multisensory environment were powerful and threatened among western Europeans as these artists matured. In the second decade of the twentieth century, abstractions that drew upon visual components of those familiar sites – in particular the brilliant color of luminous stained glass – provided a compelling direction for artists searching for meaningful and crucial content. This was also a time when artists were interested in the relationship between the senses, exemplified by synaesthesia. The cathedral with its music, light, and hushed interior was a spectacular chamber of sensory stimulation that tapped into the emotions and developing neurological webs. Delaunay, Kupka, and Kandinsky all connected cathedrals with musical memories.

The spiritual component of early abstraction is difficult if not impossible to experience today, because circumstances and memories have changed. By way of example, I am going to briefly discuss how a well-known neurologist, Semir Zeki, and an art historian, Yves-Alain Bois, discount the spiritual message which Mondrian repeatedly claimed was behind his style. Zeki has used brain imaging techniques to demonstrate that a contemporary viewer of a Mondrian shows activation in the early visual cortices – mainly areas VI and V4, where cells register color and linear orientation.[26] In this mechanistic model, no area of the brain is activated that has to do with deep memory or recognizable imagery (for our purposes cathedrals, stained glass, communal ritual spaces, or even Mondrian's constant references to resonant universal principles). Zeki celebrates this about Mondrian – he is likened to a neurologist who seeks essentials. Bois is similarly

25 See, for example, Griffiths and Stolz: "How the Mind Grows", pp. 29–51.

26 Mondrian is one of the artists whom Zeki repeatedly invokes in *Inner Vision: An Exploration of Art and the Brain*. See especially pp. 198–201.

formalist in orientation. In *Painting as Model*, in developing the ideas of Hubert Damisch, Bois claims for the viewer that "the eye is ceaselessly lead back to the painting's constituent elements, line, color, design."[27] He quotes Damisch: "One cannot give way to reverie in front of a Mondrian painting, nor even to pure contemplation….Each time perception thinks it can go beyond what is given to see toward what it would constitute as meaning, it is immediately led back to the first experience…"[28] Neurologist and art historian are not necessarily incorrect in their claims, but they are accurate only insofar as they address today's viewer.

If barren to viewers today of the spiritual content Mondrian meant to include, then the abstract modernist project as it existed in the second decade of the twentieth century is not the one we see and experience today. Something of the possibility of what the historical Mondrian could still mean in the middle of the twentieth century can be found at the chapel at Ronchamp by the aging architect Le Corbusier, friend and admirer of Mondrian (figure 5). There the south wall is pierced by rectangular apertures of stained glass panels, further divided into rectangles of red, yellow, and blue along with the occasional green, set off against clear glass. Though only "Mondrians" by association, they are nevertheless unlikely to have been realized without his example. Clearly le Corbusier still understood the spiritual potential of a Mondrian. At Ronchamp, contemplation and reverie are invited.

Behind those optical treatises of Chevreul, Helmholtz, Wilhelm Ostwald, and others that these artists read, was a deeper history of exposure to "pure" color with emotional and social connections. I would argue that the modernist painters' interest in optical theory was *shaped* by early exposure to a colorful, luminous sacred environment, and that mystical *lux nova* is a central component of their vision. Mondrian, Kupka, Delaunay, and Kandinsky did not move exclusively into radical progressive territory in lockstep with new scientific information, or bohemian religious ideas with little real relevance for society at large, as the narrative of modernism is often told, but in fact in seeking profound meaning were engaged in the most resonant, deeply historical, and communally revered spaces in the west – underscoring just how crucial the embodied eye is in artistic practice.

I would like to thank Mary Shepard, Elizabeth Emerye, and Laura Morowitz for their helpful comments on this essay.

27 Bois: *Painting as Model*, p. 248.
28 Ibid.

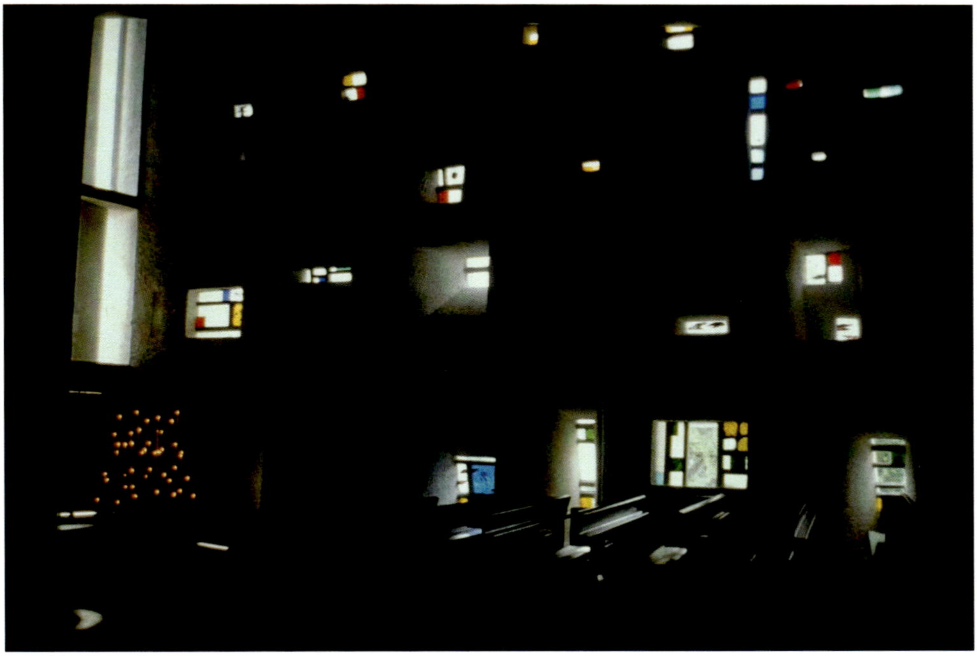

Fig. 5 : Le Corbusier, Interior, Notre-Dame-du-Haut, south wall, 1950–54.

Bibliography

Andel, Jaroslav / Dorothy Kosinski, (eds.): *Painting the Universe: František Kupka: Pioneer in Abstraction*, Dallas (Dallas Museum of Fine Arts) 1997.

Blotkamp, Carel (ed.): *De Stijl: The Formative Years, 1917–1923*, trans. by Charlotte Loeb, Cambridge (MIT Press) 1982.

Blotkamp, Carel: "Annunciation of the New Mysticism: Dutch Symbolism and Early Abstraction", in: Maurice Tuchman et al. (eds.): *The Spiritual in Art: Abstract Painting, 1890–1985*, exh. cat., Los Angeles (Los Angeles County Museum of Art) 1986, pp. 89–112.

Bois, Yve-Alain: *Painting as Model*, Cambridge (MIT Press) 1990.

Buckberrough, Sherry (ed.): *Sonia Delaunay: A Retrospective*, exh. cat., Buffalo, New York (Albright Knox Gallery) 1980.

Cheetham, Marc: *The Rhetoric of Purity: Essentialist Theory and the Advent of Abstract Painting*, New York (Cambridge University Press) 1991.

Damasio, Antonio: *Descartes' Error: Emotion, Reason and the Brain*, New York (Putnam) 1994.

Griffiths, Paul / Karola Stolz: "How the Mind Grows: A Developmental Perspective on the Biology of Cognition", in: *Synthese* 122 (2000), pp. 29–51.

Johnson, James: "The Stained Glass Theories of Viollet-le-Duc", in: *The Art Bulletin*, vol. 45 (1963) 2, pp. 121–34.

Joosten, Joop (ed.): *Piet Mondrian: Catalogue raisonné of the Work of 1911–1944*, vol. II, New York (Harry Abrams, Inc.) 1996.

Kandinsky, Wassily / Marc Franz: *The Blaue Reiter Almanac*, New York (Thames and Hudson) 1974.

Kandinsky, Wassily: "Reminiscences (1912–13)", in: Kenneth Lindsay / Peter Vergo (eds.): *Kandinsky, Complete Writings on Art (1901–21),* Vol. 1, Boston (G. K. Hall) 1982, pp. 368–69.

Kupka, František / Meda Mladek / Margit Rowell: *František Kupka, 1871–57: A Retrospective*, New York (Solomon R. Guggenheim Museum) 1975, p. 158.

Long, Rose-Carol Washton: "Kandinsky and Abstraction: The Role of the Hidden Image", in: *Artforum* 10 (1972), pp. 42–50.

Marchi, Riccardo: *Pure Painting in Berlin, 1912–1913: Boccioni, Kandinsky, and Delaunay at der Sturm*, PhD dissertation, University of Chicago, 2002.

McLeod, Hugh: *Secularization in Western Europe, 1848–1914*, New York (St. Martin's Press) 2000.

Nolan, Barbara: *The Gothic Visionary Perspective*, Princeton (Princeton University Press) 1977.

Ringbom, Sixten: *The Sounding Cosmos: A Study in the Spiritualism of Kandinsky and the Genesis of Abstract Painting*, vol. 38, no. 7, Åbo (=Turku) (Åbo Akademi) 1970.

Spate, Virginia: *Orphism: The Evolution of Non-Figurative Painting in Paris, 1910–1914*, Oxford (Clarendon Press) 1979.

Viollet-le-Duc, Eugène: "Entretiens sur l'architecture (1863–72)", in: Eugène Viollet-le-Duc, *Entretiens sur l'Architecture (Edition Intégrale)*, Wavre (Mardaga) 1995.

Viollet-le-Duc, Eugène: *Dictionnaire raisonné de l'architecture française du XIe au XVIe siècle*. Paris, 1854–1868.

Welsh, Robert: "Piet Mondrian. The Subject Matter of Abstraction", in: *Artforum* 11 (1973) 8, pp. 50–53.

Whitehouse, Harvey: *Arguments and Icons: Divergent Modes of Religiosity*, New York (Oxford University Press) 2000.

Whitehouse, Harvey: *Modes of Religiosity: A Cognitive Theory of Religious Transmission*, New York (Altamira Press) 2004.

Whitehouse, Harvey / McCauley, R. (eds.): *Mind and Religion: Psychological and Cognitive Foundations of Religion,* New York (Altamira Press) 2005.

Whyte, Ian Boyd: "The Expressionist Sublime," in: Timothy Benson (ed.): *Expressionist Utopias: Paradise, Metropolis, and Architectural Fantasy,* exh. cat., Los Angeles (Los Angeles County Museum of Art) 1993, pp. 118–37.

Zeki, Semir: *Inner Vision: An Exploration of Art and the Brain*, Oxford (Oxford University Press) 1999.

List of figures

Fig. 1 František Kupka, *The Cathedral*, 1912–13, oil on canvas, 180 x 150 cm. Signed I. I.: Kupka. From the Collection of the Museum Kampa. The Jan and Meda Mladek Foundation, Prague, Czech Republic.

Fig. 2 Mondrian, Piet (1872–1944) © HCR International Church Facade. (1914) (inscribed 1912). Charcoal on paper, 39 x 25" (99.0 x 63.4 cm). The Joan and Lester Avnet Collection. The Museum of Modern Art, New York, NY, U.S.A. Digital Image © The Museum of Modern Art / Licensed by SCALA / Art Resource, NY.

Fig. 3 Interior Chartres Cathedral.

Fig. 4 Wassily Kandinsky, *All Saints* I, 1911, glass painting, 34.5 x 40.5. Städtische Galerie in Lenbachhaus, Munich.

Fig. 5. Le Corbusier, Interior, Notre-Dame-du-Haut, south wall, 1950–54. Photo: akg-images / L. M. Peter. ©2010 Artists Rights Society (ARS), New York/ADAGP, Paris/F.L.C.

Towards Embodiment-Based Research on Musical Expressiveness

JIN HYUN KIM

I. Prologue

Over the last decades, music has increasingly become a research topic in different disciplines and interdisciplinary projects. Most particularly, psychologists' and neuroscientists' involvement in music research has expanded to a high degree. Among other things, a growing interest in 'emotions' in current scientific research, especially by those scientists empirically investigating human mind and brain has attracted their attention towards music, taken as an excellent stimulus to induce emotions. On the other hand, musicologists, whose primary research object is 'music', take a substantially different perspective on the relationship between music and emotion when contributing to music and emotion research. Their research questions focus on whether and how music *is* emotionally expressive rather than on how music *induces* emotions; although more concrete questions would differ among musicologists according to their historical, systematic and ethnological approaches, the difference between musicologists' interest in the topic 'music and emotion' from that of psychologists and neuroscientists might be generalized as briefly summarized above.

This chapter attempts to discuss what conceptual framework and methods for investigating the relationship between music and emotion, when focusing on 'music', might be most appropriate, against the background of a number of current empirical studies on music and emotion.[1] From a musicological point of view, a main focus of this chapter lies on a generalizing research approach in systematic musicology, which is to a considerable degree close to that in psychology and neuroscience, though it should be acknowledged that a careful examination using a historical and cultural approach to music and emotion in historical musicology and ethnomusicology would be profitable as well. At the same time, however, a main discussion of this chapter is directed toward a new framework for investigating 'music' integrating the processes of human mind and brain as well as socio-cultural and historical aspects, especially by taking into account a recent approach of music research which has given rise to a sub-

1 Cf. Juslin and Sloboda: *Music and Emotion*; *Handbook of Music and Emotion*.

discipline of systematic musicology called 'cognitive musicology'[2] and a new paradigm of embodiment in cognitive science and media theory.[3]

First, to what extent a framework integrating traditional natural science and the humanities can be developed within cognitive musicology will be discussed. To elaborate the term 'Geistiges', which comes to focus in cognitive musicology, in conjunction with a newer discourse on embodied mind, an important variant of meaning of the term 'embodiment' will be introduced. Based on the discussion on embodiment, several dominant hypotheses and methods of recent psychological and neuroscientific studies on music and emotion are third critically discussed. Finally, it will be considered what methodologies might be appropriate to embodiment-based research on 'music', and especially on musical expressiveness.

II. Cognitive musicology: A new framework for fundamental music research

In traditional systematic musicology, in which musical acoustics serves as the basis for its research program, 'music' is treated as a phenomenon generated as an acoustic wave, perceived as musical information and apprehended as meaningful or aesthetic, which subsumes different musical forms in the history and in other cultures. Due to its widest extension of 'music' and its generalizing research methods compared to singularizing methods of historical musicology and ethnomusicology, some researchers assign a role of fundamental music research to systematic musicology[4] – that means that systematic musicology should deal with the question of on what foundations 'music' can be defined; for instance, the question of whether 'music' might be defined on emotional foundations may arise, when considering the topic of this chapter.

It is however most likely that traditional systematic musicology based on an audio-centered research, starting from a physical-acoustic phenomenon, hardly succeeds in undertaking the role of fundamental music research, taking into account the fact that the latter should make it possible to give foundational explanations on 'music', which cannot be reduced to an acoustic substrate, as the German musicologist Carl Dahlhaus already pointed out;[5] foundational music research should also be directed towards the understanding of music as 'Geist' or

2 Laske: *Music, Memory and Thought*; Leman: *Music and Schema Theory*; Seifert: "Cognitive Science"; *Systematische Musiktheorie und Kognitionswissenschaft.*

3 Kim: *Embodiment in interaktiven Musik- und Medienperformances.*

4 Wiora: "Musikalische Grundlagenforschung"; Seifert: *Systematische Musiktheorie und Kognitionswissenschaft*; "Naturalisierte Hermneutik der Musik".

5 Dahlhaus: *Einführung in die systematische Musikwissenschaft.*

as culture. A 'Geist'/culture-nature dichotomy in musicology goes back to the 19th century, in which an epistemological program of the humanities ('Geisteswissenschaft') was founded, bordering that of natural science. This dichotomy is still dominant in the disciplines established in the academic institutions, although the importance of inter- and transdisciplinarity has been emphasized at the latest since the 1990s and a discussion on convergence between different scientific approaches has very recently begun.

Musicology belongs to one of the disciplines integrating approaches adapted from natural science and the humanities, since 'music' is a complex phenomenon with relation to which both explanation and understanding should be used complementarily. An important question, however, is how fundamental music research is possible, not reducing 'music' to a phenomenon of nature, history or culture, but taking into account different approaches of music research and integrating them into a converging approach. Traditional systematic musicology may have failed in fundamental music research since it has not developed an integrative approach.

A new perspective on generalizing and fundamental music research, however, seems to be provided by a recent approach of systematic musicology adapted from cognitive science. Cognitive musicology investigates 'music' as a phenomenon of the mind and its cognitive mechanisms. What the 'mind' means in cognitive science might be a core question in order to consider cognitive musicology as fundamental music research. In classical approaches of cognitive science, the mind has been treated as the individual mind, which has been investigated in terms of mental/neural representation of the 'outer' world. Considering the fact that the questions of cognitive science are concerned with how humans have language or music faculties and how they learn language or music, among other things, however, such questions cannot be investigated merely by looking into the mechanisms of the individual mind, which seem to have become the focus at first, because understanding them by a computational modeling approach, a basic approach of cognitive science, has proved to be complex enough.[6]

A newer approach of cognitive science pursued since the end of 1980s and recently discussed intensively, which takes into account the social nature of a cognitive system that is embodied and embedded in a biological and sociocultural environment and interacting with other systems, makes it possible to investigate the 'objective mind' that the term 'Geist' originating from a German tradition of the humanities ('Geisteswissenschaft') includes.[7] When 'music' is not reduced to an acoustic substrate, but refers to the process of 'Geistiges' including (collective) knowledge, learning, conscious experience, concept formation etc., investigating the whole process of 'Geistiges' appears a promising approach of fundamental music research. In order to investigate 'music' as the

6 Cf. Clark: *Being There.*

7 Cf. Seifert: "Naturalisierte Hermeneutik der Musik".

process of 'Geistiges', the methods of natural science and the humanities are both indispensable; they should complement one other.

Before discussing appropriate methods, attention is to be paid to the extent to which the process of 'Geistiges' is based on the body and embedded in both biological and socio-cultural environments, taking into account current discourses on embodiment.

III. Being embodied: A new perspective on "embodiment"

A growing interest in the research paradigm of embodiment, which is mostly due to a newer approach in cognitive science, called embodied cognition,[8] situated cognition[9] or interactionism,[10] has recently led to new research questions and methods in different disciplines including musicology.[11] There are, however, still different notions with regard to the understanding of the term 'embodiment', which do not give rise to a definition of this term in a strict sense yet. A tentative definition available at present emphasizes the bodily basis of mind, cognitive processes and cultural phenomena.[12] How can, however, 'the bodily basis' be understood? By introducing two different variants of meaning of 'embodiment' that the cognitive musicologist Uwe Seifert and the author have very recently elaborated,[13] a new perspective on 'embodiment' may be discussed.

The first variant of meaning of 'embodiment' is based on Cartesian mind-body dualism and therefore characterized by a result of the process of embodying a non-bodily substance – in short: by 'embodiment of'.[14] 'Embodiment' refers to corporeal processes including an interactive process with the environment, which the body is embedded in. Such corporeal processes are conceived of as those of embodying abstract or non-material entities. Though the processuality of an action or a process is assigned to 'embodiment' in this context, this processuality only relates to corporeal processes that obtain a secondary and subsequent status. Several research programs of cognitive robotics in fact pursue an embodied approach in the sense that corporeal processes *concretely* embodying cognitive

8 Clark: *Being There*; Calvo and Gomilla: *Handbook of Cognitive Science.*

9 Robbins and Aydede: *The Cambridge Handbook of Situated Cognition.*

10 Agre: *Computation and the Human Mind.*

11 See e.g. Kim: Trace Theory of Mind and Musical Expressivity"; Kim and Seifert: "Embodiment"; "Embodiment and Agency"; Leman: *Embodied Music Cognition and Mediation Technology*; Schmidt: "Towards an Embodied Cognitive Science of Music"; *Embodied Cognitive Science of Music.*

12 Cf. Frank: "Introduction: Sociocultural Situatedness".

13 Seifert & Kim: "Embodiment".

14 Seifert & Kim: "Embodiment".

capacities are incorporated in order to study human *abstract* cognition. Such research approach following the first variant of meaning of 'embodiment' might extend cognition research to a certain degree, but it does not scrutinize an epistemological and an ontological dualism; as a result, it does not provide a really new framework for cognition research.

This first variant of meaning of 'embodiment' is also supported by traditional representationalist approaches to corporeality and materiality of signs and media: A sign or a medium is conceived of as a means of conveying information, meanings, emotional states etc. as if these existed, preceding a semiotic or medial act. In short, a two-world ontology is presupposed, incorporating a transcendental world that can be made available subsequently through its appearance and a world of experience that makes the former appear and therefore makes it available.

The second variant of meaning of 'embodiment' which is characterized in the sense of 'being embodied'[15] opens up the possibility of dissolving a mind-body dichotomy: 'Embodiment' is conceived of as a starting state rather than as a final state resulting from an action or a process. In other words, what has been considered a final state of a process and that process which has been conceived of as goal-directed constitute a unity. This idea is related to the concept of entelechy developed in Aristotle's philosophy. Actuality (Greek: energeia; Latin: actus/actualitas), which is the process of achieving a goal, is distinguished from potentiality (Greek: dunamis; Latin: potentia/possibilitas) to achieve a goal. Aristotle uses the term 'entelechy' (Greek: entelecheia; Latin: actualitas) to refer to actualization in general or resulting actuality or perfection of something in particular as opposed to its mere potentiality, in which the goal (Greek: telos) to be achieved, the achieved goal or function (Greek: ergon), and the process of achieving the goal (Greek: energeia) become unified.[16]

In sum, 'embodiment' which can be understood in the sense of entelechy does not separate the goal to be achieved (e.g. percept; Greek: aisthêton), the function achieved (e.g. perception as the mental function; Greek: aisthêma) and the process of achieving the goal (e.g. the act or process of perception; Greek: aisthêsis) from each other. Rather, they become one unity of an embodied being. According to this second variant of meaning of 'embodiment', 'Geistiges' can be conceived of at best as "the processuality of an embodied being"[17].

This understanding of 'Geistiges' implies for cognitive musicology that the processuality of a *musically* embodied being becomes the object of music research. This means that all aspects constituting a unity (telos, ergon and energeia) by embodiment (entelecheia) should be carefully investigated, for which the dichotomy of natural science and the humanities institutionalized in the disciplines since the 19th century no longer appears tenable. Cognitive musicology, adapted

15 Cf. Seifert & Kim: "Embodiment".

16 Cf. Seifert & Kim: "Entelechy and Embodiment in (Artistic) Human-Computer Interaction", pp. 933f.

17 Seifert & Kim: "Embodiment".

from cognitive science in conjunction with its recent paradigm of embodiment, seems to be able to provide an epistemological and methodological basis as well as an integrative framework for investigating 'music', without presupposing a dualism of natural science and the humanities.

IV. Performance-based research approaches to music and emotion: Critical discussions

It must be obvious after having introduced the two variants of meaning of 'embodiment' introduced in section III that only a research approach following the second variant of meaning of 'embodiment' might be able to bring forth a paradigm shift in music research. By advocating the meaning of 'embodiment' understood in the sense of 'being embodied', current approaches to music and emotion research, especially in the context of music performance, may be critically discussed.

A starting point of discussion is that musical features that most empirical studies on music and emotion have focused on have been assumed to be a kind of code manifesting emotions, which can be shared by performers and by listeners. In other words, musical features have been conceived of as externalizing a performer's expressive (internal) intentions that can be expressed during music-making and deciphered by listeners during music perception.[18] Hence, the relationship between musical features and emotional states of performer/listener has become the focus, based on the notion that musicians communicate with listeners by means of expressive musical features, which may vary in music performance.

Those stimuli typically used in experimental studies which are intended to investigate such a relationship consist of the same performer's expressions of different emotions, mostly using basic emotion categories such as happy, sad, angry etc., manipulated by performing the same compositional fragment; listeners act as test persons whose task is to choose which emotions are represented in each performance fragment or induced by each stimulus. Recent studies have also considered the performer's corporeal gestures as expressive musical features additionally to acoustic musical features.[19] Hence, performance-based music research incorporates not only an auditory phenomenon, but also a bodily gesture as an object of research. Though expressive musical features – whether acoustic

18 E.g. Schaeffer: "Cognition and Affect in Musical Performance"; Gabrielsson: "Expressive Intention and Performance"; Scherer: "Expression on Emotion in Voice and Music"; Juslin and Sloboda: *Music and Emotion*; *Handbook of Music and Emotion*; Sloboda: *Exploring the Musical Mind*.

19 E.g. Dahl and Friberg: "Expressiveness of Musician's Body Movements"; "Visual Perception of Expressiveness in Musicians' Body Movements".

or gestural features – may be investigated within a new framework of cognitive musicology, when they are understood in terms of 'being embodied', current psychological and neuroscientific studies on the relationship between musical features and perceived or induced emotions are mostly based on the representationalist model of communication. This model goes back to the information theory developed by Claude E. Shannon,[20] in which communication is defined as the transmission of a signal between transmitter and receiver (see figure 1), assigning a secondary status to the process of communication, and where information is considered as already being encoded before it goes through via a communication channel.

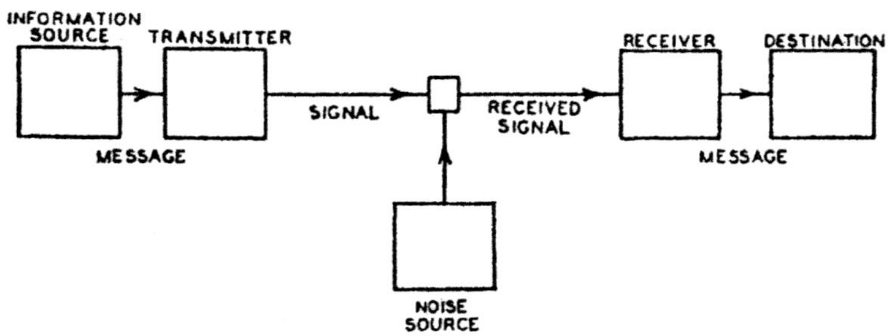

Figure 1: "schematic diagram of a general communication system" (Shannon and Weaver 1962 [1949]: 5, figure 8).

In most studies following the transmitter-receiver model of communication theory, some kind of expressiveness is presupposed which is pre-existent and independent of musical embodiment. Musical communication is conceived of as a process during which the musician's internal music-independent expressiveness is externalized and conveyed. Accordingly, musical features are considered a code of musical (expressive) intentions preceding the acts of music performance. The idea of a common set of signs developed in further studies of information theory such as those by Werner Meyer-Eppler[21] or Max Bense[22] seems to be generally taken for granted in current empirical studies on music and emotion (see figure 2): A common set of internal music-free expressive states, e.g. emotions, is assumed as the basis for musical communication.

20 Shannon: "A Mathematical Theory of Communication".

21 Meyer-Eppler: *Grundlagen und Anwendungen der Informationstheorie.*

22 Bense: *Einführung in die informationstheoretische Ästhetik.*

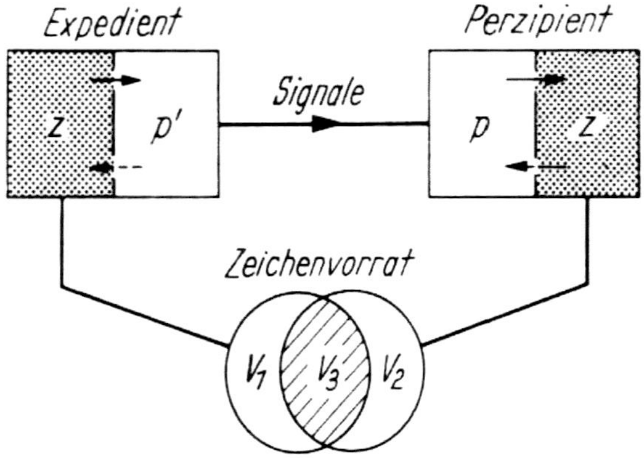

Figure 2: "model of communication chain" – V_1: active set of signs ("Zeichenvorrat") of transmitter ("Expedient"), V_2: passive set of signs of receiver ("Perzipient"), V_3: common set of signs (Meyer-Eppler 1959: 2, figure 3).

Furthermore, studies on music performance following the transmitter–receiver model of communication theory up to the present have mostly treated music production and perception as separate research areas, conceiving of music-making as encoding and music perception as decoding.[23] Music performance is considered as a communication channel through which separate processes of encoding and decoding are mediated. In experimental designs, the results of music-making have been used as stimuli, which are to be tested by listeners. Accordingly, most experimental studies on music and emotion have focused on listener's responses, which are interpreted as decoding. Furthermore, the conditions of encoding of emotions through musical features used as test stimuli have been artificially modified within a limited time span and by means of short musical passages.

Taking into account the second variant of meaning of 'embodiment' discussed in section III, basic ideas and methods of recent empirical research on musical expressiveness introduced in this section do not seem to cope with the concept of '*Geistiges* as the processuality of a (musically) embodied being' as suggested in section III. In most psychological and neuroscientific research on music, a mental/neural process realized as a material product such as a musical piece or manifested through a material form such as expressed musical features has come to the foreground. The concepts underlying this kind of performance-based music research fit in with the first variant of meaning of 'embodiment' which maintains the Cartesian mind-body dualism. Investigating the processuality of a (musically) embodied being can, however, hardly start from an abstract, music-free expressiveness. The starting state should rather be the actualization of musical expressiveness that unifies intended emotions, the perception and expe-

23 Cf. Kim: "Trace Theory of Mind and Musical Expressiveness".

rience of musical expressiveness as well as perceived and experienced expressiveness. Investigating the processuality underlying embodied musical expressiveness necessarily challenges the research questions and methods that up to present have been dominant in experimental studies on related topics. Hence, appropriate research questions, hypotheses and methods for investigating embodied musical expressiveness are subjects to discuss.

V. Considerations on embodiment-based research on musical expressiveness and 'music'

In music performance, expressive musical features may not be merely seen as the recovery of pre-existent (internal) expressiveness. Rather, musical expressiveness seems to emerge from the recurrent sensorimotor patterns that enable action and perception to be guided by each other due to embodied processing of musical expressiveness. Thus the ongoing process of music performance in which motor and sensory processes are inseparable and musical expressiveness emerges should become the focus. Hence, music-making and music perception should be treated as integrative processes: On the one hand, the process of music perception is necessary for music-making, especially for musical expressiveness experienced during music-making. During music-making, the action of music production is first guided by a number of internal kinesthetic and proprioceptive senses, then accompanied by a further perception loop of acoustic stimulus mediated by the outer ear. Hence, perceptually guided loops of motor and auditory feedback are underlying in music-making. On the other hand, listeners' music perception involves musically meaningful actions that might take place on a neural level in the form of inner coaction, and can often be observed through external behaviors. The Norwegian musicologist Rolf Inge Godøy points out that listening to music or even imaging music is "a process of incessant mental re-enactment of musical gestures"[24]. He focuses on the process of simulation of body movement during music perception to investigate how action and perception are coupled in music listening.[25]

In neuroscientific research on music performance, the coupling of auditory and motor processes in music-making and listening has recently become a relevant topic: Hauseisen and Knösche[26] demonstrated with MEG (magnetoencephalography) that well-trained pianists, while listening to piano music, exhibit invo-

24 See the website of one of his former research projects: <http://www.hf.uio.no/imv/forskning/forskningsprosjekter/musicalgestures/about.html>.

25 Cf. Godøy: "Motor Mimetic Cognition"; "Gestural Imagery in the Service of Musical Imagery".

26 Hauseisen and Knösche: "Involuntary Motor Activity in Pianists".

luntary motor activity involving the primary motor cortex. Scheler et al.[27] designed an fMRI (functional magnetic resonance imaging) experiment for motor-to-audio-processing. The expert violinists, while tapping out the first 16 bars of Mozart's violin concerto in G major, had significant activity in primary auditory regions. Bangert, Haeusler and Altenmüller[28] investigated in an fMRI study the auditory-sensory-motor co-presentation in a professional pianist. The result showed that listening to piano music activates sensory-motor areas, additionally to auditory brain regions, and that playing on a mute keyboard activates left auditory areas. Further brain imaging studies have given evidence for trained musicians' highly developed auditory-motor integration capacity in music-making and perception.[29]

The role of action-perception loops in perceiving and experiencing musical expressiveness, however, has rarely been taken into account in music research yet, in spite of some results of neuroscientific studies on the coupling of auditory and motor processes in music-making and listening. A case study indirectly investigating the role of coupled mechanisms of action and perception in music-making for musical expressiveness as experienced by the performer, guided by her or his self-perception during the ongoing processes of performance, has been carried out by the author and colleagues.[30] This study was conducted in cooperation with the Institute of Psychoacoustics and Electronic Music (IPEM) at the University of Ghent during summer 2009. A hypothesis of the case study was that music performance by professional musicians would not merely be an act of expression of the performer's own emotions or imagined emotions, but rather a process of going along with music, devotion of the self to the music, largely based on automatic processes available through embodied knowledge of the relationships between how to play, how this playing sounds, and how that sound feels, and guided by the self-perception of the performer during her or his performance actions.

To test this hypothesis, a sight-reading performance and a practiced performance of the same piece, which the test persons had never previously played, were taken as two different conditions of music performance which may impact the embodied process underlying music performance. The case study was carried out with three professional musicians – a gamba player, clarinetist, and singer. They were instructed to play unfamiliar two pieces, the style of which they were conversant with. Each piece was first sight-read, then reperformed after 20 minutes' worth of practicing. The test persons' self-reports on musical expressive-

27 Scheler et al.: "Musician's Brain".

28 Bangert, Haeusler and Altenmüller: "On Practice".

29 E.g. Bangert and Altenmüller: "Mapping Perception to Action in Piano Practice"; Bangert et al.: "Shared Networks for Auditory and Motor Processing"; Haslinger et al.: "Transmodal Sensorimotor Networks"; Warren et al.: "Sounds Do-Able"; Zatorre et al.: "When the Brain Plays Music".

30 Kim et al.: "Performance Micro-Gestures Related to Musical Expressiveness".

ness experienced during the ongoing processes of music performance were collected through post-performance oral interviews. In addition, the musicians' first-person reports were taken into account when analyzing the musicians' bodily micro-gestures as recorded by motion capture devices.

From a methodological point of view, the detailed post-performance oral interview was taken to collect and assess different aspects related to musical expressiveness that the test persons experienced during the ongoing processes of performance, including the conscious monitoring of music performance; musical interpretations; and automatic bodily and visceral reactions. To help the test persons recall the experience in the moment of music performance, a questionnaire was completed immediately after the performance; the following day, the interviewer related the oral interview to each of the test persons' literal reports, asking further oral questions that took the musicians deep into their recall of the ongoing processes of music performance. The interviewer's task was to direct the test persons' recall into their experiences only in relation to the concrete events occurring during the performance, and to help them make their experiences explicit—not based on knowledge of how to perform a piece, but instead recalling what concrete processes related to experienced musical expressiveness look like. This method, called an explication interview,[31] has an advantage over the questionnaire method; the first-person reports reveal multifaceted aspects related to experienced musical expressiveness proceeding over time, and are not purely subjective, since these reports on first-person experience are accomplished with the help of another person (interviewer) and therefore obtained from a second-person perspective.

To compare the collected self-reports to the gestural data measured from a third-person perspective, both the sight-reading and practiced performances of each performer were filmed using a Casio EX-F1 digital camera, enabling a high-speed video recording at 300fps to observe the performers' micro-gestures in detail, and a Motion Capture system (Optitrack, Natural Point) installed in the laboratory of Institute of Psychoacoustics and Electronic Music (IPEM) at the University of Ghent to analyze significant performance micro-gestures. The focus on performance micro-gestures was based on an assumption that there would only be very slight differences in overall macro-gestures between the same performer's sight-reading and practiced performance, given that professional musicians are capable of playing music on sight in an expressive manner when they are familiar with the musical style.

The results of this case study showed that the music performances shown through monitoring and/or felt by the professional musicians to be more expressive – in this case: practiced performance, without exception – comprise preparatory and retrospective micro-gestures featuring intra-personal properties related

31 Vermersch: "Introspection as Practice"; Petitmengin: "Describing One's Experience in Second Person".

to each performer, such as horizontally wide movements of the gamba player's left upper arm and the clarinetist's movements raising the clarinet using a large range of space.[32] From a methodological point of view, combining the analysis of measured or observed data from a third-person point of view and the access to first-person experience using the method of a second-person interview, and at the same time incorporating the result of interviews into the analysis of the data gained by measurement or observation appears a very promising empirical approach to embodied music processing, since the processuality of a (musically) embodied being also includes a conscious subjective experience, which has rarely been explored in the disciplines empirically investigating human mind and brain. What is of greater interest is the opportunity to incorporate the reports on first-person experience into the analysis of data gained from a third-person perspective, since this appears to be one of most appropriate research methods within the framework of embodiment, in case the subjective mind still comes to the foreground in investigating the complex processuality of 'Geistiges'.

A further methodological consideration might be briefly introduced with regard to computational modeling, an essential method of cognitive science. Recently, the importance and necessity of the use of robots in computational modeling has been emphasized in music research, especially in cognitive musicology pursuing an embodied approach.[33] Modeling a musically embodied being which is also embedded in a socio-cultural environment and interacting with other entities, combining empirical studies focusing on socio-cultural interaction and computational modeling using robots, appears an appropriate approach to investigating 'music' in general and embodied musical expressiveness in particular. In the department of systematic musicology of the institute of musicology at the University of Cologne, which provides study modules related to cognitive musicology in Germany, a new research method called (artistic) human-robot interaction design has recently been under development, following an approach that might be called hypothetical modeling.[34] Using interactive music and media performances and New Media Art as a test bed for theories of 'music',[35] musical conscious behavior exhibited by interacting entities is systematically observed with the help of a coding scheme[36] and the result of this observational study is incorporated into further strategies of computational modeling.[37] As yet less is known about the mechanisms underlying musical sensorimotor interaction, e.g., expres-

32 See Kim et al.: "Performance Micro-Gestures Related to Musical Expressiveness" for a detailed discussion on the result of this study.

33 Schmidt: "Towards an Embodied Cognitive Science of Music"; *Embodied Cognitive Science of Music.*

34 Crombie: "Styles of Scientific Thinking".

35 Seifert and Kim: "Entelechy and Embodiment in (Artistic) Human-Computer Interaction".

36 Bakeman and Gottman: *Observing Interaction.*

37 Seifert and Kim: "Towards a Computational Framework and an Empirical Methodology in Research on Artistic Human-Computer and Human-Robot Interaction"; Buch et al.: "'playing_robot'"; Kim et al.: "'playing_robot'".

sive playing of a musical instrument, and musical social interaction, e.g., playing music and dancing together or communicating with one other by means of musical sounds: There still seems to be a long way to go in approaching the understanding of 'music'. At least, a research program with a new methodological approach to investigating the processuality of a musically embodied being, however, seems to be epistemologically and methodologically established.

References

Agre, P. E.: *Computation and the Human Mind*, Cambridge (Cambridge University Press) 1997.

Bakeman, R. / J. M. Gottman: *Observing Interaction. An Introduction to Sequential Analysis.* 2nd Edition, Cambridge (Cambridge University Press) 1997.

Bangert, M. / E. Altenmüller: "Mapping Perception to Action in Piano Practice: A Longitudinal DC-EEG Study", in: *BMC Neuroscience*, 4 (2003) 26, pp. 1–14.

Bangert, M. / U. Haeusler / E. Altenmüller: "On Practice: How the Brain Connects Piano Keys and Piano Sounds", in: *Annals of the New York Academy of Science*, 930 (2001), pp. 425–428.

Bangert, M. / T. Pescheland / G. Schlaug et al.: "Shared Networks for Auditory and Motor Processing in Professional Pianists: Evidence from fMRI Conjuction", in: *NeuroImage*, 30 (2006), pp. 917–926.

Bense, M.: *Einführung in die informationstheoretische Ästhetik*, Reinbek (Rohwohlt) 1969.

Buch, B. / P. Coussement / L. Schmidt et al:. "'playing_robot': An Interactive Sound Installation in Human-Robot Interaction Design for New Media Art", in: *Proceedings of the Conference on New Interfaces for Musical Expression 2010,* (2010), pp. 411–414.

Calvo, P. / T. Gomilla (eds.): *Handbook of Cognitive Science: An Embodied Approach*, Amsterdam (Elsevier) 2008.

Clark, A.: *Being There: Putting Brain, Body and World Together Again*, Cambridge, MA (MIT Press) 1997.

Crombie, A. C.: "Styles of Scientific Thinking in the European Tradition", in: *British Journal for the History of Philosophy*, 3/2, (1995), pp. 409–419.

Dahl, S. / A. Friberg: "Expressiveness of Musician's Body Movements in Performances on Marimba", in: Camurri, A. / Volpe, G. (eds.), *Gesture-Based Communication in Human-Computer Interaction*: 5th International Gesture Workshop, GW 2003, Genova, Italy, April 15–17, 2003, Selected Revised Papers, LNAI 2915, Berlin/Heidelberg (Springer) 2004, pp. 479–486.

Dahl, S. / A. Friberg: "Visual Perception of Expressiveness in Musicians' Body Movements", in: *Music Perception*, 24 (2007) 5, pp. 433–454.

Dahlhaus, C.: *Einführung in die Systematische Musikwissenschaft*, Cologne (Gerig) 1971.

Frank, R. M.: "Introduction: Sociocultural Situatedness", in: T. Ziemke / J. Zlatev / R. M. Frank (eds.): *Body, Language and Mind, Vol. 2: Embodiment*, Berlin (de Gruyter) 2007, pp. 1–18.

Gabrielsson, A.: "Expressive Intention and Performance", in: R. Steinberg (ed.): *Music and the Mind Machine*, Berlin (Springer) 1995, pp. 35–47.

Godøy, R. I.: "Motor-Mimetic Music Cognition", in: *LEONARDO*, 36 (2003) 4, pp. 317–319.

Godøy, R. I.: "Gestural Imagery in the Service of Musical Imagery", in: A. Camurri and G. Volpe (eds.), *Gesture-Based Communication in Human-Computer Interaction: 5th International Gesture Workshop, GW 2003, Genova, Italy, April 15–17, 2003, Selected Revised Papers, LNAI 2915*, Berlin/Heidelberg (Springer) 2004, pp. 55–62.

Haslinger, B. / P. Erhard / E. Altenmüller et al.: "Transmodal Sensorimotor Networks during Action Observation in Professional Pianists", in: *Journal of Cognitive Neuroscience*, 17 (2005) 2, pp. 282–93.

Haueisen, J. / T. R. Knösche: "Involuntary Motor Activity in Pianists Evoked by Music Perception", in: *Journal of Cognitive Neuroscience*, 13 (2001) 6, pp. 786–792.

Juslin, P. N. / J. A. Sloboda (eds.): *Music and Emotion: Theory and Research*, Oxford (Oxford University Press) 2001.

Juslin, P. N. / J. A. Sloboda (eds.): *Handbook of Music and Emotion*, Oxford (Oxford University Press) 2010.

Kim, J. H.: "Trace Theory of Mind and Musical Expressivity", in: *Proceedings of the 2nd International Conference of the Asia-Pacific Society for the Cognitive Science of Music (APSCOM-02)*, 2005, pp. 122–129.

Kim, J. H.: *Embodiment in interaktiven Musik- und Medienperformances – unter besonderer Berücksichtigung medientheoretischer und kognitionswissenschaftlicher Perspektiven*, Osnabrück (epOs), in press.

Kim, J. H. / U. Seifert: "Embodiment: The Body in Algorithmic Sound Generation", in: *Contemporary Music Review*, 25 (2006) 1–2, pp. 139–149.

Kim, J. H. / U. Seifert: "Embodiment and Agency: Towards an Aesthetics of Interactive Performativity", in: *Proceedings of the 2007 International Conference of Sound and Music Computing (SMC'07)*, 2007, pp. 230–237.

Kim, J. H. / M. Demey / D. Moelants et al.: "Performance Micro-Gestures Related to Musical Expressiveness", in: *Proceedings of the 11th International Conference on Music Perception and Cognition (ICMPC-11)*, in press.

Kim, J. H. / S. H. Chang / L. Schmidt et al.: "'playing_robot': Investigating Situated Cognition in (Artistic) Human-Robot Interaction Design", in:

Proceedings of the 1st IROS 2010 Workshop on Robots and Musical Expressions 2010 (IWRME-01), in press.

Laske, O.: *Music, Memory, and Thought: Explorations in Cognitive Musicology,* Ann Arbor, MI (Bell & Howell) 1977.

Leman, M.: *Music and Schema Theory: Cognitive Foundations of Systematic Musicology*, Berlin (Springer) 2005.

Leman, M.: *Embodied Music Cognition and Mediation Technology.* Cambridge, MA (MIT Press) 2007.

Meyer-Eppler, W.: *Grundlagen und Anwendungen der Informationstheorie*, Berlin (Springer) 1959.

Petitmengin, C.: "Describing One's Subjective Experience In the Second Person: An Interview Method For the Science of Consciousness", in: *Phenomenology and Cognitive Science*, 5 (2006), pp. 229–269.

Robbons, P. / M. Aydede (eds.): *The Cambridge Handbook of Situated Cognition*, Cambridge (Cambridge University Press) 2009.

Schaeffer, L. H.: "Cognition and Affect in Musical Performance", in: *Contemporary Music Review*, 4 (1989), pp. 381–389.

Shannon, C. E.: "A Mathematical Theory of Communication", in: Shannon, C.E. *Collected Papers*, New York (IEEE Press) 1933, pp. 5–83.

Shannon, C. E. / W. Weaver: *The Mathematical Theory of Communication*, Urbana (University of Illinois Press) 1949/1962.

Scheler, G. / M. Lotze / V. Braitenberg et al.: "Musician's Brain: Balance of Sensorimotor Economy and Frontal Creativity [abstract]", in: *Soc. Neurosc. Abstr.*, 27 (2001) 76, p. 14.

Sherer, K. R.: "Expression on Emotion in Voice and Music", in: *Journal of Voice*, 9 (1995) 3, pp. 235–248.

Schmidt, L.: "'Towards an Embodied Cognitive Science of Music': Incorporating Mobile Autonomous Robots Into Musical Interaction", in: *Proceedings of the 2nd Asia-Pacific Society for the Cognitive Science of Music* (APSCOM-02), 2005, pp. 148–154.

Schmidt, L.: *Embodied Cognitive Science of Music: Modelling Experience and Behavior in Musical Context*, Cologne: PhD Thesis, Institute of Musicology, University of Cologne, 2008.

Seifert, U.: "Cognitive Science: A New Research Program for Musicology", in: *Journal of New Music Research*, 21 (1992) 3–4, pp. 219–238.

Seifert, U.: *Systematische Musiktheorie und Kognitionswissenschaft: Zur Grundlegung der kognitiven Musikwissenchaft*, Bonn (Verlag für Systematische Musikwissenschaft) 1993.

Seifert, U.: "Naturalisierte Hermeneutik der Musik – Kognitive Musikwissenschaft als Interpretationswissenschaft", in: von Blumröder, Ch. / Steinbek, W. (eds.): *Musik und Verstehen*, Laaber (Laaber Verlag) 2004, pp. 262–276.

Seifert, U. / J. H. Kim: "Entelechy and Embodiment in (Artistic) Human-Computer Interaction", in: Jacko, J. A. (ed.): *Human-Computer Interaction,*

Part I, HCII 2007, Lecture Notes in Computer Science 4550, Berlin/Heidelberg (Springer) 2007, pp. 929–938.

Seifert, U. / J. H. Kim: “Towards a Conceptual Framework and an Empirical Methodology in Research on Artistic Human-Computer and Human-Robot Interaction”, in: I. Pavlidis (ed.): *Advances in Human-Computer Interaction*, Vienna (In-Tech Education and Publishing 2008) pp. 177–194.

Seifert, U. / J. H. Kim: “Embodiment”, in: C. Bartz / L. Jäger / M. Krause et al. (eds.): *Signaturen der Medien. Ein Handbuch zur kulturwissenschaftlichen Medientheorie*, Munich (Fink) in press.

Sloboda, J. A.: *Exploring the Musical Mind. Cognition, Emotion, Ability, Function*, Oxford (Oxford University Press) 2004.

Vermersch, P.: “Introspection as Practice”, in: Varela, F. J. / Shear, J. (eds.): *The View from Within: First-Person Approaches To the Study of Consciousness*, Exeter, UK (Imprint Academic) 1999, pp. 17–42.

Warren, J. E. / R. J. Wise / J. D. Warren: “Sounds Do-Able: Auditory-Motor Interactions in Music Perception and Production”, in: *Nature Reviews Neuroscience*, 8 (2005), pp. 547–558.

Wiora, W.: “Musikalische Grundlagenforschung (Systematische Musikwissenschaft) ”, in: *MGG* Vol. 9 (1961), pp. 1199–1203.

Zatorre, R. J. / J. L. Chen / V. B. Penhune: “When the Brain Plays Music: Auditory-Motor Interactions in Music Perception and Production”, in: *Nature Reviews Neuroscience*, 8 (2007), pp. 547–558.

natur, wissenschaft und die künste
nature, science et les arts
nature, science and the arts

Edited by

Julia Burbulla, Bernd Nicolai, Ana-Stanca Tabarasi-Hoffmann,
Philip Ursprung & Wolf Wucherpfennig

Vol. 1 Julia Burbulla
Allumfassende Ordnung. Gartenkunst und Wissenschaft in Gotha unter Ernst II. von Sachsen-Gotha-Altenburg (1772–1804).
ISBN 978-3-0343-0038-4. 2010.

Vol. 2 James King
Beyond *The Great Wave*. The Japanese Landscape Print, 1727–1960.
ISBN 978-3-0343-0317-0. 2010.

Vol. 3 Sabine Flach, Daniel Margulies & Jan Söffner (eds)
Habitus in Habitat I. Emotion and Motion.
ISBN 978-3-0343-0530-3. 2010.

FSC
www.fsc.org
MIX
Papier | Fördert gute Waldnutzung
FSC® C083411

Kolibri 360 GmbH
Ferdinand-Jühlke-Straße 7
99095 Erfurt, Deutschland
produktsicherheit@kolibri360.de